BROKEN STRUCTURES

BROKEN STRUCTURES: Severe Personality Disorders and Their Treatment

---

Salman Akhtar, M.D.

JASON ARONSON INC.
Northvale, New Jersey
London

Production Editor: Judith D. Cohen

10 9 8 7 6 5 4 3 2

Library of Congress Cataloging-in-Publication Data

Akhtar, Salman, 1946 July 31–.
Broken structures : severe personality disorders and their treatment / by Salman Akhtar.
p. cm.
Includes bibliographical references and index.
ISBN 0-87668-538-6
1. Personality disorders. 2. Personality disorders – Treatment.
I. Title.
[DNLM: 1. Identification (Psychology) 2. Personality Disorders–therapy.
3. Psychoanalytic Therapy–methods. WM 190 A315b]
RC554.A24 1992
616.89 – dc20
DNLM/DLC
for Library of Congreess 91-47121

ISBN 0-7657-0255-X (softcover)

Printed in the United States of America on acid-free paper. For information and catalog write to Jason Aronson Inc., 230 Livingston Street, Northvale, NJ 07647-1726, or visit our website: www.aronson.com

To

my brother

Javed Akhtar

Ex voto

CONTENTS

PART II: THE PERSONALITY DISORDERS

FOREWORD

*Otto F. Kernberg, M.D.**

The most important contributions to the contemporary understanding of the symptoms, psychopathology, diagnosis, and treatment of personality disorders stem from the psychoanalytic exploration in depth of patients with significant character pathology. The dramatic deployment of pathological character traits as transference resistances has constituted the raw material for our understanding of this area of psychopathology. Our developing understanding of the frequency of these disorders in the general population, their relationships to other types of psychopathology, and their etiological factors has come from two broad sources: infant research and descriptive psychiatry. Infant research has, in turn, been stimulated by psychoanalytic investigation.

It might have been expected that these converging approaches—particularly psychoanalysis and descriptive psychiatry—would have

*Associate Chairman and Medical Director, New York Hospital-Cornell Medical Center, Westchester Division. Professor of Psychiatry, Cornell University Medical College. Training and Supervising Analyst, Columbia University Center for Psychoanalytic Training and Research.

cross-fertilized each other; in practice such has not however been the case. This failure has had frustrating, negative effects on the integration of knowledge in the area of character pathology and the personality disorders. As a consequence, important findings in the psychoanalytic investigation of a broad spectrum of patients with personality disorders has not been adequately incorporated into the descriptive phenomenology and the psychiatric classification of these disorders. At the same time, important findings derived from empirical research on severe personality disorders and from epidemiological studies of the pathology of early development have not found their way into the mainstream of psychoanalytic thinking.

In this elegant volume, Dr. Akhtar has sought to bridge this gap and to integrate, at a sophisticated level of contemporary knowledge, the findings from descriptive psychiatry and from the psychoanalytic study of severe personality disorders. His is not an eclectic combination of disparate findings and thinking; to the contrary, Dr. Akhtar critically analyzes the developments in both psychodynamic and descriptive psychiatry, and establishes a historical frame of reference for the approaches in both fields, one that separates out the essential from the marginal and even trivial.

Dr. Akhtar has cogently selected the clinically most prevalent severe personality disorders and reviewed the significant contributions from descriptive psychiatry and psychoanalysis, including a broad spectrum of continental European psychiatric thinking as well as the more familiar English and American literature in this field. At a time when the study in depth of descriptive psychiatry has tended to be neglected in favor of listing the principal symptomatic constellations found in clinical practice, Dr. Akhtar brings back the rich contributions to descriptive phenomenology of classical psychiatry, providing the clinician with sophisticated, subtly discriminating tools. Dr. Akhtar also reviews critically the psychoanalytic contributions to the understanding of the major personality disorders from both structural and dynamic perspectives. Bringing together the findings from contemporary ego psychology, object relations theory, self psychology, and interpersonal psychoanalysis, he replicates here the same broad, international perspective that characterizes his review of descriptive psychiatry.

In condensing and integrating these areas and approaches for each of the major personality disorders, Dr. Akhtar, with a remarkable clarity and economy of style, provides an enormous amount of information without ever overwhelming the reader. The result is a comprehensive update on the principal personality disorders, ongoing controversial issues, research in progress, and a critical analysis of *DSM-III-R*. By adding a careful differential diagnosis, he gives the clinician valuable instruments with which to assess the patients' psychopathology, prognosis, and treatment indications.

A significant, original contribution is Dr. Akhtar's presentation of a comprehensive frame that permits a comparison of these personality disorders from six viewpoints: the patient's self concept, his interpersonal relations, his social adaptation, his functioning in the area of love and sexuality, his ethics and ideals, and his cognitive style. This approach clearly transcends counting descriptive traits in order to arrive at a diagnostic formulation.

At the same time, Dr. Akhtar leaves open the challenging, still unresolved issue of a satisfactory classification of personality disorders that would integrate both categorical and dimensional criteria. He points to the importance of considering the ways in which some of the personality disorders differ in degree of severity rather than structurally, but he also stresses the categorical nature of several personality disorders. A fully satisfactory classification of personality disorders will require a clear understanding of the mechanisms of their development and crystallization, of the interaction of genetic, neurophysiological, early developmental, familial, and, above all, psychodynamic and psychostructural features that should permit such an integration. Dr. Akhtar's book gives the reader a comprehensive overview of the evidence currently available in all these fields, without attempting premature closure.

Dr. Akhtar also addresses the methodology of clinical evaluation of patients with personality disorders. He conveys valuable advice to the diagnostician, illustrated with lively clinical examples, and then proceeds to spell out his own approach to psychoanalytic psychotherapy. The reader might or might not agree with Dr. Akhtar's approach to the psychotherapy of personality disorders. The richness, cogency, and fairness of his review of alternative psychotherapeutic approaches, however, always permit the reader to reach his own conclusion.

The study of severe personality disorders transcends the interest of the clinician. The shadow of these disorders falls on the vast territory of alcoholism and drug abuse, delinquency and family pathology, and, in terms of the influence of the personality of leadership on the destiny of groups and organizations, on the social process as well. Dr. Akhtar's careful synthesis of our knowledge of this field should be of great interest to those who deal with all these problematic areas.

I believe Dr. Akhtar has made a path-breaking contribution to a new synthesis of descriptive psychiatry and psychoanalysis, to the diagnostic study of patients with character pathology, and an invaluable contribution to all clinicians and researchers in the field of personality disorders.

PREFACE AND ACKNOWLEDGMENTS

This book is a work of synthesis. I have written it with three purposes in mind. First, by combining the descriptive and psychoanalytic observations on severe personality disorders, I have attempted to develop deeper, theoretically sounder clinical profiles of these conditions than were hitherto available. In attempting such a synthesis, I have tried to show that descriptive psychiatry and clinical psychoanalysis are not conceptual adversaries and have much to offer each other. Second, by casting my net wide, I have included a large number of classics from both descriptive psychiatry and psychoanalysis to demonstrate the continuing validity of these earlier observations as well as their occasionally striking correspondence with contemporary literature. Finally, in discussing the techniques of evaluation and treatment of severe personality disorders, I have attempted to highlight the productive dialectics between the two approaches euphemistically termed *medical* and *psychoanalytic* in current professional debates. Thus, in all three areas—diagnosis, evaluation, and treatment—I have sought to emphasize the mutual interdependence of psychiatry and psychoanalysis.

On a deeper level lies the synthesis that writing this book has achieved for me personally. It has brought together, in a reasonably harmonious gestalt, the three phases of my own professional training. These include a rigorous descriptive psychiatry-oriented residency in Chandigarh, India, a five-year transitional period at the University of Virginia, and my psychoanalytic training at the Philadelphia Psychoanalytic Institute. As I reflect upon this long journey toward the consolidation of my professional identity, I find myself deeply grateful to many teachers who guided me along the way. Prominent among them are Drs. Jagdish S. Teja, Vijoy K. Varma, and especially N. N. Wig (Chandigarh, India); Drs. Wilfred Abse, John Buckman, Dan Josephthal, and especially Vamık Volkan (Charlottesville, Virginia); and Drs. Eugene Baum (late), Alexis Burland, Harry Cohen (late), Newell Fischer, Selma Kramer, Eric Lager, Henri Parens, Sydney Pulver, Joseph Rudolph, Morton Schwab, and William O'Brien (Philadelphia Psychoanalytic Institute). Along with many others, these outstanding individuals have taught me most of what I know today and I remain indebted to them. Drs. Seymour Rabinowitz and (late) Steven Hammerman helped me in profound ways during my Charlottesville days and upon my arrival in Philadelphia respectively and I wish to thank them here. I have also greatly benefited from my discussions with a number of gifted colleagues over the many years of my training, especially Drs. B. C. Khanna (Chandigarh), J. Anderson Thomson, Jr. (Charlottesville), Edward Hicks, and Thomas Wolman (Philadelphia Psychoanalytic Institute).

Following my training, I have continued to participate in two psychoanalytic study groups. One of them is comprised of my seniors: Drs. Morris Brody, Ted Cohen, Joan Gross, Ruth Fischer, Eric Lager, Louis Leaff, and Leo Madow. The other is made up of my contemporaries: Drs. Ira Brenner, Marc Lipschutz, Barbara Schwartz, Neal Shore, and Dan Wallace. Although what I have been learning from these groups is perhaps more evident in my psychoanalytic writings than in the material contained in this book, their sustaining value over many years of my professional identity consolidation has been enormous and I wish to acknowledge this debt here.

I wish to thank Dr. Troy Thompson, chairman of the Department of Psychiatry at Jefferson Medical College, for creating and sustaining an intellectual environment conducive to such academic endeavors. Many others on the Jefferson faculty have also facilitated my writing this book. Dr. Harvey Schwartz, the department's residency training director, some years ago asked me to give senior residents a seminar on severe personality disorder. Many ideas expressed here took shape in teaching this seminar over the years. Drs. Abraham Freedman, Gregg Gorton, Frank Maleson, Dilip Ramchandani, and Steven Samuel offered helpful suggestions in informal discussions. Dr. Stephen Schwartz provided the epigraph for one of the chapters. To all these individuals, my sincere thanks.

Drs. Albert Kaplan and Melvin Singer, both of the Philadelphia Association for Psychoanalysis, were also very helpful. Dr. Kaplan read initial drafts of many chapters and offered useful feedback. Dr. Singer pointed out a very significant omission on my part and thus saved me from later embarrassment. I am deeply thankful to both of them.

My gratitude to my secretary, Ms. Gloria Schwartz, is beyond customary acknowledgment. She deciphered my handwriting, typed and retyped numerous drafts, and conducted library searches with remarkable skill, patience, and good humor. My work was made easier by her attitude, and I remain very thankful for this.

Of course, there are still others, including my family, my training analyst, and my patients, whose silent but indisputable contributions to my knowledge, my personal strength, and my work-ego, I must acknowledge only in the privacy of my true self.

If we throw a crystal to the floor, it breaks; but not into haphazard pieces. It comes apart along its lines of cleavage into fragments whose boundaries, though they were invisible, were predetermined by the crystal's structure. Mental patients are split and broken structures of this same kind.

Sigmund Freud, 1932

Part I

IDENTITY

1

IDENTITY AND ITS ORIGINS

A novice beginning yet experient of myriads of seasons,
Of every hue and caste am I, of every rank and religion,
A farmer, mechanic, artist, gentleman, sailor, quaker,
Prisoner, fancy-man, rowdy, lawyer, physician, priest.

—"Song of Myself," Walt Whitman

The growing number of borderline and narcissistic patients who call on psychoanalysts and other psychotherapists for help has led to a rising interest in the problem of identity and identity diffusion. Such patients frequently present with poorly synthesized identities and contradictions in their self-images, aspirations, and interpersonal relationships. Indeed, many analytic theoreticians (Jacobson 1964, Kernberg 1967) regard disturbances of identity as a sine qua non of borderline and narcissistic character disorders. However, the literature pertaining to various clinical phenomena associated with such disturbance remains scattered and ill-synthesized.

In this chapter, I will attempt to bring together the various writings on the topic of identity. I will also comment upon the various developmental processes contributing to the origins of personal identity. However, a clarification of the very concept of identity and its admittedly ambiguous place in psychoanalytic theory seems necessary at the very outset.

THE CONCEPT OF IDENTITY

The term *identity* was introduced into the psychoanalytic literature by Tausk (1919), who examined how the child discovers his self and asserted that man must, throughout life, constantly find and experience himself anew. Freud, according to Erikson (1958), referred to the concept of identity only once. Not insignificantly, that was in his address to B'nai B'rith (Freud 1926a). The fact that identity was necessarily a two-sided term with intrapsychic as well as social ramifications perhaps contributed to its not gaining much acceptance and usage in subsequent psychoanalytic literature. In the 1950s Erikson (1950a, 1956, 1958, 1959) resurrected the term in his contributions to character formation. Around the same time, the concept appeared in the object relations and developmental models of personality formation of Jacobson (1964) and Mahler (1958a,b, 1968), respectively. In 1967, Kernberg, in a seminal contribution on borderline personality organization, emphasized the psychostructural and diagnostic significance of identity diffusion in patients with severe character pathology. Later, in 1980, he declared that "it is the presence or absence of identity diffusion that most clearly differentiates borderline from non-borderline conditions" (p. 14).

Erikson

Despite these more recent recognitions and emphases, the concept of identity is still poorly understood and, in view of its social interface, ambivalently regarded in psychoanalytic circles. For clarification, then, it may be useful to begin with Erikson himself. Erikson (1956) used the term *ego identity* to denote "both a persistent sameness within oneself (selfsameness) and a persistent sharing of some kind of essential character with others" (p. 12). He later dropped the prefix *ego* in part to accommodate Hartmann's (1950) differentiation between ego and self. Erikson emphasized that identity could have many connotations and may refer at one time to

> *a conscious sense of individual identity;* at another to an unconscious striving for a *continuity of personal character;* at a third, as a criterion for the silent doings of *ego synthesis;* and finally, as a maintenance of an inner *solidarity* with group's ideals and identity. [p. 102]

While he noted that identity formation is a lifelong development, with its roots going back to the earliest self-recognition, Erikson emphasized the period of adolescence in consolidating one's identity. This view was shared by Eissler (1958) and subsequently enriched by Blos's (1962) work. Erikson saw the adolescent as attempting to integrate what he knew of himself and his world into a stable continuum of past knowledge, present experiences, and future goals in order to elaborate a cohesive sense of personal feeling. Failure in this task led to a chaotic sense of personhood, both in its subjective and its social sense.

Although Erikson's terminology gained wide acceptance and his work gave considerable impetus to psychoanalytic study of identity, there remained areas that needed further clarification. These included the relative significance of infantile and adolescent phases in identity consolidation, the distinctions between the usual identity crisis of adolescence and identity diffusion, and finally the correlation between the latter syndrome and the more traditional classifications of character pathology. Jacobson (1964) and Kernberg (1967, 1976, 1980b) later recognized these limitations and attempted to fill the lacunae. However, Erikson's contribution still remains one of pioneering significance in the study of identity.

Erikson's work was subsequently extended in two directions: one emphasizing the social-cultural and the other emphasizing the uniquely personal, childhood origins of identity. Prominent among the contributors to the sociocultural determinants of personal identity are Fromm (1955), Wheelis (1958), Lynd (1958), Lifton (1971), Lasch (1978), and Kovel (1981). These authors use the term *identity* in its usual descriptive sense rather than its psychoanalytic sense. They emphasize the social aspect of this admittedly Janus-faced concept. They view the search for identity as a general problem for the whole present generation, a problem caused by the breakdown of the past value systems in our time.[1] The works of these authors seem to have two foundations. The first is more manifest in their writing style; the second, in the content of their propositions. Their stylistic foundation is in the poignantly subjective and almost solipsistically experiential tradition of the existential literature and philosophy. The authors raise questions that appear answerable only by a god, for example, Who am I?, What is the meaning of life? Their queries about human identity seem more metaphysical than psychological. On the other hand is their second foundation, more manifest in their content, which emanates from an overly sociological perspective. Thus their hypotheses about identity disturbance frequently remind one of the Marxist depictions of the individual's alienation in a society of free enterprise (Marx 1867), as well as of the Durkheimian concept of individual "anomie" being consequent upon rapid environmental change and social fragmentation (Durkheim 1951).

Lichtenstein

This existential-sociological paradox of the above-mentioned authors can be viewed as yet another testimony to the two-sidedness of the very concept that they are dealing with. Lichtenstein (1961) points out that this tension also exists in Erikson's work. He notes that Erikson's (1958) writings contain two views of identity: *ego identity,* the personal identity that results from self-objectivation, and *existential identity,* the personal identity that is defined by the "relationship of each soul to its mere existence" (p. 177). While the relative emphasis on these two aspects does reflect two phases of Erikson's thought, the fact remains that he always underscored that the concept of identity involves both self-objectivation and the subjective "experience of inner continuity in change" (Lichtenstein

[1]This implies that such questions as Who am I? were easily answered by those of earlier generations. Clearly, this is not so. Individuals have always struggled with such issues, and to negate this is to fuel a nostalgic cynicism that protects an infantile, idealized view of parents.

1963). The inherent ambiguity in the concept of identity is acceptable to Erikson (1958), who stated that he "can attempt to make the subject matter of identity more explicit only by approaching it from a variety of angles—biographic, pathographic, and theoretical; and by letting the term identity speak for itself in a number of connotations" (p. 102).

Lichtenstein (1961, 1963) also believes that the conflict between identity as self-objectivation and identity as pure existential awareness without any external referent has to be accepted as such. He further proposes two opposing forces as being active in connection with identity. The first is what he refers to as the *identity principle,* or the perpetual drive of man to maintain his historical existence and his self-defined, self-created identity. Lichtenstein sees the symbiotic mother-child relationship as the beginning of human identity formation and states:

> The mother does not convey a *sense* of identity to the infant but an *identity;* the child is the organ, the instrument for the fulfillment of the mother's unconscious needs. *Out of the infinite potentials within the human infant, the specific stimulus combination emanating from the individual mother "releases" one, and not only one, concrete way of being this organ, this instrument.* It would, however, be a mistake to see this "organ" or "instrumental" identity as too narrowly defined. The mother imprints upon the infant not *an* identity, but an *"identity theme."* This *theme* is irreversible, but it is capable of variations, variations that spell the difference between human creativity and "a destiny neurosis." [1961, p. 208]

Juxtaposed to the driving pressure of this "identity theme" is a second force, which, according to Lichtenstein, is the longing to abandon the human quality of identity (see also Searles 1960 in this connection). Lichtenstein recognizes that the abandonment of identity produces confusion and anguish, but he also indicates that this loss can be experienced as liberation and ecstasy. For the loss of human quality of identity, he proposes the term *metamorphosis.* Lichtenstein sees identity and metamorphosis as two limits of human experience incompatible with one another but complementary, since human life exists in an oscillation between these two extremes.[2] Sexual union, for Lichtenstein, amply demonstrates these two opposing forces at work insofar as it necessitates that an individual become "an instrument for the fulfillment of another one's needs" (1961, p. 209), thus living out the symbiotic "identity theme" on the one hand and surrendering one's identity altogether and undergoing metamorphosis on the other.

While Lichtenstein's work is largely in the philosophical phenomenological realm, his ideas about "identity theme" and the impact of early mother–child interactions have significant bearing upon the ontogenetic development of personal identity.

THE DEVELOPMENTAL ORIGINS OF PERSONAL IDENTITY

Freud

It is difficult to summarize Freud's contributions to the current understanding of the origins of identity. There are two reasons for this. The first involves his choice of the term *das Ich,* translated into English as the *ego,* and the second, his usage of the word *identity.* As far as the term *ego* is concerned,

[2]Bach (1985) later correlated such "oscillations between subjective and objective self-awareness" with the vicissitudes of the separation-individuation process. He pointed out that individuals who have difficulty experiencing themselves subjectively *and* objectively at the same time also experience the chronic dilemma in terms of "self-love or object-love, of isolation or merger, of sadism or masochism, and it is accompanied by a mirroring (controlling) transference or by an idealizing (submissive) transference. The sadomasochism, of course, reflects the fact that the object line of rapprochement overlaps with the instinctual line of anality, and the coercion of the object serves to reduce or deny the awareness of separation" (p. 71). Besides etiologically correlating the oscillations between internal and external self-experience with the works of Balint (1968), Kohut (1977), and, most importantly, Mahler et al. (1975), Bach describes in eloquent detail the painful handicaps in the love and work life of "the patient [who] can either be lost in an absorbed state without being aware of himself or is constantly aware of himself without being able to lose himself" (p. 72).

> it seems possible to detect two main uses: one in which the term distinguishes a person's self as a whole (including, perhaps, his body) from other people, and the other in which it denotes a particular part of the mind characterized by special attributes and functions. . . . It is not always easy, however, to draw a line between these two senses of the word. [editor's introduction, Freud 1923a, pp. 7–8]

If one assumes the former meaning of *ego* as being akin to *identity,* one would be compelled to review Freud's views about ego development in general. Such a daunting task, besides being beyond the scope of this brief survey, might also lead one far afield. The second difficulty in summarizing Freud's contributions to identity is exactly opposite in nature. Freud rarely used the term *identity* in a technical manner. In fact, of the ninety-two times that Freud used the word *identity* (Guttman et al. 1980, pp. 310–311), ninety-one were in a colloquial and/or literal sense. On the one occasion (Freud 1926a) when he did invoke the concept as it is under consideration here, it was in passing. As a result, the choice seems to be between reviewing practically all of Freud's writings on ego or dropping the matter altogether. My preference is to strike a compromise. I will do so by citing a few brief statements of Freud that highlight what might have been his stance about identity.

> In the process of a child's development into a mature adult there is a more and more extensive integration of his personality. . . . [1921, p. 18] . . . the ego is first and foremost a bodily ego. [1923a, p. 26] . . . the character of the ego is a precipitate of abandoned object-cathexes and . . . it contains the history of those object choices. [1923a, p. 29] . . . the ego ideal is . . . the heir of the Oedipus complex. [1923a p. 36] . . . Anatomy is Destiny. [1924, p. 178] . . . all human individuals, as a result of their bisexual disposition and of cross-inheritance, combine in themselves both masculine and feminine characteristics. [1925b, p. 258]

Freud also spoke directly of his own sense of identity in an address to B'nai B'rith:

> Whenever I felt an inclination to national enthusiasm I strove to suppress it as being harmful and wrong, alarmed by the warning examples of the people's among whom we Jews live. But plenty of

> other things remained over to make the attraction of Jewry and Jews irresistible—many obscure emotional forces, which were the more powerful the less they could be expressed in words, as well as a clear consciousness of *inner identity,* the safe privacy of a common mental construction. [Freud 1926b, pp. 273–274, emphasis added]

While the word *identity* appears infrequently here, these brief statements succinctly portray Freud's implicit view of the genesis and consolidation of identity. This view is a comprehensive one and accommodates somatic underpinnings, gender differences, early identifications, the role of the Oedipus complex and its resolution, the ongoing synthetic function of the ego, and ethnic and moral dimensions. What remained implicit yet palpably present in Freud was to be developed by his followers.

Fenichel

In elaborating on Freud's (1923a, 1926b) speculations on the early development of ego, Fenichel (1937) suggested that the image of our self originates from two sources: the direct awareness of our inner experience and the indirect perception of our bodily and mental self as an object. He gave equal importance to somatic foundations and identifications in the origin of the ego (identity) and declared that, for the growing infant, the "sum of representations of his own body and its organs which arises in the process, the so-called 'body image,' is of fundamental importance for the further development of his ego" (1937, p. 29). Fenichel also noted that into "the formation of every ego there have gone many identifications" (1945, p. 77).

Other early analysts made significant contributions. Federn's (1952) concept of early "ego feeling" approximated the more contemporary notion of rudimentary self-representations forming the building blocks of identity. This was similar to Glover's (1950) concept of "ego nuclei," or islets of executive function, and object-related awareness that subsequently fuse to form the coherent structure of the ego. Spiegel (1959) talked about the "pooling" of isolated self-representation as underlying solid identity formation. However, the emphasis in this early literature on "ego identity" (Erikson 1956) remained on the *ego* rather than on *identity*. It was not until the contributions of Greenacre, Mahler, Jacobson, Winnicott, Kernberg, Chasseguet-Smirgel, and Blos that the infantile and developmental origins of personal identity became clearer. Before discussing these authors' views, it may be worthwhile to point out that while the role of gradually unfolding primary autonomous functions is recognized in the following account, the focus of discussion is on affective and intrapsychic rather than cognitive factors.[3]

Greenacre

Greenacre (1958a) pointed out that the sense of identity always involves some relation to others. This is because identity includes self-observation by the person himself and through another person. Knowing and assimilating "I am different" with "I am similar" are thus essential for cohesive identity. She saw a continuum of development from body image through self-image to identity.

Greenacre (1958a,b) also emphasized the importance of the habitual taking in through vision of the opposite-sex genitals and the fusion of this part image with that of the subject's own body. An early and repeated exposure to the genitals of the opposite sex among twins, for instance, may lead to their marked primary incorporation. This may influence later identifications and create problems of identity, which may be more marked if such exposure occurs largely in the phallic and oedipal phases. It is in this period that Greenacre conceptualized the child as beginning to have a preliminary sense of identity, though she acknowledged that identity

[3]A bridge between the literal-cognitive and the mythic-dynamic forces in the acquisition of identity is provided by one's name. Although Abraham (1911a) had commented on the "determining power" of names vis-à-vis individual character, subsequent literature makes little reference to the child's discovery of his name and the organizing effect of this discovery on his identity. Also interesting in the name issue is that most individuals live peacefully with many names: first name, last name, nickname, title, sometimes pen name, addresses by intimates ("honey," "dear," etc.), and relatives, with the latter changing and evolving over the life span ("Uncle," "Grandpa," etc.). Clearly, a smoothly operative synthetic function of the ego and a cohesive identity underlie the comfort with which multiple names can exist together.

consolidation is incomplete until adolescence resolution and that there might be further reformulations of identity later in life.

By emphasizing perception and experience, bodily sensations and their interpretations, and by adding an experiential dimension to the origins and resolution of bisexuality, Greenacre provided for both preformation and epigenesis in identity formation.

Mahler

Based on extensive observational studies done alone or in collaboration with her colleagues, Mahler (1958a,b, 1968, Mahler et al. 1975) distinguished the psychological birth of the human infant, that is, the beginning in the child of the sense of personhood, from its biological birth. She postulated a sequence of developmental and maturational events through which a child must pass before becoming separate enough from the mother and acquiring a fairly stable sense of being a unique entity. Very briefly, these phases are the *autistic phase,* in which the neonate is self-contained and encased as if by a psychophysiological stimulus barrier; the *symbiotic phase,* in which a dual unity exists between the mother and the infant and the psychological self of the child begins in a state of enmeshment with the mother's self; the *differentiation phase,* in which the child starts to learn about his psychological separateness through rudimentary explorations of the self as well as the mother's environment; the *practicing phase,* in which the toddler elatedly enjoys his newfound psychic autonomy and motoric freedom and appears to be involved in the "conquest of the world"; and the *rapprochement phase,* in which the child learns that his separateness, autonomy, and motor abilities have their limits and that his world is more complex than he imagined. The realities of the external world appear harsher in this phase as the child regresses in the hope of reestablishing the lost symbiotic bliss with the mother. This return, however, is ambivalent, since the drive of individuation is at work with greater force. The resulting "ambitendency" accounts for the alternating cycles of dependence and flight characteristic of a child in this phase. If overcome, the rapprochement phase is followed by a period designated *on the road to object constancy,* in which a deeper, somewhat ambivalent, but more sustained object representation is internalized, the libidinal attachment to which does not get seriously compromised by temporary frustrations. This is accompanied by a more realistic and less shifting view of the self.

Mahler emphasized that two conditions must be met for organization of the ego and neutralization of drives to arrive at a sense of identity: (1) the enteroceptive-proprioceptive stimuli must not be so continual and so intense as to prevent structure formation; thus a shift from viscera-centered splanchnic innervation to the external rind of body ego is essential for self boundary formation, and (2) the mother must be able to buffer and organize inner and other stimuli for the infant. She suggested that the libidinal ministrations of the mother during the symbiotic phase and the aggressive hurts and bumps during the practicing phase both constitute the outlines, as it were, of the child's bodily self-awareness. However, it is not until the end of the rapprochement subphase of separation-individuation, an event occurring at approximately two years of age, that "self constancy" or a stable sense of one's unique and separate personhood comes into being. The renewed clinging as well as the valiant self-assertion of the toddler during this phase must, according to Mahler, be met with a constant but empathic stance from the mother. Internalization of this maternal attitude permits the needy and the omnipotent self-images of the child to unite and form a realistic view of the self. Failures of this process result in the persistence of contradictory self-images, thus laying the foundation for identity disturbances later in adult life.

According to Mahler and colleagues (1975), "self-constancy" consists of an awareness of being a separate entity and a beginning awareness of a gender-defined identity. The former sense begins in the differentiation subphase and is consolidated with the termination of the rapprochement subphase. The latter sense emanates from the "constitutionally predestined gender-defined differences in the behavior of boys and girls" (1975, p. 224), which are further elaborated in the phallic-oedipal phase of psychosexual development. Body image representations now emerge from pregenital libidinal positions and bisexual identifications to firm establishment of sexual identity. Successful separation-individuation, manageable amounts of castration anxiety, successful identification with the parent of the same sex, and the emotional attitudes of both parents to the child's sexual identity are of paramount importance here. This specific area of gender identity consolidation has received significant contributions from Stoller (1968, 1972), Galenson and Roiphe (1971), and Meyer (1980), among others.

Jacobson

Jacobson's well-known monograph "The Self and the Object World" (1964), as well as her many papers that preceded it (Jacobson 1953a, 1954a,b, 1957, 1959), contains a wealth of ideas regarding the child's discovery of his identity. Jacobson combined her findings from the treatment of affective disorders and severe adolescent identity disturbances with the metapsychological works of Freud (especially 1914, 1923a, 1924, 1926a), Fenichel (1945), Hartmann (1948, 1950, 1952, 1955), and Hartmann, Kris, and Loewenstein (1946), as well as with the developmental hypothesis of Mahler (1952, 1957, 1958) and Spitz (1957). Based on this synthesis, Jacobson formulated a "complex and highly elaborate" (Kernberg 1980b) developmental framework with wide-ranging theoretical implications.

Jacobson's contributions to the understanding of the development of identity can be divided into five categories: (1) the concept of self- and object representations, (2) the notion of a fused self-object representation as the first intrapsychic structure, (3) the emergence of identity from primitive identifications and its, in turn, facilitating further, more refined identifications, (4) the role of aggression in self-delineation, and (5) the modifications of the theory of oedipal resolution and superego formation. Jacobson introduced the concept of self-representations, which are the endopsychic images of the bodily and mental self in the system ego. By using the word *representation,* she clarified the distinction between the self as experienced and the self in reality (she similarly used the term *object representation*). This improved theoretical precision, insofar as it emphasized that these were intrapsychic and not interpersonal matters.

Jacobson proposed that intrapsychic structure is a fused self-object representation that evolves through primary, libidinal identifications with the mother. Gradually, differentiation between self- and object representations begins; the propensity for defensive refusion of self- and object representations is marked during this phase and, if not overcome adequately, lays the foundation for a psychotic core to the self. With differentiation comes recognition of painful experiences and subsequently their repudiation by denial, splitting, and projection. The inner world thus comes to be populated by pleasurable and unpleasurable self and object representations. The next developmental step consists of the integration of "good" and "bad" object representations into a more realistic self representation. With this, identity comes into existence. The discovery of identity, in turn, facilitates more complex interactions with what are now perceived as "total" parental objects. Discovery and acceptance of sexual differences further renunciation of symbiotic wishes because heterosexuality and oedipal strivings become predominant. Curiosity regarding parental sexual behavior and resulting disappointments induce identifications with the rival, further strengthening the sexual identity.

To the already known fact that superego derives from the incorporation of parental prohibitions, Jacobson added that the motive for superego formation is not only fear of the father's prohibitory behavior but also identification first with the mother, then with the father. She emphasized that the superego is not simply the precipitate of aggressively tinged internalizations; it includes libidinally invested identifications. Thus loving aspects of relationship with both parents contribute to superego, which Jacobson saw as both deepening and maintaining the identity.

Finally, Jacobson (1964) pointed out another growth-promoting feature of the aggressive drive. She indicated that

> passing through many frustrations, disappointments, failures, and corresponding hostile experiences of envy, rivalry and competition, the child eventually learns the difference between wishful and more or less realistic and self and object-images. Thus not only the loving but also the hostile components of the infantile self and object directed strivings furnish the fuel that enables the child to develop his feelings of identity. . . . [p. 61]

Winnicott

Although Winnicott did not use the term *identity* specifically, his views on early development are of great significance to the formation of identity. His work provides the developmental basis for (1) authenticity; (2) "corporeality" (Khan 1983), or a deeply assimilated and personalized bodily foundation for one's self-experience; and (3) the experience of temporal continuity in the self. It is, however, the development of the first of these three aspects that Winnicott's work addresses most penetratingly. Winnicott suggested that the infant's spontaneous gestures and personal ideas emanate from his "true self." If the infant's mother is "good enough" (Winnicott 1960) and can meet his omnipotence by empathically making sense of it, and if she does this repeatedly, then what feels real and is real in the infant begins to have life. However, if the mother fails to decode the infant's overture and replaces it by her own gesture, then the process is reversed. The infant is forced to give sense to the mother's gesture by compliance and by splitting off (actually, Winnicott uses the term *dissociation* more frequently than *splitting*) his original, authentic self-assertion. Such compliance gives birth to a "false self." Winnicott posits that if the latter sequence of mother–child interaction is the usual one, then the child's true self withdraws inwardly and the child develops an outwardly compliant but inauthentic self. Winnicott described at some length the various clinical pictures associated with such "false personalities" and at the same time emphasized the defensive nature of the inauthentic persona, which seeks to hide and protect the "true self."

Through his developmental views Winnicott (1949) shed light on the essential somatic contribution to the self-experience from the earliest infancy. He emphasized that the infant was a "psychosomatic being" (1960, p. 144) and that the true self comes from "the aliveness of body tissues and working of body functions" (1960, p. 148). He also pointed out that in individuals with a "false self" a peculiar mind–body split occurs and only the mind becomes the locus of identity, with the body being relegated to the status of a disowned vestige. Mental functions in such individuals take on somatic meanings, and the body becomes an inevitable, but hollow, experiential burden.

One can discern the earliest ontogenetic roots of the temporal continuity that Erikson (1956) and Lichtenstein (1963) emphasize as a central characteristic of a sound identity in the following comment by Winnicott:

> All the processes of a live infant constitute a *going-on-being,* kind of blueprint for existentialism. The mother who is able to give herself over, for a limited spell, to this her natural task, is able to protect her infant's going-on-being. Any impingement, or failure of adaptation causes a reaction in infant, and the reaction breaks up the going-on-being. If reacting to impingements is the pattern of an infant's life, then there is a serious interference with the natural tendency that exists in the infant to become an integrated unit, able to continue to have a self with past, present and future. [1960, p. 86]

Obviously, more underlies the future adult's sense of temporal discontinuity. Continued defects of the ego's synthetic function, haphazard layers of unfinished developmental tasks, and contradictory identifications sequestered by splitting mechanisms are various factors that working in unison may result in such a temporally fractured identity. Yet the foregoing comment of Winnicott does seem to hint at the earliest and prototypical beginning of such an occurrence.

Kernberg

Kernberg (1967, 1976, 1980b) proposed, in essential agreement with Jacobson (1964), that the development of ego identity is based on the internalization of early object relationships. He clarified that the early ego has to accomplish two essential tasks for such internalization to take place. The first is the differentiation of self images from object images that form part of early introjections. The accomplishment of this task depends on the maturation of primary autonomous functions, as well as on the gratification and/or frustration of early instinctual needs, since "libidinal gratification draws attention cathexes to the interaction between self and objects and fosters the differentiation in that area, and because frustration brings to awareness the painful absence of the fulfilling objects and thus contributes to differentiate self from non-self" (Kernberg 1975a, p. 26).

The second task for the developing ego is that the self- and object images built under the libidinal drives have to be integrated with self and object images built under the influence of aggressive drives.

In the beginning, the self- and object images formed under the loving influences exist separately from those built under depriving influences. The experience of the self is simplistic and often contradictory, being overly dependent on the affects related to gratification or the lack of it from an external object. However, with growing memory skills, increasing synthetic ability of the ego, manageable amounts of constitutional aggression, and a predominance of "good" introjects, the two contradictory self-images are mended. Partial introjections and identifications along libidinal and aggressive lines coalesce. The resulting ambivalent but deeper and realistic view of the self forms the rudimentary substratum of the ego identity. The concomitant deepening of the awareness of others as distinct and unique individuals facilitates more varied interactions with them than were hitherto possible. Meanwhile, the discovery of anatomical differences between sexes lays the foundation of gender identity, and the vicissitudes of the oedipal phase give it an object-related direction. Through these developments and interactions in later childhood, the earlier concrete identifications with parents are replaced by more selective identifications with parental roles, ideals, and prohibitions. Identity, thus enriched, is finally consolidated in adolescence, when further individuation through "disidentification" with primary objects, role clarification, and psychosexual self-definition takes place.

By integrating the works of Klein (1948), Erikson (1950a,b, 1958, 1962), Jacobson (1964), and Mahler (1968, 1971, 1975) with his own views, Kernberg formulated a three-step process of identity formation. The first step in the process is *introjection,* whereby certain affectively charged, specific attributes of others are internalized without being fully assimilated into the self-image. Such "an organized cluster of memory traces" (Kernberg 1976, p. 29) includes an object image, a self-image, and the affective coloring of the interaction binding the self and the object. The second step is *identification,* which implies a less concrete and more role-oriented internalization of significant others in relationship to oneself. Identifications, unlike introjects, do not feel like a "foreign body" in the self; topographically speaking, identifications are situated "deeper" in the self-system than introjects, which in their experiential aspects are often preconscious. Clearly, a more sophisticated ego, with more advanced cognitive and perpetual abilities, is involved in identification than in introjection. The third step is *identity formation,* whereby the childhood identifications are synthesized into a harmonious gestalt. In this process, individual identifications become "depersonified" (Jacobson 1964); that is, they lose their concrete similarities with their original sources. This selective repudiation and mutual assimilation of earlier identifications leads to a new psychic configuration, the ego identity.

Kernberg (1978) also described the distinctions between the adolescent identity crisis and the syndrome of identity diffusion, which he correlated with a borderline level of character organization. In addition, Kernberg (1980b) delineated the new dimensions that middle age adds to the consolidation of ego identity. He suggested that middle age brings about a renewed recognition of personal myths, a deeper reworking of oedipal tasks, an acceptance of the limits of one's creativity, and a shift in time perspective. He eloquently described this later phase in the consolidation of ego identity, which at this stage

> also integrates the knowledge of what one will not be able to do or be; and it also includes a painful and yet illuminating awareness of where one's creativity should or could lead next—and yet will not. Paradoxically though, self acceptance . . . now also means to accept the adventurous part of living, knowing that the road one takes has its dangers and limits and yet accepting that this is one's destiny. [Kernberg 1980, p. 128]

Chasseguet-Smirgel

Chasseguet-Smirgel's (1983, 1984) views on ego-ideal formation and on what she calls "perverse" character organization have significant bearing on the issues of identity consolidation. According to her, an oedipal child has two routes open to him. The first, or the "long path," consists of his accepting the tragedy of chronological lag between his erotic longing for his mother and his attainment of full genital capacity. This deepens the acceptance of reality, with the resulting narcissistic injury being compensated by the projection of infantile narcissism onto the parents and the formation of ego ideal. The ego ideal implies hope, promise, and future. It thus enhances ability for delayed gratification and facilitates the child's "entrance into a temporal order" (1984, p. 28). These developments are accompanied by the child's taking the father as his model, accepting the father's rule, sublimating pregenital libido, and acquiring a sense of filiation and generational (and therefore, historical) continuity.

The other outcome, leading to a perverse character, is through what Chasseguet-Smirgel calls the "short path." Here the child, often with the aid of a fixatingly seductive mother, comes to believe that it is not necessary to wait for the height of sexual development in order to reinstate the fusion with the mother. The young child mistakenly believes that he is already a man. "Forward projection" of infantile narcissism does not occur and the father is not idealized. Ego and ego ideal are fused. The "fatal character of the Oedipus complex" (1984, p. 26) is bypassed; sublimation is circumvented and the

> lack of the Ego due to the faulty introjection and assimilation of the paternal attributes—an unconscious process which involves a relationship full of love, admiration and closeness—is repaired not by an imitation of the father and his attributes (which are necessarily decathected) but by an attempt to free oneself completely from all filial links. [1984, p. 74]

Chasseguet-Smirgel thus emphasizes the role that object relations of the oedipal phase play in identity consolidation. Her views have special relevance to the experience of temporality, filiation, authenticity, and generational continuity that others have found central to a solid identity. Most importantly, her views help place the issues of filial legacy and thus ethnic and historical continuity squarely within psychoanalytic developmental psychology. This rectifies the not infrequent mistake to view these aspects of identity as merely social epiphenomena and hence not worthy of metapsychological attention.

Blos

In a series of contributions, Blos (1962, 1965, 1967) outlined the various intrapsychic processes and phases of adolescence in terms of the positions and movements of drive and ego. He elucidated the cathectic shifts and the stabilizing mechanisms typical of adolescence and emphasized the decisive role of this economics in final personality formation. Three aspects of Blos's enormously important work have particular significance to identity consolidation. First is what he called the *second individuation process of adolescence.* Dovetailing Mahler's (1968, 1975) hypothesis that the child gains psychological separateness from the mother by internalizing her homeostatic functions, Blos suggested that the acquisition of such separateness in adolescence requires a reverse process. Emotional disengagement from the internalized infantile objects becomes necessary at this stage. With this disengagement come not only a certain instability and estrangement but also "radical alterations" (Blos 1967, p. 166) in the ego structure, which becomes increasingly autonomous and self-reliant. The superego also loses some of its power, specificity, and rigidity. The result is an individual with a greater sense of solidity, inner constancy, and abstract morality independent of the values imparted by childhood parents.

The second area that Blos's work elaborates on is the consolidation of sexual identity. This he sees as being accomplished by (1) the renunciation of the primary love objects (the parents) as sexual objects, (2) the reconciliation of activity and passivity, and (3) the resolution of bisexual identifications. For the boy, the latter involves the renunciation of the envy of the procreative mother, the countercathexis of passive sexual aims, and the mastery of negative oedipal tendencies through idealizing friendships and aim-inhibited homosexual attachments. For the girl, the resolution of bisexuality depends on the final giving up of the illusory penis, the abandonment of a narcissistic position, and the deepening of her identification with her mother.

Finally, relevant to the issue of identity consolidation are Blos's (1972, 1974, 1984) views on the formation of ego ideal. Blos proposed a biphasic resolution of the Oedipus complex. He agreed with the classical position that the positive Oedipus complex is resolved in childhood, leading to the formation of the superego and the onset of latency. He suggested, however, that the negative Oedipus complex, especially in boys, is not resolved until adolescence. Blos postulated that powerful, precompetitive libidinal attachment to the father forms the basis for the negative oedipal attitude in the boy and that this object-libido is propelled by sexual maturation to undergo a transformation into the psychic structure, the ego ideal. The ego ideal, according to Blos, is "guarded as a cherished and beloved personality attribute whose archaic origin lies in father attachment, father idealization or, briefly in the negative Oedipus complex; that is, the adult ego ideal is the heir of the negative Oedipus complex" (1984, p. 319).

In an earlier developmental context, both Loewald (1951) and Mahler (1975) had pointed out the necessity for a growing toddler of a stable relationship with the father to protect himself against the threat of this precompetitive, libidinal tie, thus highlighting the significant role of the father in psychic structuring and identity consolidation.

CONCLUSION

The term *identity,* owing to its intrapsychic and interpersonal ramifications, has had a somewhat ambiguous place in psychoanalytic theory. The tension between the views of identity as self-objectivation and as a relationship of the soul to its mere existence is obvious in most writings on the topic. Different investigators have emphasized different facets of identity and elucidated various aspects of its developmental origins. Identity is seen to emanate within the earliest infant–mother interactions; to gain further structure from primitive introjections; to refine itself through differentiation from early objects and with more selective later identifications; to acquire filiation, generational boundaries, and temporality in passage through the Oedipus complex; and to arrive at its more or less final shape through further synthesis of contradictory identifications, greater individuation, and renunciation of negative oedipal tendencies during adolescence. Cross-sectionally, a solid identity consists of the following characteristics: (1) a sustained feeling of self-sameness displaying roughly similar character traits to varied others, (2) temporal continuity in the self-experience, (3) genuineness and authenticity, (4) a realistic body image, (5) a sense of inner solidity and the associated capacity for peaceful solitude, (6) subjective clarity regarding one's gender, and (7) an inner solidarity with an ethnic group's ideals and a well-internalized conscience. Disturbances in these areas of functioning comprise the syndrome of identity diffusion.

2

THE SYNDROME OF IDENTITY DIFFUSION

The mean man thinks: "I am so generous."
The shallow man: "I am profound."
Sometimes God will sigh: "I am a worm."
The worm hisses: "I am God."

—"The Face Behind Face," Yevgeny Yevtushenko

The term *identity diffusion* was first used by Erikson in 1950 to denote the failure during adolescence to integrate earlier identifications into a harmonious psychosocial identity. In a later paper (1956) he described the clinical phenomena associated with identity diffusion. These included impaired capacity for intimacy and mutuality, diffusion of time perspective, diminished sense of workmanship, hostility toward roles offered as desirable by one's family, and pronounced conflicts regarding one's ethnic origins. Erikson suggested that adolescents with identity diffusion had been raised by intrusive, appearance-conscious mothers and weak, insecure fathers. Defensively withdrawing from their mothers and painfully disillusioned by their fathers, they developed an early identity hunger. This intense need for a personal definition, combined with little opportunity for healthy identifications, laid the foundation of subsequent identity diffusion. In this chapter, I will outline the criteria to discern identity diffusion and highlight the clinical usefulness of recognizing such psychopathology.

CLINICAL FEATURES

The syndrome of identity diffusion involves both subjective and behaviorally manifest phenomena and can be viewed from three perspectives: developmental, dynamic, and descriptive. *Developmentally,* identity diffusion results from a separation-individuation process that has been arrested at the rapprochement subphase (Mahler 1968, 1975), a distorted and unresolved Oedipus complex resulting in faulty filiation and a regressive attachment to an "anal universe" (Chasseguet-Smirgel 1983), and a failure during adolescence to integrate earlier identifications into a harmonious gestalt of relatively consistent self-feeling (Blos 1962, Eissler 1958, Erikson 1950a). *Dynamically,* identity diffusion signifies the continued active presence of "magic identifications" (Reich 1954), "unmetabolized introjects" (Kernberg 1967), and contradictory identifications, as well as the predominance of splitting over repression as a defense against object-related ambivalence or ego-dystonic self-attributes. *Descriptively,* identity diffusion denotes a more or less characteristic constellation of clinical signs and symptoms in the area of one's identity and self-experience. I had earlier described (Akhtar 1984) the following manifestations as constituting the syndrome of identity diffusion. To that list, I now add a feature that pertains to the subtle disturbances of body image and sensations frequent among those with severe identity conflicts.

Contradictory Character Traits

Individuals with identity diffusion display incompatible personality attributes. Marked tenderness toward others can coexist with extreme indifference toward them. Naivete and suspiciousness, shyness and exhibitionism, greed and self-denial, and arrogance and timidity are among other contradictory character traits observed in individuals with identity diffusion. Subjective awareness of these contradictions is associated with perplexity and often an experience of oneself as a "chronic misfit" (Goldberg 1983). The lack of an integrated self-concept is also associated with impaired integration of the concept of significant others. Individuals with identity diffusion cannot integrate cognitively and affectively the observed behavior of others into a dynamic, composite conception that would reveal the constant aspect of others' personalities. Such patients lack this condition for normal empathy, which is the cause of their need to focus excessively on the immediate behavior of other people in order to "read" them.

Concurrently pursuing multiple vocational goals, at times to the extent of remaining or becoming an "eternal dilettante" (Levy 1949), may also betray characterological contradictions. For instance, the persistence into adulthood of equally strong desires to become a physician and a movie star represents an ill-organized ego identity. Such a cleavage in the self is different from the genuine versatility one may see in association with normality. In the latter, there is one dominant identity and the other interest is relegated to the status of a hobby. No significant conflict between the two is experienced. The shifts from one to the other are purposive, pleasurable, and not disruptive of the person's basic self-image.

An important matter to keep in mind, therefore, is that a healthy and cohesive identity does *not* imply a rocklike, monolithic homogeneity.[1] Indeed a normal, well-integrated and well-functioning self is comprised of many subsets of self-representations (Eisnitz 1980). Some of these are close to action, others to contemplation; some are nearer to affect, others to thought. What differentiates a cohesive self with multiple self-representations from a poorly integrated identity is the former's overall synthesis, comfortable transition between various aspects, and optimal mixture of reality principle and ego ideal–dictated life direction in manifestation or nonmani-

[1]Indeed, a rigid and caricatured consistency may be a defense against internal chaos. Such was the case with a narcissistic businesswoman who felt confused and directionless on weekends unless she wore her usual business clothes, which provided her an identity.

festation of various self-representations. The difference is that which exists between a necklace and a loose set of beads; in identity diffusion, the beads are not connected by a meaningful and adaptive thread.

Some patients, whose disjointed attributes have undergone fantasy elaboration and personification, may present with features of multiple personality. The overlap between borderline personality, a condition with profound identity diffusion, and multiple personality was implicit in Freud's pointing out that contradictory identifications in the ego could lead to different pathological outcomes. Freud (1923a) stated that if the ego's object identifications

> become too numerous, unduly powerful and incompatible with one another, a pathological outcome will not be far off. It may come to a disruption of the ego in consequence of the different identifications becoming cut off from one another by resistances; perhaps the secret of the cases of what is described as "multiple personality" is that the different identifications seize hold of consciousness in turn. Even when things do not go as far as this, there remains the question of conflicts between various identifications into which the ego comes apart. [pp. 30–31]

Fast (1974), Abse (1983), Buck (1983), and Benner and Joscelyne (1984) have more recently emphasized the similarities and differences between identity diffusion and multiple personality.

Temporal Discontinuity in the Self

The capacity to maintain an essential core of self-awareness amid change and with passage of time has been emphasized by Erikson (1950a, 1956, 1959) and Lichtenstein (1963) as the hallmark of a sound identity. Such temporal continuity is impaired in individuals with identity diffusion. The past, present, and future are not integrated into a smooth continuum of remembered, felt, and expected existence for these patients. They experience themselves as very young and at the same time old beyond rejuvenation. Intense nostalgia alternates with frantic planning for the future, with the result that the present becomes disconnected from both the past and the future. All real experience thus becomes uncannily contemporary. Time acquires a personalized yet fragmented quality (Bach 1977), and a longitudinal anamnesis reveals "a life lived in pieces" (Pfeiffer 1974).

In younger patients this chronological rupture manifests as an inability to project themselves into the future and make consistent goals. Striking geographical motility and vocational zigzags may betray such a discontinuous self. In middle-aged patients, a peculiar dissociation from their own younger selves can be observed. Certain so-called mid-life crises,[2] especially those involving dramatic changes in lifelong vocations and interpersonal affiliations, also result from having kept a highly cathected, temporally dissociated self-representation in abeyance for a long time. Kramer's (1955) and Niederland's (1956) descriptions of the "little man" phenomena perhaps refer to similar experiences, though on an intrapsychic level and hence a different level of abstraction. Keeping chronological photo albums, writing personal diaries, frequently referring to oneself by name, chronically searching one's "roots," and exhibiting hyperreflectiveness about external events (Klass and Offenkrantz 1976) are often used as defenses against the disturbing subjective sense of temporal discontinuity in the self.

[2]Underlying the mid-life crisis are many other pathological factors. These include pathologic narcissism impeding the acceptance of one's psychosomatic limits and reawakened incestuous anxieties leading to a failure in a deeper reworking of oedipal tasks (Kernberg 1980b). However, despite being pathological and painful, the mid-life crisis can result in a meaningful reorganization of identity. Erikson's (1959) concept of "passive identity," through which man regains his active position in the face of nothingness, is relevant here. The experience of "passive identity" or "hitting rock bottom" is indicative of a profound crisis leading to a retreat "far below the trust position in infancy [to a] return to state of symbiosis with the matrix" (Erikson 1958, p. 14). From this regression a decisive reorganization may emerge. Lichtenstein (1963) aptly points out the similarity between Erikson's "passive identity" and Lynd's (1958) view of experiences of shame. Lynd believes that these "can lead in two different directions: (i) They can lead to protection of the exposed self and the exposed society at all costs—refusing to recognize the wound, covering the isolating effect of shame through depersonalization and adaptation to any approved codes. (ii) If experiences of shame can be fully faced, if we allow ourselves to realize their import, they can inform the self, and become a revelation of oneself, of one's society, and of the human situation" (p. 71).

Lack of Authenticity

Individuals with identity diffusion display feelings, beliefs, and actions that are caricaturelike. In a given situation, they act as someone else they know would act, not in a manner that is genuinely their own. They lack originality and readily acquire gestures, phrases, ideologies, and life-styles from others. However, this tendency toward mimicry based on susceptibility to external influence is not the only source of their inauthenticity. The continued presence in their inner worlds of unsynthesized early identifications (Jacobson 1964, Kernberg 1967, 1976) also renders the self experientially fragmented and inauthentic.[3] Commenting on this phenomenon, Kernberg (1975a) writes that although

> their identifications are contradictory and dissociated from each other, the superficial manifestations of these identifications persist as remnants of behavior dispositions in the ego. This permits some of these patients to "re-enact" partial identifications . . . if this appears useful to them. . . . A chameleon-like quality of their adaptability may result, in which what they *pretend* to be is really the empty dressing of what at other times they have to be in a more primitive way. [p. 39]

Helene Deutsch's (1942) classic paper on the "as-if" personality describes such pathology in its extreme form. Deutsch outlines four characteristics of the "as-if" individual: (1) a passive plasticity and a tendency to rapidly identify with others, (2) a shallow and easily shifting morality, (3) an automatonlike suggestibility, and (4) a splitting off of aggression, lending "an air of negative goodness [and] of mild amiability" (p. 305). Deutsch pointed out that despite the outward appearance of relative normalcy, an "as-if" individual lacks any genuine feelings. She emphasized that such emotional incapacity is different from

[3]It is fascinating to note that, from a completely atheoretical and descriptive stance, almost exactly the same phenomenon has been described as *memory echopraxia* in the British psychiatric literature. The term points to the fact that the echopraxic does not limit his mimicry to those around him but may imitate those he remembers.

> the coldness of repressed individuals in whom there is usually a highly differentiated emotional life hidden behind a wall, the loss of affect being either manifest or cloaked by overcompensations. . . . [while] in the "as-if" individual it is no longer an act of repression but a real loss of object cathexis. The apparently normal relationship to the world corresponds to a child's imitativeness and is the expression of identification with the environment, a mimicry which results in an ostensibly good adaptation to the work of reality despite the absence of the object cathexis. [p. 304]

While the clinical picture outlined by Deutsch is prototypical of the more severe disturbances of authenticity, milder pathology of the same sort can be seen in most borderline, narcissistic, antisocial, schizoid, and schizotypal patients. The writings of existential writers on the "alienated man," summarized by Johnson (1977), are replete with descriptions of such inauthenticity. Similar absence of depth is implied in the descriptions of the schizoid individuals by Fairbairn (1944) and Guntrip (1969), the "false self" by Winnicott (1960), the "divided self" by Laing (1965), the "narcissistic personality disorder" by Akhtar and Thomson (1982a), and the "hidden selves" by Khan (1983).

Subtle Body Image Disturbances

Individuals with a well-established identity have a realistic body image and a comfortable somatic foundation of their overall self-experience. These bodily foundations of the ego identity have been immortalized in Freud's (1923a) statement that "the ego is first and foremost a bodily ego." Winnicott (1949, 1960), Jacobson (1964), Mahler (1968, 1970, 1975), and Kernberg (1967, 1976) have all taken this matter into account while developing their ideas on personal identity.[4]

It is therefore somewhat surprising to note that the tendency in psychoanalytic and especially psychiatric literature has been to almost reflexively associate body image disturbances with either the

[4]Kohut's (1977) self psychology is a notable exception in this regard since it completely ignores the role of body in the formation of the psychological self. I have elsewhere (Akhtar 1988) elaborated on this neglect in Kohut's work.

structural conflicts of the hysteric or the anthropomorphized ego fragmentations of the psychotic. The fact remains that one frequently sees body image disturbances in individuals with identity diffusion, that is, individuals whose character organization is midway between those of neurotics and psychotics (Kernberg 1970a). Some of these patients feel that they exist only from their neck up—only their heads are real to them. Others make erroneous assessments of their weight, height, voice, appearance, skin complexion, and so on. Still others feel their genitals to be inadequate or not even belonging to them. The frequent coexistence of anorexia nervosa (Knight 1954) and transsexualism (Socarides 1970, Volkan 1980b) with underlying borderline personality organization testifies to the disturbance of body image in identity diffusion. Kretschmer's (1925) noticing motor clumsiness in schizoid individuals, Stern's (1938) reference to the "bodily rigidity" of borderline patients, and Bach's (1977) pointing out the "peculiar thermal sensitivity and skin masochism" in narcissistic individuals are some other examples. In general, it can be assumed that the more severe the identity-related conflicts, the greater the likelihood of an associated body image disturbance.

Feelings of Emptiness

Individuals possessing a subjective sense of continuity and inner solidity can sustain themselves in the absence of any social contact. When alone, they can draw on inner resources and have a peaceful solitude. Individuals with identity diffusion, however, especially those with schizoid features, experience a sense of inner emptiness under such circumstances (Kernberg 1975, Singer 1977a,b). They feel that they are "hollow," "empty," or "just a shell" (Guntrip 1969, Johnson 1977, Kernberg 1975a, Levy 1984).

Defensive operations used by such individuals to protect themselves from the despondency of emptiness vary greatly. In some patients, there develops a hungry and insistent "preoccupation with aliveness" (Singer 1977b) or a heightened "manic-defense," to use Winnicott's (1935) phrase, which may manifest in their being constantly active and never passive, their avoiding aloneness and silent contemplation, and their incessant talking and compulsive socializing. Bulimic episodes, drinking, drug ingestion, impulsive sexual encounters, and even provocative behavior that ultimately "fills" one with rage are other various measures that may be used to ward off feelings of emptiness (Kernberg 1975, Singer 1977b). Khan (1983) feels that such "outrageousness" is a frequent flamboyant persona for a missing inner solidity. In the same vein, though more regressively, self-mutilation may be another way of combating inner emptiness. Perhaps belonging on the same spectrum are individuals who use frequent urination to assure themselves of being full of something and thus not empty (Agoston 1946).

The feeling of emptiness is distinct from that of loneliness, which many neurotic and even normal individuals can experience. Loneliness is characterized by a painful longing for a fantasized object or situation not permitted by one's conscience or not currently available in reality. The inner world, though mournful, is populated with fantasies and alive with emotions. Emptiness, with its absence of longing, is a more deeply frightening and dehumanizing experience. This emphasis upon the object-relations aspect of the experience of emptiness should not, however, be taken to negate the fact that the isolated complaint of being empty, in an individual with a "higher level" (Kernberg 1970a) character organization, may be a symbolic communication of an unconscious fantasy related to a drive defense-type, structural conflict. Singer (1977a), and more recently Levy (1984), reviewed the literature on various meanings of the complaint of emptiness from such a traditional position of the instinct theory.

Gender Dysphoria

Individuals with a solid identity possess a subjective clarity regarding their gender. A well-consolidated sense of gender consists of three aspects: *core gender identity* (Stoller 1968), or an awareness of belonging to one sex and not to another; *gender role* (Tyson 1982), or one's overt behavior in relationship to other people with respect to one's gender; and *sexual partner orientation* (Green 1975), or one's preferred sex of the love object. A cohesive gender identity is concordant with one's biological sex and shows harmony between core gender identity, gender role, and sexual partner orientation. This translates into heterosexual object choice and an overall gender-appropriate demeanor including attire, gestures, roles, social priorities, sexual behavior, and interpersonal relationships. Such solid gender identity emerges from the interplay of constitutional givens and cultural factors, with deep acceptance of the distinction between the sexes, predominance of identifications with the same-sex parent, and a recognition of the complementarity of the opposite sex (Galenson and Roiphe 1971, Mahler et al. 1975, Stoller 1968, Tyson 1982).

Individuals with identity diffusion, having failed to accomplish these developmental tasks, display weakness of gender identity. This may be manifest in their difficulties with heterosexuality or their displaying overt behaviors deemed more appropriate for the opposite sex. Or they may fail to convey a deep sense of possessing any gender at all, thus displaying a state of psychic eunuchoidism. The gender confusion may, however, be restricted to their subjective experience of themselves, especially in their sexual fantasies. The observation that many transsexuals seeking sex-reassignment surgery display borderline personality organization (Meyer 1982, Socarides 1970, Volkan 1980b) attests to the frequent coexistence of gender dysphoria and identity diffusion.

Inordinate Ethnic and Moral Relativism

A healthy identity possesses an ethnic component. Through exposure to the family's cultural mores and ensuing identifications, the growing child acquires a sense of ethnicity, which provides a feeling of belonging to a larger group and imparts historical continuity to the child's existence (Erikson 1950a, 1956). A successful or near-successful resolution of the Oedipus complex adds to the child's entry into the father's universe (Chasseguet-Smirgel 1984). The resulting idealization of the father imparts an understanding of generational differences and provides impetus for familial and communal filiation. This early ethnic sense, which may border on ethnocentricity, is diluted during adolescence, when a certain disidentification with parental mores occurs. The greater interaction with diverse social and ethnic groups during adolescence further facilitates the toning down of the childhood ethnocentrism. However, ethnicity and the accompanying pride survive past adolescence and add depth to the healthy identity in adulthood.

Individuals with identity diffusion display a peculiar pallor of ethnicity. This lack of an important historical-cultural basis of identity results in a peculiarly polymorphous sense of ethnicity, which becomes evident in a vague and uneven sense of history, generational filiation, cultural norms, group affiliations, object choices, lifestyle, and child-rearing practices. Devoid of an ethnic anchor, identity acquires a falsely liberal attitude with potentially perverse implications.

A related finding in such individuals is that of inordinate moral relativism. In contrast to the expectable flexibility of the postadolescent superego, the conscience displays an exaggerated latitude. These individuals manifest surprising contradictions in their value systems (Kernberg 1967) and, at times, a peculiar absence of any genuine inner values altogether (Deutsch 1942). They may function with a "sphincter morality" (Ferenczi 1926a), that is, governance of social behavior with expectations of reward and punishment from external sources rather than from inner standards that induce guilt and concern. At other times, their ideals and convictions are simply reflections of another person's view of what is good and bad. Overenthusiastic adherence to a certain moral principle can therefore be quickly and completely replaced by a contradictory one without an inward transformation if the individual's circle of acquaintances changes. Absence of inner morality increases the need for direction from others and sometimes involves a heightened vulnerability to esoteric religious cults. This correlation between weak, inauthentic identity and the existence of superego defects has been commented upon by Abraham (1925), Deutsch (1942), Greenacre (1958b), and, more recently, Chasseguet-Smirgel (1984).

DIFFERENTIAL DIAGNOSIS

Psychotic Disturbances of Identity

Identity diffusion needs to be distinguished from disturbances of self-awareness seen in psychotic disorders (Hamilton 1974). The psychotic identity disturbances[5] (e.g., feelings of being someone else or being many people simultaneously) occur in the setting of gross personality disorganization with regressive loss of self and object boundaries. The symptoms are usually bizarre and of delusional proportions. Even when the identity-related issues seem to be the only presenting manifestations, careful inquiry often reveals the presence of disorder affect, hallucinations, and other thought disorders. Individuals with identity diffusion, on the other hand, are not psychotic and show no impairment of reality testing.

Multiple Personality

The syndromes of identity diffusion and multiple personality may coexist and do have some phenomenological overlap (Abse 1983, Benner and Joscelyne 1984, Buck 1983, Fast 1974). Both conditions involve a lack of integrated self and contradictions in personality. However, the two conditions are far from identical. Individuals with identity diffusion do not have the gross hysterical phenomena, for example, fugues, anesthesias, trancelike states, physiognomic alterations, automatic writing, that are often associated with cases of multiple personality (Fast 1974). They do not display the elaboration, naming, personification, and dramatization of their dissociated attributes that is typical of individuals with multiple personality. Also, they do not have the amnesia that keeps apart the various identities in multiple personality (Abse 1983). Indeed, it is in the cases of multiple personality without such dissociative amnesia that the presence of identity diffusion, borderline personality organization (Kernberg 1967), or even schizophrenia should be suspected.

Clearly, it is conceivable to view the case with identity diffusion, multiple personality, and psychotic disturbances of identity on a spectrum of quantitative severity as manifested by the predominance of primary process, failure of the ego's synthetic function, distortion of self-experience, and ego's detachment from reality. In

[5]While these have not been labeled as such, existing parallel to the well-recognized *world*-destruction and *world*-reconstruction fantasies in psychosis (Fenichel 1945) are always *self*-destruction and *self*-reconstruction fantasies.

this connection a curious group is constituted by those individuals who chronically use aliases and those who deliberately change their names to erase previous identities. Their psychopathology perhaps lies somewhere between identity diffusion and multiple personality. Infrequently seen in psychoanalytic practice, especially in their flagrant forms, these individuals are often the subject of startling newspaper stories of deceit and hidden identities. Abraham (1925), Greenacre (1958b), Deutsch (1955), and, more recently, Gediman (1985) and Chasseguet-Smirgel (1984) have written in meaningful detail about such persons as well as the dynamics of an ordinary individual's fascination with them.

Adolescent Identity Crisis

A more difficult and subtle differential diagnosis for identity diffusion is adolescent identity crisis. Kernberg (1978) suggested that the term *identity crisis* should be reserved for the phase-specific and expectable resurgence of doubts, regression in behavior, and reorganization of identity that occurs during adolescence. In agreement with Masterson (1967) and Offer (1969, 1971), Kernberg emphasized that adolescents undergoing an identity crisis do not display deep-seated, chronic pathology of object relationships. Even during behavioral chaos, such adolescents manage to maintain feelings of authenticity and the ability to view others with ambivalence rather than as caricatures of good and evil. Their idealizations, though intense, are often based on surprisingly deep knowledge about their heroes. Also, their heroes are temporary way stations to real object investments (Blos 1967) and not substitutes for the latter. Their conflicts involve their psychosocial roles and vocational choices and do not permeate the totality of their self-experience. They do not display defects of "core gender identity" (Stoller 1968), and, while they may find themselves lonely, they do not experience the dreadful and malignant emptiness associated with the syndrome of identity diffusion.

The term *identity diffusion* designates more severe pathology originating in chronic frustrations during early childhood. In individuals with identity diffusion, splitting predominates over repression as the main defensive operation. Their selves are poorly formed and contain unintegrated introjections and identification of a markedly contradictory nature. Their idealizations are fantastic and based on meager knowledge of their heroes; often, such idealized attachments substitute for real object choices. Object relationships are markedly disturbed, and the capability for experiencing ambivalence is severely compromised. Superego functions are archaic, contradictory, and often experienced as emanating from the external environment rather than from within oneself. The dependence on external objects for a cohesive self-feeling is great, leading to a vulnerability to the subjective experience of emptiness.

Both identity crisis and identity diffusion may first become manifest during adolescence. However, the symptoms of identity diffusion are not restricted to that phase and may be seen in adults of all ages. Also, although identity crisis could occur during the adolescence of relatively normal and neurotic individuals, identity diffusion betrays severe character pathology.

CONCLUSION

A well-consolidated identity is comprised of characterological homogeneity and persistent "self-sameness" (Erikson 1956), temporal continuity, authenticity, psychosomatic partnership, inner fullness, gender clarity, and deep ethnic and moral standards. In addition, the individual with a solid identity has a sense of filial connections and generational continuity, which peacefully coexists with a sense of his own autonomy and uniqueness. Minor contradictions do exist in the self system but are well coordinated by the synthetic function of the ego. Shifts between the various self-representations are neither disavowed nor allowed to impede the overall guiding direction of the individual's ego ideal.

Individuals with identity diffusion, on the other hand, have defects in all these areas. They display contradictory character traits, feelings of emptiness, lack of authenticity, gender dysphoria, temporal discontinuity of the self-experience, and inordinate ethnic and moral relativism consequent upon weak filiation and impaired generational continuity. However, the degree to which identity diffusion is readily manifest varies greatly. Borderline individuals may display these phenomena more overtly than narcissistic patients, who are better integrated. Also, the various manifestations of identity diffusion may not occur to an equal degree in all patients with identity diffusion. Narcissistic patients may display more inauthenticity, borderline patients more temporal discontinuity, and schizotypal patients more feelings of emptiness, for instance. Such clinical impressions, if operationalized and replicated, may help in developing better phenomenological profiles of these conditions. This may, in turn, be used to generate etiologic hypotheses and psychotherapeutic techniques more specific to various subtypes of these severe personality disorders.

While such advances in clinical theory are awaited, the exploration of identity-related issues remains an important aspect of diagnostic evaluations. Three clinical advantages result from exploring identity-related issues in a diagnostic interview, especially from recognizing the syndrome of identity diffusion. First, it helps in differential diagnosis of personality disorder. The syndrome is present in borderline, narcissistic, schizoid, paranoid, hypomanic, schizotypal, and antisocial personality disorders but not in obsessional, hysterical, and avoidant or phobiclike character disorders (Akhtar 1987, 1988, 1989, Kernberg 1967, 1970a). The symptoms of identity diffusion therefore help distinguish two basic groups of personality disorders. Indeed, these disorders can be distinguished further by assessment of the nature of conflicts and the degree of conflict internalization (Akhtar and Byrne 1983, Dorpat 1976), the developmental history (Masterson and Rinsley 1975, Rinsley 1978), and the depth of object relationships (Jacobson 1964, Kernberg 1967, 1976, Mahler 1975, Volkan 1976).

The second advantage is that the presence of identity diffusion alerts the clinician to the guarded nature of prognosis. Individuals without serious disturbances of identity develop firmer therapeutic alliances and benefit more from psychotherapeutic treatment—supportive or psychoanalytic—than those with identity diffusion (Adler 1981, Kernberg 1975a).

Third, the recognition of this syndrome helps the psychotherapist select a therapeutic strategy. In conditions with no identity diffusion, the exploration of unconscious dynamics through the vehicle of transference and its interpretations is the main therapeutic task. In personality disorders with identity diffusion, on the other hand, such work should be preceded by active confrontation and clarification of the faulty basic assumptions about the self and others (including, of course, the analyst). Conflict defenses surrounding the issues of "being" need to be explored before those related to issues of "doing." Only after the cohesive identity has been established, creating the possibility of deeper object relationships, can psychotherapy or analysis in a traditional interpretive manner begin.

It should be pointed out that the object-relations emphasis here on the various individual manifestations of identity diffusion (e.g., emptiness and inauthenticity) does not exclude the contributions of oedipally determined, structural conflicts to each of these symptoms. Thus inauthenticity, for instance, may be a schizoid technique to deal with the tragically thwarted "true self" (Winnicott 1960), a result of weak object identifications (Deutsch 1942), a manifestation of unsynthesized and "unmetabolized" introjects (Kernberg 1967), or, as I have seen in some cases, an identification with parents whose own marked inauthenticity was transparent to the child. However, it may also have oedipal roots insofar as it may betray a negation of the oedipal realities and the rule of the father (Chasseguet-Smirgel 1983) or a regressive defense against authenticity, which may be unconsciously equated with parricide (Gedimen 1985). The same logic is equally applicable to any other of the manifestations mentioned above. Each is subject to the "principle of multiple function" (Waelder 1930) and means many things simultaneously. Which of these meanings, and therefore which developmental root, is most important cannot be determined by viewing the symptom in isolation but by taking into account the entire character organization and its unfolding in the transference–countertransference axis.

Part II

THE PERSONALITY DISORDERS

3

NARCISSISTIC PERSONALITY DISORDER

In public he is so powerful, so sophisticated! Natty
As a Doberman pinscher in his neat cuffs,
He tells us he is only a poor folk
Looking for its mate,
But living with him is like living in the ten stomachs
of a snake.

—"Mea Culpa," Patricia Goedicke

In this chapter, I will attempt to develop a multifaceted phenomenological profile of narcissistic personality disorder. Though I will refer to developmental, dynamic, and psychostructural concepts, it will only be to the extent of their impact on the disorder's phenomenology. I will not discuss the conflicting hypotheses about the etiology of the disorder (Grunberger 1975, Kernberg 1970b, Kohut 1971, 1977) or the various ways in which the term *narcissism* has been used in psychoanalytic literature (Pulver 1970, van der Waals 1965). I will use the term in its descriptive sense, that is, "a concentration of psychological interest upon the self" (Moore and Fine 1967, p. 62). My focus will remain on the descriptive aspects of narcissistic personality disorder and its differentiation from other personality disorders. My aim is to elaborate on an earlier effort (Akhtar and Thomson 1982a) by taking up areas that remained unaddressed in it and by including the relevant literature since that paper's publication. However, to trace the evolution of narcissistic personality disorder as a nosological entity, I will begin with the earliest writings on this subject.

FREUD AND THE EARLY ANALYSTS

Freud first used the term *narcissism* in a 1910 footnote to "Three Essays on the Theory of Sexuality" (p. 145). Four years later, in his seminal paper "On Narcissism" (1914), Freud outlined the profoundly significant concepts of primary and secondary narcissism, the nature of narcissistic object choices, and the narcissistic foundation of ego ideal as a psychic structure. While avoiding character typology in that paper, Freud did refer to individuals who "compel our interest by the narcissistic consistency with which they manage to keep away from their ego anything that would diminish it" (p. 89). However, it was not until 1931 that he described the "narcissistic character type":

> The subject's main interest is directed to self-preservation; he is independent and not open to intimidation. His ego has a large amount of aggressiveness at its disposal, which also manifests itself in readiness for activity. In his erotic life loving is preferred above being loved. People belonging to this type impress others as being "personalities"; they are especially suited to act as a support for others, to take on the role of leaders and to give a fresh stimulus to cultural development or to damage the established state of affairs. [p. 5]

This description is generally viewed as the pioneering portrayal of narcissistic personality disorder. However, the fact remains that two earlier papers, by Jones (1913) and Waelder (1925), contained significant information on the phenomenology of this condition. Although the term *narcissistic personality disorder* does not appear in it, Jones's description of individuals with a "God complex" is perhaps its first detailed portrayal. According to Jones, such an individual displays

> an excessive admiration for and confidence in one's own powers, knowledge and qualities, both physical and mental . . . the wish to display the own person or a certain part of it . . . omnipotence phantasies . . . a peculiar interest in any methods that promise a short-cut . . . an attitude of disinclination towards the acceptance of new knowledge . . . [and] an exaggerated desire to be loved . . . [and] for praise and admiration. [pp. 244–265]

Such an individual also displays contempt for others by an unwillingness to participate in group activities, a disregard of others' time, and a tendency to not answer letters. More important to the contemporary psychoanalytic mind is Jones' sophisticated observation that narcissistic grandiosity is at times masked by an "unusually strong series" of opposing tendencies. Among these are a caricatured modesty, a social aloofness, and a pretended contempt for money in real life. Jones also outlined cognitive peculiarities, which include, on the one hand, articulateness, excellence in lecturing, and love of language and, on the other hand, a lengthy and circuitous form of diction, subtle learning defects, and inattention to objective aspects of events.

Waelder (1925) characterized "narcissistic personality" as displaying condescending superiority, intense preoccupation with self-regard, and a peculiar absence of concern for others. This lack of empathy is most apparent in sexuality; intercourse is a purely physical pleasure, the partner being less an individual than a means to an end. Even the individual's morality is governed by narcissistic motives. Unlike the usual superego dictate, "I must not do or think this, for it is immoral, my parents have forbidden it," narcissistic morality prompts something like "This may not be, for it would humiliate me; it does not accord with my lofty and noble personality" (p. 262). Waelder indicated that narcissistic individuals frequently display preference of concepts over facts and an overvaluation of their mental processes.

Wilhelm Reich (1933) described the "phallic-narcissistic character" as someone warding off a deep-seated feeling of inferiority. He portrayed such a person as arrogant, energetic, often promiscuous, and reacting to any offense to his vanity by "cold disdain, marked ill-humor, or down-right aggression" (p. 218). Reich indicated such persons' tendency toward sadistic perversions, sexual impotence, homosexuality, addictions, and superego defects. He regarded this character pathology to be more common among males and pointed out that their level of social functioning varies greatly. Some acquire fame and social power, while others tend toward daydreaming, addiction, and criminality. Reich distinguished the narcissistic character from the compulsive character by pointing out the former's lack of "reaction-formations against his openly aggressive and sadistic behavior" and "its greater boldness and less thoroughness with respect to details" (pp. 218–219).

Twelve years later, Fenichel (1945) described a patient whom he labeled "The Don Juan of Achievement" (p. 502). Generalizing from this case, he portrayed such individuals as being compelled to run from one achievement to another. However, their successes provide no inner satisfaction to them. They wish to be great men and are always in a hurry. They lack tenderness and are unfaithful to their romantic partners. Although Fenichel viewed such drivenness as an attempt to undo unconscious guilt based on early maternal seduction and a partial oedipal victory, he emphasized the overwhelming narcissistic defects in such individuals. In a different context, Fenichel described narcissistic characters as displaying omnipotent behavior, undue independence, and leadership qualities. He agreed with Olden's (1941) observation that narcissistic personalities frequently exert a fascinating effect upon others. Fenichel also indicated the superego defects of such individuals and suggested that some of them, the "narcissistic psychopaths" (1945, p. 373), may even adapt a criminal lifestyle.

Olden (1946) described a specific type of intellectual disturbance under the suggestive designation of "headline intelligence." The characteristics of this disturbance are

> gathering catchwords or headlines in one dashing glance; a certain ability to combine the few and superficially collected bits; an ability to apply these pieces of knowledge in a skillful way so that they

> appear to be profundities . . . [and being] incapable of thorough studying and learning in any one field. [p. 263]

Although Olden emphasized the oedipal anxieties underlying this desire to not know details, this kind of shallow exhibitionistic knowledge is perhaps even more characteristic of narcissistic personalities.

A. Reich (1960) later described narcissists as "people whose libido is mainly concentrated on themselves at the expense of object-love" (p. 217). Such individuals have an unduly high opinion of themselves, "exaggerated, unrealistic, i.e., infantile inner yardsticks" (p. 219), excessive unneutralized aggression, and overdependence on approval from outside. They are preoccupied with fantasies of self-aggrandizement. They manifest a driven quality in their work, inability to wait, hypochondriasis, and perverse sexual practices. Such self-inflation, Reich pointed out, is a defense against narcissistic injuries during both preoedipal and oedipal periods of development.

Following this, Nemiah (1961) described an individual with a "narcissistic character disorder" as displaying great ambition, unrealistically high goals, intolerance of imperfections, and an insatiable craving for admiration. The individual does little because of authentic inner motivation; all actions are influenced by what he thinks will make others like him. Nemiah saw the origin of this disorder in parental high demands and harsh criticism of the child, which become internalized in the latter's developing character. As an adult, the individual becomes "a prisoner of his aspirations, his needs and his harsh self-criticism" (p. 163).

Tartakoff (1966) then described individuals with a "Nobel Prize complex," exemplified by their burning ambition to win the coveted award or to attain great wealth, win an Oscar, be the president. Many such persons were quite gifted and were often the first, if not the only, child in their families. They displayed the active fantasy of being the "powerful one" and the passive fantasy of being the "special one," chosen by virtue of their exceptional gifts to perform outstanding deeds. The latter fantasy is reminiscent of the "clever baby" dream earlier reported by Ferenczi (1923), which betrayed a belief that one was born wise, "knowing it all." Tartakoff pointed out the frequent circumvention of oedipal conflict among narcissistic individuals. This led to their being cocky, promiscuous, and irreverent toward authority figures.

Finally, mention should be made of Fairbairn's (1944) and Guntrip's (1969) analysis of schizoid patients, Winnicott's (1965) work on the development of "false self," and Khan's (1983) theoretical and technical innovations, although these investigators were perhaps dealing with relatively more withdrawn states than are usually associated with narcissistic personality.

In summary, the early literature contains the following information: (1) narcissistic personality disorder is clearly recognized though, at times, without being properly designated as such; (2) among its features are not only grandiosity, constant search for glory, drivenness, boldness, and articulateness but also impaired capacity for love, superego defects, tendency toward promiscuity and perversion, and cognitive peculiarities; (3) its central feature, grandiosity, is seen as defensive against feelings of inferiority; (4) this inferiority is traced to severe frustrations in both preoedipal and oedipal phases of development; and (5) varying levels of social functioning are associated with narcissistic personality disorder.

KERNBERG

According to Kernberg (1970b), the main characteristics of narcissistic personalities are their excessive self-absorption, intense ambition, grandiosity, and inordinate need for tribute from others. Such patients experience little concern for others and obtain no enjoyment from life other than from the admiration they receive from others or from their own grandiose fantasies. They feel bored when external glitter wears off and no new sources feed their self-esteem.

Kernberg (1975a) emphasizes the coexistence of feelings of inferiority with notions of grandiosity and stresses the "presence of chronic intense envy, and defenses against such envy, particularly devaluation, omnipotent control and narcissistic withdrawal" (p. 264). These defenses appear in the individuals' contempt for, anxious clinging to, or social avoidance of secretly admired others. Kernberg stresses the pathological nature of their inner worlds, regardless of their superficially well-adapted behavior. This internal pathology is evident in their emotional shallowness, defective empathy, extreme contradictions in self-concept, and incapacity for experiencing mournful longing and sadness when faced with separation and loss. Such individuals possess a capacity for consistent hard work and may become socially successful. Yet their work is in the service of exhibitionism, done in order to obtain admiration. Kernberg terms this tendency "pseudosublimatory" (p. 229) and distinguishes it from mature, honest work consequent upon actual sublimations. In addition, narcissistic persons display a corruptible conscience and readiness to shift values quickly to gain acceptance by idealized or needed others. They experience others as "basically dishonest and unreliable, or only reliable because of external pressures" (p. 232); such a concept of themselves and others plays an important part in the transference developments during their treatment.

Kernberg stresses that the narcissism of these patients is highly pathological. Normal narcissism is associated with capacity for deep object relations. Pathological narcissism, on the other hand, is associated with a deterioration in the capacity for object relationships. Kernberg emphasizes the importance of severe frustrations with significant early objects in the defensive genesis of narcissistic personality disorder. He further notes that narcissistic personality is both strikingly similar to and specifically different from borderline personality organization. The similarity resides in the predominance of splitting over repression as the ego's main defensive operation. The difference resides in the narcissistic personality having a cohesive, albeit highly pathological, grandiose self, which hides the inner identity diffusion and aimlessness. Kernberg (1970b, 1975a, 1984) also distinguishes narcissistic personality from obsessional and hysterical personalities, whom he sees as being organized around repression rather than splitting, and as having better integrated superegos and a greater capacity for genuinely reciprocal object relations.

Kernberg (1975) differentiates three levels of social functioning among narcissistic personalities. First, there are narcissistic personalities who, possessing talents and high intelligence, may achieve outstanding social success. The constant admiration they receive keeps them going and they may never seek treatment. "One might say that their gains from their illness often compensate for the disturbances that stem from the pathology of their object relations" (p. 333). Second, there are the narcissistic patients who seek treatment for impaired capacity for maintaining long-term relationships and a nagging aimlessness despite reasonable success. This group constitutes the majority of narcissistic individuals. The third group consists of the narcissistic patients who function on an overt borderline level and display nonspecific manifestations of ego weakness, that is, deficiencies in the areas of anxiety tolerance, impulse control, and sublimation.

Finally, Kernberg (1980b) poignantly describes the effects of pathological narcissism on the specific conflicts posed by the onset of middle age. He states that, viewed within a long-term perspective of time,

> the grandiose self always has been, and remains, alone and in a strangely atemporal world of repeating cycles of wants, temporary idealizations, greedy incorporation, and disappearance of supplies by spoiling, disappointing, and devaluation. The overall effect of these mechanisms on the aging process is a gradual deterioration of the narcissistic patient's internal past . . . compounded by the gradual painful awareness that the narcissistic gratifications of youth and past triumphs are no longer available, and in order to avoid painful envy of his own past, the narcissistic patient is forced to devalue his own past achievements and accomplishments. [p. 138]

Denial of the limits posed by aging may lead the narcissistic person to adopt a grotesquely youthful lifestyle. A major mid-life crisis with dramatic vocational shifts and inappropriate love affairs is often the result. The sexually inhibited narcissistic personality of young adulthood may now begin to be promiscuous or even perverse. On the other hand, the middle-aged narcissist with a long history of promiscuity may begin to be maritally more stable, though this may be accompanied by a subtle depreciation of the marital partner. Middle age also necessitates a recognition of the burgeoning sexuality and independence of one's children and one's own realistic needs for dependence, as well as one's finiteness and mortality. These tasks are painfully difficult for the narcissist, who responds by undue envy and hatred of his youthful offspring, anxious negation of his dependent needs, and unrealistic clinging to youthfulness or a cynical withdrawal into "splendid isolation."

KOHUT

In contrast to Kernberg, Kohut suggests few empirical diagnostic criteria for narcissistic personality disorder. Kohut (1971) specifically disavows "the traditional medical aim of achieving a diagnosis in which a disease entity is identified by clusters of recurring manifestations" (pp. 15–16), holding that "the crucial diagnostic criterion is based not only on the evaluation of the presenting symptomatology or even of the life history, but on the nature of the spontaneously developing transference" (p. 23). His two monographs on narcissism are devoted to the elucidation of these specific narcissistic transferences and their ontogenetic antecedents in faulty parental empathy, first within the theoretical confines of traditional psychoanalysis, and then under the domain of his provocative and controversial self psychology (Kohut 1977). Kohut's (1984) posthumously published book-length rebuttal to critiques of his self psychology also contains few comments on the descriptive aspects of narcissistic personality disorder. However, in a paper written with Wolf (Kohut and Wolf 1978), he did provide greater detail in this regard.

Kohut (1971) noted that narcissistic patients may complain of disturbances in several areas: sexually, they may report perverse fantasies or lack of interest in sex; socially, they may experience work inhibitions, difficulty in forming and maintaining relationships, or delinquent activities; and personally, they may demonstrate a lack of humor, little empathy for others' needs and feelings, pathologic lying, or hypochondriacal preoccupations. These patients also display overt grandiosity in unrealistic schemes, exaggerated self-regard, demands for attention, and inappropriate idealization of certain others. Reactive increase in grandiosity because of perceived injury to self-esteem may appear in increased coldness, stilted speech, and painful self-consciousness.

Following this, Kohut (1972) described the phenomenon of "narcissistic rage," a profoundly angry reaction to injured self-esteem. Among its central features, Kohut included the "need for revenge, for righting a wrong, for undoing a hurt by whatever means, and a deeply anchored, unrelenting compulsion in the pursuit of all these aims" (p. 380). Another affective feature, in the description of which Kohut (1971) anticipated others (Bach 1977, Grunberger 1975, Svrakic 1985), involves the narcissistic individual's tendency toward hypomanic exaltation. Kohut portrayed it as an anxious excitement, sometimes associated with trancelike ecstasy and near-religious feelings of transcendence. This emotion is often precipitated by favorable occurrences in reality, which stir up the narcissist's as yet untamed exhibitionism and flood his psyche with archaic grandiosity.

Kohut and Wolf (1978) introduced a distinction between "narcissistic behavior disorders" and "narcissistic personality disorders." Unlike "borderline states," where "the break-up, the enfeeblement, or the functional chaos of the nuclear self" (p. 415) was permanent or protracted, both narcissistic behavior disorders and narcissistic personality disorders displayed such pathology on a transient basis. The distinction between the two was that in the latter "the symptoms—e.g., hypochondria, depression, hypersensitivity to slights, lack of zest—concern, not primarily the actions and interactions of the individual, but rather his psychological state" (p. 416). Whether the two conditions are to be regarded as degrees of clinical severity of narcissistic personality disorder itself remains unclear from this distinction.

In the same paper, Kohut and Wolf (1978) described five narcissistic personality types: (1) *mirror-hungry personalities,* who are constantly impelled to display themselves and to evoke others' admiration to counteract their inner sense of worthlessness; (2) *ideal-hungry personalities,* who are forever searching others they can admire for their prestige, skills, or power and from whom they can draw emotional sustenance; (3) *alter-ego personalities,* who need a relationship with someone conforming to their own values and thus confirming the reality of their selves; (4) *merger-hungry personalities,* who have a relentless desire to control others in an enactment of their need for inner structure; and (5) *contact-shunning personalities,* perhaps the most frequent of the narcissistic types, who avoid social contact to combat their powerful and frightening need for others.

Two comments seem necessary here. First, after describing the first three of these narcissistic character types, Kohut and Wolf (1978), in an unexplained reversal, stated that these should "in general, not be considered as forms of psychopathology, but rather as variants of normal human personality, with its assets and defects" (p. 422). By contrast, the latter two of the five types must be considered as "lying within the spectrum of pathological narcissism" (p. 422). Second, in line with Kohut's customary avoidance of usual psychiatric terminology, the potential overlap that "merger-hungry" and "contact-shunning" narcissistic types may have with borderline and schizoid personalities, respectively, is not commented on, thus missing an opportunity for linking these eloquent psychoanalytic observations with psychiatric nosology.

OTHER CONTEMPORARY AMERICAN ANALYSTS

I will now briefly comment on the views of Mahler, Bach, Volkan, Modell, Horowitz, Cooper, Bursten, and Rothstein, since these appear to provide substantial additional insights into narcissistic personality disorder.

From her child observational studies, Mahler (1970, Mahler and Kaplan 1977) concluded that narcissistic personalities do not proceed in the ordinary way through the early developmental process of separation-individuation, which culminates in a well-defined Oedipus complex. She pointed out that the adequacy of narcissistic libido, manifested in a healthy self-regard, depends upon soothing ministrations by the mother during the symbiotic phase, as well as upon her "emotional refueling" of the child during the later differentiation and early practicing subphases of separation-individuation. In addition, the autonomous activities of the later practicing subphase provide narcissistic enhancement from within. It is, however, during the rapprochement subphase that the growing child's narcissism is especially vulnerable. Maternal unavailability to empathically support the child's contrasting strivings for autonomy and fusion during this subphase may lead to a shattering collapse of the child's omnipotence. A fixation point is created with persistent splitting of self- and object representations. Renunciation of infantile omnipotence becomes difficult (Kramer 1974), and attainment of self and object constancy suffers. This, in turn, has deleterious effects on the nature and outcome of the Oedipus complex.

Phenomenological correlates of Mahler and Kaplan's (1977) developmental understanding of the narcissistic character include a continued search for perfection in oneself and others, intolerance of ambivalence, exquisite sensitivity to realistic setbacks, persistence of contradictory self-images of omnipotence and angry inferiority, and a constant vacillation between withdrawal from external objects and coercive attempts to subjugate and control them.

Bach (1977) indicates that the narcissistic person has defects in five areas: (1) perception of self; (2) language and thought organization; (3) intentionality and volition; (4) regulation of mood; and (5) perception of time, space, and causality. The disturbance in self includes a splitting of self; the split-off self-representation may even have a distinct psychophysical embodiment, such as a double. Even when such a personification does not occur, the split-off self shows a "mirror complementarity" with conscious complaints. An individual who has feelings of weakness and vulnerability may secretly harbor a grandiose and dangerously powerful split-off self, and one who exhibits paranoid arrogance may secretly fear the timid, dependent child-self. Among these individuals there is a relative predominance of self-oriented reality perception and a tendency toward excessive self-stimulation in the form of libidinized thinking, self-touching, and masturbation.

Like Jones (1913) and Waelder (1925), Bach highlights the cognitive peculiarities associated with narcissistic personality disorder. The narcissistic individual uses language in an autocentric manner for regulating self-esteem rather than for communicating or understanding. There is a peculiar gap between words and percepts, and the person gives the impression that he is talking to himself or that his words endlessly circle. A loss of flexibility in perspective results in overabstractness, concretization, or fluctuations between these extremes. Bach points out the subtle learning problems and memory defects seen in narcissistic individuals; the learning process, in its assumption of ignorance, inflicts an intolerable narcissistic injury. Along with these defects are restrictions in volition, spontaneity, and intentionality, often masked by fruitless pseudoactivity. For narcissistic individuals, time loses its impersonal, abstract quality and is reckoned by its internal, personal impact. Similarly, a causal relationship may be seen to exist between events solely because they occur simultaneously. Bach also points out that in narcissistic persons mood regulation is excessively dependent on external circumstances, with many ups and downs. These mood swings, however, differ from the classical cyclothymia, insofar as they are characterized by limited duration and rapid vacillations, with relative maintenance of insight and the general integrity of the personality.

Volkan (1976, 1980a, 1982, 1986), who has extensively applied his understanding of pathological narcissism to the study of sociopolitical processes, bases the diagnosis of narcissistic personality disorder on three criteria: "the surface picture, which reflects the patient's grandiose self, . . . the clinical picture, which reflects the other side of the coin, and the patient's constant attempts to protect and keep the cohesion of his grandiose self" (p. 338). His description of the first two aspects is in accordance with the literature already covered. It is in the third area that he makes original contributions. Volkan describes two specific maneuvers that narcissistic individuals use to keep their illusory greatness intact: the glass bubble fantasy and the transitional fantasy. In the glass bubble fantasy, narcissistic individuals feel that they are living by themselves in a glorious, albeit lonely, fashion enclosed by impervious but transparent protection. They can see others but cannot be meaningfully "touched" by them. Transitional fantasies (Volkan 1976, 1982) consist of imaginary and rather banal tales of personal glory that narcissistic persons habitually indulge in when faced with a threat to their self-esteem or when there is a regression to their ego control (e.g., while falling asleep). Their manner of using these fantasies, Volkan notes, is reminiscent of a child's use of transitional objects.

Modell (1984) bases his formulation largely on Winnicott's work (1965) and holds that narcissistic individuals were traumatized as children when their sense of self was developing. Deficient maternal empathy at that stage necessitates the establishment of a precocious and vulnerable sense of autonomy, which is supported by fantasies of omnipotence around which the grandiose self develops.

Horowitz (1975) offers three sets of criteria for the diagnosis of narcissistic personality. The first two refer to traits and interpersonal relations and include the clinical characteristics described by Kohut and Kernberg. The third refers to the information-processing style, which Horowitz sees as consisting of paying undue attention to praise and criticism, maintaining incompatible psychological attitudes in separate clusters, and using characteristic coping devices when faced with threats to self-esteem. The narcissist denies, disavows, or negates disappointing experiences or "slides around the meaning of events in order to place the self in a better light" (p. 171). Such fluid shifts in meanings, while permitting an apparent logical consistency, lead to a shaky subjective experience of ideas.

Cooper (1988) suggests that narcissism and masochistic tendencies are closely intertwined in the course of development. He believes that a single nosological entity, "the narcissistic-masochistic character" (p. 137), better integrated the vast literature existing on narcissistic and masochistic personalities separately. Masochistic satisfaction includes an element of narcissistic control, and narcissistic pursuit of attention often results in feeling painfully abandoned. Although in a given person one or the other of the tendencies may be more overt, they have a certain kind of characterological unity.

Bursten (1973a) attempted definition and even subclassification of narcissistic personality disorder. His definition is similar to those outlined above. However, his subclassification of the disorder into four subtypes (craving, paranoid, manipulative, and phallic) seems too inclusive in that it subsumes such diverse character pathologies as passive-aggressive, antisocial, and paranoid under one nosological rubric. In all fairness to Bursten, however, it should be acknowledged that similarities do exist between narcissistic personality disorder and paranoid, antisocial, hypomanic, and borderline characters. However, these disorders also have significant differences, which I will highlight in the section on differential diagnosis.

One last point regarding the nature of the Oedipus complex in narcissistic personality and its impact on the disorder's phenomenology. While many investigators, for example, W. Reich (1933), A. Reich (1960), Mahler and Kaplan (1977), and Kernberg (1970b, 1975a), have commented on this aspect, it has received more focused attention from Rothstein. Reporting on a number of male narcissistic patients, Rothstein (1979) states that a combination of maternal seduction and paternal failure frequently exists in these individuals' background, which leads them to experience a positive oedipal victory. Such a situation results in intense castration anxiety, patricidal guilt, and self-destructiveness, as well as a lifelong hunger for an admirable father. Contradictory attitudes regarding oedipal realities persist and give rise to unconscious guilt and impaired genital sexuality on the one hand, and an atemporal life-style, irreverent bravado, promiscuity, and perverse formations on the other.

Before ending this section, I should like to mention some other recent publications that have significant, though at times indirect, bearing on the phenomenology of narcissistic personality disorder. These include Gediman's (1985) paper on the multidetermined nature of feelings of imposture and fraudulence, Rinsley's (1980, 1981) synthesis of various etiological models of borderline and narcissistic conditions, Singer's (1977a,b) papers on the subjective experience of emptiness, Spruiell's (1975) distinction of three separate developmental strands (i.e., self-love, self-esteem and omnipotence) within the concept of narcissism, Stone's (1980) construction of multidimensional personality profiles, Tyson and Tyson's (1984) paper on superego and narcissistic pathology, and finally my own descriptions of the behavioral correlates of splitting (Akhtar and Byrne 1983) and identity diffusion (Akhtar 1984).

RECENT EUROPEAN CONTRIBUTIONS

Contemporary European psychoanalysts have made significant contributions to the understanding of narcissistic personality disorder. Prominent among them are Rosenfeld and Kinston from England; Freeman from Scotland; Grunberger, Green, and Chasseguet-Smirgel from France; Miller from Switzerland; and Svrakic and Starcevic from Yugoslavia.

Rosenfeld (1964, 1971) describes narcissistic object relations as characterized by omnipotence, preponderance of identification, and defenses against any recognition of separateness between self and the object. The narcissist's omnipotence is manifest in his ruthless use of others with concomitant denial of any dependence on them, since its recognition implies vulnerability to love, separation, and envy of what others have to offer. By introjective identification, the desirable aspects of others are claimed as belonging to himself; by projective identification, undesirable aspects of the self are deposited into others. An idealized self-image is maintained, and anything interfering with it is vehemently defended against. When the idealization of libidinal aspects of the self predominates, the individual feels that he is loved by everyone, or should be loved by everyone, because he is so lovable. Such an individual feels humiliated on discovering goodness in others and defends himself by devaluing them or avoiding contact with them. A more malignant situation prevails when destructive aspects of the self become idealized. Such patients attempt to destroy whatever love is offered them in order to maintain their superiority over others. In becoming completely identified with the omnipotent destructive aspect of their selves, they kill off their sane, loving and dependent self. At times, they are wistfully aware of this inner imprisonment and feel that there is nothing anybody can do to change the situation.

According to Kinston (1980, 1982), the narcissist's identity disturbance, feelings of uncertainty, and self-doubt have their roots in the absence of maternal investment in the individual's authentic experience during childhood. The weakened inner security and the accompanying wish to control the maternal object under such circumstances give rise to increased vigilance, excessive attention to the environment, interpersonal oversensitivity, and defenses against these states. The mother's repeated and excessive use of the child for her own needs results in the latter's tendency toward inauthentic compliance, pathological omnipotence, incapacity to depend upon others, and seemingly generous, bountiful grandiosity.

Freeman (1964) believes that pathological narcissism emanates as a defensive response to early frustrations; the self is loved because objects in childhood were disappointing. He further suggests that while both typically neurotic and psychotic individuals may show pathological narcissism, it is in the cases that fall between these extremes (for instance, the cases of perversion) that pathological narcissism is most evident.

Grunberger (1975) likens the narcissist to the fetus, which exists in a seemingly self-sufficient, oblivious, and parasitic economy where it receives everything but has to give nothing in return. He posits that a fundamental conflict exists throughout life, between the longing to return to such narcissistic bliss and the unavoidable human necessity for emotional dependence on others. The narcissistic individual, more than others, continues to yearn for unconditional indulgence from his world, uniqueness, omnipotence, and unlimited autonomy. Such a person is frequently preoccupied with desires for invulnerability, infiniteness, and immortality. He loathes the acknowledgment of his dependence on others, considering himself the incarnation of perfection, existing spontaneously and denying any rational causation.

This theme also finds expression in the writings of Green (1986), who suggests that narcissism manifests itself in three realms: physical, intellectual, and moral. Physical narcissism manifests in undue preoccupation with one's appearance, exhibitionism, and hypochondriacal concerns. Intellectual narcissism becomes evident in a feeling of omnipotence, a libidinization of thinking, and a tendency to dominate others by intellectual prowess. Moral narcissism gives rise to a yearning to be pure, above ordinary human needs, and free of attachment to others. Green distinguishes such narcissistic asceticism (which I propose might be a more frequent presentation of narcissistic personality in Oriental cultures) from masochism on two grounds. First, the moral narcissist suffers from shame over his having ordinary needs, while the moral masochist suffers from guilt over the nature of his desires. Second, the moral narcissist attempts to impoverish his object relationships in order to restore his infantile megalomania of self-sufficiency, while the moral masochist maintains a tormented but rich tie to his objects.

Chasseguet-Smirgel (1984, 1985) regards the narcissistic character to be a malady of ego-ideal formation. In her view, the recognition of sexual differences and generational boundaries inevitably causes the growing child a narcissistic injury. Under ordinary circumstances, this is compensated by the child's idealization of his father and, in seeking to become like him, by the formation of the ego ideal. The child accepts his own smallness, learns to wait, and develops a plan for the future. However, if the mother collusively conveys to the child that he is superior to the father, is already a man, then "forward projection" of infantile narcissism does not occur and the father is not idealized. Ego and ego ideal are fused. The narcissistic injury of one's smallness is "repaired not by an imitation of the father and his attributes . . . but by an attempt to free oneself completely from all filial links" (1984, p. 74). Upon becoming an adult, such an individual displays disregard of generational boundaries, lack of comprehension of incest taboo, promiscuity, perversions, impatience, and pervasive intolerance of the limits imposed on him by reality. However, Chasseguet-Smirgel, like Rothstein (1979), notices the inner hollowness, inauthenticity, and unconscious guilt in such narcissistic personalities.

The narcissist's inner world of feelings has been poignantly described by Miller (1981). According to her, while narcissistic individuals might have been overindulged in their childhood, they were not actually loved as persons in their own right. They were used for parental glorification, as substitutes for parental missing structures, and did not receive an empathic acceptance in which their developing authentic self could unfold. Loneliness felt in the parental home, under such circumstances, later comes to be the narcissist's isolation within himself. Undue accommodation to parental needs leads to a loss of affective aliveness and spontaneity. The vaguely depressive pain over the loss of the real self is defended by grandiosity and addiction to external acclaim. However, as admiration is not the same as love, these achievements bring no inner peace and the narcissist continues to envy those whose internal lives are richer.

Another attempt at systematization of emotional features of narcissistic personality was made recently by Svrakic (1985, 1986), who distinguished between primary and secondary narcissistic emotions. The former include chronic envy, unprovoked periodic rage, and feelings of emptiness and boredom. Among the latter, Svrakic included narcissistic rage, when there was an injury to self-esteem, and hypomanic exaltation, when there was ample gratification of narcissistic needs. Svrakic noted that, with a few exceptions, most narcissistic patients decompensate in late mid-life when external narcissistic supplies begin to diminish. They may then present with depression, boredom, and pessimism. In some cases, however, the image of "pessimistic hero" itself becomes "a new nucleus around which, through an old pattern, the subjective experience of grandiosity organizes itself again" (1986, p. 269).

Finally, Starcevic (1989) states that narcissistic personality is a defensive organization against "a pervasive fear of somatic vulnerability" (p. 314) and an equally profound mistrust in one's bodily worth.

DSM-III AND *DSM-III-R*

DSM-III listed narcissistic personality disorder as a separate, distinct nosological entity and in doing so, while it was yet to be mentioned in the major psychiatric textbooks, demonstrated a progressive tendency. It listed the following diagnostic criteria (1980, p. 317) and specified that these were characteristic of the individual's long-term functioning and not limited to episodic behavior.

A. Grandiose sense of self-importance or uniqueness, e.g., exaggeration of achievements and talents, focus on the special nature of one's problems.

B. Preoccupation with fantasies of unlimited success, power, brilliance, beauty, or ideal love.

C. Exhibitionism: the person requires constant attention and admiration.

D. Cool indifference or marked feelings of rage, inferiority, shame, humiliation, or emptiness in response to criticism, indifference of others, or defeat.

E. At least two of the following characteristic of disturbances in interpersonal relationships:

(i) entitlement: expectation of special favors without assuming reciprocal responsibilities, e.g., surprise and anger that people will not do what is wanted

(ii) interpersonal exploitativeness: taking advantage of others to indulge own desires or for self-aggrandizement; disregard for the personal integrity and rights of others

(iii) relationships that characteristically alternate between the extremes of overidealization and devaluation

(iv) lack of empathy: inability to recognize how others feel, e.g., unable to appreciate the distress of someone who is seriously ill.

These criteria failed to include certain important features of the disorder. These include chronic, intense envy and defenses against it; an exhibitionistic motivation to work; corruptibility of value systems; a tendency toward promiscuity; and cognitive peculiarities, including seeming articulateness; "sliding of meanings" (Horowitz 1975), egocentric perception of reality; pathological lying (Kohut 1971); soft learning defects; autocentric use of language, and inattention toward objective aspects of events (Bach 1977, Jones 1913, Waelder 1925).

DSM-III-R presents a revised outline. It portrays the disorder as a pervasive pattern of grandiosity, hypersensitivity, and defective empathy manifested by at least five of the following criteria (1987, p. 351):

(i) reacts to criticism with feelings of rage, shame, or humiliation (even if not expressed)

(ii) is interpersonally exploitative: takes advantage of others to achieve his or her own ends

(iii) has a grandiose sense of self-importance, e.g., exaggerates achievements and talents, expects to be noticed as "special" without appropriate achievement

(iv) believes that his or her problems are unique and can be understood only by other special people

(v) is preoccupied with fantasies of unlimited success, power, brilliance, beauty, or ideal love

(vi) has a sense of entitlement: unreasonable expectation of especially favorable treatment, e.g., assumes that he or she does not have to wait in line when others must do so

(vii) requires constant attention and admiration, e.g., keeps fishing for compliments

(viii) lack of empathy: inability to recognize and experience how others feel, e.g., annoyance and surprise when a friend who is seriously ill cancels a date

(ix) is preoccupied with feelings of envy

The inclusion of chronic feelings of envy is an improvement over *DSM-III*. However, the removal of the tendency toward overidealization and devaluation of others from the list weakens the description. Moreover, superego defects, pseudosublimation, cognitive peculiarities, and disturbances in sexual and romantic life are once again omitted from the diagnostic criteria. Finally, like *DSM-III, DSM-III-R* does not emphasize the coexistence of mutually contradictory stances in almost all areas of psychosocial functioning, a central feature of the condition (Akhtar and Thomson 1982a). The following composite profile of the disorder covers these important aspects omitted in *DSM-III* and *DSM-III-R*.

AN ATTEMPT AT SYNTHESIS

The literature surveyed above was combined and synthesized in order to develop a true picture of narcissistic personality disorder. According to this profile (Table 3–1), which is an elaboration of an

TABLE 3–1. Clinical Features of Narcissistic Personality Disorder

Clinical Features	*Overt Characteristics*	*Covert Characteristics*
I. *Self-Concept*	Grandiosity; preoccupation with fantasies of outstanding success; undue sense of uniqueness; feelings of entitlement; seeming self-sufficiency	Inferiority; morose self-doubts; marked propensity toward feeling ashamed; fragility; relentless search for glory and power; marked sensitivity to criticism and realistic setbacks
II. *Interpersonal Relations*	Numerous but shallow relationships; intense need for tribute from others; scorn for others, often masked by pseudohumility; lack of empathy; inability to genuinely participate in group activities, in family life; value children over spouse	Inability to genuinely depend on others and trust them; chronic envy of others' talents, possessions, and capacity for deep object relations; lack of regard for generational boundaries; disregard for others' time; not answering letters
III. *Social Adaptation*	Socially charming; often successful; consistent hard work done mainly to seek admiration (pseudosublimation); intense ambition; preoccupation with appearances	Nagging aimlessness; shallow vocational commitment; dilettantelike attitude; multiple but superficial interests; chronic boredom; aesthetic taste often ill-informed and imitative

IV.	*Love and Sexuality*	Marital instability; cold and greedy seductiveness; extramarital affairs and promiscuity; uninhibited sexual life	Inability to remain in love; impaired capacity for viewing the romantic partner as a separate individual with his/her own interests, rights, and values; inability to genuinely comprehend the incest taboo; occasional sexual perversions
V.	*Ethics, Standards, and Ideals*	Caricatured modesty; pretended contempt for money in real life; idiosyncratically and unevenly moral; apparent enthusiasm for sociopolitical affairs	Readiness to shift values to gain favor; pathologic lying; materialistic lifestyle; delinquent tendencies; inordinate ethnic and moral relativism; irreverence toward authority
VI.	*Cognitive Style*	Impressively knowledgeable; decisive and opinionated; often strikingly articulate; egocentric perception of reality; love of language; fondness for shortcuts to acquisition of knowledge	Knowledge often limited to trivia ("headline intelligence"); forgetful of details, especially names; impaired in the capacity to learn new skills; tendency to change meanings of reality when facing a threat to self-esteem; language and speaking used for regulating self-esteem

earlier attempt (Akhtar and Thomson 1982a), the clinical features of narcissistic personality disorder involve six areas of psychosocial functioning: (1) self-concept, (2) interpersonal relations, (3) social adaptation, (4) love and sexuality, (5) ethics, standards, and ideals, and (6) cognitive style. In each of these areas, there are overt and covert manifestations. This conceptualization of the clinical features as being both overt and covert should be regarded as a forward step, since it serves to

> underline the centrality of splitting in narcissistic personalities and to emphasize their divided self. This not only gives sounder theoretical underpinnings to the disorder's phenomenology but also prepares the clinician for the mirror complementarity of the self that Bach (1977) noted. Patients with narcissistic personality disorder may sometimes initially display some of the usually covert features, while most of the usually overt ones remain hidden in the first few interviews, but the therapist's awareness of the dichotomous self will encourage further inquiry and prevent misdiagnosis. [Akhtar and Thomson 1982a, p. 17]

It should be pointed out that the overt and covert designations in this context do not necessarily imply their conscious or unconscious existence, though such topographical distribution might also exist; Kohut's (1971) concept of the occasional "horizontal splitting" of the grandiose self addresses this point. In general, however, the overt and covert designations denote seemingly contradictory phenomenological aspects that are more or less easily discernible. Moreover, these contradictions are not restricted to the individual's self-concept but permeate his interpersonal relations, social adaption, love life, morality, and cognitive attitudes. The individual with a narcissistic personality disorder is overtly grandiose, scornful of others, successful, enthusiastic about ideologies, seductive, and often strikingly articulate. However, covertly he is doubt-ridden, envious, bored, incapable of genuine sublimations, unable to love, corruptible, forgetful, and impaired in the capacity for genuine learning.

This manner of organizing symptomatology, however, is not entirely problem-free. For instance, there is a risk of the overt and covert designations being completely equated with conscious and unconscious aspects despite reminders to the contrary. The risk is heightened by the fact that covert features are by definition difficult to discern and may not be immediately apparent. Also, the lack of actuarial data on the frequency of various clinical features makes their relative diagnostic weight difficult to ascertain at this time. These reservations notwithstanding, the profile of narcissistic personality disorder remains superior to ordinary checklist methods since it (1) includes both phenomenological and psychodynamic observations, (2) values depth and complexity over descriptive oversimplification, and (3) establishes a connection between the descriptive and psychostructural, hence developmental, aspects of the narcissistic pathology. While it does not fully resolve the general difficulties in describing any personality disorder (Frances 1982), this detailed profile may lend itself better to the prototypal model of classification proposed by Frances and Widiger (1986) as the only way to salvage a categorical system of personality diagnosis. Finally, this profile helps in more meaningful differential diagnosis of narcissistic from other related personality disorders.

DISTINCTION FROM BETTER INTEGRATED PERSONALITY DISORDERS

Distinguishing narcissistic personality disorder from personality disorders with a "higher level" (Kernberg 1970a) character organization (e.g., obsessional and hysterical personalities) should not be very difficult, since the resemblances are only superficial. For example, individuals with obsessional and hysterical personality disorders do not give the history of a deeply traumatized childhood. Unlike narcissistic characters, they display the evidence of a successful separation-individuation process, greater internalization of conflict, better superego integration, consolidation of identity, predominance of repression over splitting as the main defensive operation, and capacity for deep object relationships. However, on a behavioral level narcissistic personality does resemble obsessional and hysterical personalities. This makes distinguishing them necessary.

Obsessional Personality

Both narcissistic and obsessional personalities display high ego ideals, great need for control, perfectionism, and a driven quality to their work. Important differences, however, exist in the inner lives of the two (Akhtar 1984, Akhtar and Thomson 1982a, Kernberg 1970a,b, 1975a, Volkan 1976, 1982). The obsessive person seeks perfection; the narcissist claims it. The obsessive loves details, which the narcissist casually disregards (W. Reich 1933). The obsessive does not devalue others, while the narcissist shows contempt for others. The obsessive has a high, even undue, regard for authority, while the narcissist has frequent difficulty with those having power over him. The obsessive is modest, the narcissist haughty. The obsessive is rigidly moral, while the narcissist is corruptible. Finally, although somewhat bland on the surface, the obsessive has genuine moral and sociopolitical beliefs; the narcissist shows apparent enthusiasm about such issues while lacking authentic commitment to them.

Hysterical Personality

Many authors (Akhtar and Thomson 1982a, Kernberg 1975a, Volkan 1976) have stated that narcissistic individuals seem like hysterical individuals. Both tend to be demonstrative, exhibitionistic, dramatic, and, at times, seductive. However, the narcissistic patient's exhibitionism and seductiveness have an exploitive, cold quality; the hysterical person is more human, playful, and warm. The hysteric is capable of tolerating ambivalence and does not display "narcissistic rage" (Kohut 1972) when crossed. Also, the affectualization of the hysteric is usually restricted to instinctually exciting, triangulated situations. The narcissist, on the other hand, is constantly bubbling with sadistically tinged exhibitionistic affects. Indeed, both obsessional and hysterical individuals, unlike narcissists, retain the capacity for empathy, concern, and love for others.

DISTINCTION FROM OTHER SEVERE PERSONALITY DISORDERS

Narcissistic personality disorder also needs to be distinguished from borderline, schizoid, paranoid, hypomanic (Akhtar 1987), antisocial, and as-if (Deutsch 1942) personalities. Although they differ in their phenotypal presentations and, to some extent, in their developmental background and psychostructural characteristics, all these disorders imply a "lower level" (Kernberg 1970a) of character organization. Developmentally, individuals suffering from them show a history of preoedipal trauma; an aborted separation-individuation process; much pregenital aggression; a distorted and unresolved Oedipus complex; uneven, defective, and poorly internalized superego functions; failure to establish an optimal state of latency; and a more than usually troubled adolescence (Akhtar 1984, Erikson 1959, Fairbairn 1944, Guntrip 1969, Kernberg 1970a, 1975a, Khan 1983, Klein 1975, Mahler 1970, 1975, Mahler and Kaplan 1977). Psychostructurally, all these disorders imply identity diffusion (Akhtar 1984, Erikson 1959, Kernberg 1975a, 1980a), although the degree to which various features of this syndrome are readily manifest varies (Akhtar 1984). Dynamically, splitting or active dissociation of mutually contradictory self- and object representations (Akhtar and Byrne 1983, Kernberg 1975a, Mahler and Kaplan 1977) is a major defensive operation in all these conditions. Descriptively, patients with these personality disorders exhibit vacillating interpersonal relationships, defective empathy, inability to love, egocentric perception of reality, sexual difficulties, and moral defects. Despite these remarkable similarities, important differences between these personality disorders exist.

Borderline Personality

More devastating traumatic events during childhood (e.g., parental divorce, desertion or death, and familial alcoholism or violence) usually characterize the developmental background of borderline patients (Gunderson 1985a, Shapiro et al. 1975, Walsh 1977). With narcissistic patients, one usually gets the history that, as children, they were treated by their parents in an unempathic, cold, and even spiteful but nonetheless "special" manner (Robbins 1982, Volkan 1976). This is perhaps because many of them did, from the very beginning, possess special attributes (e.g., talent, outstanding intelligence, or physical charm) that drew admiration from their otherwise unempathic early environment.

Moreover, in narcissistic disorder, the self is more cohesive and less in danger of regressive fragmentation (Adler 1981, Kohut 1971). In borderline personality, the self is poorly integrated and at risk of dissolution into psychoticlike states during stress or under the influence of psychoactive substances (Adler 1981, Gunderson 1985a,b, Kohut 1971). In narcissistic patients, the inflated self-concept hides the shame-laden, hungry self-representation (Kernberg 1970a, 1975a, Volkan 1976), while in borderline patients, a core of omnipotence is hidden behind the overt, devalued self-representation (Kernberg 1975a). Identity diffusion is manifest in borderline personality, while it is masked in narcissistic personality by an enthusiastic yet shallow vocational commitment. Because of their greater cohesiveness, narcissistic personalities show a greater tolerance for aloneness (Adler 1981), a better work record, and greater social adjustment. Also, narcissistic individuals show better impulse control and anxiety tolerance than borderline patients. Self-mutilation and persistent overt rage, frequent in borderline personality (*DSM-III* 1980, *DSM-III-R* 1987, Gunderson 1985a, Gunderson and Kolb 1978, Gunderson and Singer 1975) are not features of the narcissistic disorder.

Schizoid Personality

Both narcissistic and schizoid individuals prefer ideas over people. Both display intellectual hypertrophy and a corresponding lack of wholesome rootedness in their bodily existence. Both lack warmth, feel awkward in intimate situations, and avoid encounters that require genuinely spontaneous responses (Akhtar 1987, Akhtar and Thomson 1982, Bach 1977, Fairbairn 1944, Guntrip 1969, Khan 1983). Important differences, however, exist between the two conditions (Akhtar 1987). The narcissist exploits others for his dependency needs, while the schizoid hides his dependency needs (Nemiah 1961). The narcissistic individual is ambitious and competitive (Kernberg 1970b, 1975a), while the schizoid is resigned and fatalistic (Akhtar 1987, Fairbairn 1944, Guntrip 1969, Khan 1983). The narcissist compensates for his defective object relations by compulsive socialization. The schizoid individual has given up the external search for an omnipotent love object only to replace it with an ongoing involvement with highly valued internal objects. As a result, the narcissist is active, restless, flamboyant, and chronically in pursuit, while the schizoid is passive, cynical, overtly bland, or, at best, vaguely mysterious.

Paranoid Personality

A facade of cold grandiosity is present in both narcissistic and paranoid personalities. Devaluation of others, difficulty in accepting criticism, restricted affectivity, defective empathy, chronic envy, and a sense of entitlement are all shown by both narcissistic and paranoid individuals. However, the paranoid person lacks the attention-seeking charm and seductiveness of the narcissist. The narcissist, on the other hand, does not display the paranoid's pervasive mistrust and search for hidden demeaning intentions of others (Shapiro 1965). The narcissist can indulge in superficial banter, though craftily; the paranoid lacks all sense of humor and cannot relax with others. Finally, the cognitive style of the two individuals shows important differences. The narcissist, often inattentive to real events, is forgetful of details and unable to learn well (Bach 1977, Jones 1913, Waelder 1925). The paranoid, in contrast, has a biased but acute and highly vigilant cognition (*DSM-III* 1980, *DSM-III-R* 1987, Shapiro 1965).

Antisocial Personality

The narcissistic person may indulge in substance abuse, promiscuity, manipulativeness, and antisocial behavior. Also, he may display occasional pathological lying (Kohut 1971) and may distort events to suit his purposes (Horowitz 1975). However, these behaviors are sporadic. The narcissistic patient is devoid of the consistent, pervasive, calculated, and ruthless disregard for social standards evident in the sociopathic individual (*DSM-III* 1980, *DSM-III-R* 1987). Unlike the sociopathic individual, the narcissistic patient retains the ability for consistent work and job-related success.

Hypomanic Personality

Both narcissistic and hypomanic individuals overtly display grandiosity, self-absorption, social ease, articulateness, seductiveness, and moral, aesthetic, and vocational enthusiasm. Covertly, both experience feelings of inferiority, boredom, uncertainty, and aimlessness. However, they differ in important ways (Akhtar 1988). The narcissist overtly devalues others while secretly envying them; the hypomanic, on the surface, is everyone's friend yet privately holds them in contempt. The narcissist is devoid of constant elation, verbosity, pervasive denial, compulsive humor, and object hunger that characterize the hypomanic. The hypomanic, on the other hand, lacks the seething vindictiveness of "narcissistic rage" and either explodes in anger when crossed or, using extensive denial, is all too eager to forgive and forget. While both are ambitious and overactive, the narcissist comes across as dedicated, haughty, humorless, and steadfast in his pursuit of perfection, while the hypomanic appears playful, suggestible, digressive, and more impaired in his capacity for sadness and mature aloneness (Akhtar 1988).

As-If Personality

Inauthenticity, inordinate moral relativism, and a tendency to imitate idealized others are seen in both "as-if" (Deutsch 1942, Meissner 1982, Ross 1967) and narcissistic personalities. The latter disorder, however, lacks the intense suggestibility of the as-if personality. Also, the degree to which aggression is sequestered is much greater in the as-if personality. Narcissistic patients can become quite oppositional and even vindictively enraged (Kohut 1977, W. Reich 1933). The bleak, rapidly shifting, and shallow childhood environment often associated with the as-if personality sharply contrasts with the tormented but colorful childhood of the narcissistic individual. Moreover, as Meissner (1982) points out the as-if personality has not achieved a "strong enough oedipal involvement" in childhood, while the narcissist has a distorted but intense Oedipus complex (Chasseguet-Smirgel 1984, 1985, Rothstein 1979). Its evidences are manifest in the narcissist's inability to genuinely comprehend incest taboo and to respect generational boundaries (Chasseguet-Smirgel 1984, 1985), as well as in his intense castration anxiety and incapacity for mature, genital sexuality (Rothstein 1979).

COMMENT

One final aspect of narcissistic personality disorder as a nosological entity now remains to be addressed. This pertains to its demographic correlates. The disorder seems to have a greater prevalence among males. This is implicit throughout the literature surveyed above and has been explicitly noted by some investigators (Akhtar and Thomson 1982a, W. Reich 1933). The reasons for this finding are, however, unclear. Could it simply be a reflection of the fact (Pulver 1978) that more men than women are undergoing psychoanalysis? After all, practically all these descriptions do come from largely analytic practices. Or is there a diagnostic bias whereby more men are diagnosed as having narcissistic personality, while women with similar features are labeled otherwise? Or is there a referral artifact? In other words, do narcissistic men more often than narcissistic women seek treatment? If so, then what might be the reasons for this? Finally, is there a genuinely greater incidence of narcissistic personality in men? In that case, could it be that male psychosexual development, or perhaps even the gender-determined differences in the separation-individuation process of two sexes (Mahler 1970, 1975), contribute to this difference? Clearly, these are provocative questions, but few definitive answers exist at this time.

A second demographic issue pertains to birth order. There is considerable evidence in the literature that a large proportion of narcissistic patients are either the firstborn or the only child in their families. The meaning of this finding is unclear. Is it possible that being the first or only child renders the growing child's psychic structure more vulnerable to parental anxieties and to conscious or unconscious demands for perfection? To what extent does the birth order actually affect separation-individuation, oedipal conflict, and identity consolidation?

The final demographic issue is whether narcissistic personality disorder is merely a sociocultural epiphenomenon related to contemporary Western culture. Hankoff (1982), for instance, states that

> narcissistic personality features refer more often to cultural attitudes and values than to a psychological or psychopathological entity. . . .

> If the society at large reflects the themes and behaviors that characterize narcissism, are we not looking at a sociocultural phenomenon rather than an intrapsychic one? [p. 1078]

Similar implications with subtle variations can be found in Lifton's (1971) portrayal of the "protean man," Wheelis's (1966) poignant description of the "illusionless man," Johnson's (1977) existential portrait of the "alienated man," and Lasch's (1978) sociological study of "the culture of narcissism." This approach, however, is misleading. It ignores the fact that narcissistic patients were clearly recognized long before the so-called me generation. It also overlooks the existence of narcissistic personality disorder in individuals raised and residing in non-Western cultures (Akhtar and Thomson 1982a). Certainly, societal attitudes facilitate the expression of someone's pathological narcissism, but it is a fallacy to equate cultural individualism with a pathologic personality formation that has a tormented (and tormenting) life of its own. I hope this chapter has amply elucidated and firmly established the nosological entity consequent upon such pathological narcissism.

4

BORDERLINE PERSONALITY DISORDER

My secrets cry aloud.
I have no need for tongue.
My heart keeps open house,
My doors are widely swung.
An epic of the eyes
My love, with no disguise.

—"Open House," Theodore Roethke

The literature on borderline personality disorder is enormous. Besides numerous descriptive papers, quantitative research studies, and psychoanalytic essays, it includes at least three edited, multi-authored volumes (Grotstein et al. 1987, Hartocollis 1977, Mack 1975) and seventeen books by individual investigators (Abend et al. 1983, Adler 1985, Chatham 1986, Grinker and Werble 1977, Grinker et al. 1968, Gunderson 1984, Kernberg 1975a, Kroll 1988, Masterson 1972, 1976, Meissner 1984, Rinsley 1982, Searles 1986, Stone 1980, Volkan 1976, 1986, Wolberg 1973). These wide-ranging contributions pertain to the disorder's genetics, phenomenology, nosological boundaries, psychodynamics, developmental background, and treatment by psychopharmacological agents or psychoanalytic psychotherapy. To review this vast literature is clearly beyond the scope of this chapter. Here I will focus on the disorder's phenomenology. Even in this realm, I will sacrifice comprehensiveness for clarity. I will stay close to the primary sources and cite only those review articles (Gunderson and Singer 1975, Liebowitz 1979, Mack 1975, Perry and Klerman 1978) that provide a significantly unique synthesis of prior literature. I will survey both the descriptive and psychoanalytic contributions separately and attempt to trace the evolution of this elusive nosological concept. I will then synthesize the various views into a composite clinical picture of the disorder and discuss its distinctions from other severe personality disorders.

DESCRIPTIVE STUDIES

Early Literature

In 1835, Prichard expanded the horizons of clinical psychiatry forever by pointing out that, in addition to the traditional forms of insanity, there is "a form of mental derangement in which the intellectual faculties appear to have sustained little or no injury." Prichard called this disorder "moral insanity" and described it as

> madness consisting in a morbid perversion of the natural feelings, affections, inclinations, temper, habits, moral disposition, and natural impulses, without any remarkable disorder or defect of the intellect of knowing and reasoning faculties, and particularly without any insane illusion or hallucination. [Prichard, quoted in Mack 1975, p. 2]

Prichard's concept of "moral" faculties included will and temperament in addition to conscience (Mack 1975), and his "moral insanity" was a broadly inclusive entity. However, later interpretations of his concept became restricted to antisocial individuals only, leading to a gradual inattention toward other severely dysfunctional personalities.

Kraepelin (1905) revived interest in this area by his description of "morbid personalities." He viewed these conditions as "borderline states" between insanity and day-to-day eccentricities of normal individuals. According to Kraepelin, there were numerous forms of morbid personality that showed "every possible combination of inefficiency with healthy and even with exceptionally gifted dispositions" (p. 295). However, only a few, especially those with legal difficulties, came to psychiatric attention. Acknowledging a referral artifact to his sample, Kraepelin described three types of individuals in this group: (1) those with an instability of will, (2) morbid liars and swindlers, and (3) pseudoquerulous individuals. The latter two groups represent antisocial and paranoid personality disorder, respectively, while the first seems to resemble borderline personality. The patient Kraepelin described under this designation had a "checquered career . . . [was] childishly unstable . . . presumptuous, overbearing and unmanageable. . . . want of all perseverance and resistance to temptation. . . . shortsighted selfishness. . . . complete want of sympathy with others . . . [and] occasional great irritability" (pp. 296–299). Whether this describes borderline personality is debatable, but what remains clear is that among "morbid personalities" Kraepelin included antisocial ("morbid liars"), paranoid ("pseudoquerulous"), borderline ("those with instability of the will"), and even narcissistic ("exceptionally gifted" and "striking") types. However, this breadth was lost sight of by later investigators and the term *psychopathic personality,* which had replaced *morbid personalities* in Kraepelin's (1921b) subsequent writings, became restricted to antisocial individuals. The broad area of other severe personality disorders became neglected again.

A decade later, an incentive to explore this understudied area came from Bleuler and Kretschmer. Bleuler (1911) questioned the pessimism inherent in the Kraepelinian designation *dementia praecox.* He renamed the syndrome *schizophrenia,* implying that a disorganization of psychic functions rather than an ultimate demented state was its outstanding characteristic. Moreover, Bleuler described two nonpsychotic forms of the disorder, namely, simple and latent schizophrenias. Individuals suffering from them did not suffer from hallucinations and delusions. However, they did display oddities of behavior attributable to an underlying tendency to turn away from reality and live in a world of fantasy. Although Bleuler's concepts of latent and simple schizophrenia are now largely subsumed under schizotypal personality disorder, their value lies in having further opened up the area of nonpsychotic yet severe oddities of behavior for investigation.

Kretschmer's (1925) detailed descriptions of the "cycloid" and "schizoid" temperaments associated with manic-depressive and schizophrenic psychoses, respectively, furthered this line of investigation. I would highlight his conceptualizations in the chapters on schizoid and hypomanic personalities. Here I wish to emphasize that beginning with Prichard and continuing in the works of Kraepelin, Bleuler, and Kretschmer, one notices an expansion of the purview of clinical psychiatry and an increasing interest in severely impaired personality types, especially as these related to classical psychoses. Inherent in their contributions are the seeds of antisocial, paranoid, cyclothymic, hypomanic, schizoid, and schizotypal personality disorders.

Some other early contributions also deserve mention. Zilboorg (1941) described individuals suffering from "ambulatory schizophrenia." He included in this group psychopathic personalities, sexual perverts, and murderers, as well as relatively mild-mannered, unobtrusive, and ineffective people. In most cases of "ambulatory schizophrenia," there was an outward appearance of normality accompanied by shallow emotionality, incapacity for true friendships, dereistic thinking, and inability to settle on one job or life pursuit. Zilboorg, however, discarded the label *borderline* and regarded this condition as a muted variant of schizophrenia.

A few years later, Hoch and Polatin (1949) described a somewhat different condition under the designation *pseudoneurotic schizophrenia.* Individuals suffering from this disorder appeared neurotic, but hidden behind this facade were the core features of schizophrenia. These patients displayed pananxiety, pansexuality, and panneurosis. No area of their functioning was free from conflict and tension. Their sexual life was characterized by promiscuity and perversions. They displayed multiple and severe neurotic symptoms. In addition, they were exquisitely sensitive to criticism and often seething with ill-concealed rage. Hoch and Polatin emphasized that theirs was not a borderline group but a genuine subtype of schizophrenia. Their concept, however, did not gain much popularity and gradually faded away from nosological debates. One thing it did accomplish was to highlight the overlap of apparently neurotic symptomatology with an inwardly sicker state of affairs.

Two other sources provided impetus to search for clarity in this realm. First, much information about "sicker patients" began to pour in from clinical psychoanalysis. This data, besides deepening the understanding of intrapsychic dynamics of borderline patients, helped define these patients with greater phenomenological clarity. Second, studies involving psychological testing (Rapaport et al. 1945, 1946; see also the summary of psychological testing literature by Singer 1977) suggested that there existed a seemingly nonpsychotic, though considerably maladjusted, group of individuals who reveal a predominance of primary-process thinking in unstructured situations. These two sources, combined with the earlier descriptive literature, which had already begun tentative mapping of the borderline realm, set the stage for the first systematic, empirical investigation in this field.

The Study by Grinker and Colleagues

In 1968, Grinker and colleagues undertook a study of fifty-three hospitalized patients in order to establish objective criteria for the borderline diagnosis. They investigated these patients for ninety-three behavioral criteria and finally arrived at four fundamental characteristics of what they termed the "borderline syndrome." These were (1) chronic anger, (2) defective interpersonal relationships, (3) identity disturbance, and (4) depression based on feelings of loneliness. Cluster analysis of their data yielded four subcategories of the borderline syndrome. The first, the "psychotic border," consisted of patients displaying marked deficiencies in identity and reality testing, inappropriate appearance and behavior, negativism, rage outbursts, and depression. The second, the "core borderline" group, included patients with vacillating relationships, chronic rage, impulsive self-destructiveness, and an awareness of their identity coexisting with behavior inconsistent with this identity. The third group consisted of affectless, "as-if" individuals who lacked authenticity, tended to mimic others, and, though superficially well adjusted, led meaningless, false lives. The last group, seen by

Grinker et al. to be near the neuroses, consisted of patients with chronic anxiety and anaclitic depression.

Although Grinker et al. did not establish clear inclusion and exclusion criteria or weighted scales for the diagnosis of their borderline syndrome, their study remains a landmark in the evolution of the borderline concept. It was the first attempt to introduce contemporary research methods to the study of these patients. Gunderson (1984) correctly declares the study by Grinker et al. to have been the "springboard for a whole series of empirical descriptive studies in the 1970s" (p. 3).

Significant Contributions from 1970 to 1990

For nearly a decade following Grinker et al.'s (1968) study, the trend to view borderline psychopathology as a variant of schizophrenia persisted; the adoptive studies (Kety et al. 1975, Rosenthal et al. 1971, Wender et al. 1974) that suggested a genetic link between schizophrenia and a characterologically disturbed group lent further support to such conceptualization. To this line of thinking was added the view that borderline conditions were in fact atypical affective disorders (Klein 1975, 1977). This view held that the constant pursuit of romantic and exciting relationships displayed by borderline individuals was actually an attempt to stabilize their mood, and that their tendencies to abuse drugs and alcohol and to feel suicidal when feeling rejected were secondary manifestations of their underlying affective instability.

The appearance around this time of a significant synthesis of previous literature by Gunderson and Singer (1975) helped refocus attention on borderline psychopathology as a distinct entity in its own right. Their paper appeared when the use of the borderline diagnosis was increasing but there was little agreement on its definition. By pooling clinical observations of numerous previous investigators, Gunderson and Singer developed a list of six criteria for a discrete syndrome designated *borderline personality disorder*. These six criteria were (1) intense affect, usually of a strongly hostile or depressed nature; (2) impulsive behavior with self-destructive results; (3) social adaptiveness, which masks a disturbed identity; (4) brief psychotic experiences, especially during drug use or in unstructured situations and relationships; (5) bizarre and primitive responses to projective psychological tests; and (6) disturbed interpersonal relationships, which typically "vacillate between transient, superficial relationships and intense, dependent relationships that are marred by devaluation, manipulation and demandingness" (Gunderson and Singer 1975, p. 8). Gunderson and Singer concluded by expressing hope that their work would facilitate further research that would generate even more reliable diagnostic criteria for the disorder.

Two other outstanding reviews of literature that appeared soon afterward, however, questioned the validity of the Gunderson and Singer stance. Perry and Klerman (1978) conducted a comparative analysis of four sets of diagnostic criteria (Grinker et al. 1968, Gunderson and Singer 1975, Kernberg 1967, Knight 1953) and found that a total of 104 diagnostic criteria had been mentioned in association with the psychosocial functioning of the borderline patient. Half of these criteria were mentioned in only one of these four studies. Perry and Klerman felt, therefore, that apart from the concept delineated by criteria common to all four studies, there were many subtypes emphasized by different authors. They concluded that further empirical research was needed before the nosological status of borderline personality could be finally decided upon. A somewhat similar conclusion was arrived at by Liebowitz (1979), who found that the borderline label was being variously used as (1) a discrete syndrome distinguishable by behavioral criteria, (2) a marginal variety of schizophrenia, (3) a group of atypical affective disorders, and (4) a psychostructural substrate underlying most forms of severe character pathology. Liebowitz felt that the "available data do not weigh conclusively for or against borderline's status as an independent entity" (p. 35).

These dissenting voices notwithstanding, the delineation of the "core borderline" group by Grinker et al. (1968) and the development of the diagnostic criteria by Gunderson and Singer (1975) gave a strong impetus to searching clinical features that would clearly discriminate borderline personality from related conditions. In 1977, Grinker and Werble added fourteen new borderline patients to their earlier study and reaffirmed their findings. Two years later, Grinker (1979) compared his sample of borderline patients with a group of schizophrenics. He found that the psychotic breaks borderline patients had were largely ego-dystonic, brief, and reversible. Grinker concluded that "the borderline syndrome represents an independent entity" (1979, p. 51). Around the same time, Gunderson, working in collaboration with a National Institutes of Mental Health group of researchers, found that borderline patients have more anger and more dissociative experiences than schizophrenics (Carpenter et al. 1977, Gunderson and Singer 1975). In a later study, which compared borderline with schizophrenic and neurotically depressed patients, Gunderson and Kolb (1978) isolated seven distinguishing characteristics of borderline patients: (1) low school and work achievement; (2) impulsivity, especially pertaining to substance abuse and sexual promiscuity; (3) manipulative suicidal gestures; (4) heightened affectivity, which involves not only chronic anger but also "multiple intense affects" (p. 795); (5) mild psychotic experiences; (6) high socialization based on an intolerance of being alone; and (7) intense interpersonal relationships characterized by "devaluation, manipulation, dependency and masochism" (p. 795).

Following Gunderson and Kolb's (1978) study, two other groups of investigators developed diagnostic criteria for borderline personality. Spitzer and colleagues (1979) drew a seventeen-item list derived largely from the Gunderson and Kolb criteria. They sent the list to 4,000 members of the American Psychiatric Association and asked them to judge the list's discriminating ability. The 808 members who responded indicated that the list would accurately discriminate borderline from nonborderline patients 88 percent of the time. The notion of an identifiable borderline personality was thus supported. Spitzer et al. (1979) then proposed eight diagnostic criteria for borderline personality, although they somewhat idiosyncratically labeled the condition "unstable" character. These eight criteria were (1) anger; (2) unstable affect, including depression, irritability, and anxiety; (3) chronic feelings of emptiness and boredom; (4) identity disturbance; (5) intense emotional relationships showing manipulativeness and shifts between devaluation and idealization; (6) intolerance of aloneness; (7) impulsivity, often resulting in substance abuse; and (8) physically self-damaging acts. A ninth criterion that was found by the respondents to be highly discriminatory for this group consisted of dissociative experiences, referential ideas, and paranoid tendencies. This, however, later became a part of the description of the schizotypal personality disorder (see Chapter 8).

The second group of investigators (Sheehy et al. 1980) compared borderline patients with a matched control group of individuals with other personality disorders. This was an advance since, until then, control groups had consisted of schizophrenics and depressives. Sheehy and colleagues found that impulsivity, intense affects, and interpersonal difficulties constituted the triad that most clearly distinguished borderline patients from the others. An unstable identity was also found to be a useful criterion. Overall, their list of discriminating criteria included twelve features: (1) poor affect, (2) intense feelings and impulses, (3) unstable sense of self, (4) devaluation and idealization, (5) periodic social withdrawal, (6) impulsivity, (7) substance abuse, (8) chaotic sexual life with a tendency toward promiscuity, (9) projective mechanisms rendering reality testing weak, (10) absence of hypochondriasis, (11) absence of obsessive-compulsive symptoms, and (12) bizarre sexual fantasies.

In 1980, the diagnosis of borderline personality disorder received an "official" status by being included in *DSM-III*. In the years that followed, there occurred an explosion in empirical studies of the newly recognized disorder. In 1985 alone, for instance, 105 articles were published on the subject (Blashfield and McElroy 1987). A great deal of this literature concerned itself with the boundary between borderline personality and affective disorders. The demonstration of comorbidity of borderline personality disorder with affective disorders received three explanations: (1) borderline personality predisposes to affective disorder (Gunderson 1984), (2) borderline personality is itself a subaffective disorder (Akiskal et al. 1983), and (3) affective disorders are independent conditions that often coexist with severe personality disorders (McGlashan 1983). However, further studies (Barasch et al. 1985, Pope et al. 1983) revealed that a substantial proportion of borderline patients do not develop a major affective disorder and that core symptoms of borderline personality do not respond significantly to antidepressant medications (Soloff et al. 1989).

Among other areas addressed by recent research are demographic correlates of the diagnosis (Akhtar et al. 1986, Widiger and Frances 1989), development of diagnostic assessment instruments for it, and comparisons of various diagnostic schemes. There are now five diagnostic instruments available for borderline personality: the Diagnostic Interview for Borderlines (Gunderson 1982, 1984, DIB; Gunderson et al. 1981), Structured Interview for DSM-III Personality Disorders (SIDP; Pfohl et al. 1986), Schedule for Interviewing Borderlines (SIB; Baron et al. 1981), Personality Interview Question-II (PIQ-II; Widiger et al. 1986), and Diagnostic Interview for Personality Disorders (DIPD; Zanarini et al. 1987). Discussion of these instruments is beyond the scope of this chapter, and I refer the reader to articles by Reich and Noyes (1987) and Widiger and Frances (1987) on this subject. In keeping my focus on the cross-sectional picture of borderline personality, I will also forego consideration of the many studies on the course of borderline personality disorder. Suffice it to say that Stone (1989), who has meaningfully reviewed this literature, concludes that self-discipline, talent, likableness, attractiveness, and high IQ contribute to a favorable outcome, while substance abuse, aggressivity, parental victimization via incest or cruelty, and antisocial tendencies tend to be associated with a poor outcome.

Summary

After being associated with marginal forms of schizophrenia and atypical affective disorders, the term *borderline* is being used increasingly in the context of a personality disorder. Borderline personality disorder is viewed as a nosological entity consisting of (1) unstable sense of self or identity disturbance, (2) disturbed interpersonal life characterized by vacillating but intense relationships, (3) a superficially neuroticlike picture associated with a tendency toward occasional mild psychotic breaks, (4) contradictory presence of intense affects with a dreadful sense of inner emptiness, (5) impulsivity, (6) chronic rage at others coupled with self-destructiveness, (7) intolerance of being alone leading to compulsive socialization and yet a tendency toward periodic withdrawal from others, (8) chaotic sexual life, and (9) inordinate sensitivity to rejection by others. These nine features ultimately refer to major contradictions in the realms of self-image, mood regulation, and interpersonal relationships.

PSYCHOANALYTIC VIEWS

Early Literature

In a ground-breaking paper entitled "Character and Anal Erotism," Freud (1908a) extended the scope of psychoanalysis from the in-depth investigation of symptomatic neuroses to a similar understanding of certain personality attributes. Among the early exponents of his work, Abraham (1923, 1924b, 1926) and Jones (1913, 1918) became prominent in extending such investigation to other character traits. These investigators attempted to map out various libidinal stages and the intricate connections between particular erotic drive components and specific personality types. Freud (1914) also began to appreciate the role of narcissism in more severe mental disturbances and of such defenses as projection and denial, through which the individual tries to maintain self-regard and the integrity of his personality even at the cost of distorting reality and his relationships with others. Two years later, Freud (1916) described further character types whose functioning was largely governed by their unconscious feelings of guilt or by their having been exposed to massive misfortunes during childhood. Still later, Freud (1923a) developed the structural theory of the mind, described the ego and its defenses, clarified the mechanism of identification and the role it plays in the genesis of the ego, and outlined the central role of intrapsychic conflict in the formation of pathological psychic structures. While Freud did not specifically speak of borderline personality, his work laid the foundation for the subsequent psychoanalytic understanding of severe character pathology.

Perhaps the first psychoanalytic description of borderline personality can be attributed to Wilhelm Reich. In a 1925 paper, which remained untranslated into English until 1974, Reich clearly described the intense ambivalence, the dominance of pregenital aggression, the marked ego and superego impairments, and the primitive narcissism associated with a severe personality disorder. Although Reich termed such individuals *impulsive characters,* he explicitly recognized that they constituted "borderline cases" between psychosis and health.

The term *borderline* was subsequently given a formal status by Stern (1938), who outlined the characteristics of patients who did not do well in, or responded adversely to, classical psychoanalysis. His list of ten criteria remains an outstanding description of borderline personality disorder. Stern's criteria included (1) narcissism, (2) psychic bleeding and a tendency to give up in the face of crises, (3) inordinate hypersensitivity, (4) psychic and bodily rigidity, (5) tendency to respond negatively to helpful and correct interpretations, (6) a deeply ingrained deficit of self-esteem and accompanying feelings of inferiority, (7) masochism and depressive mood swings, (8) organic insecurity or a constitutional incapacity to tolerate much stress, (9) preponderance of projective mechanisms, and (10) difficulties in reality testing.

Another significant early contribution was the description of "as-if" personalities by Deutsch (1942). These patients, according to Deutsch, generally maintain a firm grip on reality and appear quite normal. However, they lack inner authenticity and display a tendency toward rapid narcissistic identifications with others. These identifications are not assimilated into the self-system but are acted out in a superficial manner. This tendency to mimic others is aimed at denying any conflict with them and to assure their continued support. Aggressive tendencies are split off, giving such individuals an "air of mild amiability" (Deutsch 1942, p. 305). Inauthenticity, neediness, and mimicry also contribute to a corruptible value system. Social groups and ideologies valued one day can readily be discarded in favor of other, often contradictory affiliations if circumstances change. Deutsch's description is not entirely congruent with the current nosological group designated as borderline; the latter are more overtly negativistic and hostile. However, the importance of her description lies in its emphasis on the pathology of internalized object relations.

This inner realm of patients with severe character pathology was further mapped out by Klein (1934, 1940, 1946) and Fairbairn (1944), although these influential contributors did not specifically use the term *borderline* in their writings. I will comment on Fairbairn's contributions while discussing schizoid personality (see Chapter 5), since he seems to have been dealing with more withdrawn individuals than those generally considered borderline. Here it is sufficient to note that Fairbairn made enormous contributions to the understanding of early internalization processes, which he saw as always involving a bipolar unit of an ego fragment and an internal object (self- and object representations, in current terminology). Moreover, he emphasized the role of early caretakers in facilitating a growing child's move from total dependence to mature interdependence. Fairbairn also noted how apparently hysterical and obsessional manifestations were often mere techniques to satisfy deeper needs consequent upon intense frustrations with the earliest objects of infancy.

More relevant are Klein's contributions, which provide the earliest descriptions of the splitting of object representation and projective identification, two mechanisms regularly associated with borderline personality organization. In Klein's view, the neonate is threatened from within by the destructive potential of the death instinct. This is projected outward, resulting in persecutory anxiety. In a subsequent defensive maneuver, the external object is split into "all-good" and "all-bad" versions. Such division protects the "good" object from aggression and preserves a safe ego core. Further defensive idealization of the "good" object leads to megalomanic aspirations, undue optimism, and hypomanic tendencies. Compartmentalized maintenance of "bad" objects results in paranoia, contempt, and sadistic devaluation of others. Later, the infant becomes capable of forming a unified conception of external objects. In Klein's terminology, this is the move from the earlier "paranoid position" to a "depressive position." Such developmental advance also changes the affective life from one governed by envy, greed, and fear to one regulated by sadness, guilt, gratitude, and reparation. When this progress is not made, the paranoid position remains the functional template of all behavior. Splitting predominates over repression and the individual remains vulnerable to seeing others only in idealized or devalued terms. Under such circumstances, there is little real knowledge of others. The inner world is populated by mere caricatures of self and others. In addition, there is an impairment for capacity for genuine sadness, guilt, and mourning, since no aggression is owned and "badness" is seen to reside externally. Through the mechanism of projective identification, unacceptable attributes of the self are deposited into others, who are subsequently manipulated to live out these attributes.

Klein's conceptualizations present three problems. First, in an overemphasis on constitutional sources of aggression Klein overlooks the role of severe early frustrations in the genesis of these mechanisms. Second, Klein's attributing a highly elaborate fantasy life to young infants—a tendency that contributes to her idiosyncratic language—is questionable in the light of current knowledge of neonatal cognitive development. Finally, Klein places the occurrence of these developments in the first year of life, a timetable that appears too early. Nonetheless, Klein's description of splitting and projective identification remains extremely relevant to the understanding of borderline psychopathology. Even her postulated move from the paranoid to the depressive position may have resonance with other theoretical models (Kernberg 1975a, Mahler et al. 1975), which deal with the child's capacity to experience and sustain ambivalence regarding himself and others.

Fenichel (1945) included "queer psychopaths, abortive paranoids . . . [and] apathic individuals" (p. 444), or schizoid personalities, under the broad rubric of "borderline cases." He viewed them as a barely compensated group vulnerable to a psychotic breakdown under stressful conditions. According to Fenichel, such individuals retain much primitive narcissism and respond to frustration by denial, defensive grandiosity, or loss of object relationships. They lack authentic emotions, have few friends, and often remain surprisingly untouched by affect-laden situations. At other times, they explode into "sudden and incomprehensible emotional spells" (p. 445). Their language usage is idiosyncratic; their inner psychic tension is often translated into motor stiffness. They often feel empty and enraged but may appear relatively normal as long as certain conditions of security are fulfilled.

In 1947, Schmideberg described a group of "borderline" patients. She felt that these patients remained true to their type over time and were "stable in their instability." They displayed unconventional behavior, could not stick to routines, and led chaotic lives. Something dreadful was always happening to them. When they did seek psychoanalytic help, they showed poor motivation, were often late for appointments, and failed to free associate.

A few years later, Knight (1953) brought further clarity to the nosological status of borderline patients. He emphasized that a careful assessment of various ego functions was necessary in order to establish this diagnosis. Borderline states, according to Knight, often present with neurotic symptoms, but underneath this picture lies severe ego weakness. Among the ego functions that are severely impaired are those involved with "integration, concept formation, judgment, realistic planning, and defending against eruption into conscious thinking of id impulses and their fantasy elaborations" (Knight 1953, p. 6). Knight emphasized that only a face-to-face interview, often extending over several sessions, can provide the opportunity to evaluate the total ego functioning of the patient. In such situations, borderline patients are evasive and minimize intrapsychic conflict. They often appear unconcerned about their predicament and oblivious to the obvious implications of what is being said. They may exhibit thought blocking, arbitrary inferences, and linguistic oddities. Knight disapproved of the term *borderline* and explicitly stated that these cases "involve schizophrenic tendencies of some degree" (p. 2).

Following the publication of Knight's paper, the American Psychoanalytic Association gave the borderline issue official recognition by holding two all-day panel discussions in May 1954 and December 1955 on "The Borderline Case" (Rangell 1955, Robbins 1956). In these meetings, Zilboorg and Zetzel objected to the borderline diagnosis, while Schmideberg made an attempt to relate the borderline concept to character disorders. More importantly, Frank suggested during the course of these discussions that borderline states might be better understood using the concepts of Winnicott rather than the classical psychoanalytic approaches. This line of thinking was to be developed later by Modell (1963), who clarified that the interpersonal relationships of borderline persons were characterized by (1) a state of transitional relatedness, since their objects are not perceived in their reality but "owe their lives, so to speak, to processes arising within the individual" (p. 285); (2) a tendency to endow certain objects, for example, their therapists, with magical omnipotence; (3) a divided self-image composed of two portions: a helpless infant and someone who is omnipotently giving or omnipotently destructive; (4) an intense dependence on others and yet an illusion of self-sufficiency; and (5) the "harrowing dilemma" (p. 286) of extreme dependence coupled with an intense fear of closeness, hence a chronic struggle to achieve proper distance in relationships.

The subsequent years also witnessed the significant contributions of Erikson, Jacobson, and Mahler to the understanding of the borderline psychopathology. Erikson (1956, 1959) outlined the epigenetic sequence of identity formation and described the syndrome of identity diffusion. A healthy sense of identity, according to Erikson, consists of a sustained sense of self-sameness, a sharing of similar character traits with varied others, a temporal continuity in the self-experience, and a feeling of affiliation with an ethnic and communal group. Identity diffusion, on the other hand, consists of deficiencies in all these areas. This syndrome was to be recognized as the "key anchoring symptom" (Kernberg 1984, p. 33) of borderline personality organization. Jacobson (1953a, 1954a, 1964) not only further elucidated the psychostructural correlates of early introjections and identifications leading to identity formation (see Chapter 1) but also described the pathological internalized object relations of borderline patients and the relationship of this early pathology to the vicissitudes of ego and superego formation in such individuals. According to Jacobson, serious identity conflicts are not characteristic of neurotics but of borderline patients. These individuals

> at times experience their mental functions or their bodily organs as belonging to their own self and, at other times, as objects, i.e., foreign bodies which they want to expel. Or they may at one time attach part of their own mental or body self to external objects, and at another time attribute realistic object qualities to the latter. [Jacobson 1964, p. 48]

In Jacobson's view, identity disturbance and primitive object relations are the hallmark of borderline personality. Jacobson also pointed out that such individuals retain the "adolescent fluidity of moods" (1964, p. 159) even in their adulthood and display a preponderance of shame, inferiority feelings, and paranoid fears of exposure over genuine guilt reactions.

Mahler and her colleagues (Mahler 1966a, 1967, 1970, Mahler et al. 1975) provided significant understanding regarding the genesis of borderline personality. According to them, the toddler's growing awareness of his separateness from his mother causes his narcissism to be most vulnerable during the rapprochement subphase of separation-individuation. Moreover, his object relations at this time are intensely ambivalent. On the one hand, the toddler asserts his autonomy; on the other hand, he seeks to retain the "already toppling delusion or illusion of exclusive union with mother" (Mahler et al. 1975, p. 93). During the rapprochement subphase, the child shows an increased anguish at being left alone, a tendency to use mother as an extension of the self, and alternations between demands for autonomy and for closeness. Splitting mechanisms, which protect the "good" mother image from aggression, predominate, and internalization of a sustaining maternal image is rudimentary. Discovery of sexual differences and "psychical consequences" (Freud 1925b) further complicates the child's fantasy life around this time. Mahler et al. found that a lack of optimal emotional availability on the part of the mother during this phase was frequently associated with a future borderline personality. Under such circumstances, infantile omnipotence is not renunciated and the search for an "all-good" mother persists in later life. Alternating behaviors of coercive clinging and negativistic withdrawal impede establishment of "optimal distance" (Bouvet 1958) in interpersonal relationships. Object constancy is not achieved, nor is a sustained sense of the individual's own identity. Instead, there persists an inordinate dependence on external objects to maintain a cohesive self-experience. Mood regulation suffers, and realistic setbacks are responded to with intense negative mood swings.

Finally, Balint's (1968) description of the area of "basic fault" appears relevant to understanding borderline psychopathology. According to Balint, the characteristics of this level are

> (a) all the events that happen in it belong to an exclusively two-person relationship—there is no third person present; (b) this two-person

> relationship is of a particular nature, entirely different from the well-known human relationships of the oedipal level; (c) the nature of the dynamic force operating at this level is not that of a conflict; and (d) adult language is often useless or misleading in describing events at this level, because words have not always an agreed on conventional meaning. [pp. 16–17]

Balint further described interpersonal relationships of individuals with "basic fault." There is an overcathexis either of objects (ocnophilia) or of ego functions (philobatism) with resulting oddities in interpersonal distance. Balint noted that while fitting in with a desired object produced, in such individuals, only a tranquil well-being, separation from that object evoked "highly vehement and loud symptoms" (p. 17).

Kernberg

In 1967, Kernberg published his seminal paper "Borderline Personality Organization." This personality organization is not a transitory state fluctuating between neurosis and psychosis. Despite its chaotic appearance, this is a stable pathological state. Kernberg proposed its diagnosis to be based on three sets of criteria: descriptive, structural, and genetic-dynamic. The *descriptive features,* which constitute presumptive evidence of borderline personality organization, include (1) chronic, diffuse anxiety; (2) polysymptomatic neurosis with multiple phobias, relatively ego-syntonic obsessive-compulsive phenomena, bizarre conversion symptoms, and hypochondriasis; (3) polymorphous perverse sexuality; (4) classical prepsychotic personalities (e.g., schizoid, paranoid, and hypomanic personalities); (5) impulse neuroses and addictions; and (6) lower level character disorders, including "infantile," narcissistic, as-if, and antisocial personalities. Among the *structural characteristics,* Kernberg included (1) nonspecific manifestations of ego weakness (poor anxiety tolerance, lack of impulse control, and inadequate sublimation), (2) primary process thinking in unstructured situations, (3) specific defensive operations, and (4) pathological internalized object relations. The *genetic-dynamic analysis* reveals a specific condensation between pregenital and genital conflicts and a precocious development of oedipal conflicts from the second or third year on. Oral and anal rage contaminate the object images of the oedipal phase. A positive Oedipus complex is seriously interfered with and there is vulnerability, in both sexes, to an orally derived greedy promiscuity or a negative oedipal outcome with overt homosexuality.

In a subsequent contribution, Kernberg (1977) highlighted the constellations of preoedipally distorted oedipal conflicts in borderline patients. These include (1) an excessive aggressivation of oedipal conflicts, (2) an undue idealization of the heterosexual love object in the positive oedipal relation and of the homosexual love object in the negative oedipal relation, (3) a highly unrealistic quality to the fantasied relations with either of these objects, (4) a pregenital agenda to seemingly genital strivings, and (5) a premature oedipalization of preoedipal conflicts. Kernberg noted that while these instinctual characteristics are reflected in the borderline individual's sexual behavior, fantasies, and interpersonal relations, their value for diagnostic purposes is less than that of the psychostructural and defensive characteristics of these patients.

It is the description of these defensive operations and pathological internal object relations that gives Kernberg's contribution its unique stamp. According to Kernberg, the defenses in borderline personality organization center on splitting or the defensive keeping apart of contradictory self- and object representations in order to avoid anxiety consequent upon intense ambivalence. Splitting leads to the division of external objects into "all good" and "all bad" ones, with the concomitant possibility of abrupt shifts of an object from one extreme compartment to the other. It also results in a selective ego-syntonic impulsivity, intensification of affects, and extreme oscillation between contradictory self-concepts. The mechanism of splitting is buttressed by primitive idealization, projective identification, primitive denial, and omnipotence and devaluation. Primitive idealization refers to the tendency to see certain external objects as "all good" in order to gain protection against other, "all bad" objects. Primitive idealization is not reaction formation, since it does not include a conscious or even unconscious acknowledgment of aggression toward the object. Instead, it is the direct result of a primitive fantasy built for protective functions and to serve as a recipient of omnipotent identification. Projective identification ize "all bad" self- and object images, but since there is k of self- and object differentiation in this area, the sing this defense continues to experience an uncanny empat[illegible] ith his "enemy" alongside a need to control the latter. Primitive denial refers to the fact that while the borderline individual is aware that his perceptions, thoughts, and feelings about himself or others at a certain time are completely opposite those he had before, his memory fails to have any emotional relevance to him. A peculiar disregard for a sector of one's subjective experience results. Omnipotence is manifest in these patients' ruthless and possessive control of others, as well as in the conceit and grandiosity that is frequently hidden underneath their feelings of inferiority and self-criticism. Devaluation is a corollary of omnipotence: "If an external object can provide no further gratification or protection, it is dropped and dismissed because there was no real capacity for love of this object in the first place" (Kernberg 1967, p. 672).

Kernberg described the internal object relationships of borderline individuals in detail. Their inner world is populated by dissociated ego segments, each of which contains a self-image, a part-object image, and an affect disposition. Although self-object differentiation is by and large intact, the self-experience is far from cohesive. Capacity for comprehending objects in totality is impaired, and affects pertaining to ambivalence, mourning, and genuine sadness are deficient. Superego integration is minimal. Internalized bad object images, forming superego forerunners of a sadistic kind, are easily projected, creating frightening persecutors. Overidealized self- and object images create fantastically high, unachievable ideals, which fail to provide benevolent inner guidance. Persistence of contradictory identifications means that an integrated self-concept cannot develop. Persistence of contradictory object representations impedes realistic evaluation of the external objects. All this represents the syndrome of identity diffusion, a central characteristic of borderline personality.

It is important to note that Kernberg's "borderline personality organization" referred not to a discrete nosological entity but to a level of personality organization that existed underneath all severe character pathology, including narcissistic, schizoid, hypomanic, paranoid, antisocial, as-if, and infantile personality disorders.

While this breadth helped to highlight the structural and dynamic similarities among various severe personality disorders, it also caused a bit of confusion, especially because descriptive psychiatrists were busy, around the same time, tightening the criteria for a specific personality disorder under the same name.

While maintaining his view of borderline personality organization, Kernberg did later distinguish it from narcissistic personality disorder (1975a) and from the identity crisis associated with a turbulent adolescence (1978). Also, he tightened the criteria for borderline personality organization into identity diffusion, primitive defenses, and intact reality testing, thus excluding the presumptive descriptive signs and the genetic-dynamic analysis from the diagnostic arena. Kernberg (1970a) distinguished this organization from a neurotic-level personality organization and a psychotic-level personality organization on various psychodynamic and structural characteristics. He devised a specific interviewing technique, the "structural interview" (Kernberg 1977), to distinguish between these levels. Later, Kernberg and his colleagues (1981) attempted to empirically test the validity of his structural interview, comparing it with the Diagnostic Interview for Borderlines (Kolb and Gunderson 1980). Finally, Kernberg (1984) critically evaluated the *DSM-III* stance on borderline personality and noted the omission of brief psychotic regressions from its definition.

Contributions of Other Contemporary Psychoanalysts

Abend, Porder, and Willick (1983) based their findings on four analyzed "borderline" patients discussed in detail at the meetings of the Kris Study Group of the New York Psychoanalytic Institute. They carefully reviewed the literature in this area and critically evaluated Kernberg's formulations. While acknowledging substantial agreement among prior psychoanalytic descriptions of borderline cases, Abend et al. questioned the usefulness of the term *borderline* to denote a specific diagnostic category. They disagreed with Kernberg's formulation that all patients with borderline personality organization share similar defensive operations, ego structures, and internalized object relations. Abend et al. felt that these patients' psychopathology can be understood in terms of traditional defenses in the setting of profound ego weakness and identifications with disturbed parents. They emphasized that defenses in general should not be viewed as primitive or advanced but considered alongside the overall ego organization of each patient. Finally, Abend et al. noted that previous psychoanalytic investigators had minimized the significance of oedipal phase conflicts in the genesis of borderline personality. In their view, preoedipal conflicts are not crucial etiological determinants of these patient's psychopathology but regressive defenses against deeply disturbing oedipal issues. Their position in this regard, owing perhaps to their having dealt with somewhat healthier patients than are ordinarily described as borderline, stands in contrast to the views of other contemporary analytic investigators.

Prominent among this latter group is Adler (1985), who presents a view of borderline psychopathology derived from a combination of Piaget's (1937) and Fraiberg's (1969) work on cognitive development, Mahler's (1968, 1975) separation-individuation theory, Winnicott's (1960, 1965) notions about the holding environment and capacity for aloneness, and Kohut's (1977) self psychology. Adler posits that the fundamental pathology of the borderline personality consists in not having achieved a solid evocative memory in the realm of object relations. This results in an inability to hold on to introjects that provide soothing sustenance to the self. Adler distinguishes his views from those of Kernberg, which emphasize a failure in synthesizing introjects of contradictory affective valence and the subsequent use of this failure as a defense against intolerable ambivalence. In his view, borderline patients suffer from a "*primary* inner emptiness based upon a relative *absence* of positive introjects around which the self is organized" (Adler 1985, p. 12). This inner emptiness leads borderline patients to desire intense attachments. When their dependent relationships are endangered, these patients experience a threat to their entitlement to survive; this "annihilatory panic" in turn causes intense rage. This results in further deterioration of the inner sustaining world, with the loss now not only of evocative memory but of recognition memory as well. At this stage of profound emptiness, panic, and rage, patients may fail to recognize a friend or a therapist even while in the individual's physical presence.

Masterson (1972, 1976) derived his ideas regarding borderline personality by synthesizing Bowlby's (1969, 1973) attachment theory, Mahler's (1975, 1978) views on separation-individuation, and Kernberg's (1975a, 1976) object relations-based conceptualizations of the psychic structure. Masterson proposed that the mother of the borderline individual was herself a borderline who encouraged symbiotic clinging and withdrew her love when the child displayed strivings toward independence. The situation was complicated by an absence of the usual counteracting pull of the father toward reality. The child was thus caught in a dilemma: to be himself was to risk losing mother's love, while to retain this love was to risk losing his independence. Masterson believed this dilemma to be the core issue in the borderline makeup. Such an individual will keep searching for a clinging tie with a mother substitute. If such a relationship, however transient or illusory, is established, there will follow a feeling of safety. Soon, however, the unfinished developmental task of individuation will reassert itself. This then upsets the balance, since such assertiveness is intrapsychically associated with abandonment. The result is a lifelong picture of unstable relationships, chronic search for blissful unions, and repeated ruptures leading to enraged or empty states of depression.

Meissner (1978a,b, 1982, 1984) attempted to arrange various "borderline conditions" on a hierarchical continuum. In his view, this continuum exists separately on hysterical and schizoid dimensions. The hysterical dimension includes pseudoschizophrenia, psychotic character, borderline personality, and primitive hysteric. The schizoid dimension includes schizoid personality, false self-organization, and as-if personality. This scheme remotely echoes the two lines of thinking in descriptive psychiatry that view borderline personality as related either to schizophrenia or to affective disorders. What remains puzzling is Meissner's inclusion of pseudoschizophrenia and psychotic character in the hysterical but not the schizoid dimension. In any case, Meissner notes that all borderline conditions share certain basic characteristics and that each individual type functions at a more or less stable level of personality functioning. He views the borderline personality proper as being of intermediate severity between the psychotic character and the primitive hysteric. Individuals with borderline personality have chronic difficulties in relating to others. They display shifting levels of ego functioning, have a certain passivity, and continually experience a sense of inner emptiness and loneliness. They seem extraordinarily sensitive to the unconscious fantasies and impulses of others around them. Meissner believes that borderline individuals retain a relatively good adaptation to reality and show regression only while under the effect of drugs or during severe developmental crises. At times, progressive developments in a psychotherapeutic relationship precipitate such regressions. In Meissner's view, the primary defect in borderline personality lies in the organization of the constituents of the self. The chief pathogenic configurations involve a victim-introject, an aggressor-introject, and narcissistically determined traits of grandiosity and inferiority. Sadomasochism and the motif of suffering therefore play a cardinal role in borderline personality disorder.

Rinsley, working at first in collaboration with Masterson (Masterson and Rinsley 1975) and then independently (Rinsley 1977, 1978, 1982), also believes that the mother of the future borderline is herself a borderline, whose ambivalence-ridden interactional pattern with her infant becomes introjected by the latter and serves as the basis of what Masterson and Rinsley (1975) termed the "split object relations unit." This is comprised of two substructures. One, the "withdrawing object relations unit," consists of a critical and withdrawing maternal image, an affect of anger and frustration, and a part self-representation of being inadequate, bad, and helpless. The other is the "rewarding object relations unit," which consists of an approving maternal image, good feelings, and a self-image of being passive and compliant. Persistence of these structures has eight consequences (Rinsley 1977): (1) a view of the object world as either "all good" or "all bad," (2) a state of psychic transitivism necessitating further primitive defenses, (3) perceiving whole objects as part objects, (4) inadequate capacity to mourn and work through losses and separations, (5) persistence of primitive ego and superego forerunners, (6) deficiency of normal developmental phase specificity, (7) stunted ego growth, and (8) a hypertrophied sensory-perceptual ego function directed toward the early detection of the fearsome possibility of abandonment. In translating these psychostructural characteristics into phenomenological terms,

Rinsley by and large follows Grinker et al.'s (1968) descriptive categories of the borderline syndrome, which were outlined earlier.

Robbins (1983) observed that the adjustment of borderline individuals depends on one or more obligatory relationships with persons who are quite inaccurately perceived. Although these relationships are clearly destructive, the borderline individual is dependent on them. According to Robbins, such primitive personalities also display (1) a lack of inner resources to be peacefully alone; (2) an inability to genuinely experience intrapsychic conflict; instead, they experience conflictual elements in discrete components; (3) an inconstancy in perceptions of themselves and others, (4) occasional misperceptions about the origins of a given experience; and (5) despite excessive hostility, a peculiar inability to feel anger in appropriate situations. Robbins highlights the contradictory features of the borderline individual who is dependent yet resourceful, aggressively controlling yet sometimes dramatically compliant, socially adapted yet refractory to learning, and affectively intense yet strangely unable to discriminate bodily sensations and emotions.

Searles (1969, 1978, 1979, 1986) eloquently described the pathological ego structure of borderline patients and its effects upon their identity, thought processes, language, and interpersonal relations. He points out that the borderline individual is pervasively unable to differentiate, at more than a superficial level, between dreams and reality, between emotions and sensations, between thoughts and actions, between past and present, between symbolic and concrete communications, and between self and nonself. However, these difficulties are "fascinatingly subtle" (1986, p. 58) and often become evident only in the course of therapy. The borderline individual rapidly loses the internalized images of valued others unless an image receives repeated perceptual reinforcement from outside. He also has much difficulty in integrating feelings regarding change and loss. His incomplete differentiation between inner and outer reality gives rise to an unconscious conviction that his thinking possesses an omnipotent power. "This reification of his thoughts greatly complicates his ability to think freely, for he fear[s] the tangible power of his thought to do harm either to himself or others" (1986, p. 64). The borderline individual's self-concept contains many unintegrated representations that range from being omnipotently malevolent to being utterly vulnerable. There is a constant fear of an invading outer world that has the power to completely mold his identity. Multiple identity functioning and poor differentiation from the nonhuman environment also manifest in frequent depersonalization, use of the pronoun *we* for himself, and references to himself as a thing.

Such dehumanized qualities of the borderline's experience are viewed differently by Singer (1977a,b, 1979). According to him, borderlines fear not only that their inner world will become devoid of objects, whether loving or hating, but also that it will become devoid of themselves. This dreaded loss of self-experience and the subjective feeling of emptiness are eloquently described by Singer. He also delineates various protective mechanisms used by borderline individuals to avoid this disconcerting state of affairs. Feeling nonhuman is one such defensive device. Singer notes that

> dehumanized experiences of the self, whether animate or inanimate, alive or dead, were effective manoeuvers or primitive defences to combat threats of dissolution, since in these mechanical, dissociative, depersonalized-like states, human vulnerabilities were absent. . . . Likewise, the motive for extreme self-centredness, chronic low-level anxiety and masochistic states was to provide a continuous focus of attention and awareness of oneself to ensure an intact self-representation, be it mind or body, to prevent dissolution. [Singer 1979, p. 495]

Various merger fantasies, incessant talking, social clinging, and sadomasochistic involvements are among other attempts to keep the feeling of emptiness in abeyance. While pointing out other psychostructural characteristics of the borderline personality (e.g., inadequately developed signal anxiety, deficient participation of secondary process thinking in problem-solving techniques, perceptual-affective chaos resulting from unintegrated and rapidly shifting self- and object representations), Singer emphasizes the centrality of the vulnerable self-experience in borderline personality. He distinguishes the emptiness experience from loneliness, where the inner world remains populated with fantasy and mournful longing, and depersonalization proper, where a hypercathexis of self-perception occurs for defensive purposes.

Finally, mention must be made of Volkan's (1976, 1980b, 1981, 1987) important contributions. Although his work pertains predominantly to the metapsychology and psychoanalytic treatment of borderline patients, it also enriches the phenomenological profile of their condition. Volkan eloquently describes the introjective-projective relatedness of borderline individuals who repeatedly externalize their split self- and object representations only to reinternalize the resulting distorted object images. He points out such individuals' vulnerability to emotional flooding, the first manifestation of which

> is usually an accumulation of memories and fantasies (flooding in the ideational field) that support the same emotion. The patient can refer to these memories or fantasies only in a kind of "shorthand"—fragmentary sentences, or a single word. He may then begin stuttering and lose the power of intelligible speech altogether. It is impossible at this point to distinguish between flooding in the emotional, actional, or ideational field. The patient may scream and exhibit diffuse motor activity; he may seem to have lost his human identity. . . . Patients capable of reporting their experience of emotional flooding after the event usually indicate that strange perceptual changes took place. They underwent a "metamorphosis" during the experience, becoming monstrous and diabolical when signal affects were replaced by primal affects closely related to the aggression drive. [Volkan 1976, pp. 179, 183]

Under favorable circumstances, however, primal affects closer to libidinal drive may be activated, causing an exhilarating, hypomaniclike transformation. Volkan highlights the borderline individual's attachment to, and use of, external objects (including pets) in sustaining a vulnerable self-experience.

Volkan (1980b) also points out that many individuals seeking sex-reassignment surgery are borderline in their character organization. In addition, Volkan (1981, 1986) outlines three types of early environment associated with the characteristic impairment of the ego's integrative function in borderline personality organization: (1) single-parent relationships, where the child was exposed to intense frustrations due to maternal unavailability and hence was unable to integrate contradictory self- and object representations; (2) multiple mothering, which evokes varied, often contradictory, identifications hard to integrate into a composite whole; and (3) situations in which the child experienced himself as a depository of a representation of someone else as it existed in the mind of his parents. Such poorly integrated "deposited representations" (Volkan 1987, p. 42) may also underlie the splitting of self-representations so often seen in borderline individuals.

Summary

The psychoanalytic literature lacks nosological congruence with the general psychiatric description of borderline personality disorder. It describes a somewhat loose group of severe character pathology under this designation, although more recent writings tend to be somewhat more specific in this regard. There appears to be controversy regarding the etiological model for this condition, with some authors emphasizing the developmental deficiencies and others focusing on conflicts surrounding ambivalence. There is greater agreement regarding the psychostructural and phenomenological characteristics. Among various features noted are (1) a substrate of excessive aggression originating from constitutional factors and from severe, sustained preoedipal trauma; (2) an aborted separation-individuation process and therefore a lack of self- and object constancy and intense vulnerability to separation anxiety; (3) a failure to achieve oedipal phase dominance, condensation of preoedipal and oedipal conflicts with a sadomasochistic tinge, and a tendency toward promiscuity and perverse formations; (4) a predominance of dyadic, object-relations conflicts over internalized, structural conflicts; (5) a persistence of split of self- and object representations and associated mechanisms of primitive denial and projective identification; (6) a syndrome of identity diffusion; and (7) an uneven, poorly internalized superego function, resulting in the instinctual life being restrained by shame and fear rather than by genuine inner guilt and concern for others. In essence, the emphasis of the psychoanalytic literature is on the pathology of the internal object relations, especially identity diffusion, as it affects the cohesiveness of self-experience and the capacity for deep relationships with others.

DSM-III AND *DSM-III-R*

DSM-III (1980, pp. 322–323) officially introduced the term *borderline personality disorder* into psychiatric nomenclature. It listed eight criteria for the diagnosis and specified that these characterized the individual's long-term functioning and caused either significant impairment in social or occupational functioning or subjective distress. The criteria included the following:

A. At least five of the following are required:

(i) impulsivity or unpredictability in at least two areas that are potentially self-damaging, e.g., spending, sex, gambling, substance use, shoplifting, overeating, physically self-damaging acts

(ii) a pattern of unstable and intense interpersonal relationships, e.g., marked shifts of attitude, idealization, devaluation, manipulation (consistently using others for one's own ends)

(iii) inappropriate, intense anger or lack of control of anger, e.g., frequent displays of temper, constant anger

(iv) identity disturbance manifested by uncertainty about several issues relating to identity, such as self-image, gender identity, long-term goals or career choice, friendship patterns, values, and loyalties, e.g., "Who am I?", "I feel like I am my sister when I am good"

(v) affective instability: marked shifts from normal mood to depression, irritability, or anxiety, usually lasting a few hours and only rarely more than a few days, with a return to normal mood

(vi) intolerance of being alone, e.g., frantic efforts to avoid being alone, depressed when alone

(vii) physically self-damaging acts, e.g., suicidal gestures, self-mutilation, recurrent accidents or physical fights

(viii) chronic feelings of emptiness or boredom

B. If under 18, does not meet the criteria for Identity Disorder.

It should be noted that the *DSM-III* entity of borderline personality disorder resulted from the division of the hitherto heterogeneous and ill-defined borderline group into two categories: schizotypal and unstable. Indeed, the American Psychiatric Association's Task Force on Nomenclature and Statistics preferred the term *unstable personality disorder* and yielded only after much discussion to the proponents of the term *borderline personality disorder.* The diagnostic criteria themselves appear adequate. They include identity disturbance, troubled interpersonal relationships, chronic rage, self-destructiveness, inability to be alone, unmitigated boredom, wild affective swings, and generalized impulsivity. However, a closer look at the criteria reveals the "noteworthy omission" (Leichtman 1989, p. 239) of items related to psychoticlike episodes or disturbed thinking and communication. This omission is disconcerting, since a large number of studies (O'Connell et al. 1989, Perry and Klerman 1980, Pope et al. 1985, Sheehy et al. 1980) have repeatedly demonstrated the occurrence of magical thinking, referential ideas, and psychoticlike episodes among borderline patients. A certain recklessness in decision-making processes, resulting from the underlying splitting mechanisms (Akhtar and Byrne 1983), is also a characteristic of the borderline cognition missing from the *DSM-III* description. Incapacity for ambivalence, inordinate moral and ethnic relativism, subtle body-image disturbances, and a tendency toward hypomanic exhilaration under favorable circumstances are other clinical features of the borderline condition

(Akhtar 1984, Akhtar and Byrne 1983) that do not find a place in the *DSM-III* description.

DSM-III-R (1987, p. 347) criteria are, by and large, a replication of those in *DSM-III.* In a largely semantic move, the criterion of "intolerance of being alone" was changed to "frantic efforts to avoid real or imagined abandonment." The entire *DSM-III-R* criteria set reads as follows:

A pervasive pattern of instability of mood, interpersonal relationships, and self-image, beginning by early adulthood and present in a variety of contexts, as indicated by at least five of the following:

(i) A pattern of unstable and intense interpersonal relationships characterized by alternating between extremes of overidealization and devaluation

(ii) impulsiveness in at least two areas that are potentially self damaging, e.g., spending, sex, substance use, shoplifting, reckless driving, binge eating (Do not include suicidal or self-mutilating behavior covered in [v].)

(iii) affective instability: marked shifts from baseline mood to depression, irritability, or anxiety, usually lasting a few hours and only rarely more than a few days

(iv) inappropriate, intense anger or lack of control of anger, e.g., frequent displays of temper, constant anger, recurrent physical fights

(v) recurrent suicidal threats, gestures, or behavior, or self-mutilating behavior

(vi) marked and persistent identity disturbance manifested by uncertainty about at least two of the following: self-image, sexual orientation, long-term goals or career choice, type of friends desired, preferred values

(vii) chronic feelings of emptiness or boredom

(viii) frantic efforts to avoid real or imagined abandonment (Do not include suicidal or self-mutilating behavior covered in [v].)

Once again, cognitive peculiarities, hypomanic end of mood swings, inability to experience ambivalence, body-image disturbances, weak ethnicity, and superego disturbances are omitted from the phenomenological profile of the condition. Although the description correctly emphasizes a stable pattern of instability in mood, self-image, and interpersonal relationships, it does not underscore the centrality of splitting and identity diffusion in the condition. Since only five of the eight criteria are required for making the diagnosis, it appears theoretically possible to diagnose an individual borderline even if he or she does not display identity disturbance. This lack of assigned greater weightage to the identity diffusion criterion is a major weakness of the *DSM-III-R* description of borderline personality.

The following clinical profile includes what is omitted in *DSM-III* and *DSM-III-R* and thus rectifies the shortcomings of their descriptions. Moreover, by taking the centrality of splitting and identity diffusion into account, this profile emphasizes the coexistence of mutually contradictory stances in almost all areas of psychosocial functioning of the borderline individual.

AN ATTEMPT AT SYNTHESIS

The literature reviewed here was pooled and synthesized in order to develop a composite clinical profile of borderline personality disorder. According to this profile (Table 4–1), the clinical features of borderline personality belong to six areas of psychosocial functioning: (1) self-concept; (2) interpersonal relations; (3) social adaptation; (4) ethics, standards, and ideals; (5) love and sexuality; and (6) cognitive style. Akin to the situation in narcissistic personality disorder (see Chapter 3), each of these areas has overt and covert features. However, since borderline personality disorder lacks the cohesion of narcissistic personality, its overt and covert features are less rigidly separated. In borderline personality, overt and covert features often rapidly alternate in becoming surface phenomena.

Other caveats regarding the organization of symptomatology along these lines have already been mentioned in connection with narcissistic personality. These have equal application here as well. Nonetheless, in emphasizing the centrality of splitting and identity diffusion and in including cognitive style, superego elements, and the dimensions of ethnicity and body image, the scheme provided here is richer and theoretically more sound than the checklist approach of *DSM-III* and *DSM-III-R*. According to this profile, borderline individuals overtly view themselves as victims, are righteously indignant and chronically enraged, are intensely involved in idealizing and hating others, are superficially adapted to reality although highly impulsive, are transiently zealous about moral and ethical issues, are very romantic and sexually promiscuous, and are recklessly decisive and smugly knowledgeable. However, covertly they feel inherently defective, are frequently suicidal, are incapable of truly depending on others, are impaired in their capacity for mature aloneness, are unable to experience genuine guilt, are incapable of sustained love, and are vulnerable to magical thinking and psychoticlike episodes. This comprehensive portrait meaningfully links descriptive and psychoanalytic data on borderline personality and facilitates the distinction from related conditions.

DIFFERENTIAL DIAGNOSIS

Borderline personality disorder should be distinguished from narcissistic, histrionic, antisocial, and schizotypal personality disorders. All these syndromes represent severe character pathology and have overlapping phenomenology, psychodynamics, psychic structure, and developmental background. Descriptively, individuals with all these disorders exhibit troubled interpersonal relationships, defective empathy, inability for sadness, mourning, and mature love, egocentric perception of reality, sexual difficulties, and moral defects. Dynamically, splitting of contradictory self- and object representations is a major mechanism in all these conditions. These personality disorders also display the use of denial, projective identification, and primitive idealization. Psychostructurally, they imply identity diffusion, although the degree to which features of

TABLE 4–1. Clinical Features of Borderline Personality Disorder

Clinical Features	*Overt Characteristics*	*Covert Characteristics*
I. *Self-Concept*	Self-image of one cruelly victimized by past and contemporary figures; a portrait of injured grandiosity; self-righteously enraged; bitter and cynical	Feeling of inherent defectiveness, lacking substance, empty, "bad"; frequently suicidal; intense feelings of inferiority; subtle disturbances of gender identity and body image
II. *Interpersonal Relations*	Intense involvements that oscillate between idealization and devaluation; clinging and dependent; keeping an inner list of hated enemies and worshipped others; difficulty maintaining "optimal distance" in relationships	Mistrusting, incapable of truly depending on others; failure to genuinely comprehend the separate existence and independent motivations of others; periodic futile vows of withdrawing from interpersonal relations
III. *Social Adaptation*	Superficially adapted to reality; compulsive socialization; marked impulsivity in stressful situations; unable to resist any promise of ecstasy, hence vulnerable to substance abuse; erratic academic and vocational record	Unpredictable and often inappropriate in social situations; incapable of peaceful solitude; dramatic shifts in vocational career; much geographical mobility over time; unclear about life goals

IV.	*Love and Sexuality*	Seemingly hedonistic and very romantic; frequent intense infatuations; sexually precocious and promiscuous	Can easily fall out of love; those "loved" are not actually known and accepted in their separate details and are merely idealized; sexual interest wanes in monogamous relations; tendency toward perversions
V.	*Ethics, Standards, and Ideals*	Transiently enthusiastic about moral and ethical ideas; idiosyncratic beliefs; interest in obscure religious systems; inner restraints on behavior center around shame, fear, and a paranoid dread of exposure	Inability to experience genuine, inner guilt; easily corruptible; lack of solid ethnic and communal affiliation; hunger for benevolent guidance; vulnerable to charismatic preachers and esoteric cults
VI.	*Cognitive Style*	Recklessly decisive although frequently with later regret and reversals; smugly knowledgeable with premature closure of information processing; things seen in black-and-white terms; brief and reversible psychotic breaks	Egocentric perception of reality; tendency toward much primary-process thinking in unstructured situations; magical thinking; ideas of reference; at times may possess significant artistic and poetic creativity

this syndrome (see Chapter 2) are readily manifest varies. Developmentally, individuals with such "lower level character organization" (Kernberg 1970), regardless of its specific phenotypal presentation, reveal a history of severe preoedipal trauma, an aborted separation-individuation process, much pregenital aggression, a distorted and unresolved Oedipus complex, defective and poorly internalized superego functions, a failure to establish an optimal phase of latency, and a more than usually troubled adolescence. Despite these remarkable similarities, important differences do exist between them.

Narcissistic Personality Disorder

In borderline personality disorder, the self is poorly integrated and at chronic risk of dissolution into psychoticlike states (Gunderson 1984, Gunderson and Singer 1975, Kohut 1977); interpersonal stress or psychoactive substances frequently unmask this vulnerability. In narcissistic personality, however, the self is more cohesive and less in danger of regressive fragmentation (Adler 1985, Kernberg 1975a, Kohut 1977). The borderline individual feels inferior to everybody else, although his frequently conceited attitude often betrays hidden grandiosity (Kernberg 1967). The narcissistic patient, in contrast, is overtly self-assured and grandiose only to be privately shame-laden, hungry, and insecure. Identity diffusion (Akhtar 1984, Erikson 1950a, Kernberg 1975a) is more overt in borderline disorder than in narcissistic disorder, where an enthusiastic, yet shallow, vocational commitment hides the inner aimlessness. Because of their greater cohesion, narcissistic personalities show better occupational functioning (Akhtar and Thomson 1982a, Kernberg 1975a), greater tolerance for aloneness (Adler 1985), and better impulse control and anxiety tolerance (Kernberg 1975a) than borderline personalities. Self-mutilation and persistent rage, frequent in borderline personality (Gunderson 1984, Gunderson and Singer 1975), are not associated with narcissistic personality. Much like the paranoid personality, the narcissist shows a sharpened reasoning when angry (Kohut 1972), whereas the borderline when enraged becomes flustered, illogical, and chaotically explosive.

The developmental background of the two is also different. With narcissistic patients, one usually gets the history that, as children, they were treated by their parents in an unempathic, cold, even spiteful but nonetheless "special" manner (Kernberg 1975a, Robbins 1982, Volkan 1976). This is perhaps because many of them were either firstborn or only children, possessed special attributes (e.g., talent, outstanding intelligence, or physical charm), or occupied a particularly meaningful place in the mythic history of the family. Borderline individuals, in contrast, frequently come from families broken due to parental death or divorce. As children, they suffered extreme frustrations, traumatic ruptures of the caretaking environment, and even physical and sexual abuse.

Histrionic Personality Disorder

Like borderline individuals, histrionic patients are dramatic, impulsive, often sexually promiscuous, corruptible, and vulnerable to temper tantrums (see Chapter 8 for more details). In their clinging attitude, manipulativeness, and constant need for attention, histrionic patients resemble borderline patients. However, they do not display the chronic rage and self-destructiveness characteristic of borderline individuals (Gunderson 1984). The intense suggestibility of the histrionic individuals makes them easier to get along with interpersonally and overtly less disturbed. A longitudinal view, however, reveals a pattern of unstable relationships, checkered vocational career, questionable morality, and inappropriate sexual involvements in both conditions (Kernberg 1985).

Antisocial Personality Disorder

Both borderline and antisocial individuals display impulsivity, intolerance of frustration, and failure to sustain socially productive lives (Gunderson 1984). Both manipulatively use others. However, the borderline individual does so desperately and is often secretly shameful or guilty about it, whereas the antisocial does so in a smooth, guiltless manner for material gains. Borderline individuals develop intense attachments from which, despite fluctuating extremes of idealization and devaluation, they find it hard to disengage themselves. Antisocial individuals, in contrast, tend to be more disaffiliated and self-absorbed and can easily trade one relationship for another (Gunderson 1984, Wolman 1987). Finally, while both borderline and antisocial individuals commit delinquent and illegal acts, this tendency is more nonchalant and sustained in the latter.

Schizotypal Personality Disorder

The overlap between borderline and schizotypal personality disorders is the subject of much scrutiny in current literature. The two disorders were originally separated (Spitzer et al. 1979) on the basis that while the schizotypal personality shows oddities in perception and thinking, the borderline personality displays instability across several areas of functioning. Further studies (Clarkin et al. 1983, Gunderson and Siever 1983, McGlashan 1986, Pope et al. 1983), however, revealed considerable overlap between the two disorders. Both types of patients show perceptual and cognitive distortions, such as magical thinking, ideas of reference, and oddities of communication (Gunderson 1984, Gunderson and Siever 1983, Rosenberger and Miller 1989). The main areas of their distinction are genetic linkage to schizophrenia, more evident in the schizotypal patients (Kendler et al. 1981, Torgersen 1985), and interpersonal behavior. The schizotypal patient is socially isolated and lacks the heightened emotionality and intense involvements typical of the borderline individual (Gunderson and Siever 1983, Kendler 1984, Torgersen 1984). Suspiciousness, detached affect, and obviously eccentric behavior are also more usual of the schizotypal than the borderline patient (Rosenberger and Miller 1989).

COMMENT

The term *borderline* had its beginnings as a "poorly defined, idiosyncratically employed catchall term for difficult patients" (Gunderson 1989, p. 123). It was initially used in connection with subclinical forms of schizophrenia and later in relation to its potential linkage with major affective disorders. However, the current usage of the term is in the context of personality disorders. In this realm there are two different though overlapping uses of the term: borderline personality disorder and borderline personality organization. Borderline personality disorder is a descriptive phenomenological designation that refers to a more or less specific psychiatric syndrome characterized by diffuse impulsivity, chronic anger, unstable interpersonal relationships, identity disturbance, feelings of emptiness and boredom, and proclivity toward self-destructive acts. Borderline personality organization, in contrast, is a broader concept with definite psychostructural and developmental implications. It refers to a character structure that shows identity diffusion, predominance of splitting (buttressed by denial, projective identification, and primitive idealization) over repression as the ego's main defensive operation, and an arrested separation-individuation process with resultant unstable self-concept, lack of object constancy, much pregenital aggression, and marked preoedipal coloration to the Oedipus complex. Clearly, the two concepts are on different levels of abstraction, although they do overlap and can indeed be synthesized. A borderline personality organization underlies all cases of borderline personality disorder. However, not all cases of borderline personality organization present phenotypically as borderline personality disorder. Borderline personality organization also underlies narcissistic, paranoid, schizoid, antisocial, hypomanic, and "as-if" personalities.

Finally, the term *borderline* itself needs comment. In my opinion, these cases are borderline in five different ways: (1) their symptomatic severity is of an intermediate level between neuroses and psychoses; (2) while unlike psychotics, individuals suffering from these conditions retain capacity for reality testing—they do not display a well-integrated self-concept typical of the neurotic level organization; in other words, their ego functions are of an intermediate level; (3) the traumatic events (and associated fantasies and defensive operations) usually held responsible for the development of the borderline condition seem to occur at developmental phases that lie between the ones whose disruption is associated with either neuroses or psychoses; (4) while neurotic disorders are held to be predominantly psychogenic and psychotic disorders predominantly constitutional in etiology, the borderline disorder perhaps derives an equal share from constitutional givens and severe early frustrations in its etiology; and (5) the disorder lies on the far borders of what can assuredly be treated with either classical psychoanalysis or conventional psychopharmacology. The term *borderline,* therefore, is particularly apt for this malady.

5

SCHIZOID PERSONALITY DISORDER

Solitude won't hurt you.
Solitude means no offense.
Solitude understands
As a man cannot understand.
Solitude can embrace
As a man cannot embrace.
But the dress is worn on bare
Nerves
and all its hooks are red-hot!

—"Love of Solitude," Yevgeny Yevtushenko

The recent renewal of interest in schizoid personality has two somewhat divergent roots. First is the controversy (Kernberg 1984, Livesley et al. 1986, Millon 1981) that surrounds the *DSM-III* distinctions of schizoid, schizotypal, and avoidant personality disorders. Second is the need generated by recent advances in psychoanalytic understanding of severe character pathology (Bach 1985, Guntrip 1969, Kernberg 1967, 1970, 1976, Khan 1974, 1983, Kohut 1971, Kohut and Wolf 1978, Mahler 1968, Mahler and Kaplan 1977, Mahler et al. 1975) for a fresh look on the phenomenology of the schizoid disorder. The need for such a reconsideration is strengthened by the absence of a comprehensive overview of the schizoid condition in recent general psychiatric literature.

In this chapter, I will attempt to highlight various views of schizoid personality and to integrate the contemporary psychoanalytic observations on severe character pathology with the corresponding descriptive views. My aim is to develop a phenomenological profile of schizoid personality disorder that will synthesize the classic and contemporary writings and correlate the behavioral characteristics of the condition with its underlying psychostructural organization.

DESCRIPTIVE STUDIES

The term *schizoid* was coined by Eugen Bleuler in 1908 to designate a natural component of man's personality that directed his attention toward his own inner life and away from the external world. A morbid but nonpsychotic exaggeration of this tendency was labeled the *schizoid personality.* Such persons were quiet, suspicious, "comfortably dull and at the same time sensitive" (Bleuler 1908, p. 441), and incapable of discussion. Bleuler emphasized that the inner lives of schizoid individuals were characterized by "a lack of uniformity of the affectivity and actual coexistence of different, nay, contrasting strivings" (p. 175).

About the same time, Hoch (1909, 1910) described the "shut-in" personality, which he claimed was frequently associated with schizophrenia. He viewed it as displaying secretiveness, inclination toward mystical pursuits, shyness, sensitivity, and excessive daydreaming. Hoch also stated that such individuals had a tendency toward "a poorly balanced sexual instinct . . . [and] strikingly fruitless love affairs" (1910, p. 467).

These ideas found a receptive exponent in Kretschmer (1925), who pointed out that such persons frequently were lovers of books, unathletic, ectomorphic, motorically clumsy, and quite unpractical in ordinary matters of life. He observed that schizoid individuals were "either in ecstasies or shocked, either enthusiastically attracted to a person or his mortal enemy" (p. 178). They could be lazy and yet act with passionate energy in certain matters. They were socially withdrawn or eclectically sociable without deep psychic rapport and yet could develop deep friendships with a select few in a sort of "enlarged autism among people of same persuasion" (p. 162). Most striking were their contradictory emotional states behind an apparently detached facade. While Kretschmer referred to hyperaesthetic and anaesthetic emotional attitudes in the schizoid character, he did not suggest its division into two separate groups. Indeed, he believed that the tension between these extremes lay "at the heart of schizoid pathology" (Livesley et al. 1986). Kretschmer (1925) recognized that schizoid individuals were always sensitive, though the extent to which they overtly displayed this inner trait varied considerably. He emphasized that

> even in that half of our material, which is primarily cold, and poor in affective response, as soon as we come into close personal contact with such schizoids, we find, very frequently, behind the affectless numbed exterior, in the innermost sanctuary, a tender personality-nucleus with the most vulnerable nervous sensitivity, which has withdrawn into itself and lies there contorted. [p. 153]

Following Kretschmer's important contributions, Kasanin and Rosen (1933) described schizoid individuals as having few friends, preferring solitary activities, being closemouthed, being followers rather than leaders in group situations, and possessing inordinate sensitivity. A related concept was described by Terry and Rennie (1938) under the somewhat idiosyncratic designation of "parergasic personality." Besides noticing inappropriate ambitions and shyness, these authors emphasized the incongruity between the snobbish exterior and the internal sensitivity of such individuals. They also pointed out the occurrence of compulsive masturbation and perverse sexuality in them.

Kallman (1938) used the term *schizoid psychopath* to describe certain nonpsychotic relatives of his schizophrenic patients. These persons were characterized by impulsive delinquent acts of illogical nature, secretiveness, and social withdrawal. A similar group among the adult children of schizophrenic mothers was subsequently reported by Heston (1966).

Fisher (1944) provided an eloquent description of the powerful need for attachment that underlies the schizoid's tendency to withdraw from others:

> Upon becoming interested in others, . . . he tends to become too interested. He suddenly finds himself bound by the strength and tenacity of his own feelings. Then, in an effort to break the suffocating bondage imposed by his incapacitating affective tensions, he unwittingly resorts to emotional withdrawal. [p. 365]

Asperger (1944) described "autistic psychopathy," a syndrome recognizable from early childhood onwards. His work has been resurrected recently under the varying titles of "autistic personality disorder" (Wing 1981) or Asperger's syndrome (Mawson et al. 1985, Wolff and Chick 1980). The syndrome consists of gaze abnormalities, autistic intelligence, solitariness, asexuality, and extreme personal sensitivity associated with indifference, even cruelty toward others. Asperger did not regard the condition as preschizophrenic but did relate it to the preexisting descriptions of "introverts" (Jung 1923) and "schizoids" (Kretschmer 1925).

Surveying the literature and adding his own opinions, Nanarello (1953) concluded that schizoid personality had three essential traits: feelings of inadequacy, social withdrawal, and a tendency toward autistic thinking. He also pointed out that the sexual life of such individuals was either "inactive or polymorphous and chaotic but hardly ever smooth-flowing" (p. 247).

Manfred Bleuler (1954) stated that "many schizoid traits resemble the symptoms which, in schizophrenia, are blown up to psychotic proportions" (pp. 381–382). He pointed out that schizoid personality is a frequent precursor of schizophrenia and occurs more often among the relatives of schizophrenics. Subsequent genetic studies of schizophrenia, comprehensively summarized by Rosenthal (1975), confirmed these ideas.

Heston (1970) attempted to distinguish behavioral and intrinsic attributes of the schizoid condition. Among the former, he included social aloofness, sexual deviation, suspiciousness, tendency toward heavy drinking, and odd crimes. Among the latter, he listed rigid thinking, exquisite sensitivity, blunted affect, and "micropsychotic" episodes. A more recent attempt to develop "core characteristics" of schizoid personality by Wolff and Chick (1980) yielded five criteria: solitariness, impaired empathy and emotional detachment, increased sensitivity, rigidity of mental set, and an unusual or odd style of communication. These investigators suggested that schizoid individuals were both unempathic and sensitive at the same time and were either uncommunicative or overtalkative and lacking in guardedness. They thus emphasized a certain contradiction to be inherent in the nature of schizoid condition.

Summary

The descriptive psychiatry literature suggests that schizoid personality is genetically, developmentally, and phenomenologically related to schizophrenia. It characterizes the condition with (1) social withdrawal, (2) vivid internal life, (3) contradictory presence of sensitivity and callousness, (4) sexual chaos, (5) moral unevenness, (6) cognitive peculiarities, (7) vagueness of pursuits, and (8) fluctuations in attachment to others, from extreme involvement to complete withdrawal. Finally, almost all authors note the discrepancy between the outer and inner worlds of the schizoid individual and emphasize the "divided self" (Laing 1965) of such a person.

PSYCHOANALYTIC VIEWS

Early Literature

Freud's (1931) description of the "narcissistic" type is generally viewed as an antecedent of the narcissistic personality disorder. However, certain aspects of this type also apply to the schizoid personality. These include preoccupation with self-preservation, freedom from ordinary moral restraints, low frustration tolerance, and predisposition to psychosis. Freud did not discuss the schizoid personality per se, but clearly his ideas—especially his notions about early ego development, the mechanisms of splitting, projection, and identification, and the ego's conflicting allegiance to internal wishes and external reality—underlie all the work that followed.

Reich (1933) emphasized that the psychic contactlessness of the schizoid person was itself a compromise between a wish for and against involvement. This wall kept others away but also evoked curiosity and attention.

The most significant early contribution was that of Melanie Klein (1946), who suggested that splitting was the fundamental characteristic of the schizoid condition. She viewed the origin of such splitting—the keeping apart of contradictory self- and object representations—in a defensive maneuver against infantile persecutory anxieties consequent upon projection of inborn aggression. Splitting was buttressed by denial of contradictions and by the use of "projective identification" (Klein 1946, 1955). Parts of self, viewed as unacceptable or in danger of being experientially drowned by contradictory self-images, were expelled into the outer world and deposited into others. This resulted in the creation of frightening persecutors and idealized external representatives of one's own goodness. Such an introjected-projected relationship and its inevitable narcissistic orientation led to the need to control others. Under the sway of a deflected drive to control parts of himself, the schizoid individual clung to or shrank away from others.

Klein regarded the absence of anxiety in schizoid individuals as only apparent since

> it is kept latent by the particular method of dispersal. The feeling of being disintegrated, of being unable to experience emotions, of losing one's objects, is in fact the equivalent of anxiety. This becomes clearer when advances in synthesis have been made. The great relief which a patient then experiences derives from a feeling that his inner and outer worlds have not only come more together but back to life again. At such moments it appears in retrospect that when emotions were lacking, relations were vague and uncertain and parts of the personality were felt to be lost, everything seemed to be dead. All this is the equivalent of anxiety of a very serious nature. [Klein 1946, p. 21]

An important contribution to follow was Deutsch's (1942) description of the as-if personalities that, in her opinion, were muted characterological variants of schizophrenia. Deutsch outlined four characteristics of such individuals: a tendency to rapidly identify with others, an easily shifting morality, an automationlike suggestibility, and a defensive splitting of aggression lending to them an air of negative goodness and mild amiability. The importance of her contribution lay in its emphasis on the pathology of the internal world of these patients. Indeed, Deutsch pointed out that as-if personalities may appear quite normal on the surface, thus emphasizing the dissociation between the inner and outer aspects of such individuals.

Fenichel (1945) described "schizoid characters" as responding to narcissistic hurts with denial, narcissistic withdrawal, and temporary loss of object relationships. He noted further that schizoid individuals tended to supplant their defective object relations by pseudocontacts and pseudoemotions, an aspect of their emotional lives much emphasized in the British school of psychoanalysis.

The British School

More than any other psychoanalyst, Fairbairn (1940) delved into the phenomenology and dynamics of the schizoid condition. He viewed schizoid individuals as displaying an attitude of omnipotence, emotional detachment, and preoccupation with inner reality. He pointed out that such social isolation and overvaluation of thought processes may have beneficial results, especially for those engaged in scientific and intellectual pursuits. In his psychoanalytic work with schizoid patients, Fairbairn found

> (i) that in early life they gained the conviction, whether through apparent indifference or through apparent possessiveness on the part of their mother, that their mother did not really love and value them as persons in their own right; (ii) that, influenced by a resultant sense of deprivation and inferiority, they remained profoundly fixated upon their mother; (iii) that the libidinal attitude accompanying this fixation was one not only characterized by extreme dependence, but also rendered highly self preservative and narcissistic by anxiety over a situation which presented itself as involving a threat to the ego; (iv) that through a regression to the attitude of the early oral phase, not

> only did the libidinal cathexis of an already internalized "breast-mother" become internalized, but also the process of internalization itself became unduly extended to relationship with other objects; and (v) that these resulted in general overvaluation of the internal at the expense of the external world. [p. 23]

Fairbairn elaborated on the phenomenological consequences of such a fixation. The regressive substitution of mother as a person by a more easily controllable part object, the breast, led in such individuals to an overall tendency to treat other people as less than persons with an inherent value of their own. This powerful tendency toward a simplification of relationships often resulted in their substituting bodily for emotional contacts. The persistence of this early attitude also manifested in the predominance of taking over giving in the emotional life. Fairbairn pointed out that schizoid individuals feel exhausted after social contacts and defend against their difficulty in emotional giving by playing roles that replace giving by showing.

Fairbairn stated that "the attraction of literary and artistic activities for individuals with a schizoid personality is partly due to the fact that these activities provide an exhibitionistic means of expression without involving direct contact" (p. 16). However, he pointed out that schizoid individuals have another reason for keeping their love to themselves. Schizoids fear that the vigor of their needs can deplete others and therefore come to regard loving as dangerous. To hide their love and to protect themselves from others' love, rendered dangerous by projection, schizoid individuals erect defenses against loving and being loved. They feel compelled to distance others by seeming indifferent or by being rude, even hateful. According to Fairbairn (1940), this substitution of loving by hating has two motives, one immoral, the other moral:

> The immoral motive is determined by the consideration that, since the joy of loving seems hopelessly barred to him, he may as well deliver himself over to the joy of hating and obtain what satisfaction he can out of that. . . . The moral motive is determined by the consideration that, if loving involves destroying, it is better to destroy by hate, which is overtly destructive and bad, than to destroy by love, which is by rights creative and good. [p. 27]

Fairbairn thus viewed schizoid individuals as suffering from three tragedies. The first is that they feel that their love is destructive. The second is that they exhibit a defensive compulsion to hate and be hated while longing deep down to be loved. The third is that the situation thus necessitates an "amazing reversal of moral values" (p. 27).

Another major contributor to the understanding of schizoid personality was Winnicott, who proposed the notions of "true" and "false" selves. Winnicott (1960) suggested that if the infant's mother can meet his spontaneous gestures empathically, then what is real in the infant begins to have life. However, if the mother fails to decode the infant's overture and replaces it by her own gesture, then the process is reversed. The infant is forced to comply and renunciate his authentic self-assertion. Winnicott posited that when this latter sequence is the usual mother–child interaction, then the child's "true-self" withdraws inwardly and the child develops an outwardly compliant but "false-self." He further suggested that only when all goes well in infancy does the "person of the baby start to be linked with the body and the bodily functions" (Winnicott 1963), and that where a "false-self" predominates there is also a mind–body split. The mind becomes the locus of identity and the body a disowned experiential vestige.

Winnicott viewed schizoid personality as a variety of "false-self" organization. He suggested that behind the overtly compliant persona of such individuals lie concerns over "(i) going to pieces, (ii) falling forever, (iii) having no relationship to body, [and] (iv) having no orientation" (Winnicott 1965, p. 58). He emphasized that the "false-self" was not just a mask; it was also a caretaker of the "true-self." It provided a secret life for the "true-self" while continuing to

> search for conditions which will make it possible for the True-Self to come into its own. If conditions cannot be found then there must be organized a new defense against exploitation of the True-Self, and if there be doubt then the clinical result is suicide. Suicide in this context is the destruction of the total self in avoidance of annihilation of the True-Self. When suicide is the only defense left against betrayal of the True-Self, then it becomes the lot of the False-Self to organize the suicide. [Winnicott 1965, p. 143]

The work of Fairbairn and Winnicott was further elaborated by Guntrip and Khan. Guntrip (1969) outlined nine characteristics of the schizoid personality: introversion, withdrawal, narcissism, self-sufficiency, a sense of superiority, loss of affect, loneliness, depersonalization, and tendency toward regression. More importantly, he described the peculiar object relations of the schizoid individual who, when separated from his love objects, feels utterly insecure and lost but, when reunited, feels swallowed, smothered, and absorbed. Thus the schizoid must always be rushing into a relationship for security and at once breaking out again for freedom and independence. Guntrip suggested that the propensity to withdraw from external relationships emanated from (1) tantalizing refusal by early caretakers that aroused hungry impulses so powerful as to be feared as devouring, (2) impingement by a hostile object that evoked direct fear of the outer world, or (3) emotional desertion by parental figures that necessitated seeking gratification within oneself.

Khan (1963, 1974, 1983) further highlighted the peculiar mother-child relationship that led to the development of schizoid personality. On the one hand, the mother repeatedly failed in her function as a protective shield for the growing child, causing a pathogenic "cumulative trauma" (1963) of anaclitic betrayals. On the other hand, through indulgences and collusion, the mother maintained an intense focal, often physical, closeness with the child, a "symbiotic omnipotence" (1974), which actively discouraged involvement with other objects. Khan outlined the behavioral consequences of both "cumulative trauma" and "symbiotic omnipotence" in the adult schizoid personality. These included, respectively, (1) pseudocompliance, self-sufficiency, intellectual defense, withdrawal, and autoeroticism; and (2) an ability to mobilize hopefulness in others, magical thinking, omnipotence, secret optimism, and an expectancy of oversensitive rapport from others.

Other Psychoanalytic Contributions

The views of Erikson (1950a), Jacobson (1964), and Mahler (1968, 1975) on the development of a separate sense of self and identity have a significant, though somewhat indirect, bearing on understanding the phenomenology of schizoid personality. According to these views, schizoid personality belongs to a group of character disorders that show an incompletely developed sense of self, poorly consolidated identity, continued presence of unsynthesized contradictory identifications, and a persisting dependence on external objects for cohesiveness of the self-experience.

Kernberg more directly associated schizoid personality with a borderline personality organization (1967) or a "lower level" (1970) character pathology. At this level of character organization superego integration is minimal, and the synthetic function of the patients' ego is seriously impaired. Splitting is the central defensive operation of the ego instead of repression. There is a general lack of restriction of the conflict-free ego, and primary-process thinking infiltrates cognitive functioning. Kernberg portrayed schizoid individuals as being unable to understand themselves and others in ambivalent totality. Consequently, their inner worlds were populated by idealized and horrible aspects of others and shameful and exalted self-images. Kernberg emphasized the subjective unreality, drifting, and identity diffusion of schizoid patients. Coupled with a defensive dispersal of affect, these characteristics led to chronic feelings of inner emptiness, a frequent schizoid complaint discussed in detail by Singer (1977a,b).

In Kohut's (1971) view, schizoid personality was a defensive organization that resulted from the individual's "[pre]conscious awareness not only of his narcissistic vulnerability, but also, and specifically, the danger that a narcissistic injury could initiate an uncontrollable regression" (p. 12). Kohut viewed schizoid individuals as being capable of meaningful contact and possessing considerable libidinal resources, which they defensively channeled into nonhuman interests. While he distinguished schizoid personality from narcissistic personality, his later description of "contact-shunning personalities" (Kohut and Wolff 1978) showed the phenomenological overlap of the two conditions.

Rey (1979) described the "schizoid personality organization" in detail, though at times using "schizoid" and "borderline" labels interchangeably. He viewed such patients as vulnerable to rapid identification with their objects, with resulting anxiety over loss of identity. Rey pointed out that these patients lack a firm sexual identity and are susceptible to body-image disturbances. They lack normal reparative concerns toward others or express these in concrete ways. Their communication is peculiarly asymbolic and takes place "at a level of 'merchandise,' a sort of barter agreement in which the subject feels himself to be given 'things,' made to accept 'things,' where 'things' are done to him, etc." (p. 452).

Finally, mention must be made of Burland's (1986) description of the "autistic character disorder." Basing his conceptualizations on Mahler's (1968, Mahler et al. 1975) scheme of the separation-individuation process, Burland suggested that an early, severe, and sustained deprivation of maternal care resulted in an incomplete "hatching" of the infant from the normal autistic phase. A gratifying symbiotic phase did not follow as the child failed to establish a libidinal object. Consequently, the subsequent phases of separation-individuation leading to self- and object constancy were miscarried. This multifaceted developmental arrest manifested in interpersonal unrelatedness, cognitive lag, pathological narcissism, and higher than normal levels of destructive aggression. Although Burland described the syndrome mainly in maternally deprived ghetto children, he did suggest that it was recognizable in adults by their affectionlessness, fragmented identity, cognitive impotence, and mindless hedonism.

Summary

The psychoanalytic literature characterizes the schizoid personality as displaying (1) evidence of considerably severe, sustained preoedipal trauma; (2) an aborted separation-individuation process and therefore a lack of self- and object constancy; (3) predominance of object relations and dyadic conflicts over internalized, structural conflicts; (4) persistence of severe splitting of self-representations and related mechanisms of repudiation, projection identification, primitive idealization, and so on; (5) the condensation of preoedipal and oedipal conflicts, with a sadomasochistic tinge and tendency toward perverse formations; (6) the syndrome of identity diffusion; and (7) an uneven superego, with an unrealistic ego ideal formed, not by idealization of parental objects but in lieu of them. In essence, the emphasis of the psychoanalytic literature is on the defensive nature of the schizoid withdrawal, underlying which is the inordinate need for human contact and the poorly formed self of such an individual.

DSM-III AND *DSM-III-R*

DSM-III

DSM-III (p. 311) recognized schizoid personality disorder as a distinct nosological entity with the following diagnostic criteria:

A. Emotional coldness or aloofness, and absence of warm, tender feelings for others.

B. Indifference to praise or criticism or to the feelings of others.

C. Close friendships with no more than one or two persons, including family members.

D. No eccentricities of speech, behavior or thought characteristic of schizotypal personality disorder.

E. Not due to a psychotic disorder such as Schizophrenia or Paranoid Disorder.

F. If under 18, does not meet the criteria for Schizoid Disorder of Childhood or Adolescence.

Leaving the self-explanatory negative statements (D through F) aside, one is left with three diagnostic criteria which, on close scrutiny, seem ambiguous and repetitious. For instance, criterion A appears a mere rewording of criterion B. Also, how can individuals with "absence of warm, tender feelings for others" (criterion A) have "close friendships" (criterion C), even if these are limited in number? Similarly, can "close friendships" (criterion C) be entered into by someone with "indifference to . . . the feelings of others" (criterion B)? It appears that two (A and B) of the three diagnostic criteria overlap remarkably, and the third (C) does not fit comfortably with either.

To complicate matters, one notices significant omissions in these criteria. No mention is made of the chronic dilemma in which the schizoid individual finds himself, namely, that he can neither be in a relationship nor be out of one without fearing engulfment or intense aloneness (Burnham et al. 1969, Guntrip 1969). Also omitted is the rich fantasy life that underlies the apparent detachment of the schizoid individual (Cameron 1963, Kernberg 1984). *DSM-III* also did not refer to the moral unevenness and sexual chaos that characterize schizoid personality.

The explanation for this phenomenological pallor lies in the designation schizoid personality being used in an extremely restricted sense. What had customarily been understood as schizoid personality was, in *DSM-III,* broken into three separate syndromes: the schizoid, the avoidant, and the schizotypal. Millon (1969, 1981, Millon and Millon 1974), from whose theoretical constructs these distinctions were largely derived, clarifies the *DSM-III* stance.

> The designation "schizoid" is limited to personalities characterized by an intrinsic defect in the capacity to form social relationships. The label "avoidant" represents those who possess both the capacity and desire to relate socially, but who fear humiliation and disapproval, and, hence, distance themselves from such relationships. The term "schizotypal" is reserved for individuals who are noted by the eccentric character of their social communications and behaviors, and for an ostensive genetic linkage to schizophrenia. [1981, p. 274]

This typology, though didactically appealing, posed many conceptual difficulties besides fostering an artificial dichotomy between conflict (avoidant) and deficit (schizoid) models of psychopathology. The schizotypal concept (see Chapter 8), though having some phenomenological overlap (Pfohl et al. 1986, Siever and Klar 1986) with the schizoid diagnosis, presents less difficulties in this regard since it may have greater resemblance to the older concepts of simple and latent schizophrenia (Kernberg 1984, McGlashan 1983, Plakum et al. 1985). It is the *DSM-III* distinction of schizoid and avoidant character types that drains more from phenomenology of the schizoid condition.

The main difference between the avoidant and schizoid alities (Grinker et al. 1968, Millon 1981) is supposed to be that the avoidant person wishes social involvement and is hypersensitive, while the schizoid prefers aloneness and is impervious to acceptance or rejection by others. This distinction is a dubious one in my clinical experience. Kernberg (1984) also questions the assumption that schizoid personalities do not desire social involvement. He believes that schizoid individuals experience an acute awareness of their surrounding environment, an emotional attuneness to others, and a guilty sense of unavailability of their feelings for others.

Criticism of the schizoid-avoidant distinction has come from other avenues as well. In a thorough reexamination of the influential writings of Kretschmer (1925), Livesley et al. (1986) point out that the active and passive social avoidance, the inner hypersensitivity and the callous persona, and the vigilant and the absent-minded attitudes are various facets of the same condition. Reich and Noyes (1986), in a study of 82 patients on multiple personality inventories, also found the *DSM-III* separation of schizoid and avoidant personalities to be questionable. A similar conclusion was arrived at by Morey (1985), who, using detailed interpersonal-style inventories, found similar affection and affiliation-seeking scores in the *DSM-III* avoidant and schizoid personalities. Morey concluded that *DSM-III* misjudged the importance of interpersonal relationships for persons it labeled as schizoid.

DSM-III-R

DSM-III-R (pp. 339–340) retains schizoid personality disorder as a distinct nosological entity and provides the following criteria for its diagnosis:

A. A pervasive pattern of indifference to social relationships, and restricted range of emotional experience and expression, beginning by early adulthood and present in a variety of contexts, as indicated by at least four of the following:

   (i) neither desires nor enjoys close relationships, including being part of a family

(ii) almost always chooses solitary activities

(iii) rarely, if ever, claims or appears to experience strong emotions, such as anger and joy

(iv) indicates little if any desire to have sexual experiences with another person (age being taken into account)

(v) is indifferent to the praise and criticism of others

(vi) has no close friends or confidants (or only one) other than first-degree relatives

(vii) displays constricted affect, e.g. is aloof, cold, rarely reciprocates gestures or facial expressions, such as smiles or nods

B. Occurrence not exclusively during the course of Schizophrenia or Delusional Disorder.

A richer picture of schizoid personality disorder emerges from this description. The improvement over *DSM-III* criteria is discernible in three areas. First, requiring a greater number of clinical features from the diagnosis reduces the risk of oversimplification. Second, difficulties in the expression of sexuality and overt aggression have been given their due recognition. Third, the addition of qualifiers ("appears," "claims," "indicates," "displays") to the schizoid indifference and lack of feelings subtly accommodates the view that these may be only surface phenomena. This allowance softens the rigid separation of the schizoid and avoidant types. A corresponding shift in the *DSM-III-R* version of avoidant personality is a greater emphasis on its phobiclike rather than schizoidlike qualities. This too minimizes the *DSM-III* schizoid-avoidant split, while presenting a newer version of avoidant personality that is more akin to the "phobic character" (Fenichel 1945) discussed below.

While these are major improvements, the retention in *DSM-III-R* of a lack of desire for human relationships as a criterion for schizoid personality remains open to question. Also, the inclusion of superego defects, hidden perverse tendencies, characterological contradictions, and profound identity conflicts may have rendered the clinical profile of schizoid personality deeper and more comprehensive.

Summary

DSM-III schizoid personality disorder was descriptively anemic. Diagnostic criteria were sparse and failed to include certain well-recognized clinical features of the condition. Surface phenomena, such as social withdrawal, were taken on face value, and the importance of human relationships for schizoid individuals was misjudged. The deficiencies resulted from the introduction of a "schizoidlike" avoidant personality disorder. In contrast, *DSM-III-R* presents a more vivid description of schizoid personality disorder. It also minimizes the schizoid-avoidant split by (1) suggesting that the indifference and withdrawal even in schizoid personality may be more apparent than real, and (2) subtly shifting the avoidant personality toward a "phobiclike" disorder.

AN ATTEMPT AT SYNTHESIS

The literature surveyed above was synthesized in order to develop a true picture of schizoid personality disorder. According to this profile (Table 5-1), the clinical features of schizoid personality involve six areas of psychosocial functioning: (1) self-concept; (2) interpersonal relations; (3) social adaptation; (4) love and sexuality; (5) ethics, standards, and ideals; and (6) cognitive style. In each of these areas, there are overt and covert manifestations. These designations do not imply conscious or unconscious but denote seemingly contradictory aspects that are phenomenologically more or less easily discernible. Moreover, "such contradictions are not restricted to the schizoid's object-relatedness but permeate his morality, emotional attitudes and the view of his self" (Akhtar 1986b). Thus the schizoid individual is "overtly" detached, self-sufficient, absentminded, uninteresting, asexual, and idiosyncratically moral, while "covertly" exquisitely sensitive, emotionally

TABLE 5–1. Clinical Features of Schizoid Personality Disorder.

Clinical Features	*Overt Characteristics*	*Covert Characteristics*
I. *Self-Concept*	Compliant; stoic; noncompetitive; self-sufficient; lacking assertiveness; feeling inferior and an outsider in life	Cynical; inauthentic; depersonalized; alternately feeling empty, robotlike, and full of omnipotent, vengeful fantasies; hidden grandiosity
II. *Interpersonal Relations*	Withdrawn; aloof; having few close friends; impervious to others' emotions; afraid of intimacy	Exquisitely sensitive; deeply curious about others; hungry for love; envious of others' spontaneity; intensely needy of involvement with others; capable of excitement with carefully selected intimates
III. *Social Adaptation*	May prefer solitary occupational and recreational activities; marginal or eclectically sociable in groups; vulnerable to esoteric movements, owing to a strong need to belong; tendency to be lazy and indolent	Lacking clarity of goals; weak ethnic affiliation; usually capable of steady work; sometimes quite creative and may make unique and original contributions; capable of passionate endurance in certain spheres of interests

IV.	*Love and Sexuality*	Asexual, sometimes celibate; free of romantic interests; averse to sexual gossip and innuendo	Secret voyeuristic and pornographic interests; vulnerable to erotomania; tendency toward compulsive masturbation and perversions
V.	*Ethics, Standards, and Ideals*	Idiosyncratic moral and political beliefs; tendency toward spiritual, mystical, and parapsychological interests	Moral unevenness; occasionally strikingly amoral and vulnerable to odd crimes, at other times altruistically self-sacrificing
VI.	*Cognitive Style*	Absentminded; engrossed in fantasy; vague and stilted speech; alternations between eloquence and inarticulateness	Autistic thinking; fluctuations between sharp contact with external reality and hyperreflectiveness about the self; autocentric use of language

needy, acutely vigilant, creative, often perverse, and vulnerable to corruption.

This manner of organizing symptomatology emphasizes the centrality of splitting and identity diffusion in schizoid personality. This stance is not idiosyncratic. The foregoing review of literature amply demonstrates the support of such a position within both the descriptive and psychoanalytic traditions in psychiatry. However, a description of schizoid personality along these lines is not entirely problem-free. There is a risk of the overt and covert designations being equated with conscious and unconscious aspects despite reminders to the contrary. This risk is heightened by the fact that covert features are difficult to discern and may not be apparent in one or two interviews. Also, the lack of actuarial data on the frequency of various clinical features makes their relative diagnostic weight difficult to distinguish at this time. Finally, it is possible that studies with larger samples may show that in some schizoid individuals the usually covert features are overt or vice versa.

These reservations notwithstanding, the description of schizoid personality provided here (Table 5-1) does seem to have many advantages over those outlined in *DSM-III* and *DSM-III-R* insofar as it (1) maintains historical continuity in the use of the term *schizoid,* (2) includes both descriptive and psychoanalytic observations, (3) values depth and complexity over descriptive oversimplification, and (4) has sounder theoretical underpinnings since it establishes a connection between the descriptive and psychostructural (therefore, developmental) aspects of the schizoid pathology. Finally, this profile helps in more meaningful differential diagnosis of schizoid from related personality disorders.

DIFFERENTIAL DIAGNOSIS

Phobic Character

Fenichel (1945) coined the term *phobic character* for individuals "whose reactive behavior limits itself to the avoidance of the *situations* originally wished for" (p. 527, emphasis added). Mackinnon and

Michels (1971) also pointed out that more common than the symptomatic phobia is the use of fearful avoidance as a characterological defense, adding that such an individual is "constantly imagining himself in *situations* of danger while pursuing the course of greatest safety" (p. 49, emphasis added). Most recently, Stone (1980) recognized a "phobic-anxious" personality type that displays extremes of "such qualities as fearfulness and avoidance of the most harmless objects and *situations*" (p. 332, emphasis added). While resembling schizoid individuals in their restricted life-style, phobic characters are different in important ways. *They avoid situations, not people.* Their avoidance of certain situations (e.g., visit to an amusement park, travel on a highway, overnight stay at a friend's house) may lead to the false appearance of discomfort with people in general. The fact is that outside these situations, they can have deep, empathic, and meaningful affective interchange with others.

Using the term *avoidant* for such a phobic organization, I earlier (Akhtar and Byrne 1983) pointed out other significant differences between this syndrome and the schizoid personality. Those with a phobic character do not display identity diffusion (Akhtar 1984, Erikson 1950a, Kernberg 1975a), nor do they manifest a predominance of splitting over repression and its related defense mechanisms. Conceptually, therefore, a phobic personality should be regarded as a "higher level" or neurotic character organization (Kernberg 1970) and "an ego-syntonic characterological counterpart" (Akhtar 1986b) of the phobic neurosis. Schizoid personality, on the other hand, shows a "lower level" (Kernberg 1970) or borderline character organization with prominent splitting, impaired object relations, and severe identity diffusion.

Compulsive Personality

Both schizoid and compulsive personality disorders display rigidity, inordinate self-reliance, excessive caution in emotional expression, and a tendency toward hidden omnipotence. The two disorders, however, are actually quite distinct. Unlike the schizoid, the compulsive individual is capable of deep object relations, mature love, concern, genuine guilt, mourning, and sadness (Kernberg 1970, Volkan 1976). Also, the compulsive personality does not manifest defensive splitting and the syndrome of identity diffusion; both of these are regular features of the schizoid makeup. The compulsive's strict morality is even, the schizoid's uneven. Moreover, the compulsive has not suffered the deeply traumatizing events generally associated with the childhood of the schizoid individual.

Narcissistic Personality

There are many similarities between the narcissistic and schizoid personality disorders (see Chapter 3). Developmentally, both show arrested separation-individuation, a distorted Oedipus complex, and an uneven superego, resulting in less than optimal latency and adolescence (Guntrip 1969, Jacobson 1964, Kernberg 1970, 1975a, Khan 1974, 1983, Mahler 1968). Dynamically, both display a predominance of splitting over repression as the main defensive operation. Identity diffusion is present in both, although in the narcissistic disorder it is masked by a pathological grandiose self. Descriptively, both narcissistic and schizoid individuals prefer ideologies over deep relationships. Both display intellectual hypertrophy (Bach 1985, Khan 1974) and a corresponding lack of wholesome rootedness in their bodily existence. Also, both lack warmth, feel awkward in intimate situations, and avoid encounters that require spontaneous responses.

Important differences, however, exist between the two conditions. The narcissist exploits others for his dependency needs, while the schizoid hides his dependency needs (Nemiah 1961). The narcissistic individual is ambitious and competitive (Akhtar and Thomson 1982a, Kernberg 1975a, Kohut 1971), while the schizoid is resigned and fatalistic (Cameron 1963, Guntrip 1969). A narcissistic individual frequently deposits inferiority and shame-laden self-representations into others, causing others to experience such feelings. A schizoid individual, on the other hand, deposits optimistic and sane attributes into others for safekeeping and thus mobilizes hope, curiosity, and rescue fantasies in the latter (Akhtar 1991a). The narcissist compensates for his defective object relations by compulsively socializing and seeking admiration. The schizoid individual has given up the external search for an omnipotent love object only to replace it with an ongoing involvement with highly valued internal objects. As a result, the narcissist is active, restless, flamboyant, and chronically in pursuit, while the schizoid is passive, cynical, overtly bland, or, at best, vaguely mysterious.

Borderline Personality

The recognition of an overlap between schizoid and borderline conditions is implicit in Millon's choice of such terms as *detached-borderline* (1969) and *borderline-schizoid* (Millon and Millon 1974). It is more explicit in Kernberg's (1967) seminal paper on borderline personality organization and his subsequent (1970) classification of personality disorders. On both these occasions, Kernberg associated schizoid personality with the borderline personality, viewing both of these as lower level character organizations. The overlap between schizoid and borderline conditions was also revealed in the empirical investigation of the syndrome by Grinker et al. (1968). Most recently, Gunderson (1985) suggested that role confusion and psychoticlike ideation occur in both borderline and schizoid personalities, and Plakum et al. (1985) noted the coexistence of the *DSM-III* borderline and schizoid diagnoses.

Despite some similarities, the two conditions are behaviorally quite distinct. The borderline is overtly rageful, the schizoid merely cynical. The borderline is given to sexual promiscuity, while the schizoid is vulnerable to erotomania and autistic love affairs. Finally, the manner of handling strong affects is different in the two conditions. The borderline gives in to them and explodes, while the schizoid negates, shelves them away, and thus remains seemingly unperturbed.

COMMENT

One other aspect of the schizoid disorder needs attention here. This refers to the variations of schizoid symptomatology over an individual life span. There is some evidence that the disorder is recognizable from early childhood onwards (Essen-Moller 1946,

Wolff 1973) and may persist in subdued (Morris et al. 1954) or completely unchanged (Wolff and Chick 1980) forms into early adult life. Relatively little is known about the manifestations of schizoid personality during middle and old age. Bergman (1978), who has studied the presence of personality disorders in the elderly, suggests that schizoid patients make better adjustments to aging than would be expected form their psychopathology.

One little-noted phenomenon is an occasional crossover in the phenomenology of schizoid and narcissistic personality disorders during middle age. At this time certain narcissistic patients begin to show an emotional introspection, a painful awareness of aloneness, a new sense of humility, and a self-effacing abandonment of their previous grandiosity (Kernberg 1980b). These changes, coupled with a defensive withdrawal from external reality, may render them phenomenologically akin to schizoid individuals. Certain gifted schizoid individuals, on the other hand, become more comfortable in overtly manifesting their hitherto secret grandiosity, inner sensitivity, need for attachment, and sexual longing during middle age. Combined with their cumulative social accomplishments, this dynamic shift may make such schizoid individuals look like those with a narcissistic personality.

The crossover is not surprising. Until middle age the narcissist has pursued external glory and suppressed his morose self-doubts, while the schizoid has maintained an ascetic persona and negated his sensitive but omnipotent self-representation. Middle age, by introducing a powerful shift in time perspective, necessitates a final and deeper consolidation of identity (Kernberg 1980b), which may be difficult for those with "hidden selves" (Khan 1983). The temptation now to travel the road not taken during earlier consolidation of identity is great for such individuals and may explain the symptomatic shift described earlier.

Clearly, life phase–specific variations in the symptomatology of personality disorders are not restricted to the schizoid and narcissistic types. The somewhat better than expected adjustment of paranoid personalities (Bergman 1978), the diminution in delinquency of antisocial personalities (Robins 1966), and the anergic state of borderline personalities (Snyder et al. 1983) in later age are other examples of this tendency. All this suggests that a greater psychodynamic fluidity and phenotypal variability than have hitherto been suspected may exist within severe character pathology. However, before this can be investigated, it is essential to develop comprehensive psychodynamically based phenomenological profiles of the personality disorders involved. The outline developed in this chapter is a step in that direction.

6

PARANOID PERSONALITY DISORDER

Today my voice is choked and mute is my flute.
My world has disappeared in an evil dream.
Therefore with tears I ask thee:
"Those who have poisoned thine air
And extinguished thy light,
Hast thou forgiven them?
Hast thou loved them?"

—"A Question," Rabindranath Tagore

Paranoid personality disorder is a well-established nosological entity. It is listed in *DSM-III-R* and was included in all previous versions of *DSM*. References to it are scattered throughout the vast descriptive literature on schizophrenia and paranoid psychoses. Psychoanalytic literature also recognizes such a character type. Yet there is a paucity of papers specifically devoted to the phenomenology of paranoid personality disorder. Unlike other severe personality disorders, where attempts have been made to synthesize the descriptive and psychoanalytic contributions, these two views of paranoid personality disorder continue to exist independently of each other.

My aim in this chapter is to provide a comprehensive survey of the descriptive and psychoanalytic literature on the subject and to synthesize the two in order to develop a multifaceted phenomenological profile of paranoid personality disorder. Such a delineation would have sound developmental and psychostructural underpinnings. It would also help in meaningful differential diagnosis of paranoid from other related personality disorders.

DESCRIPTIVE STUDIES

The influential French psychiatrist Magnan (1893) divided paranoid psychoses into two types: chronic delusional state of systematic evolution and delusional states of the degenerates. He divided the latter category into three subtypes: paranoia associated with mental defect, chronic delusional states with a good long-term prognosis, and the delusional states of degeneracy or *bouffée delirante des degeneres*. The last condition was characterized by sudden onset, affective coloring, clouded sensorium, and rapid remission. According to Magnan, such short-term paranoid developments emanated from a constitutional degeneracy, or a "fragile personality," which showed idiosyncratic thinking, undue sensitivity, hypochondriasis, referential thinking, and suspiciousness. Magnan's description is perhaps one of the earliest portrayals of paranoid personality disorder in psychiatric literature.

Closely related in time is Kraepelin's (1905) description of a pseudoquerulous personality type who is "always on the alert to find a grievance, but without delusions" (p. 309). Such an individual is vain, self-absorbed, sensitive, irritable, litigious, obstinate, and living at strife with the world. Kraepelin (1921a) renamed the condition *paranoid personality* and provided its more detailed description. He characterized such individuals as displaying marked distrust, feeling unjustly treated by everyone, and regarding themselves as the object of hostility, interference, and oppression. Such individuals were chronically irritable and behaved in a boastful, impatient, and obstinate manner. Though mostly unromantic, they could show "great sexual excitability" (p. 270) and were vulnerable to erotomanialike secret love affairs. Kraepelin also observed a peculiar contradiction in such persons. On the one hand, they think that their unusual actions are quite in order and hold stubbornly to their ideas. On the other hand, they are often extremely credulous and accept without hesitation every piece of gossip as truth.

Following Kraepelin, Bleuler (1908) described "contentious psychopathy" or "paranoid constitution" as displaying the characteristic triad of suspiciousness, grandiosity, and feelings of persecution. He too emphasized that the false assumptions of such individuals do not attain the form of a real delusion. Bleuler referred to their narrow field of vision, inordinate sensitivity, irritability, and attempts at solving difficulties of life by geographical moves.

Kretschmer (1927) emphasized the sensitive inner core of the paranoia-prone personality. According to him, such individuals feel shy and inadequate, but accompanying this is an attitude of entitlement. Sometimes these contradictory attitudes pertain to the individuals' estimation of their sexual prowess. They overtly attribute their failures to the machinations of others but secretly to their own inadequacies. Their lives are characterized by constant tension between feelings of self-importance and experiences of the environment as unappreciative and humiliating.

Jaspers (1949), the influential German phenomenologist whose work of the 1940s remained untranslated into English until recently, did not use the term *paranoid personality.* However, his description of "self-insecure personalities" bears a close resemblance to the paranoid personality disorder. A paranoid individual, according to Jaspers, leads a life of inner humiliation brought about by outside experiences and his interpretation of them. The helpless urge to get some external confirmation of this grinding self-depreciation makes him see intentional insults in the behavior of other people. He suffers immensely from every slight, for which he once more seeks the real reason in himself. Self-insecurity of this sort leads to attempts at overcompensation. Compulsive formality, strict social observances, and exaggerated displays of assurance are all masks for this inner bondage.

Schneider (1950) described a group of individuals under the designation of "fanatic psychopaths"; the descriptor *psychopath* was used by him as an equivalent of the current term *personality disorder.*

According to Schneider, there were two types of fanatic psychopaths: combative and eccentric. The combative types are unpleasantly insistent about their false notions and are actively quarrelsome. They complain bitterly, constantly seek justice, and are frequently litigious. The eccentric types are passive, secretive, vulnerable to esoteric sects, but nonetheless harboring suspicious and false assumptions about others.

Leonhard (1959) emphasized that the paranoid individuals overvalue their abilities and readily attribute their failure to the ill will of others. They are ambitious, driven, and inordinately sensitive to criticism. Following this, in a study of morbid jealousy, Shepherd (1961) provided a thorough profile of paranoid personality disorder. Such individuals constantly feel mistreated. They accumulate trivial incidents and make every effort to furnish proof of their accusations. Their interpersonal relations are extremely disturbed, and they are in constant conflict with their spouses, friends, or legal authorities.

Polatin (1975) described individuals with paranoid personality disorder as rigid, suspicious, watchful, self-centered, and rather selfish. Although they are inwardly highly sensitive, they appear emotionally undemonstrative. Polatin also noted that such individuals tend to be arrogant, secretive, critical, humorless, and inconsiderate. Often these characteristics are covered by a facade of affability. However, if there is any difference of opinion, the facade shatters readily and the underlying mistrust, authoritarianism, hate, and rage burst through.

Subsequent textbook descriptions of paranoid personality continued to be relatively uniform, although some (Hamilton 1974, 1984, Salzman 1974, Stanton 1978) offered greater clarity than others (Slater and Roth 1977, Winokur and Croewe 1975). For instance, in elaborating on Fish's earlier work, Hamilton (1974, 1984) distinguished two kinds of paranoid personality: sensitive and querulous. The former was characterized by subdued resentment and cynicism, the latter by open defiance and litigiousness. Another aspect frequently noted was the existence of contradictions in the paranoid makeup. Slater and Roth (1977) pointed out the paranoid individual's "contradictory pride and lack of self-confidence" (p. 149). Salzman (1974) noted the coexistence of feelings of superiority and inferiority. Stanton (1978) pointed out the paranoid individual's overt stubbornness and hidden self-doubt. He also observed that while such individuals are contemptuous of others' naivete, they themselves have a remarkable, though latent, gullibility.

In the 1980s more attention was paid to paranoid psychoses than to paranoid personality disorder. When the latter was addressed, the focus remained on its potential relationship with paranoid schizophrenia (Kendler et al. 1984, Kendler and Grunberger 1982) or paranoid disorders (Rettersol 1985, Winokur 1985), not on its phenomenological details. Even the major reviews of recent personality disorder literature (Morey 1988, Widiger and Frances 1985) paid scant attention to the paranoid type. Widiger and Frances (1985) attributed such omission on their part to a relative lack of controversy about paranoid personality disorder. However, this lack of controversy was not because the condition is thoroughly understood but because it has remained understudied. A computer search of personality disorder literature from 1985 to 1988, for instance, yielded over 1,200 citations, and not one was specifically devoted to the phenomenology of paranoid personality disorder (Gorton and Akhtar 1990). The only significant descriptive contribution of this decade was that of Millon (1981), who divided the features of paranoid personality into four categories. These included (1) behavioral characteristics of vigilance, abrasive irritability, and counterattack; (2) complaints indicating oversensitivity, social isolation, and mistrust; (3) the dynamics of denying personal insecurities, attributing these to others, and self-inflation through grandiose fantasies; and (4) a coping style of detesting dependence and hostile distancing of oneself from others. Millon, like many other investigators mentioned above, noted that "the confidence and pride of paranoids cloak but a hollow shell . . . [and their] arrogant pose of autonomy rests on insecure footings" (p. 383). Yet another contradiction displayed by such individuals was recently pointed out by Tobak (1989), who observed the frequent coexistence of an expedient mendacity with moralistic self-righteousness in the paranoid character.

Summary

The descriptive psychiatry literature suggests that paranoid personality is genetically and phenomenologically related either to paranoia ("delusional disorder") or paranoid schizophrenia. Further, it characterizes the condition with contradictory presence of (1) profound mistrust with naive gullibility, (2) arrogant demandingness with hidden inferiority, (3) emotional coldness with marked sensitivity, (4) superficial asexuality with vulnerability to erotomania, (5) moralistic stance with potentially corrupt attitudes, and (6) acutely vigilant attention with inability to see the whole picture. Almost all authors note this discrepancy between the outer persona and the inner world of the paranoid individual and thus subtly underscore the divided self of such a person.

PSYCHOANALYTIC VIEWS

Freud (1911) related paranoid tendencies to the repudiation of latent homosexuality through projection. Homosexual longings and accompanying feminine wishes were first transformed into their opposite. The resulting hatred was projected externally, causing the original love object to appear persecutory and hateful. This formulation has been criticized (Meissner 1978b, Ovessey 1955, Walters 1955) on the grounds that it overemphasizes libidinal factors, ignores the actual harshness faced by the paranoid individual while growing up, and minimizes the role of aggression in the genesis of paranoid tendencies. However, as Blum (1980) recently highlighted, Freud (1887–1902, 1908b) had on two earlier occasions hinted at the deep connection between sadomasochism and paranoid psychopathology. Moreover, Freud (1919) stated that people who harbor unconscious beating fantasies

> often develop a special sensitiveness and irritability toward anyone whom they can include in the class of fathers. They are easily offended by a person of this kind, and in that way (to their own sorrow and cost) bring about the realization of the imagined situation of being beaten by the father. I should not be surprised if it were one day possible to prove that the phantasy is the basis of the delusional litigiousness of paranoia. [p. 195]

In still later writings, Freud called attention to three other important factors in the genesis of paranoid pathology: an initial aggressive disposition (1923a), actual early experiences of threat to survival (1922), and marked aggression toward the mother during the preoedipal phase of development (1923).

Klein (1946) described the "paranoid-schizoid position" as the earliest developmental constellation of infantile object relations. While characteristic of the first six months of life, this position is capable of subsequent activation and may become a habitual personality style. Klein posited that the infantile ego, threatened from within by inborn aggression, resorts to extensive projection. This creates persecutory anxiety, which is defended against by splitting, denial, and primitive idealization. Splitting keeps the good and bad objects apart. Good objects are introjected and identified with, while bad objects are projected. Denial minimizes the existence of inner aggression and masks the unacceptable aspects of needed objects. Primitive idealization causes exaggeration of the desirable aspects of external objects and satisfies fantasies of unlimited gratification from them. These mechanisms result in a phenomenological picture of grandiosity, contempt, undue optimism, and an incapacity for ambivalence, mourning, sadness, and deep object relations. In the Kleinian view, the paranoid-schizoid position is the developmental substrate of all severe character pathology.

Winnicott (1952), on the other hand, emphasized the role of external environment in the genesis of paranoid traits. He posited that the infant experiences any interference with his "going-on-being" as a menace. The end of intrauterine bliss, with birth, provides the deepest template for such disturbance. However, the mother's devoted care neutralizes the resulting inchoate anxiety. A rudimentary yet authentic self begins to come into its own. For this to continue, however, the mother not only has to satisfy the infant's needs but also must provide an unobtrusive presence in the background of which the infant can gather bits and pieces of his experience. Maternal failures in either regard lead to disruption of the infant's being. Anxiety, inner withdrawal, and diminution of psychic freedom follow. Later, such a child displays suspiciousness, lack of playfulness, motor stiffness, and preoccupation with fantasies of cruelty. With the onset of adolescence, social isolation, disturbing persecutory dreams, sadomasochistic sexual concerns, and overtly paranoid fantasies are added to the clinical picture.

Erikson (1950a) also posited that paranoid trends had their genesis in overwhelming frustrations during early infancy, which impede the development of basic trust. Instead, there develops a lack of confidence, followed by increasing helplessness, pessimism, and feelings of shame and doubt. The subsequent history is punctuated by rigid superego morality, inhibition of spontaneity, deterioration of peer relationships, development of omnipotent fantasies to mask inner inferiority, and ultimately the syndrome of identity diffusion with a mixture of negativism, self-isolation, and avoidance of intimacy with others.

Heimann (1952) likened the paranoid personality to a chronic hypomanic state. Both conditions are defenses against a deep sense of unworthiness, rage, guilt, and depression. The triumphant feeling of the paranoid individual, while convicting his object of incompetence, cruelty, disloyalty, or stupidity, links the paranoid and manic state. Other similarities lie in the impaired cognitive processes, such as shallowness, changing of topics, and inability to accept a differing viewpoint. Heimann further pointed out that despite their chronic anxiety, paranoid patients retain a sufficient amount of relatively unimpaired ego functions. They display sharpness of observation, a tendency toward hairsplitting, and a rich vocabulary. Many are gifted speakers. However, their defensive operations are primitive and center on splitting, denial, and projective identification. They constantly need, and unconsciously seek, "bad" external objects on whom they might plausibly project their own split-off, unacceptable attributes. Nonetheless, these defenses remain infiltrated with disavowed drive derivatives; paranoid individuals unconsciously obtain a good deal of sadistic pleasure in situations that they consciously register as only persecutory.

Rycroft (1960) reported the psychoanalytic treatment of an individual with paranoid personality. Among its phenomenological characteristics, he included profound mistrust, pervasive contradictions, an ill-synthesized identity, and an idiosyncratic mode of speech. He also noted that the patient's pretensions to genius compensate for the lack of object love in his life. The individual denies dependent longings and vehemently guards against loving and being loved. Rycroft saw the origin of such pathology in severe infantile traumata, often an early parental loss with a shocking betrayal of the child's anaclitic needs. Under such circumstances, mistrust of others develops alongside a spurious self-sufficiency. Paranoid rage serves multiple purposes: it provides sadistic gratification in the contemporary recreations of early traumatizing relationships and guards against the dreaded betrayal that is expected with dependence on others. However, it is also the paranoid individual's only hope of salvation from his internal loneliness, since an "enemy" who can remain benevolent despite venomous attacks may, after all, turn out to be the longed for friend.

According to Cameron (1963), many paranoid individuals were actually treated cruelly during early childhood, with the result that they internalized sadistic attitudes toward themselves and others. Having grown up with frequent betrayals, the paranoid person is always on guard against sudden deception. Cameron outlined four aspects of paranoid personality: (1) hypersensitivity to the unconscious attitudes of others, (2) insensitivity to one's own motivations, (3) secret feeling of sexual inferiority, and (4) lack of self-esteem and a powerful undercurrent of unconscious guilt. Cameron noted that the paranoid individual approaches sexuality with an expectation of being rebuffed. There is also a selective hypersensitivity to unconscious homoeroticism and other pregenital trends in persons around them. Occasionally, there is a tendency to see a full-blown erotic intention in minimal libidinal cues offered by others; there is thus a vulnerability to erotomania.

Shapiro (1965) recognized two types of paranoid personality: "furtive, constricted, apprehensively suspicious individuals and rigidly arrogant, more aggressively suspicious, megalomanic ones" (p. 54). He described the paranoid cognition in detail. This includes rigidity of mental set, intentional disregard of new data, intolerance of ambiguity, search for clues that confirm a preexisting bias, and tensely directed, hyperactive, scanning attention. Associated with this is a partial loss of reality. Paranoid individuals disdain the obvious and lose a sense of proportion while focusing on narrow "clues." Shapiro regarded

> the paranoid person's construction of a subjective world as having two aspects: On the one hand, a biased seizing of "significant" clues

> form their context and, on the other hand, a loss of appreciation of that context, which is just what normally gives the small clue its actual significance. . . . A subjective world comes into being that is a peculiar blend of the autistic and the factual. The paranoid person's picture of the world is interpretively autistic, but is usually accurate in its factual details. He imposes a biased and autistic interpretive scheme on the factual world. [p. 66]

Shapiro also described the inhibition of spontaneity, the caricatured superficial affability, the motor tension, and the overall hyperintentionality of the paranoid individual. Every action has an aim; all behavior is designed, intended, and purposeful. Parallel with this is the abandonment of tenderness, sensuality, and playfulness. Lack of interest in art, music, and poetry is often accompanied by a fascination with mechanical devices, computers, electrical circuits, and automation schemes.

Jacobson (1971) observed that paranoid individuals had frequently grown up in families where there was overt cruelty and much bickering between parents. A markedly sadomasochistic family atmosphere, often focusing on a parent's marital infidelity, sets the stage for the development of the child's own sadism. Severe early frustrations prevent the building up of unambivalent object relations and stable identifications. The child's self-esteem is weakened, and there develops a sense of futility about finding love in the future.

Bursten (1973a) suggested that paranoid personality was a subtype of narcissistic personality. The fundamental dynamic issue in paranoid personalities, according to him, is their powerful unconscious longing for a reunion with the infantile parental objects. Such longing stirs up not only homosexual and incestuous fears but also a dread of the dissolution of the self. These "shameful" unconscious desires are disavowed by projection. Their further negation occurs through ruthless contempt for those who have now come to represent these attributes.

Kernberg (1975a) associated paranoid personality with a borderline personality organization or a lower level character pathology (1970). At this level of character organization, superego integration is minimal, and the synthetic function of the ego is impaired.

Splitting, denial, and projective identification are the central defensive operations of the ego instead of repression and its related mechanisms. There is a restriction of the conflict-free ego, and primary-process thinking infiltrates cognitive functioning. Kernberg (1985) also pointed out that narcissistic and paranoid personality disorder features may coexist. In such cases, the decision as to which character constellation is dominant depends on the quality of prevalent object relations. The paranoid individual is cold, aloof, and suspicious but not exploitative and envious, like the narcissistic individual.

Another major contributor to the contemporary understanding of paranoid personality has been Meissner (1978b), who points out that a frequent presentation of such cases is through a depressed and masochistic wife who can no longer tolerate what is happening at home. The husband, in such cases, has a paranoid personality and is extremely resistant to treatment. Meissner believes that in such characters a paranoid process has become highly structuralized and ego-syntonically embedded in the personality organization. This core consists of displacement of responsibility through projection, suspiciousness, defensive grandiosity, rigid conviction about one's beliefs, concern over autonomy, and troubled relationships with authority figures. While Meissner agrees with the classic view of paranoia as a defense against latent homosexuality, he posits that it is the underlying identification with the weak, passive, and victimized mother that is the central source of anxiety in both conditions.

Finally, mention must be made of Blum's (1980, 1981) recent papers, which, besides highlighting certain less-cited views of Freud in this regard, masterfully synthesize the classic with contemporary psychoanalytic writings on paranoia. According to Blum, hostility is a primary problem in this condition and not merely a defense against latent homosexual impulses. He does not exclude the reverse formulation that hostility defends against homosexuality but regards it as of secondary importance. Blum feels that a complex interplay of innate disposition, actual threats to survival during childhood, impaired object relations, and subsequent structural defects and defensive elaborations underlie the ultimate paranoid picture in adulthood. He holds that the "latent core" of paranoid personality involves preoedipal problems. Interweaving his propositions with Mahler's (1975) theory of separation-individuation, Blum points out that the lack of internalization of the comforting, constant mother is associated with a lack of ego integration, untamed infantile omnipotence, fragile self-esteem, and a tendency toward intense separation anxiety. In this context, Blum (1981) introduces his concept of "inconstant object," the ambivalently loved object that is felt to be both persecutory and needed. Such an object cannot be allowed to have an independent existence. The threat of betrayal must be tenaciously maintained. In a sense, such constant fear of persecution is the reciprocal of libidinal object constancy and a desperate effort to preserve an illusory constant object while constantly fearing betrayal and loss. Such structural substrate of untamed narcissism, intense aggression, and archaic defenses renders the mastery of oedipal tasks difficult. Masochistic, negative, and perverse solutions to the Oedipus complex predominate. Agreeing with Freud (1919) and Bak (1946), Blum posits that paranoid fantasies of persecution often gratify original masochistic desires to be beaten by the father. Blum's view, therefore, subsumes constitutional factors, drive-related issues, structural conflicts, ego deficits, separation-individuation failures, and oedipal anxieties in a widened psychoanalytic perspective on the genesis of paranoid personality.

Before ending this section, I would like to mention some other contributions that have significant, though at times indirect, bearing on the phenomenology of paranoid personality disorder. These include Anthony's (1981) delineation of the paranoid adolescent, Green's (1986) essay on moral narcissism, Kohut's (1972) description of narcissistic rage, Pao's (1969) work on morbid jealousy, Socarides's (1966) view on the affect of vengeance, Volkan's (1986) insights regarding man's need for enemies and allies, and my own descriptions of the behavioral correlates of splitting (Akhtar and Byrne 1983) and identity diffusion (Akhtar 1984).

Summary

Psychoanalytic literature characterizes paranoid personality disorder as displaying (1) evidence of severe, sustained, and actual preoedipal trauma; (2) lack of basic trust; (3) an aborted separation-individuation process and therefore a lack of self- and object constancy; (4) predominance of object-relations and dyadic conflicts over internalized, structural conflicts; (5) persistence of severe splitting of self- and object representations, along with the related mechanisms of denial and projective identification; (6) masochistic, negative, or perverse outcome of the Oedipus complex with intense unconscious beating fantasies, sadomasochistic perversions, or marked asexuality; (7) the syndrome of identity diffusion; (8) an uneven superego; and (9) a peculiar corruption of autonomous ego functions that results in a narrow, biased, rigid, and hypervigilant cognitive style. Paranoid rage, negativism, and hatred are viewed as complexly determined phenomena. These are affective concomitants of a disturbed ego, as well as measures to control external objects in an effort to compensate for the lack of inner object constancy. In addition, these defend against passive surrender to the love objects, a surrender that stirs up dread of incest, homosexuality, and dissolution of the self.

DSM-III AND *DSM-III-R*

DSM-III, like both its predecessors, listed paranoid personality disorder as a separate, distinct nosological entity. It outlined the following diagnostic criteria (1980, p. 309) and specified that these were characteristic of the individual's long-term functioning and not limited to episodic behavior:

A. Pervasive, unwarranted suspiciousness and mistrust of people as indicated by at least three of the following:

  (i) expectation of trickery or harm

  (ii) hypervigilance, manifested by continual scanning of the environment for signs of threat, or taking unneeded precautions

  (iii) guardedness or secretiveness

(iv) avoidance of accepting blame when warranted

(v) questioning the loyalty of others

(vi) intense, narrowly focused searching for confirmation of bias, with loss of appreciation of total context

(vii) overconcern with hidden motives and special meanings

(viii) pathological jealousy

B. Hypersensitivity as indicated by at least two of the following:

(i) tendency to be easily slighted and quick to take offense

(ii) exaggeration of difficulties, e.g., "making mountains out of molehills"

(iii) readiness to counterattack when any threat is perceived

(iv) inability to relax

C. Restricted affectivity as indicated by at least two of the following:

(i) appearance of being "cold" and unemotional

(ii) pride taken in always being objective, rational, and unemotional

(iii) lack of a true sense of humor

(iv) absence of passive, soft, tender, and sentimental feelings

D. Not due to another mental disorder, such as Schizophrenia or a Paranoid Disorder.

While seemingly adequate, these criteria left much to be desired. First, as Siever and Kendler (1987) pointed out, many of these criteria (e.g., "absence of passive, soft, tender, and sentimental feelings" and "exaggeration of difficulties") were less specific to paranoid personality disorder and could reflect a broad spectrum of psychopathology. Second, there remained a considerable overlap between the criteria of paranoid personality disorder and those for other Axis II diagnoses. Third, studies (Mellsop and Varghesi 1982, Spitzer et al. 1979) employing these criteria suggested a low reliability for the diagnosis of paranoid personality disorder. Finally, the *DSM-III* criteria failed to include grandiosity (Heimann 1952, Jacobson 1971, Kraepelin 1921, Kretschmer 1927, Meissner 1978b, Stanton 1978), sexual difficulties (Bleuler 1908, Cameron 1963, Hamilton 1984, Heimann 1952, Kretschmer 1927, Rycroft 1960, Stanton 1978), hidden feelings of inferiority (Bleuler 1908, Heimann 1952, Kretschmer 1927, Rycroft 1960, Stanton 1978), idiosyncratically moral attitudes (Jacobson 1971, Kernberg 1970, Shepherd 1961, Tobak 1989), and gullibility and naivete (Kraepelin 1905, Salzman 1974) that paradoxically coexist with pervasive mistrust in paranoid personality disorder.

DSM-III-R (1987, p. 339) presents a revised descriptive outline. It portrays the disorder as a generalized pattern of mistrust and suspiciousness manifested by

A. A pervasive and unwarranted tendency, beginning by early adulthood and present in a variety of contexts, to interpret the actions of people as deliberately demeaning or threatening, as indicated by at least four of the following:

    (i) expects, without sufficient basis, to be exploited or harmed by others

    (ii) questions, without justification, the loyalty or trustworthiness of friends or associates

    (iii) reads hidden demeaning or threatening meanings into benign remarks or events, e.g., suspects that a neighbor put out trash early to annoy him

    (iv) bears grudges or is unforgiving of insults or slights

(v) is reluctant to confide in others because of unwarranted fear that the information will be used against him or her

(vi) is easily slighted and quick to react with anger or to counterattack

(vii) questions, without justification, fidelity of spouse or sexual partner

B. Occurrence not exclusively during the course of Schizophrenia or a Delusional Disorder.

The reduction of sixteen items used to diagnose paranoid personality disorder in *DSM-III* to seven in *DSM-III-R* makes the list more manageable and consistent with the diagnostic criteria sets for other personality disorders. This, along with the inclusion of the new item "bears grudges or is unforgiving of insults or slights," is an improvement over *DSM-III.* However, in its emphasis on descriptive clarity, the *DSM-III-R,* like its predecessor, does not include superego unevenness, self-esteem defects, romantic and sexual difficulties, and the core of naive gullibility in the clinical picture of paranoid personality disorder. Finally, both *DSM-III* and *DSM-III-R* do not highlight the coexistence of mutually contradictory stances in almost all areas of psychosocial function, which seems to be a central feature of the condition. The following composite profile of the disorder covers these important aspects omitted in *DSM-III* and *DSM-III-R*.

AN ATTEMPT AT SYNTHESIS

The literature surveyed above was combined and synthesized to develop a true picture of paranoid personality disorder. According to this composite profile (Table 6–1), the clinical features of paranoid personality disorder involve six areas of psychosocial functioning: (1) self-concept; (2) interpersonal relations; (3) social adaptation; (4) love and sexuality; (5) ethics, standards, and ideals; and (6) cognitive style. In each of these areas, there are overt and covert manifestations. This conceptualization of clinical features as being overt and covert should be regarded as a nosologically forward step since it serves to underline the centrality of splitting and projective mechanisms in the paranoid makeup. This not only gives sounder developmental and dynamic underpinnings to the disorder's phenomenology but also prepares clinicians for the "mirror complementarity of the self" that Bach (1977) noted. Patients with paranoid personality disorder may, at times, initially display some of the usually covert features, while the typically overt ones may remain hidden, but the clinicians' awareness of these patients' divided and dichotomous self will encourage further scrutiny and prevent misdiagnosis.

It should be noted that the overt and covert designations do not necessarily imply their conscious or unconscious existence, respectively. Instead, these designations denote seemingly contradictory phenomenological aspects of the disorder that are more or less easily discernible. Moreover, these contradictions are not restricted to the individual's attitude toward others but permeate his self-concept, social adaptation, love life, morality, and cognitive attitudes. The individual with a paranoid personality disorder is overtly arrogant, mistrustful, and suspicious of others; is driven, industrious, and even successful in solitary professions; and is unromantic, idiosyncratically moralistic, and sharply vigilant toward the external environment. However, covertly he is frightened, timid, gullible, chronically experiencing interpersonal difficulties in the work situation, corruptible, vulnerable to erotomania and sadomasochistic perversions, and cognitively unable to grasp the totality of actual events in their proper context.

This manner of organizing paranoid symptomatology is not entirely problem-free. For instance, there is a risk of the overt and covert designations being completely equated with conscious and unconscious topography despite the reminder here to the contrary. The risk is heightened by the fact that covert features are by definition difficult to discern and may not be immediately apparent. Indeed, when similar phenomenological profiles of narcissistic (Akhtar and Thomson 1982), schizoid (Akhtar 1987), and hypomanic (Akhtar 1988) personalities were drawn, Frances et al. (1988) questioned their utilizability by dynamically unsophisticated psychi-

TABLE 6–1. Clinical Features of Paranoid Personality Disorder.

Clinical Features	*Overt Characteristics*	*Covert Characteristics*
I. *Self-Concept*	Arrogant; overconfident; intimidating; self-righteously indignant; contemptuous and easily enraged	Timid; frightened; doubt-ridden; guilty over aggression toward others; feels inferior and envious of others
II. *Interpersonal Relations*	Mistrustful; accusing; demanding; aloof; lacks sense of humor; superficial attempts at affability; appears emotionally cold and detached	Naive; gullible; frightened of "powerful" people; terrified of loving and being loved; detests dependence; holds grudges and seeks revenge; highly sensitive
III. *Social Adaptation*	Industrious; driven; keeps detailed records; often successful in solitary critical lines of work; prefers "hard" data offered by mechanical, electronic, or even legal professions	Frequent interpersonal difficulties; carries on personal agendas at work; unable to be genuine team member; has few friends at workplace; unable to enjoy music, poetry, and "soft" lines of work

IV.	*Love and Sexuality*	Seemingly devoid of romantic interests; either averse to sexual gossip and innuendo or crudely humorous about sex	Extremely anxious about sexual prowess; vulnerable to erotomania; unduly sensitive to pregenital trends in others; latent homosexuality; sadomasochistic perversions
V.	*Ethics, Standards, and Ideals*	Moralistic; values intellectual prowess; literal religiosity; occasional religious fanaticism	Idiosyncratic moral systems; expedient mendacity; occasional sociopathic tendencies
VI.	*Cognitive Style*	Sharp attention; hypervigilant; categorical; searching for "clues" that fit preexisting bias; rich vocabulary; ability for hairsplitting; often good public speaker; hyperamnesic	Unable to grasp the "big picture"; loses proportion and context; readily dismisses the obvious; ignores evidence contradictory to personal beliefs; recall of past events distorted by personal motives

atrists. The same, though untested, objection might be raised against the outline of paranoid personality disorder presented here. Moreover, the lack of actuarial data on the frequency of various clinical features makes their relative diagnostic weight difficult to ascertain at this time.

These reservations notwithstanding, this profile (Table 6–1) of paranoid personality disorder still remains superior to the ordinary checklist methods since it (1) includes both phenomenological and psychoanalytic observations; (2) values depth and complexity over descriptive oversimplification; and (3) establishes a connection between the behavioral and psychostructural, hence developmental, aspects of the paranoid character pathology. While it does not fully resolve the general difficulties inherent in describing any personality disorder, this detailed profile may lend itself better to the prototypal model of classification proposed by Frances and Widiger (1986) as the only way to salvage a categorical system of personality diagnosis. Finally, this profile helps in more meaningful differential diagnosis of paranoid from related personality disorders.

DIFFERENTIAL DIAGNOSIS

Psychotic Paranoid Conditions

Paranoid personality disorder needs to be distinguished from paranoid schizophrenia, reactive or acute paranoid disorders, and paranoia or "delusional disorder." The distinction from paranoid schizophrenia should not be very difficult. The paranoid schizophrenic displays a serious break with reality, bizarre delusions of persecution, grandeur, jealousy or infidelity, auditory hallucinations, symptoms of thought control, incongruous affect, and gross peculiarities of behavior. None of these are characteristic of an individual with paranoid personality disorder.

Reactive or acute development of paranoid delusions (Allodi 1982, *DSM-III* 1980, *DSM-III-R* 1987, Jack 1984, Ndtei 1986) should also be differentiated from paranoid personality disorder proper, though clearly the two conditions may coexist. An acute paranoid disorder is generally seen among individuals "who have experienced drastic changes in their environment, such as immigrants, refugees, prisoners of war, inductees into military services, or people leaving home for the first time" (*DSM-III* 1980, p. 197). Even though the delusions among such individuals are often comprehensible, resolve quickly, and rarely become chronic (Allodi 1982, Jack et al. 1984, Ndtei 1986), their condition is distinct from paranoid personality disorder, which is a nondelusional, stable state lacking a clear onset.

The line of demarcation between paranoia or "delusional disorder" (Winokur 1977) and paranoid personality disorder, however, is harder to draw. The course of both disorders shows few exacerbations or remissions. Intellectual and occupational functioning are usually preserved in both disorders. Paranoid complaints in both center on marriage, plots, and being unfairly treated. Unlike paranoid schizophrenics, individuals with paranoia rarely display "the more exotic type" (*DSM-III-R* 1987, p. 514) of paranoid beliefs; the same is true of paranoid personalities. The difference between paranoia and paranoid personality disorder seems largely quantitative (Bleuler 1908, Kraepelin 1905, 1921, Leonhard 1959, Stanton 1978), though some authors (Munro 1987) consider the two separate and very different disorders. In paranoia, there are delusions, while delusions are never part of paranoid personality disorder. Moreover, the proverbial kernel of truth is greater in the suspicions of paranoid personality. For paranoid individuals, their accusations have more plausibility; their paranoid attitudes are diffuse and less encapsulated than those of individuals with paranoia.

Phobic Character

The term *phobic character* was coined by Fenichel (1946) to designate individuals "whose reactive behavior limits itself to the avoidance of the situations originally desired for" (p. 527). Mackinnon and Michels (1971) also recognized fearful avoidance as a characterological defense, adding that an individual using such a defense is "constantly imagining himself in situations of danger while pursuing the course of greatest safety" (p. 49). Most recently, Stone (1980) described a "phobic-anxious" personality, which displays extremes n qualities as fearfulness and avoidance of the most harmless o s and situations" (p. 332). My own clinical experience affirms the existence of an ego-syntonic phobic character organization. The avoidant personality in *DSM-III-R* resembles, though with some significant differences (Akhtar and Byrne 1983), such a nosological concept.

While resembling paranoid personalities in their restricted life-styles, phobic characters are different in an important way: they avoid situations, not people. Wurmser (1981) points out three other differences between phobic and paranoid characters. In the phobic, the feeling is "It is a danger, but I do not know why. It may be for this or that reason," while in the paranoid it is "It is a danger *and I know why,* namely, such and such is his or her intention" (p. 314, author's emphasis). In other words, the phobic character does not display the personalization and intentionality of the outside menace. Second, the leading affective reactions in the two conditions are different. In the paranoid personality, it is rage, hatred, contempt, and grudge, while in the phobic character it is anxiety, guilty fears, and their somatic counterparts. Third, the paranoid reacts by attack or provocation of attack, while the phobic reacts by avoidance and flight. Moreover, those with a phobic character do not display identity diffusion (Akhtar 1986, 1987), nor do they manifest a predominance of splitting over repression and its related defense mechanisms. Conceptually, therefore, a phobic personality should be regarded as a higher level (Bak 1946) or neurotic character organization and "ego-syntonic characterological counterpart" (Akhtar 1986) of the phobic neurosis proper. Paranoid personality disorder, on the other hand, shows a "lower level" (Kernberg 1970) or borderline personality organization with pervasive splitting, denial, and projective identification in the setting of the syndrome of identity diffusion.

Compulsive Personality Disorder

While the paranoid and compulsive personalities are alike in many ways, their differences are as critical as their resemblances. Similarities in the two conditions include their rigidity, intense purpose fulness, limited affective spontaneity, restricted sexuality, and generalized difficulty with risk taking, humor, and playfulness (Shapiro 1965). Individuals with both disorders dislike surprises and prefer order and predictability in their lives. However, the compulsive knows that the pressure to conform emanates from within himself and regards his moral dictates to be unquestionably superior to his instinctual desires. The paranoid individual, on the other hand, views such demands as originating from external sources and also as unjustified. The compulsive's rebellion against his internalized moral authority is subtle, unconscious, disguised, even ego-alien (Fenichel 1945). The paranoid individual, in contrast, consciously plots against his imagined enemies.

Cognitively, the compulsive is overinclusive (Shapiro 1965), while the paranoid has a narrowly focused, biased attention (Heimann 1952, Kraepelin 1921a, Meissner 1978b, Shapiro 1965). The compulsive is chronically indecisive and doubt-ridden, while the paranoid is smugly self-assured. Interpersonally, the compulsive is capable of concern and mutuality (Kernberg 1970, Volkan 1976), while the paranoid views everyone with jealous mistrust. Psychostructurally, the compulsive displays a higher level (Kernberg 1970) character organization with well-consolidated identity, predominance of repression over splitting, capacity for genuinely triadic and reciprocal object relations, relatively intact autonomous ego functions, and a well-demarcated tripartite structure of the mind. The paranoid personality, in contrast, displays a lower level (Kernberg 1970) character organization with identity diffusion, predominance of splitting over repression, impaired object relations, contaminated autonomous ego functions, and a mind that is riddled by loosely integrated, unsynthesized, sadomasochistic introjects.

Developmental background of the two conditions is also different. The compulsive has had a successful separation-individuation process and has acquired self- and object constancy (Mahler et al. 1975). His problems emanate largely from oedipal phase difficulties, which are regressively substituted by anal phase metaphors. The paranoid individual, on the other hand, has had much actual preoedipal trauma and an unsuccessful separation-individuation process and lacks self- and object constancy (Akhtar and Byrne

1983, Kernberg 1975a). Even a superficial developmental history reveals a more traumatized and turbulent childhood in the case of paranoid versus compulsive individuals.

Narcissistic Personality Disorder

The many similarities between paranoid and narcissistic personality disorders have led Kernberg (1985) to declare their distinction to be particularly difficult. Both types of individuals are ambitious, haughty, driven, and given to "narcissistic rage" (Kohut 1972) when their pride is injured. Dynamically, both display a predominance of splitting over repression as their main defensive operation (Akhtar and Byrne 1983, Kernberg 1975a), although projective mechanisms are more marked in paranoid personalities. Developmentally, both show evidence of an arrested separation-individuation process, a distorted Oedipus complex, and a less than optimal latency and adolescent passage. Psychostructurally, subtle identity diffusion, often masked by an overzealous yet shallow vocational commitment, is discernible in both disorders. The superego in both conditions is unduly harsh, but uneven and poorly demarcated from the ego proper. It may indeed be that cases with combined narcissistic and paranoid features (Kernberg 1985, Millon 1981) are more common than their pure types.

When this overlap is not marked, however, the two conditions show many differences. Narcissistic personality does not display the pervasive mistrust, litigiousness, and self-righteous indignation of the paranoid personality (Akhtar and Thomson 1982, Kernberg 1985, Volkan 1976). Paranoid personality, on the other hand, lacks the charming social veneer, seductiveness, sexual promiscuity, and "inordinate exploitativeness" (Akhtar and Thomson 1982a, p. 9) of the narcissistic character. The narcissist hides his discomfort with spontaneity by crafty socialization (Akhtar and Thomson 1982a), the paranoid by angry negativism, haughty aloofness, or brooding withdrawal. Cognitively, the narcissist displays absentmindedness and lofty disregard for details (Akhtar and Thomson 1982, Bach 1977), while the paranoid shows an acutely vigilant, though biased, attention.

Antisocial Personality Disorder

The overlap between antisocial and paranoid personality disorders has been commented on by many early descriptive psychiatrists (Jaspers 1949, Kraepelin 1921b). Conlon (1984) emphasized it with his mnemonic description of the "paranoid psychopath" as "malicious, manipulative, mendacious, mendicant, meretricious, malignant, moralistic, mindless, [and] murderous" (p. 90) besides being "sensitive, secretive, sentimental, superior, selfish, [and] sexually disturbed" (p. 91). While a developmental, psychostructural, and dynamic overlap does exist between the two conditions, it is important to keep Reid's (1985) reminder in mind: "The person with paranoid personality characteristically lacks the chronicity of antisocial behavior—and the child to adult continuum—found in the psychopath. His acts are more consistent with projection and paranoia, without the stimulating quality usually seen in antisocial personality" (p. 3).

COMMENT

Two other aspects of paranoid personality warrant brief comment here. The first pertains to the variations of paranoid symptomatology over an individual's life span. There is indication in the literature (Anthony 1981, Winnicott 1952) that subtle paranoid tendencies are recognizable from early childhood onwards and may gather further coloration during adolescence before reaching the full-blown picture of the adult paranoid personality disorder. This needs further investigation. A bit more, perhaps, is known about the outcome of paranoid personality during middle and old age. Lowenthal (1968) and Bergman (1971, 1978), who have studied the presence of personality disorders in the elderly, suggest that paranoid individuals often make better adjustments to aging than their psychopathology would suggest. Bergman (1978) states that the fighting stance of paranoid personalities keeps them intact; failure is never their own. The world at large has to be taken on in single combat; life presents a diverting struggle against dangerous external forces, and there is little time for despair and depression.

The second issue involves subclassification within the paranoid personality disorder. Schneider (1958), Hamilton (1974, 1984), and Shapiro (1965) propose two subtypes: one weaker, passive, secretive, and cynically brooding; the other stronger, actively defiant, openly angry, and litigious. The former appears to have a kinship with schizoid personality and the latter with narcissistic personality. Such nosological linkages within the severe character pathology spectrum do make phenomenological and theoretical sense. On the other hand, it may not be a matter of subtypes but of varying level of social functioning manifested by individual paranoid patients. Akin to Kernberg's (1975a) outline of different levels of functioning in narcissistic personality, it may be that certain paranoid personalities are better compensated, achieve success in solitary professions, and are more active and open in their defiant attitudes. Others have weaker ego structures and are passive, secretive, and unable to translate their inner programs into real action. Yet another explanation for these differences might be that the two paranoid styles are sex-related. The silently resentful outcome may be more frequent among women and the blatantly defiant picture seen more often in men. There is some support of such conceptualization in the literature (Bleuler 1908, Kraepelin 1905, 1921a), although the matter is far from settled.

7

HYPOMANIC PERSONALITY DISORDER

I keep on being happy,
disclosing to nobody
my ambiguous malady:
the grief I endure for self-love,
who has never so loved in return

—"Conditions," Pablo Neruda

Three current developments in psychiatric thinking necessitate a reconsideration of the concept of hypomanic personality disorder. First, the renewed psychoanalytic interest in severe character pathology (Chasseguet-Smirgel 1985, Kernberg 1975a, 1984, Kohut 1971, 1977, Mahler 1970, Volkan 1976) and its nosological yield, in the form of narcissistic and borderline personality disorders, demands extension to less recognized forms of personality disorders. Second, the burgeoning empirical research on "soft bipolar-spectrum" disorders (Akiskal 1984, 1986, Akiskal et al. 1977, 1983) provides an opportunity for a fresh view on what affective syndromes, owing to their ego-syntonic, chronic, and stable nature, may more properly be classified under personality disorders. Finally, the inclusion of the schizotypal category, itself perhaps a "tail-end of schizophrenia" (Kernberg 1984, p. 89) and a rough equivalent of the earlier simple and latent varieties of schizophrenia, in the personality disorder section of DSM-III raises the question about similar characterological counterparts of affective syndromes.

While recognizing that the status of depressive personality (Abse 1985, Kernberg 1967, Laughlin 1956) too needs further clarification, I will restrict my attention in this chapter to the more neglected and elusive concept of hypomanic personality. I will survey the scattered literature, synthesize it into a clinical profile of the condition, and then briefly comment on its differential diagnosis.

DESCRIPTIVE STUDIES

The Greek word *hyperthyme* was adapted for clinical purposes by Ziehen (1905) when he described certain permanently cheerful, verbose, and excitable individuals as having "hyperthymic psychopathic constitution." Kraepelin (1909) also maintained that there was a group of individuals whose "constitutional excitement" manifested in their loftiness, distractibility, constant longing for change, and sexual and alcoholic excesses. He noted the similarity of this condition to hypomania but emphasized that this was a fixed personal peculiarity and not an episodic condition. In the later descriptions, however, Kraepelin (1921a,b) related such personality deviation to the manic-depressive illness and renamed the condition "manic temperament." Individuals with such temperament, according to Kraepelin, were permanently exalted, glib, restless, and inordinately confident. Their optimism knew no bounds and they were convinced of their superiority over others.

Among the affective features of the condition, Kraepelin included permanent euphoria, a tendency toward marked rage when contradicted and occasional anxious and mournful moods. Among the cognitive features, he listed distractibility, subtle learning defects, glibness, articulateness, and a peculiar hyperamnesia regarding past events that nonetheless was often colored by partiality and falsified by numerous personal additions. In addition, these individuals were unable to form a general view of their lives, felt a nagging sense of aimlessness, lacked empathy for others, were averse to deep commitments, and were vulnerable to sexual promiscuity. These inner difficulties were discernible even in the milder manic temperament seen in unevenly gifted personalities who impress others by

> their intellectual mobility, their versatility, their wealth of ideas, their ready accessibility and their delight in adventure, their artistic capability, their good nature, their cheery, sunny mood, but at the same time they put us in an uncomfortable state of surprise by a certain restlessness, talkativeness, desultoriness in conversations, excessive need for social life, capricious temper and suggestibility; lack of reliability, steadiness and perseverance in work, a tendency to build castles in the air and scheming occasional unusual activities. [1921b, pp. 129–130]

Kraepelin regarded the manic temperament to be one of the "fundamental states" (constitutionally determined muted variants) of manic-depressive illness. He believed that while some such individuals developed an overt, episodic manic-depressive illness, many others "throughout the whole of life exist as [a] peculiar form of psychic personality without further development" (1921b, p. 118). The more severe end of this stable spectrum resembled a lifelong hypomanic condition while the milder end manifested itself in a driven, energetic, ambitious, and superficially successful life-style. Finally, while Kraepelin recognized the occurrence of occasional sad moods in such individuals, it led him neither to equate their condition with cyclothymic temperament (which displayed more sustained, prominent, and frequent mood swings) nor to question the stable, characterological nature of the manic temperament.

Following Kraepelin, Bleuler (1908) recognized manic disposition as one of the many attenuated variants of the manic-depressive condition. Such individuals, according to Bleuler, infrequently came under psychiatric attention even though they were unduly cheerful, hasty, and somewhat thoughtless in their manner of living. Bleuler also noted the variation of severity within this group, stating that

> we find here on the one hand, snobbish, inconsiderate, quarrelsome and cranky ne'er-do-wells, who have no staying powers in their transactions, but on the other hand "sunny dispositions" and people endowed with great ability, amounting sometimes to genius and not rarely gifted with artistic ability who possess tireless energy. [p. 485]

Subsequent investigators continued to view characterological hypomania as a recognizable syndrome. Kretschmer (1925), while devoting greater effort to finding a characterological bridge between the hypomanic and depressive temperaments, clearly recognized the existence of the hypomanic character. He portrayed such individuals as highly sociable, daring, sharp, cheerful, humorous, and inclined to display a marked acceleration of psychic tempo. They move and talk swiftly, do not know what it means to be tired, and are often renowned for their enormous energies. However, Kretschmer also noted such individuals' tendency toward naivete, superficiality, arrogance, tactlessness, occasional recklessness, and, in some cases, surprising absence of guiding ideals. He noted that individuals with hypomanic character quickly develop strong interest in various ideas or schemes but fail to sustain this enthusiasm over time. Their cognitive functions are colored by far-reaching many-sidedness, a naive objective outlook, and poverty of systematic construction. Their mood is permanently euphoric, though at times they do display ill-sustained melancholic swings.

More important to the contemporary psychodynamic mind is Kretschmer's observation that those with a hypomanic character have a "permanent melancholic element somewhere in the background of their being" (p. 130). In the same vein, it is significant that Kretschmer preferred *hypomanic* to *manic* as a descriptive label; he also occasionally employed the term *character* rather than *temperament.* Clearly, the term *hypomanic character* has an adjectival prefix of greater phenomenological accuracy and a following noun that permits more psychodynamic thinking regarding the origins of the condition than the term *manic temperament,* in which the descriptive prefix is less apt and the following noun carries a stronger constitutional emphasis. While he may have subtly contributed to such a shift in thinking, Kretschmer himself remained committed to the

Kraepelinian view of this syndrome as a genetically determined precursor or muted variant of the manic-depressive condition.

In elaborating and operationalizing the somatic-constitutional dimension of Kretschmer's work, Sheldon (1970) recognized individuals who "remain hypomanic all through life" (p. 46). Somatotonic and cerebropenic, using Sheldon's somewhat idiosyncratic terminology, such individuals were described as bold, assertive of posture and movement, energetic, risk-taking, aggressive under the influence of alcohol, youthful, and desirous of power and domination.

Jaspers (1949), whose work of the 1940s remained untranslated in English for two decades and who generally was opposed to the notion of discrete personality disorder entities, also spoke of two related and frequently coexistent types of basic personality dispositions that approximate the concept under consideration here. Jaspers stated that an

> abnormally excitable temperament *(sanguine)* reacts quickly and in lively fashion to every kind of influence, it lights up immediately but excitement dies down equally fast. The individual leads a restless life, and likes extremes. We get a picture of vivacious exuberance or of an irritable, troubled hastiness, a restless psyche with a tendency to extremes. . . . An abnormally cheerful *(euphoric)* individual bubbles over happily. He is blissfully light hearted about everything that happens to him and is contented and confident. The happy mood brings a certain excitement with it including motor excitement. [p. 440]

Schneider (1950) described a category of "hyperthymic personalities." He described such persons as cheerful, kindly disposed, active, and optimistic but also as shallow, uncritical, hasty in decision making, prone to excessive drinking, and not particularly dependable. Schneider suggested that such individuals often get carried away by their overconfidence and undertake unduly risky business or interpersonal ventures. He pointed out that those with hyperthymic personalities are poor listeners and hence largely imperturbable. Occasionally, however, they unpredictably explode in rage when criticized or contradicted. Such rage is usually short in duration and does not result in calculated and sustained vindictive behavior. Schneider also described a tendency toward "moral defect" and pathological lying in such individuals.

According to Schneider, the hyperthymic group consists of individuals with varying degrees of psychopathology. Thus there exist "shiftless and socially unstable hyperthymes" who display much lying and petty criminal behavior, as well as "syntonic hyperthymes" whose driven, energetic work attitudes often lead to much social success and acclaim. Finally, in regard to the potential relationship between the hyperthymic and the manic-depressive groups, Schneider took a different position than his predecessors and emphasized that the relationship between the two groups is not so specific as is frequently supposed.

Over the three decades following Schneider's contributions, the concept of hypomanic personality persisted, albeit marginally, in descriptive psychiatry. The influential German psychiatrist Leonhard (1959) included a hypomanic type in his classification of personality disorders and listed overactivity, cheerfulness, and prolixity among its characteristics. British psychiatric textbooks (Fish 1978, Slater and Ross 1977) continued to mention such an entity. In the United States, Winokur and colleagues (1969) recognized hypomanic personality and described such an individual as displaying "a high energy level ordinarily with a great number of interests and an excessive amount of participation in various social interests" (p. 107). Despite this continued endorsement, however, few attempts were made to study the syndrome in a systematic fashion, and relatively little was added to its preexisting descriptions.

A notable exception in this regard is Akiskal's (1984, 1986, 1987) recent empirical research on soft bipolar-spectrum disorders. Although his work focuses mainly on dysthymic and cyclothymic patients, Akiskal does address the issue of hypomanic personality as well. Based on a study of twelve work-addicted, highly energetic, successful individuals with "chronic hypomanic adjustment" and no depressive swings, Akiskal describes the "hypomanic temperament" as follows:

> The energy and self-assured entrepreneurial attitude characteristic of hypomanic individuals places them in leadership roles where their less desirable, uninhibited and meddlesome tendencies are tolerated. Although their drivenness may drive others away, their exuberance and people-seeking skills are counterbalancing assets. Borderline judgment in social, sexual and financial spheres may hurt their loved ones and irritate associates; yet lack of insight and a hypertrophied sense of denial prevents them from seeking psychiatric help. [1984, p. 85]

Akiskal thus seems to describe hypomanic personality in its contradictory aspects: on the one hand, these include high energy, sociability, success, and cheerfulness, and, on the other, disregard of boundaries, intrusiveness, defective empathy, and potential recklessness. While Akiskal's description is superior and his demonstration of the neurophysiological (1984) and hereditary (1987) relationship of this syndrome to cyclothymic and bipolar affective disorders largely undisputed, his classifying hypomanic temperament as an affective disorder and not a personality disorder is debatable. Why should a lifelong, stable, ego-syntonic condition (even if constitutionally related to affective disorders) not be regarded as a personality disorder? More puzzling is that after having described twelve patients with chronic hypomanic lifestyle who "vigorously denied depressive and other psychiatric symptoms" (1984, p. 85), Akiskal, in his more recent writings (1986, 1987), declares "pure hyperthymic temperament without any depressive swings" to be only an "extreme theoretical possibility" (1987, p. 36). He now seems to lump hypomanic temperament with cyclothymia by demonstrating mild depressive swings in such patients and by labeling their condition "predominantly hypomanic cyclothymia" (1987, p. 36). This newer conceptualization not only disregards his own earlier data but appears a departure from Kraepelin's original, more lenient view of the manic temperament as well.

Akiskal's position is reflected in *DSM-III,* which recognizes cyclothymic disorder to be long-lasting and beginning in early life without a clear onset and yet groups it under affective disorders rather than personality disorders. This nosological stance has been questioned by others who suggest that there are certain cyclothymic patients whose disorders are more accurately considered personality disorders either because phenomenologically it makes more sense (Kernberg 1984, Nakdimen 1986) or because they do not display a close affinity with bipolar affective disorder (Simons et al. 1985).

Akiskal's ambivalent stance on "pure hyperthymia" also has a counterpart in *DSM-III,* where a "chronic hypomanic disorder" with hypomanic features of at least two years duration is mentioned but regarded as not well enough established to warrant inclusion as a distinct entity. In this context, the following comment of Faust and Miner (1986) on the premature exclusion of certain diagnostic entities from *DSM-III* is especially pertinent:

> Overemphasis on reliable measurement can result in premature abandonment of potentially important discoveries or ideas. There is mention in *DSM-III* that certain proposed diagnostic categories were eliminated during the field trials. Although it is not specified, failure to achieve reliable identification may have been one reason for doing so. Exclusion from *DSM-III,* in turn, may reduce new researchers' exposure to those proposed conditions and thus investigatory efforts. Perhaps *DSM-IV* should include a listing of "orphan" disorders that cannot yet be measured reliably but seem to offer promising leads. [p. 965]

Finally, it should be noted that the other major nosological document in psychiatry, besides *DSM-III* and *DSM-III-R,* the International Classification of Diseases (9th revision, 1980), does include "chronic hypomanic personality disorder" as a distinct and separate nosological entity.

Summary

The descriptive psychiatry literature suggests that hypomanic personality is genetically and phenomenologically related to manic-depressive illness. Though recently disputed, the condition has been by and large viewed as a stable characterological syndrome. Among its characteristics are high energy, success, work addiction, jocularity, and volubility, along with meddlesomeness, disregard of limits, a corruptible conscience, and defective empathy. Most authors agree on this. One issue that does demand further clarification, however, is whether there are two hypomanic personalities (one gifted, driven, and successful; the other inconsiderate, corrupt, and undependable) or whether the difference is only a matter of severity, perhaps dependent on the existence or the degree of genetic predisposition, within the same disorder. Or are the unempathic, potentially corrupt side and the sunny, successful side actually two facets of the same disorder, only that in the severe form the former facet is more easily discernible than in the milder form?

PSYCHOANALYTIC VIEWS

Abraham (1924a) was the first psychoanalyst to study manic-depressive illness. He found similar difficulties underlying both depression and mania, with only the patient's attitude about them being different in the two states. Depressives were weighed down by these difficulties while manics warded them off by denial. Although he acknowledged an inherited predisposition, Abraham held the essential causative factor of the condition to be a painful disappointment in the later oral stage, leading to a severe narcissistic injury. While this fixation acquired further coloring from later psychosexual phases, its oral agenda remained discernible in the impatient, cannibalistic object-hunger of the manic individual.

To these drive aspects of the conflict, Freud (1917, 1921) added the structural perspective. Freud posited that in mania the ego succeeds in freeing itself from the superego. The two fuse and the energy tied in their struggles is freed up for triumphant self-inflation. Freud's (1921) other explanatory suggestion about mania invoked a possibly biological necessity for the differentiated psychic structures to coalesce periodically, so that the part that arises later in development disappears in its part of origin. Thus in mania the superego rejoins the ego, just as the ego fuses with the id during deep sleep. As an evidence of societal recognization of this need for structural regressions, Freud cited cultural festivals that allowed transgressions of the usual moral restraints on behavior.

Freud's ideas were integrated by Abraham (1924a,b) in his

subsequent work. However, Abraham emphasized that the guilt a manic was denying emanated not from oedipal conflicts but from unresolved preoedipal aggression toward the mother. Fenichel (1939, 1945) and Rado (1927) concurred with this. Fenichel saw mania as a "cramped denial of dependencies" (1945, p. 410), a technique of extortion of love and an unstable reconciliation reached by a denial of guilt over oral sadistic impulses.

These elaborations of Freud's work, while furthering the understanding of manic-depressive illness, did not elucidate a related specific personality type. Freud himself left the issue unclear. In his discussion of mania, Freud (1921) wrote of individuals in whom this distinction may never have been established satisfactorily to begin with and whose egos preserved their "earlier narcissistic self-complacency" (p. 129). However, Freud did not label such individuals as hypomanic characters. Later, though, he described a narcissistic type (1931) whose overconfidence, activity, freedom from moral restraints, and intolerance of frustration form a phenomenological cluster frequently seen in narcissistic, hypomanic, and "perverse" (Chasseguet-Smirgel 1985) characters.

This issue of characterological or "chronic hypomania" was first addressed by Deutsch (1933), who suggested that a persistent denial underlies such a state. Such individuals depreciate what they have lost and quickly find substitute objects, thus nipping in the bud any reaction to loss. Deutsch stated that a

> continuous activity of the defense mechanism is displayed in chronic hypomania. We are shown that we are dealing with a defense mechanism by a surplus, an excess of expenditure, an exaggeration of restlessness. If we look more closely . . . we note the hollowness of their success in comparison with the energy expended, how the love relationships lack warmth, in spite of their apparent passion, how sterile the performance in spite of continuous productivity. This results from the monopolization of psychic energy in service of the goal we have described: the silencing of the narcissistic wound, of aggression, and guilt reactions. [p. 215]

In her analytic experience with chronic hypomanics, Deutsch found their rage (and subsequent guilt) to be emanating from traumas not only in the oral but also in the phallic phase of development.

Klein (1934, 1935), on the other hand, exclusively emphasized the oral determinants of this rage and guilt. She saw hypomanic personality as a pathological outcome of the "depressive position," a developmental phase characterized by integration of love and hate toward the mother and the emergence of guilt, mourning, and reparative strivings. Since the depressive position is linked with issues of dependence, ambivalence, and the awareness of an internal world, containing a highly valued internal object that can be damaged by one's aggression, manic defenses are directed against denying internal reality, dependence, and aggression and yet compelling the object to fulfill needs. Triumph is a denial of depressive feelings of valuing and caring. Contempt defends against guilt and fear of abandonment. All this is accompanied by idealization that disguises contempt and compulsive introjection, that contains the fantasy that since there are so many objects, a few less do not matter. The tendency among such individuals to think in large numbers also betrays a scornful neglect of real objects.

Winnicott (1935), in extending Klein's ideas, indicated that *manic defense* consists of four mechanisms: (1) denying inner reality; (2) fleeing to external reality; (3) keeping internalized parental imagoes in suspended animation, causing the individual to feel historically disconnected and yet vaguely hopeful of genuine affiliation; and (4) using opposites for reassurance, so that all depressive feelings are vehemently replaced by their opposites. Winnicott emphasized that the grandiose fantasies of these individuals were a defense against inner reality. Flight to fantasy, and from one fantasy to another, was a preliminary step toward flight to reality. Winnicott also hinted at ways that manic defense incorporated symbolic representatives of later psychosexual conflicts as well.

Angel (1934), in describing the psychodynamics of "chronic optimists," emphasized this latter aspect and traced bubbly, unwarranted hopefulness to a denial of castration fantasies. Lewin (1937, 1941, 1950), however, emphasized the oral substrate of the "neurotic hypomanic personalities," who

> are characterized by the immense enterprise they show in daily affairs, overfilling their time with inconsequential doings, throwing themselves vigorously into hobbies, sexual affairs, or business deals,

> to drop them all abruptly with a striking sudden loss of interest. Their analysis shows a latency period in which strong identifications are built up with a usually dead or absent parent, and a sharp, often conscious recrudescence of incestuous wishes at puberty, followed by a vehement plunge into activities as a distraction. [1937, p. 59]

Lewin suggested that the hypomanic was haunted by "the triad of oral wishes": to devour, to be devoured, and to sleep. The first wish was obvious in the hypomanic's behavior. The other two presented conflict especially because they had been contaminated by too much aggression and became equated with being murdered and dying. Therefore, these wishes either were denied through insomnia and overactivity or expressed in rapt absorption in work, a state of giving up the self.

Following Lewin's work, Cohen and colleagues (1954) published an intensive study of the character type associated with manic-depressive illness. Although the study employed terms like *cyclothymic* or *manic-depressive* character, the sample also included chronically hypomanic individuals. They were described as overactive, hard-working, frequently successful individuals who had numerous acquaintances. Close scrutiny of these relationships, however, revealed lack of genuine intimacy and mutuality. Hypomanic individuals also had a few extremely dependent relationships with an essentially narcissistic orientation. Cohen and colleagues found that such individuals, as children, were the best endowed members of a family that unduly used them to enhance its esteem. Their autonomous strivings were punished by painful withdrawal of love. As adults, they remained terrified of abandonment, emotionally hungry, and yet compulsively driven toward external achievement.

These views, though couched in an interpersonal model, bear a close resemblance to the insights generated from the child-observational studies of Mahler and her colleagues (Mahler 1966b, 1970, Mahler et al. 1975) and from the study of severe character pathology by Kernberg (1970, 1975a,b, 1984) and others (Masterson 1976, Volkan 1976). In her studies of the separation-individuation process, Mahler (1966b) found unmistakable evidence of elation being the basic mood characteristic of the practicing subphase. This is manifested in the toddler's intoxication with his own faculties, imperviousness to frustrations, and absorption in his magical omnipotence. Mahler attributed this elation to a massive shift of psychic energy into rapidly growing autonomous ego functions, the acquisition of upright locomotion being a prime example of this spurt. Mahler, did, however, note that the pervasive narcissism of the practicing phase contained a kernel of the earlier delusion of symbiotic omnipotence of the mother–infant dual unit. She also pointed out that the elation of the practicing phase was subtly contingent on the child's certainty that he can return to the mother for "emotional refueling." Mahler mentioned that gradual disillusionment with shared mother–child omnipotence must take place in the rapprochement subphase for a normally optimistic, as opposed to an unduly elated, mood to become the stable affective pattern.

In extending Mahler's observations, Pao (1971) wondered whether the elation of the practicing phase also contained an attempt to deny the loss of symbiotic bliss and whether this latter aspect (i.e., denial of the loss of symbiosis) was behind the pathological elation of hypomania. In discussing various views regarding the prolonged persistence of infantile omnipotence, Kramer (1974) forwarded a different hypothesis. She suggested that an overwhelming difficulty in the rapprochement subphase (which follows the practicing subphase and involves a relatively more complete and sad renunciation of omnipotent fantasies) may underlie a regressive clinging to the practicing subphase. The subsequent hypomanic style would, therefore, contain the now defensive elation of the practicing subphase, as well as the warded-off depression and object coercion of the rapprochement subphase. Indeed, the adult hypomanic could be characterized not only by joyous overactivity and intensified work-pleasure but also a subtly depressive, restless search for a symbiotic object.

In line with these views is the inclusion by Kernberg (1970, 1975a) of hypomanic personality in disorders characterized by an underlying borderline personality organization (1975a) or a lower level character pathology (1970). In such individuals, splitting, denial, and primitive idealization are the main defenses rather than repression and related mechanisms. Superego integration is minimal and the synthetic function of the ego is impaired. There is a general restriction of the conflict-free ego, identity formation is impeded, and the primary process infiltrates cognitive thinking. Kernberg (1975b) emphasized the pathological object relations in hypomanic personality, and, recognizing the syndrome as a distinct entity, lamented (1984) its omission from *DSM-III.*

While the foregoing review has emphasized preoedipal developmental pathology, such pathology also exerts deleterious effects upon the ability of the child to deal with the complex tasks of the oedipal phase. Persistence of denial mechanisms and impaired capacity for mourning resulting from problematic preoedipal development render the mastery of the tragic oedipal realities difficult. As a result, understanding and acceptance of incest prohibitions (and, by extension, other limits and prohibitions), as well as of generational differences, are impeded, leading to cocky, defiant, and irreverent attitudes. Chasseguet-Smirgel's work (1985) on "perverse" character organization refers precisely to such an outcome, though without clearly invoking its preoedipal basis.

Summary

Though differing in conceptual vantage points and terminology, various psychoanalytic views coalesce into portraying hypomanic personality as a syndrome of persistent infantile omnipotence, pathological object relations, identity diffusion, predominance of splitting-related mechanisms, condensation of preoedipal and oedipal conflicts, an uneven superego, and an exaggerated ego ideal that is poorly differentiated from the ego proper. Phenotypically, this translates into pathological elation, grandiosity, incapacity for deep relationships, disregard of generational boundaries, moral defects, and a chronic sense of inner doubt and restlessness.

AN ATTEMPT AT SYNTHESIS

The literature surveyed was combined and synthesized to develop a composite picture of hypomanic personality disorder. According to this profile (Table 7–1) the clinical features of hypomanic personality involve six areas of psychosocial functioning: (1) self-concept, (2) interpersonal relations, (3) social adaptation, (4) ethics, standards, and ideals, (5) love and sexuality, and (6) cognitive style. Each of these areas has overt and covert manifestations. These designations do not necessarily imply conscious or unconscious manifestations, although such topographical distribution might also exist. The overt and covert designations actually denote seemingly contradictory phenomenological aspects that are easily discernible. These contradictions are not restricted to the individual's self-concept and related affective state but permeate his interpersonal relations, morality, and cognitive style. The individual with hypomanic personality is overtly cheerful, highly social, given to idealization of others, work-addicted, flirtatious, and articulate, while covertly he is guilty about his aggression toward others, incapable of being alone, defective in empathy, unable to love, corruptible, and lacking a systematic approach in his cognitive style.

The manner of organizing symptomatology emphasizes the centrality of splitting, denial, and identity diffusion in hypomanic personality without doing injustice to its potential constitutional basis. Such a stance is not idiosyncratic. Various descriptions of hypomanic personality reviewed here provide ample support for such a descriptive framework. The approach does, however, have some potential problems. For instance, there is a risk that the overt and covert designations could be equated with conscious and unconscious aspects, despite reminders to the contrary. This risk is heightened by the fact that covert features are by definition difficult to discern and may not be immediately apparent. Also, the lack of actuarial data on the frequency of various clinical features makes their relative diagnostic weight difficult to ascertain at this time. These reservations notwithstanding, this description of hypomanic personality does seem to have an advantage over the preexisting ones insofar as it accommodates both descriptive and psychoanalytic observations and in so doing establishes a connection between the descriptive and psychostructural (and therefore, developmental) aspects of hypomanic personality. This profile also helps in a more meaningful differential diagnosis of hypomanic from other similar personality disorders.

TABLE 7–1. Clinical Features of Hypomanic Personality Disorder.

Clinical Features	*Overt Characteristics*	*Covert Characteristics*
I. *Self-Concept*	Grandiose and overconfident; robust; problem-free; unduly cheerful and optimistic	Fleeting, morose self-doubts; hidden guilt and difficulty in contemplative aloneness and sadness
II. *Interpersonal Relations*	Numerous acquaintances; loves company, rapidly develops intimacy with others; much idealization of others	Unable to empathize with others; quickly loses interest in people; has contempt for others; has one or two extremely dependent relationships; displays disregard for generational boundaries
III. *Social Adaptation*	Decisive and daring; energetic, "workaholic"; at times, quite successful, with an inclination toward leadership roles	Displays questionable judgment in social and financial matters; ill-sustained professional interests; inordinately dependent on praise and acclaim

IV.	*Love and Sexuality*	Seductive and flirtatious; fond of sexual innuendo and gossip; sexually precocious and promiscuous	Unable to be genuinely involved with a romantic partner viewed with equal regard and sustained emotional and sensual interest
V.	*Ethics, Standards, and Ideals*	Enthusiastic and zealous about various ethical and moral matters; fantastically high ideals for self and others; vulnerable to new and promising trends and philosophies	Cuts ethical corners; potentially corrupt and, at times, deliberately mocks conventional authority
VI.	*Cognitive Style*	Glib and articulate; hyperamnesic; impressively knowledgeable, especially regarding "trivia"; given to punning and playful use of language	Displays a cognitive style characterized by knowledge that lacks depth; recall of past is altered by personal motives; subtle learning defects; poverty of systematic approach and objective outlook to various plans

DIFFERENTIAL DIAGNOSIS

Cyclothymic Personality Disorder

Both cyclothymic and hypomanic personality disorders are basically disorders of mood that are felt by the individual to be integral to his character makeup. Both have a genetic affinity to bipolar affective disorder, although they do not display psychotic features themselves. The mood disturbance in both is ego-syntonic, of long duration, and of ill-defined onset. The two disorders also share many neurophysiological (Akiskal, 1984) and psychodynamic (Abraham 1924b, Cohen et al. 1954, Kernberg 1975b, Klein 1934, 1935, Rado 1927) characteristics. The distinction between them is essentially a quantitative one. In hypomanic personality, the mood is euphoric on a more permanent basis, and melancholic states, if any, are brief, infrequent and quickly warded off by manic defenses. Cyclothymic personality disorder (Kernberg 1984, Simons et al. 1985), on the other hand, displays hypomanic and depressive swings on a regular basis, with the two extreme moods being of comparable intensity and duration. In all fairness, however, it should be acknowledged that phenomenologically intermediate states between the typical cyclothymic and hypomanic extremes are perhaps more common, a point implicit in such labels as "cyclothymic personality with strong hypomanic trends" (Kernberg 1984) and "predominantly hypomanic cyclothymia" (Akiskal 1987).

Compulsive Personality Disorder

Many investigators (Akiskal 1984, Cohen et al. 1954) have commented on the superficial similarities between hypomanic and compulsive personality disorders. Both types display driven, ambitious, and perfectionistic attitudes. Individuals with both disorders may set high standards not only for themselves but also for others, making quite unreasonable demands on family and subordinates at work. Both may be prone to stubbornness to the point of obstinacy. The two disorders are, however, quite distinct. Unlike the hypomanic, the compulsive individual is capable of deep object relations, mature love, concern, genuine guilt, mourning, and sadness (Cohen et al. 1954, Kernberg 1984, Volkan 1976). The compulsive is capable of lasting intimacy but is modest and socially hesitant. The hypomanic, on the contrary, is pompous, loves company, and rapidly develops rapport with others only to lose interest in them soon afterward. The compulsive loves details, which the hypomanic casually disregards. The compulsive is tied down by morality and follows all rules, while the hypomanic, like the "perverse character" (Chasseguet-Smirgel 1985), cuts corners, defies prohibitions, and mocks conventional authority. Psychostructurally, the compulsive character is built around repression and reaction formation and does not display "the syndrome of identity diffusion" (Akhtar 1984, Erikson 1950a). In contrast, the hypomanic character shows identity diffusion and extensive use of splitting, denial, and other related primitive defense mechanisms (Kernberg 1970, Klein 1934, 1935, Rado 1927).

Narcissistic Personality Disorder

There are many similarities between the narcissistic and hypomanic personality disorders (Kernberg 1975a,b). Developmentally, both show evidence of an arrested separation-individuation process, predominance of object relations conflicts, distorted Oedipus complex, a fantastic ego ideal created not so much by the idealization of parents as by the lack of them, and uneven superego functions. Dynamically, both disorders display an underlying borderline personality organization with predominance of splitting (and related mechanisms) over repression (and related mechanisms) as the main defensive operations. Identity diffusion, frequently masked by an overly zealous vocational commitment, is present in both conditions. Descriptively, both narcissistic and hypomanic individuals overtly display grandiosity, self-absorption, social ease, articulateness, seductiveness, and moral, aesthetic, and vocational enthusiasm. Covertly, both experience feelings of inferiority, boredom, uncertainty, and aimlessness.

Despite these remarkable similarities, the two disorders differ in important ways. The narcissist overtly devalues others while secretly envying them (Akhtar and Thomson 1982a); the hypomanic, on the surface, is everyone's friend but privately holds them in contempt (Kernberg 1975b, Klein 1934, 1935). The narcissist is devoid of the verbosity, pervasive use of denial, compulsive humor, and object hunger that characterize the hypomanic. The hypomanic, on the other hand, lacks the seething vindictiveness of "narcissistic rage" (Kohut 1972) and either quickly explodes when crossed or, using extensive denial mechanisms, is all too eager to forgive and forget. While both are ambitious and overactive, the narcissist comes across as dedicated, humorless, and steadfast in his pursuit of perfection, while the hypomanic appears playful, suggestible, digressive, and more impaired in his capacity for sadness and mature aloneness.

COMMENT

There can be four objections to recognizing hypomanic personality disorder as a distinct entity: (1) the disorder is too rare to warrant recognition; (2) the individuals involved are too well adapted to be viewed as having a personality disorder; (3) the syndrome is genetically linked to bipolar affective disorder and therefore should not be classified as a personality disorder; and (4) no useful purpose is served by the concept. A brief response to each of these objections follows.

Delineation of a syndrome depends on a frequently coexistent cluster of symptoms without any bearing to its incidence at large. Invalidation of a syndrome on the basis of its rarity is thus questionable. Moreover, the allegedly low incidence may itself be spurious, a self-fulfilling prophecy in response to unfamiliarity with the concept or a preexisting bias against the disorder's frequency. Overly stringent diagnostic criteria and the use of alternate diagnostic labels may also artificially lower the incidence of a disorder. This has happened, for instance, with schizoid personality, which is being diagnosed much less frequently (Pfohl et al. 1986) after the *DSM-III* introduced the related concepts of avoidant and schizotypal personalities. The belief that hypomanic personality is seldom seen in psychiatry may similarly reflect a diagnostic bias of excluding anyone with the slightest depressive swings from this group.

Not all hypomanic personalities display good social adaptation. More importantly, underneath the charming veneer of even the most successful hypomanic personalities lie an inordinate need for socialization, defective empathy, an easily corruptible conscience, and much contempt for others. To deny hypomanic personality disorder recognition on the basis of its social success appears shortsighted and superficial.

The third argument, that hypomanic personality is genetically related to bipolar affective disorder and hence should not be classified under personality disorders, is especially puzzling. Why can it not be related to the bipolar illness *and* be a personality disorder? After all, the term *personality disorder,* especially in *DSM-III*, has no etiological implications, being only a descriptive statement regarding the stability, ego-syntonicity, and maladaptive nature of a condition. This is pointedly clear in the case of the schizotypal category, which the *DSM-III* recognizes to have an ostensive genetic linkage to schizophrenia and yet designates as a personality disorder. Why can a similar stance not be taken regarding hypomanic personality?

The final argument against the concept is questioning its usefulness. Such a view overlooks that undue reliance on pharmacological agents and limitation of psychological intervention to superficial, counseling-like approaches often follow the affective disorders label. Designating the condition as a personality disorder, on the other hand, may prevent such "biological" overenthusiasm and encourage deeper exploration of the defensive nature of the patient's elation and overactivity. Besides this clinical benefit, the concept of hypomanic personality disorder has a heuristic advantage as well. Like schizotypal personality disorder, hypomanic personality disorder links two major sectors of psychiatric nosology (psychoses and personality disorders) and draws attention to an obscure and understudied area of clinical psychiatry.

In view of these counterarguments and in light of the psychiatric and psychoanalytic literature synthesized here, hypomanic personality disorder appears to be a legitimate and useful concept. Significantly, in a commentary on an earlier appearance of this chapter as a paper (Akhtar 1988), Akiskal (1988) stated "full agreement with Akhtar's position of granting individual nosologic status for a hyperthymic disorder" and enunciated operational criteria for such an entity. These criteria included (1) indeterminate early onset, (2) subsyndromal hypomanic features with infrequent euthymia, (3) intermittent course, and (4) Schneiderian hypomanic traits of cheerfulness, overoptimism, grandiosity, vigor, volubility, impulsivity, extroversion, meddlesomeness, and promiscuity. These criteria lend further support to the diagnostic profile outlined here. However, the latter criteria more comprehensively synthesize the disorder's descriptive features with its structural substrate of identity diffusion, splitting, denial, and impaired internal object relations.

8

ANTISOCIAL PERSONALITY DISORDER

I
Make houses shrink
And trees diminish
By going far; my look's leash
Dangles the puppet-people
Who, unaware how they dwindle
Laugh, Kiss, get drunk,
Nor guess that if I choose to blink
They die.

—"Soliloquy of the Solipsist," Sylvia Plath

Antisocial personality disorder has an enormous and wide-ranging literature, with contributions from psychiatrists, psychologists, psychoanalysts, lawyers, judges, sociologists, theologians, and writers (Bergman 1968, Capote 1965, Cleckley 1941, Craft 1965, 1966, Eissler 1949a, Eysenck 1964, Frankenstein 1959, Glueck and Glueck 1956, 1959, Hare 1970, Hare and Shalling 1978, Henderson 1939, Karpman 1947, Lombroso 1876, McCord and McCord 1956, 1964, Pinel 1801, Ray 1838, Reid 1978, 1981, Robins 1966, Sheldon 1956, Thompson 1953, Wolman 1987, Yochelson and

Samenow 1976, 1977). I will not try to summarize this entire body of literature here and will refer only to the pioneering descriptive and psychoanalytic contributions in an attempt to trace the historical evolution of the antisocial personality disorder concept. I will describe the *DSM-III* and *DSM-III-R* criteria for the disorder and evaluate them in the light of my literature review. I will then attempt to synthesize a comprehensive clinical profile of antisocial personality disorder and briefly discuss its differential diagnosis.

DESCRIPTIVE STUDIES

Early Literature

Pinel's (1801) labeling of the behavior of a violent but not psychotic individual *manie sans delire* was, perhaps, the first recognition of the fact that certain antisocial behaviors emanated from mental illness. Later, Prichard (1835) described "moral insanity," a loosely put together group of socially marginal, odd, and eccentric characters, including various criminals and delinquent individuals (see Chapter 4). An American psychiatrist, Ray (1838), made a distinction between "intellectual mania" and "moral mania." Ray believed that the latter corresponded to Pinel's *manie sans delire* and Prichard's "moral insanity." Among the clinical characteristics of this condition were an inordinate propensity to lie, irresistible impulses to steal, morbid sexuality, and chronic destructiveness.

Yet another significant early contribution was Lombroso's (1876) treatise on criminality in which a certain type, "the born criminal," was identified. Links between Prichard's "moral insanity" and Lombroso's "born criminal" were later identified by Gouster (1878). However, the concept of moral insanity remained ill-assimilated in medicine until Koch (1891) renamed the condition "constitutional psychopathic inferiority." Further respectability was added to the disorder's status when the great British psychiatrist, Maudsley (1896), recognized it. He was convinced that such a disorder existed and described individuals suffering from it as egoistic, ruthless, vain, lacking true moral feelings, and governed by immoral motives.

Following these early contributions, Kraepelin (1905) described four kinds of individuals who can now be seen as antisocial personalities: (1) morbid liars and swindlers, (2) criminals by impulse, (3) professional criminals, and (4) morbid vagabonds. Morbid liars and swindlers were glib, charming, even talented but completely lacking in inner morality, perseverance, and a sense of duty. They frequently used aliases, were fraudulent and accumulated large debts. Criminals by impulse were given to periodic arson, sexual crimes, kleptomania, and other such crimes. While their acts could be dangerous, they differed from professional criminals in that they had poorer impulse control and lacked secondary gains for their criminal acts. Kraepelin's third type, professional criminals, were not impulsive. They often appeared orderly, well mannered, and polite, but inwardly they were cold, ruthless, and cruel. They displayed a strange contrast between clear intellectual understanding of their whole position and an absolute inability to put this knowledge into practice because moral incentives to action had no influence over them. The fourth type, morbid vagabonds, showed a "restless love of wandering" (p. 323), a lack of self-confidence, incapacity to tackle life's ordinary hardships, propensity toward substance abuse, and inability to work and live responsibly in one place for a sustained length of time.

A few years later, Glueck (1918) published his now famous study of the inmates of Sing-Sing prison. He noted the early onset of antisocial tendencies among such individuals and their chronic recidivism. However, Glueck's sample was diverse and included addicts, alcoholics, and sexual deviants along with more clearly antisocial individuals.

Partridge (1930) classified "psychopathic personality" into three somewhat loosely organized subgroups: (1) inadequate, (2) emotionally unstable, and (3) flagrantly antisocial. The first group included insecure, weak-willed, and asthenic personalities. The emotionally unstable group comprised contentious, excitable, paranoid, and explosive characters, and the flagrantly antisocial group included pathologic liars, swindlers, vagabonds, and sexual deviants.

In a subsequent description of antisocial characters in the military, Dunn (1941) largely followed Partridge's classification and noted that antisocial individuals are both attracted and repelled by the idea of military service. Military milieu that requires absolute obedience at times exacerbates latent antisocial tendencies. Dunn extensively reviewed the literature on antisocial personality in the armed forces and concluded that during war the behavior of such individuals might be "heroic at one time and so panicky as to be dangerous at another" (p. 256). Even when brave, they remained unreliable and untrustworthy.

Henderson (1939) offered a novel classification of psychopathic states. In his view, such characters were of three types: (1) predominantly aggressive, (2) predominantly inadequate, and (3) predominantly creative. The predominantly aggressive group comprised criminals, chronically destructive individuals, substance abusers, ill-tempered explosive persons, and sexual perverts. These were people who "throughout their life had been difficult to please, who are intolerant of routine, imperious, bad losers, petulant, egotistical, and emotionally immature" (p. 66). The predominantly inadequate group comprised individuals whose criminality was petty and never violent, and yet they were more consistently abnormal and immoral. Henderson (1939) provided an outstanding description of this group:

> Some are placid, easy-going, facile individuals who follow the path of least resistance, agree with whoever seems to be in the ascendant, and are so good-natured that they may be regarded as charming companions. They have been likened to flowers without perfume. It is only after they have failed their friends and acquaintances repeatedly and have shown an almost entire absence of warmth and honor that they are recognized as suffering from an essential lack, an inability to meet life fairly. When involved in difficulty, they rely on glib explanations and rationalizations which tell only a fraction of the truth. Others are more calm and frigid, are blunted emotionally, and may show a condition approaching apathy, but it is not so much an apathy as a self-centeredness which takes no thought of others, and has for its aim the individual's self-gratification and glorification, irrespective of what consequences may follow. They form friendships with the least desirable of their acquaintances, and have a

> facility for involving themselves in difficulties which, with a little prudence, might easily have been avoided. They are both narcissistic and exhibitionistic; altruism has little or no place, but in their own mild way they take a delight in their morbid fancies in relation to others; their wit is macabre. Remorse, if it ever is present, is short-lived and soon forgotten; they have no sense of shame of being dependent on their families even though their families have rescued them innumerable times. [pp. 78–79]

Henderson's third group, the predominantly creative psychopathic personalities, included sensitive, erratic, and unstable geniuses who showed both aggressive and inadequate tendencies. Like aggressive psychopaths, they stirred up the group around them by their novel ideas and contempt for societal mores. Like inadequate psychopaths, they were ill-organized, dependent, and poorly adapted to daily living. This admixture resulted in others holding opposing views of them. Some found them charming and charismatic, while others viewed them as unbearably self-absorbed and manipulative.

From Cleckley to *DSM-II*

Following Henderson's contribution, Cleckley (1941) outlined sixteen characteristics of the antisocial condition: (1) superficial charm and intelligence, (2) absence of the usual neurotic symptoms, (3) no psychotic symptoms, (4) unreliability, (5) lying, (6) lack of genuine guilt, (7) inadequately motivated antisocial behavior, (8) inability to learn from experience, (9) egocentricity and incapacity for love, (10) shallow emotions, (11) lack of insight, (12) superficiality in interpersonal relations, (13) fantastic behavior with drink and sometimes without, (14) impersonal and chaotic sexual life, (15) rarity of suicide, and (16) failure to follow any definite life plan. Cleckley suggested that the main issue with antisocial personality is not behavior but an underlying pathology that he termed *semantic aphasia*. This serious psychological defect involved an incapacity to symbolize and to learn, hence a propensity toward action with banal repetitiveness. Cleckley also emphasized that antisocial personality occurs in all social classes. Although some antisocial individuals might become socially successful, their inner semantic aphasia remains discernible to the experienced eye. Adequate social functioning does not rule out the presence of antisocial personality.

Karpman (1941, 1948) divided symptoms of psychopathic personality into four categories: (1) lying, (2) impulsiveness, (3) antisocial behavior, and (4) inability to profit from experience. While each of these could be present in neurotic or psychotic disorders, their occurrence in psychopathic personality was qualitatively different. For instance, the neurotic might lie in response to inner, unconscious demands, but the psychopathic individual would lie for material gains in external reality. Similarly, while impulsiveness is generally associated with psychopathy, neurotics and psychotics could be much more impulsive: "the true psychopath is in a sense the least impulsive of them all . . . rather than being hasty, the psychopath often coolly and deliberately plans his actions" (1948, p. 527).

In view of the behavioral overlap between psychopathic, neurotic, and psychotic conditions, Karpman divided psychopathy into symptomatic and idiopathic types. The former included neurotics, mild manic-depressives, and incipient schizophrenics. The former, primary psychopathy, was termed *anethopathy* by Karpman. He believed this to be the core antisocial group, with a malady that was largely constitutional in origin. There was little or no psychogenesis to this group. While this conclusion is questionable, Karpman's (1941) further classification of this group into two types is intriguing. These were the "aggressive-predatory" type and the "passive-parasitic" type. The former group included ruthless criminals, rapists, and shrewd con artists, while the latter included insatiably greedy, manipulative, dependent, lazy, and parasitic individuals.

Schneider (1950) classified psychopathic personalities into ten types: hyperthymic, depressive, insecure, fanatic, attention-seeking, labile, explosive, affectionless, weak-willed, and asthenic. However, Schneider's use of the term *psychopathic personality* correlated to the current label *personality disorder.* Only one of his ten types, the affectionless psychopath, approximates antisocial personality disorder proper. Schneider described such individuals as "lacking capacity for shame, decency, remorse, and conscience . . . [and] ungracious, cold, surly, and brutal in crime" (pp. 126, 132).

These individuals always were incorrigible and frequently were delinquent. Schneider allowed for the possibility of nondelinquent affectionless types who do "astonishingly well" in positions of power; this appears an astute, early recognition of the phenomenological overlap between narcissistic and antisocial personalities. Schneider also noted that (1) there were more male than female affectionless psychopaths; (2) childhood ruthlessness, bitterness, cruelty, and defiance often were precursors to the adult character disorder; (3) criminal tendencies of such individuals diminished with age; and (4) there were "colder, more brutal . . . more active" and "passive, unstable" types of affectionless psychopaths.

In 1952, *DSM-I* suggested the term *sociopathic personality disturbance* to serve as an umbrella concept under which could be classified antisocial reaction, dyssocial reaction, addictions, alcoholism, and sexual deviations. This overinclusive concept did not last long. Many significant contributions over the next two decades made the independent recognition of the antisocial group inevitable. McCord and McCord (1956) emphasized that the antisocial individual's defective conscience and inability to identify with others differentiate him from other social deviants. Glueck and Glueck (1956, 1959) demonstrated, through prospective follow-up studies, that antisocial personality was a distinct disorder that began early and continued far into adult life. They also presented convincing evidence of the role of environmental factors in the genesis of antisocial personality. These included maternal neglect, indifference, and alcoholism as well as sustained deprivation of emotional ties with any significant adult during childhood. Robins (1966), in a follow-up study of 524 children referred to a child-guidance clinic, found that having a sociopathic or alcoholic father was a powerful predictor of antisocial personality disorder in adult life. Interestingly, this effect was not related to whether the child had actually been raised in the presence of such a father, thus suggesting a certain genetic factor in the causation of antisocial personality disorder. Indeed, later twins and adoption studies (Cadoret 1978, Hutchings and Mednick 1974, Schulsinger 1977) lent support to such a concept. The notion of antisocial personality disorder as a separate, discrete entity was becoming strong.

Further impetus was provided by Craft (1965, 1966, 1969), who emphasized that typically neurotic or psychotic symptoms did not accompany antisocial personality. Craft characterized the antisocial individual as having an inability to love, impulsivity, a lack of remorse, an inability to learn from experience, and a peculiar lack of motivation.

It was becoming apparent that most practicing psychiatrists recognized the antisocial group of the *DSM-I*'s "sociopathic personality disturbance" as an independent entity. Reasonable consensus seemed to exist regarding its description. This was evident in an opinion survey of Canadian psychiatrists regarding the clinical features of antisocial personality (Gray and Hutchison 1964). This survey found that the following ten features were considered most significant in making this diagnosis: (1) inability to learn from experience, (2) irresponsibility, (3) inability to form meaningful relationships, (4) impulsivity, (5) absence of inner morality, (6) inability to experience guilt, (7) delinquent behavior, (8) egocentricity, (9) emotional immaturity, and (10) futility of punishment in altering behavior.

In 1968, *DSM-II* recognized antisocial personality disorder as a distinct entity. The designation was recommended for

> individuals who are basically unsocialized and whose behavior pattern brings them repeatedly into conflict with society. They are incapable of significant loyalty to individuals, groups, or social values. They are grossly selfish, callous, irresponsible, impulsive, and unable to feel guilt or to learn from experience and punishment. Frustration tolerance is low. They tend to blame others or offer plausible rationalizations for their behavior. A mere history of repeated legal or social offenses is not sufficient to justify this diagnosis. [p. 43]

This definition, largely derived from the classic descriptions of Kraepelin (1905), Henderson (1939), and Cleckley (1941), is regarded by Otto Kernberg (1989) to have been "remarkably relevant and meaningful" (p. 555). I agree with him. The *DSM-II* definition included the narcissistic features of antisocial personality. It was trait oriented and did not encourage diagnosis by listing specific behaviors. Moreover, it deemphasized the weight of criminal offenses in making the diagnosis of antisocial personality. The *DSM-II* description became well accepted.

The Last Two Decades

In the 1970s, many authors revived earlier observations regarding the cognitive aspects of antisocial personality. They noted the "unusually rich imagination" (Kolb 1973, p. 499) and the "aura of superior intelligence" (Rappeport 1974, p. 259) of such individuals, while also recognizing that the smattering of art, literature, and technical parlance was superficial and misleading. Another aspect that received attention was the manifestations of antisocial personality disorder in women. Cloninger et al. (1975) documented that the disorder was three times as prevalent in men than in women. Christ and Solomon (1974) noted the association between prostitution and psychopathy in women. Rappeport (1974) felt that although female antisocial personalities definitely existed, they were "generally not in pure form" (p. 261). This area, however, remains unclear and deserves further study. Finally, following the publication of *DSM-II,* Guze (1971) provided additional evidence to establish the child-to-adult continuum of antisocial personality disorder.

Besides the publication of *DSM-III* in 1980 and *DSM-III-R* in 1987, which will be discussed in a separate section, the 1980s witnessed the important contributions of Reid and Wolman. Reid (1978, 1981a, 1986) edited many books on the topic of antisocial personality in an effort to update and synthesize knowledge in this area. Reid (1985) added significantly to the phenomenological description of antisocial personality disorder. He concluded that it is erroneous to equate criminality and antisocial personality, since "it is likely that the subset of psychopaths who are criminal by American legal standards occupies no more than 50 percent of the entire group of those with antisocial personality" (p. 6); that symptoms of antisocial personality disorder overlap with those of borderline, narcissistic, histrionic, and paranoid personality disorders; that overemphasizing the charming, glib, and seductive aspects of antisocial personality runs the risk of overlooking the patient's inner turmoil; that underlying the gaiety and bravado of these patients are chronic feelings of depression and emptiness; and that contrary to the portrayal in early literature, the antisocial individual is vulnerable to severe depression and even suicide, especially during middle age.

Wolman (1987) addressed various aspects of antisocial personality disorder. Among those aspects pertaining to the phenomenology of the disorder, Wolman emphasized distinguishing violent from nonviolent sociopaths and described a "narcissistic-parasitic" (p. 39) type of antisocial character. Wolman noted that all antisocial individuals are selfish, manipulative, fundamentally paranoid, prone to lie, and exploitative, but that, only some are violent. Most others try to win favors by presenting themselves as victims of bad luck. They tend to be totally parasitic, "expecting the entire world to act as a milk-giving mother" (p. 42). Wolman also noted their laziness, preoccupation with sensual pleasures, and vulnerability to substance abuse. He observed that underneath their self-assured, self-entitled attitude existed low self-esteem and their seeming boldness often masked chronic hypochondriasis. Cognitively, "gifted sociopaths are more often plagiarists rather than inventors. . . . Their thinking lacks depth and their ideas are narrow" (p. 130).

Summary

Antisocial personality disorder has been given different names and varying breadths of definition in descriptive psychiatry over the last two centuries. A selective review of this literature reveals the following to be its chief clinical features: (1) selfishness; (2) lack of inner morality and incapacity for genuine guilt; (3) an easy-going, hedonistic attitude interrupted, at times, by rage, cruelty, and violence; (4) interpersonal manipulativeness and parasitic attitudes; (5) propensity toward substance abuse; (6) delinquency and criminality; (7) polymorphous perverse sexuality; (8) inability to follow a life plan (with irresponsibility, much geographical motility, and incapacity for sustained employment); and (9) superficial charm, glibness, and impressive knowledge that mask the absence of authentic interests and learning capacities. Many authors (Henderson 1939, Karpman 1941, Schneider 1958, Wolman 1987) divide the antisocial personality disorder into actively criminal and passively parasitic subtypes, but this issue remains unsettled.

PSYCHOANALYTIC VIEWS

Early Literature

Although Freud did not use the term *antisocial personality disorder,* his observations regarding the nature of crime and criminal tendencies continue to illuminate phenomenological, dynamic, and structural issues in this realm. In 1908c, he wrote:

> Our civilization is built upon the suppression of instincts. . . . Each individual has surrendered some part of his possessions—some part of the sense of omnipotence or of the aggressive or vindictive inclinations in his personality. . . . The man who, in consequence of his unyielding constitution, cannot fall in with this suppression of instinct, becomes a "criminal," an "outlaw" in the face of society—unless his social position or his exceptional capacities enable him to impose upon it as a great man, a "hero." (p. 187)

This remarkable passage contains five elements that constitute a most sophisticated understanding of the antisocial personality disorder: (1) a constitutional factor in etiology, (2) weakness of repression, (3) nonrenunciation of infantile omnipotence, (4) the fundamental role of aggression, and (5) the potential overlap between the "criminal" and the "hero" (i.e., between the antisocial and narcissistic characters). Freud (1914) mentioned the connection between excessive narcissism and sociopathy in his paper on narcissism as well. He stated that great criminals fascinate us because they maintain "a blissful state of mind—an unassailable libidinal position which we ourselves have since abandoned" (p. 89). In a subsequent contribution, Freud (1916) identified the two fundamental human crimes—incest and parricide—suggesting all other crimes to be their disguised or regressive versions. In the same paper, he differentiated between those who were "criminal from a sense of guilt" and those "who commit crimes without any sense of guilt" (p. 333). The former committed punishable deeds to relieve their vague, inner torment at the hands of unconscious guilt. The latter committed crimes because they had "developed no moral institutions." A few years later, Freud (1925a) again stated that delinquent individuals and criminals lacked "certain psychical structures" (p. 275). They were therefore not suitable for psychoanalysis and required modified interventions.

Aichhorn (1925) became the first psychoanalyst to develop such modified interventions. His famous book, *Wayward Youth,* not only detailed the practical ways of dealing with delinquent individuals but also was a pioneering psychoanalytic exposition on the phenomenology and etiology of delinquency. According to Aichhorn, two developmental defects contribute to this condition. The first involves the child's failure to move on, in the usual manner, from the predominance of pleasure principle to that of reality principle in his mental life. The second is a malformation of his *ego ideal* (a term Aichhorn used interchangeably with *superego*). Aichhorn posits that both extreme indulgence and excessive severity impede a growing child's renunciation of pleasure principle. Consequently, unquestioned longings for immediate gratification persist and instinctual impulses cannot be contained in thoughts and fantasy. The defects in the superego come from two sources: either the internalized parental norms were themselves abnormal or the internalization of parental norms suffered because the early parent–child relationship was grossly unsatisfactory. In the treatment of such individuals later on, a major task is to help them establish an idealizing relationship with the therapist even if it requires indulgences and compromises of the psychoanalytic technique. Only after being able to idealize the therapist can these individuals renunciate their narcissistic position and be amenable to usual therapeutic interventions.

Abraham (1925) suggested that impostrous and antisocial tendencies had their roots in "psychological undernourishment" (p. 304) during childhood. Most such individuals were unloved as children, and this had a deleterious effect on their capacity for object relationships. It also caused a regressive increase in their narcissism and a lifelong hatred in them for others. A normal Oedipus complex did not ensue and the structurally salutary consequences of oedipal resolution were missing from the character. This inner state of affairs manifested in an inability to form lasting bonds, self-centeredness, a great need to be admired, bragging, fraudulence, perverse and chaotic sexuality, and a chronic tendency to disappoint and betray others.

Reich (1925, 1933) explained the delinquent acts of the "instinct-ridden characters" by a mechanism he termed *the isolation of the superego*. Whereas ordinarily the ego attempts to comply with the dictates of the superego or, at times, takes steps to ward them off, here the ego appears to keep the superego actively and consistently at a distance. The ego experiences the pressures of conscience in one place or at one time but is strikingly free from them during alluring moments of instinctual temptations. The impulse is yielded to immediately before any superego inhibition is felt. Remorse is often experienced later in a displaced, frequently minor, context.

Alexander (1930) introduced the concept of *neurotic character*. In this group he included "individuals whose lives are full of dramatic action . . . adventurers . . . modern Casanovas . . . the Don Juan types . . . those who are attached to two women at the same time . . . [and] individualists who are fettered by social sentiments" (pp. 297–300, 308). Alexander noted that neurotic characters also could commit criminal acts, although such delinquency differed from "the more homogeneous, unified and antisocial personality" (p. 292). In the neurotic character, there were intrapsychic conflict, unconscious guilt, and a greater disguise of the instinctual gratification derived from alloplastic deeds. In the antisocial character, there were no conflict, little guilt, and more direct instinctual gratification.

However, in a puzzling reversal, Alexander also stated that such distinction might be largely theoretical:

> Most criminals find it necessary to content themselves with substitutive acts which they can perform without conflict. This is a sign that in the modern world even criminality has become domesticated. As a matter of fact, I am convinced of the opinion that on closer examination most of our criminals will turn out to be neurotic characters, and that the notion of pure criminality must be looked upon as a theoretical concept akin to the theory of a limit in mathematics. [p. 304]

In 1945, Greenacre, Fenichel, and Friedlander further advanced the psychoanalytic understanding of antisocial personality. Greenacre (1945) described such patients in detail, although her sample represented somewhat milder psychopathology. These patients displayed impulsivity, irresponsibility, labile affective life, a lack of practical appreciation of time, and an inability to profit from experience. They repeated the same fiascoes over and over again in a strikingly self-destructive manner. Their love life was superficial, their sexuality polymorphously perverse. They were prone to alcoholism and drug addiction. They were often glib and charming and showed a cognitive tendency toward "the substitution of the symbol of gesture or word for the accomplished act" (p. 167). They therefore felt offended when others did not accept their intentions as deeds.

Greenacre observed that these patients had highly narcissistic parents who constantly explained away or concealed their children's weaknesses. The children were always on display and were expected to be well behaved so as to reflect favorably on their parents. This distorted their sense of reality and rendered them opportunistically pleasing and manipulatively tactful. However, being used as narcissistic extensions by their parents (especially their mothers) also intensified their aggression and fueled their need for a separate, distinct identity. Projection of this aggression resulted in the creation of terrifyingly persecuting external objects. At the same time, the existence of a distant, awe-inspiring, "magic father" (p. 172) led to the formation of unrealistic and gauzy ideals. Consequently, the antisocial individual had fantastic threatening and exalted external figures with which he was constantly playing hide and seek, both in fantasy and in reality. Greenacre emphasized that the antisocial individual was not really guilt-free; he experienced guilt in a primitive and externalized manner. Besides these genetic-structural hypotheses, Greenacre also pointed out that an additional factor in such guilt feelings is that of the negative narcissistic relation to the parents. In such circumstances,

> the child is also overly attached to both parents, especially to the mother; but instead of being a specially favored part or organ of the mother, it is regarded by her with shame and as evidence of her guilt. The child seems to imbibe this from its earliest days and takes over this guilt and generally both rebels against and succumbs to it. [p. 183]

Fenichel (1945) distinguished psychopathic impulsiveness from neurotic compulsions. The former is pleasurable, ego-syntonic, and instinctual in quality, while the latter is painful, ego-dystonic, and noninstinctual in quality. Fenichel emphasized that superego in psychopathic individuals is not absent but pathological. Moreover, the reactions of the ego to such pathologic superego reflect the ambivalences and contradictions that these persons felt toward their earliest objects. Fenichel cited Reich's (1933) "isolation" of the superego as one such ego reaction and added "bribing" of the superego as another. This refers to the purchase of instinctual liberties by the antecedent or simultaneous fulfillment of an ideal requirement or of a punishment. Fenichel described psychopathic individuals as chronically dissatisfied, impostrous, hyperinstinctual, hypersexual, extremely ambivalent toward all objects, and continually fluctuating between rebellion and ingratiation. They often showed charm and seduced others to fall in love with them, only to betray them afterward. They needed repeatedly to prove themselves lovable as well as to take revenge for not having been loved by their parents in the first place. Such individuals typically had a childhood background of frequent change of milieu, as well as a loveless and highly inconsistent environment. Under such circumstances, capacity for reciprocal object relationship suffered or never developed, and Oedipus complex and its solutions were correspondingly disorganized, weak, and inconsistent.

Friedlander (1945) noted that for antisocial individuals, instinctual satisfaction was more important than an object relationship. Their impulses demanded immediate gratification and subordinated their intellectual awareness of right and wrong—hence their unreliability, the ease with which they lied, and the defects in their moral code. These character traits distinguished the antisocial individual from the neurotic. "A character structure . . . with the ego still under the dominance of the pleasure principle and with an undeveloped superego, seems in every way typical of the antisocial character" (p. 200).

Friedlander saw the genesis of such character structure in the mother's inconsistent attitude toward a child's early instinctual life, especially when augmented by the display of violent emotional outbursts among the adults of the early family setting. These factors impeded the establishment of a reality principle, injured the capacity to delay gratification, and weakened superego internalization. Further, where internalization of parental demands had not adequately taken place, relationship to subsequent authority figures also met the same fate. Later punishments did not strengthen the superego but were felt either as instinctual gratifications or as frustrations permitting further hostility against the person administering them. Little enrichment of personality therefore occurred during latency and adolescence in antisocial characters. Such character formation, however, did not exclude a parallel neurotic development. The ego could acquire a reality principle in regard to some instinctual urges and not others, and a partial development of the superego might take place. The varying proportion of the neurotic-antisocial admixture in the personality as well as intelligence, special talents, sublimatory capacity, and environmental factors decisively influenced the eventual form of character.

From Eissler to Winnicott

Searchlights on Delinquency (Eissler 1949a), a *festschrift* in honor of August Aichhorn, contained contributions from many distinguished analysts, including Anna Freud, Hoffer, Johnson, Lampl-de-Groot, Schmideberg, and Szurek. Eissler (1949b) himself contributed a masterful essay on the phenomenology of delinquency and antisocial personality. In it, and in a later contribution (Eissler 1950), he portrayed the delinquent as displaying the following characteristics: (1) a predominantly narcissistic orientation in which even the seeming "island(s) of true devotion" (1949b, p. 12) hid selfish motives; (2) a paranoid view of the world; (3) excessive sensitivity to displeasure; (4) a heightened alloplastic tendency; (5) outward directed aggression; (6) an impaired, weak, or inconsistent value system; (7) spells of infantile helplessness alternating with self-inflating omnipotence; (8) an "addiction to novelty" (1950, p. 114) and drive to experience the unknown; (9) subtle body image disturbances; and (10) cognitive peculiarities, including magic beliefs, recognition only of the concrete exchanges of money and sex as being real, and easy acquisition of delinquent skills coupled with an incapacity to learn the ordinary and the expected.

Eissler posited that delinquent acts were geared toward enhancing or restoring feelings of omnipotence that, in such individuals, had been badly injured during childhood. As children they suffered profound injustices; they were traumatically betrayed just when they began to relinquish their omnipotence in favor of idealized, anaclitic relationships with adults in their environment. Consequently, they became mistrustful, glib, evasive, narcissistic, bored, and defensively addicted to thrill seeking. However, Eissler wrote, a careful listening to the delinquent's enraptured accounts of his exploits revealed that what he described as new and surprising was really the repetition of one and the same experience. It appeared that he experienced the familiar as new and surprising. "By endowing the familiar with the quality of the new he actually escapes the experience of a truly new situation which he seems to equate with the traumatic" (1950, p. 111). These dynamic and phenomenological insights led Eissler to devise specific treatment strategies involving an element of surprise caused by the therapist to such individuals.

With the exception of Johnson and Szurek, whose independent contributions to this *festschrift* and collaborative work later on (Johnson and Szurek 1952) led to the landmark concept of *superego-lacunae,* I will mention the other contributors only briefly. Anna Freud (1949) stated that if during the first year of the child's life, the mother is absent, neglectful, or extraordinarily ambivalent, then she cannot provide steady satisfaction to the child. Under such circumstances, the child's libidinal interest cannot be lured away from his own body and its needs. There develops a lifelong tendency to lose all interest in love objects during moments of disappointment. The body and its needs retain greater importance than object relations. Such blunting of libidinal development leads to inadequate binding of aggression with resultant tendencies toward destructiveness and criminality. However, Anna Freud added that certain delinquent behaviors, especially in school-age children, result from unconscious displacement of unresolved preoedipal and oedipal conflicts from the familial to the outside world. Acting out of voyeuristic, exhibitionistic, sadomasochistic, passive-feminine, and primal-scene related fantasies especially may lead to difficult and unacceptable behavior at school. A still more grave social maladjustment may occur from the complete suppression of phallic masturbation and the consequent flooding of the ego activities with sexual content. Anna Freud thus appealed for distinction between narcissistic and neurotic types of delinquencies.

Hoffer (1949) suggested that in the impostor "idealization and the formation of an ego ideal occurs too early, [and] the formative influence of reality and of the oedipus situation ends too soon" (p. 154). The impostor's ego does not take notice of a threatening, castrating father–competitor, having fallen in love with an idealized father and internalized him unchanged into ego ideal. The oedipal struggle and its outcome is held in suspenseful abeyance. Disavowing his true feelings, the impostor blandly forgives his father's lies, deceptions and even violence. He maintains an idealized image of his father and is convinced that he himself is exactly like that. Lampl-de-Groot (1949) noted that it is the balance between the superego proper and ego ideal that determines the ultimate ratio of neurotic and antisocial manifestations in character. When superego is severe but the ego ideal is strong, aggression is turned inward and a neurotic picture results. When the superego is menacing but the ego ideal is weak, aggression is discharged outward and antisocial behavior results. Usually there is an admixture of two processes. Even the normal individual displays not only a small neurotic nucleus (and perhaps a personal delusion) but also "a minor 'psychopathic' spot in his make-up" (p. 252).

Something more ominous than this "minor psychopathic spot" was the focus of Schmideberg's (1949) contribution. She chose to discuss "major criminals," defining them as those (1) who have fundamentally antisocial attitudes and criminal associations, (2) whose criminal acts are serious, skilled, and deliberate, and (3) who live on the proceeds of crime. Schmideberg acknowledged that these individuals are often callous, explosive, dishonest, seemingly guilt-free, and tough. However, she believed that their toughness was highly defensive and that even the most hardened criminals were never totally guilt-free.

A significant new insight into the superego structure associated with antisocial behavior was provided by Johnson and Szurek (Johnson 1949; Johnson and Szurek 1952, Szurek 1942, 1949). According to them, an explanation of antisocial behavior is frequently to be found not in generalized superego weakness but in a lack of superego in certain circumscribed areas ("superego lacunae"). Johnson and Szurek proposed that often one child in a family of several children is subtly chosen as the scapegoat and unconsciously encouraged by the parents to act out their own unrealized or forbidden impulses. The parents obtain much vicarious gratification while maintaining an unconsciously permissive attitude toward the child. However, since such behavior is quite contrary to the parent's conscious self-image, it may also evoke severe punishments. The child is therefore trapped, unconsciously encouraged by the parents to act in certain ways (e.g., steal, be promiscuous, lie) and consciously discouraged to do the same. The paths open to such a child, and later adult, are a paralysis of intention or increasing cleverness in carrying out the delinquent acts (so as not to be caught by the seemingly moral parents). The former, I believe, is one explanation of the antisocial individual's bouts of laziness. The latter could explain not only the superficial charm and manipulative skills of the psychopath but also the constant "hide-and-seek" (Greenacre 1945) such an individual feels compelled to play with external and externalized authorities.

Johnson's and Szurek's ideas appear to have great merit in explaining the inner nature of delinquent behavior. Their applicability may, however, be greater in cases of milder and focal delinquencies. A more satisfactory understanding of pervasive and severe superego pathology was provided later by Jacobson (1964, 1971) and Rosenfeld (1964). Kernberg (1967, 1970, 1975a, 1984, 1989) synthesized these contributions and elaborated upon the relationship between the nature of superego pathology in narcissistic personalities to the antisocial personality proper.

Before turning to Kernberg, however, I would like to mention a significant paper by Winnicott (1956), entitled "The Antisocial Tendency." Winnicott traced the origin of the "antisocial tendency" to deprivation of ego needs during childhood. In his inimitable fashion, Winnicott suggested that insofar as it compels the environment to be important, the antisocial tendency is an expression of hope. The delinquent's outrageousness is a cry for help. Winnicott noted that there were always two trends in the antisocial tendency:

> One trend is represented typically in stealing, and the other in destructiveness. By *one* trend the child is looking for something,

> somewhere, and failing to find it seeks it elsewhere, when hopeful. By the *other* the child is seeking that amount of environmental stability which will stand the strain resulting from impulsive behavior. This is a search for an environmental provision that has been lost, a human attitude, which, because it can be relied on, gives freedom to the individual to move and to act and to get excited. [p. 310]

Winnicott emphasized the great importance of recognizing the hope implicit in antisocial tendency. A failure to recognize this hope causes intolerance of the overtly outrageous behavior, and the moment of hope withers away. Winnicott, however, clarified that treatment of the antisocial tendency is "not psychoanalysis but management, a going to meet and match the moment of hope" (p. 309).

Kernberg's Contributions

Kernberg's (1975a, 1976, 1984, 1989) outstanding contributions to the dynamic and structural understanding of severe character pathology as a whole also contain specific points of clarification regarding antisocial personality disorder. Kernberg believes that all clear-cut cases of antisocial personality show an underlying "borderline personality organization" (1967) or a lower-level character organization (1970a). At this level, superego integration is minimal and its sadistic forerunners are easily projected outward. Synthetic function of the ego is grossly impaired and the delimitations between ego and ego ideal, and ego and superego, are completely blurred. Splitting is the main defense, rather than repression. The resulting dissociation of contradictory ego states is further supported by other primitive defenses, such as protective identification, primitive denial, and the like. Object constancy has not been achieved, identity diffusion prevails, and there is a pathological condensation of preoedipal and oedipal conflicts with a preponderance of pregenital aggression. This state of affairs translates behaviorally into (1) an unstable self-concept that is a chaotic mixture of shameful and exalted images, (2) paranoid trends, (3) defective empathy, (4) markedly deficient concern and guilt, (5) repetitive patterns of contradictory behaviors (e.g., unbridled generosity and anxious miserliness, gluttonous indulgence and disenchanted asceticism) that remain dissociated from each other, (6) lack of goals and direction in life, (7) inauthenticity, and (8) erratic work record, poor sublimatory potential, and tendency toward magical thinking.

Kernberg (1970b) stated that the antisocial personality may be considered a subgroup of the narcissistic personality. Like those with a narcissistic personality, antisocial individuals displayed extreme self-centeredness, grandiosity, and a remarkable absence of interest in and empathy for others. However, the antisocial individuals showed more severe superego pathology than the usual narcissistic individuals. Kernberg (1971) acknowledged that some antisocial behavior can be seen in almost all types of severe personality disorders. For instance, it is not uncommon to notice stealing, parasitism, and exploitativeness in borderline individuals, pathologic lying in histrionic personalities, treacherousness in paranoid characters, promiscuity and self-serving distortions of reality in hypomanic and narcissistic individuals, and so on. However, the antisocial personality presents a more severe and pervasive superego pathology. Kernberg emphasized that the following questions needed to be answered before a diagnosis of antisocial personality disorder could be satisfactorily made. Does the antisocial behavior actually reflect individual psychopathology, or is it labeled as such due to a social or moral prejudice of the interviewer? Does the antisocial behavior reflect a normal adaptation to an abnormal social environment? Does the antisocial behavior reflect an adolescent turmoil (time-limited, anxiety-laden, and accompanied by other neurotic symptoms)? Does the delinquent behavior reflect a severe personality disorder other than antisocial personality disorder? The diagnosis of antisocial personality disorder should be made only if these questions have been answered in the negative. Long-term history and assessment of object relations and superego pathology is necessary for such a conclusion.

In 1984, Kernberg commented briefly on the *DSM-III* criteria for antisocial personality disorder. He found the criteria clear and reliable but noted an overemphasis on criminal behavior and a mistaken omission of such crucial factors as the individual's capacity for loyalty, guilt, anticipatory anxiety, and learning from prior experiences. A few years later, Kernberg (1989) returned to a thorough discussion of antisocial personality disorder. He reiterated that all patients with an antisocial personality disorder present typical narcissistic personality features plus a severe pathology of superego and internal object relations. To his earlier criticisms of *DSM-III* he added (now also referring to the *DSM-III-R*) that (1) the criteria were excessively concrete and behavioral, (2) the stress on criminality led to delinquents with very different character makeups being diagnosed as having antisocial personality disorder, and (3) the criteria neglected "the non-aggressive variety or the predominantly inadequate or passive type of antisocial personality disorder" (1989, p. 554). Kernberg then presented a hierarchical differential diagnosis of antisocial behavior that, from the most severe to the least severe, included the following categories: (1) antisocial personality disorder, (2) the syndrome of malignant narcissism, (3) narcissistic personality disorder with antisocial behavior, (4) other severe personality disorders with antisocial features, (5) neurotic personality disorders with antisocial features, (6) antisocial behavior as part of a symptomatic neurosis, and (7) dyssocial reaction.

Kernberg divided the manifestations of antisocial personality into four areas: (1) pathological self-love, including self-centeredness, exhibitionism, overambitiousness, and severe bouts of inferiority alternating with grandiosity; (2) pathological object relations including greed, envy, defenses against envy, entitlement, appropriation of others' ideas and property, lack of concern for others, and a total absence of nonexploitative relations; (3) a basic ego state characterized by chronic emptiness, stimulus hunger, and a diffuse sense of meaninglessness of life; and (4) severe superego pathology manifesting not only in an incapacity for self-reflective sadness and absence of guilt feelings but also in lying, swindling, forgery, and prostitution (in the passive type) and assault, robbery, and murder (in the aggressive type). Individuals with narcissistic personality disorder differed from truly antisocial individuals in showing only the passive antisocial behaviors, being capable of some guilt, working better, and planning their futures meaningfully.

The syndrome of malignant narcissism represents an intermediary group between the narcissistic and antisocial personalities.

This syndrome is characterized by "a narcissistic personality disorder, antisocial behavior, ego-syntonic aggression or sadism directed against others or even expressed in a particular type of triumphant kind of self-mutilation or suicidal attempts, and a strong paranoid orientation" (1989, p. 553). Finally, Kernberg commented on the dyssocial reaction, a normal or neurotic adjustment to an abnormal social environment. Kernberg felt that this was a clinically infrequent situation and that most such individuals present some character pathology that allows them to accept uncritically a social subgroup with antisocial behaviors.

Some Other Recent Contributions

Bursten (1973a,b, 1989), Singer (1975), Leaff (1978), Hott (1979), Gediman (1985), and Person (1986) also provide substantial additional insights into the phenomenology of antisocial personality disorder.

Bursten (1973a,b) discarded the label *antisocial personality* on the grounds that such diagnosis often reflects sociological concerns (deviance, delinquency, crime) more than inherent psychological traits (e.g., callousness, lack of remorse, and an inability to profit from experience). He preferred the designation *manipulative personality,* saying it better reflected the essential feature of such persons regardless of whether they were socially well adapted or deviant. Manipulation, in this context, is an intrapsychic phenomenon with the conscious existence of four components: (1) conflict of goals, (2) intention to influence, (3) deception, and (4) the feeling of putting something over. In addition to such manipulation, the manipulative personality is characterized by a propensity for lying, having little guilt, transient and shallow relationships, and contempt for others. Bursten pointed out that such individuals had traumatic experiences in childhood that taught them to seek safety and omnipotence only in those relationships that they can manipulate and control. Their manipulativeness is meant to exert control, deny dependence, ward off anxiety of uncertainty, and externalize their own inferiority-laden self-image by assigning it to the other person. In this regard, the manipulative personality is like the paranoid personality. However, the manipulative personality keeps up appearances by alternating his aggression and applying it to being clever.

Bursten (1989) later compared the manipulative personality (roughly *DSM-II*'s antisocial personality) with the grandiose personality (roughly *DSM-III*'s narcissistic personality). Both show self-absorption, cohesiveness, invulnerability to regressive fragmentation, and exploitativeness. Both lack "non-narcissistic affects" (p. 581) such as concern, respect, loyalty, and pity. Both have a tendency to take care of themselves even if others who depend upon them go wanting. The manipulative person, however, shows much more widespread contempt for others than does the grandiose person. His affects are shallower, his capacity for guilt more deficient, and he tends to be more socially disaffiliated than the usual grandiose personality.

Singer (1975) summarized the manifestations of milder, "middle-class delinquency" (p. 429) under three headings: (1) drive disturbances and associated fantasies, (2) disturbances of ego functions, and (3) superego defects. In the first category, Singer noted that while early deprivation of adequate maternal care was ubiquitous in such cases, more often there was a "pyramiding of conflicts" (p. 431) from all levels of psychosexual development. Stealing in such individuals, for instance, may represent not only a restoring of symbiotic omnipotence by negating the limits of ownership but also the acquiring of an aggrandized penis to undo hidden feelings of being small, castrated, impotent, and worthless. In the second category, Singer included characterological disturbances of heightened sensitivity to displeasure, alloplastic bent, disturbed reality sense, and cognitive disturbances showing inability to delay action by fantasy and contemplation. In the third category, Singer included earlier observations suggesting that the superego in such individuals was corruptible (Alexander 1930), isolated, and unusable (Greenacre 1945) and riddled with lacunae (Johnson and Szurek 1952). Singer reported that the disciplinary configuration most frequent in the background of such delinquents was that of very restrictive policy-making, loose policing, and very lenient punishing by parents. Singer wondered if internalization of such family disciplinary configuration was an additional explanation of the genesis of these patients' borderline organizations.

Leaff (1978) stated that criminality is not a psychological concept. In diagnosing antisocial personality, the defective nature of superego, not the occurrence of overt criminal acts, should be accorded greater weight. This is especially true since antisocial behavior could signify different things under different conditions. However, there did exist a core group of truly antisocial personalities. Leaff, in agreement with Bursten (1973a,b), stated that this group represented a severe form of narcissistic personality structure. Among its behavioral manifestations were selfishness, callousness, irresponsibility, impulsivity, deficient guilt feelings, poor frustration tolerance, a tendency to blame others, and poor learning from experience. Such character resulted from a chaotic mother–child relationship, with difficulties becoming evident in the rapprochement phase, and with a father who was either an active traumatizer or an inadequate protector of the child from the traumatic maternal situation. Defective object relations, defensive self-inflation, negative oedipal outcome, and a paranoid world view were other consequences of such a background.

Hott (1979) distinguished between asocial, dyssocial, and antisocial characters. Asocial characters were narcissistically withdrawn individuals who led solitary lives in remote alcoves, religious communes, or in lifelong travel. They were not delinquent, only totally incapable of social adaptation. The dyssocial group comprised individuals whose conflicts with societal norms resulted from their having been raised in a grossly abnormal moral environment. Children of cultists and professional criminals fit into this category. The core or "compulsive antisocial characters" were extremely callous, sought immediate gratifications, lacked social judgments, were unable to profit from experience, lacked the capacity for genuine guilt, and were motivated mainly by self-aggrandizement and acquisition of power. Such individuals came from unhappy, broken families where they were unwanted, unloved, and frequently beaten and abused. Hott added that while in the past antisocial personality had been more common among men, "now it appears that more women are also sharing the antisocial character problems, perhaps as part of women's newer and increasing role in society" (p. 240).

In her astute study of imposture, inauthenticity, and fraudulence,

Gediman (1985) emphasized that impostrous tendencies were complexly determined, nearly ubiquitous, and not restricted to one or the other traditional diagnostic categories. However, she did suggest a distinction between the impostor and the impostrous. Citing Deutsch (1955), Greenacre (1958b), and Ross (1967), Gediman pointed out that the true impostor literally takes on someone else's identity, while the impostrous pretends under someone else's style and role. The former is more cohesive, while the latter shows a proclivity for multiple, shifting, and unconsolidated identifications. Such impostrous tendencies are most marked in as-if personalities but may also occur as defensive structures in neurotic characters who unconsciously equate authenticity with parricide (Loewald 1979). Moving on from such macroscopic nosological issues to a finer description of impostrous tendencies and fraudulence, Gediman described their five important attributes.

> The first is verbal fluency, facility, and fluidity; the second is a hypertrophied development of a limited kind of empathy; the third is a quality of dilettantism, involvement in esoterica and artifice; the fourth is an intense disturbance in the sense of identity manifested in multiple identifications and fragmented, largely imitative, noninternalized role playing; the fifth is a paradoxically heightened sense of reality accompanying what Eidelberg (1938) has called impostrous ego states. [p. 915]

Gediman noted that these individuals have astounding verbal fluency with tendencies toward punning, glibness, and verbal web spinning. They have an uncanny capacity to "read" both the superficial and the deeply unconscious aspects of others. However, such "empathy" is quite restricted, and they have profound difficulty in perceiving the more sustained, integrated, and enduring aspects of others. There is a tendency toward rapidly shifting identifications, which is often used defensively to avoid interpersonal disagreements and conflicts. The love of trivia and esoteric jargon frequently hides an absence of in-depth knowledge. Significantly, owing to unconscious guilt, many impostrous individuals feel more real when being phony and feel phony when being real. This phenomenon is, in my opinion, more true to neurotic types of impostrous individuals than of true, hard-core antisocial personalities.

Person (1986), like Bursten (1973a,b), viewed interpersonal manipulation, motivated primarily by the need to dominate and control others, as the central feature of psychopathy. While such behavior is riddled with aggression, the antisocial individual protects himself and humiliates his victim even more by the overlay of charm. The essential purpose of psychopathic manipulativeness is to stabilize identity and self-esteem. In warding off anxiety and depression, the delinquent act resembles a drug fix or a drink. In requiring enactment with an external object, the delinquent act resembles perversion.

Person also compared antisocial individuals with entrepreneurs. Both display a narcissistic personality structure. Both are action-oriented and innovative. Both possess finely worked skills to turn interpersonal maneuvers to their own ends. However, the entrepreneur has a lesser pathology of ego ideal and the will to dominate is more removed from primitive sadistic wishes. Moreover, the superego pathology in the entrepreneur is less of developmental origin than "indicative of immersion in a subculture which does not provide a holding environment for the maintenance of superego structures" (p. 269). Person seems to be addressing the narcissistic-antisocial continuum here. Her distinguishing the two groups on the basis of sustained work-related achievement confirms this interpretation of her thinking; the entrepreneur is a successful psychopath, the psychopath, a failed entrepreneur.

Summary

Though of somewhat dubious nosological congruence with descriptive psychiatry of the severely antisocial, psychoanalytic literature has nonetheless made important contributions to the understanding of immoral, impostrous, delinquent, antisocial, and criminal tendencies. Most psychoanalytic investigators agree that the core antisocial character results largely from a severely traumatized childhood, with much actual injustice being suffered by the growing child. Internalization of abnormal parental superegos or unconscious parental encouragement of the child's delinquency are other common background factors. Disappointment in primary objects, humiliation and suffering, internalization of abnormal norms, and/or corruption by parents are various factors that work with the child's own age-specific distortions and fantasy elaborations, leading to (1) excessive narcissism and nonrenunciation of infantile omnipotence; (2) weakly invested and need-based object relationships in which there is little empathy for others and in which one relationship can be traded readily for another; (3) an aborted separation-individuation process with resulting lack of self- and object constancy; (4) paranoid trends; (5) a basic ego state characterized by chronic emptiness, stimulus hunger, and a pervasive sense of meaninglessness in life; (6) the syndrome of identity diffusion with marked inauthenticity and temporal discontinuity of the self-experience; (7) severe superego pathology manifesting in a profound lack of guilt and remorse and in active or passive criminal tendencies; and (8) a severely distorted Oedipus complex, often with a contradictory picture of sexual bravado, promiscuity, and perversions on the one hand, and a lack of fusion of tender and sexual feelings, peculiar sexual inhibitions and fears, occasional bouts of impotence, and loss of sexual interest on the other hand. Psychoanalytic literature recognizes a continuum of superego pathology that runs through neurotic delinquencies, mixed forms, and truly antisocial states. Distinction between the neurotic and antisocial types rests mainly on the extent of superego pathology, the nature of libidinal economy, object relations, identity consolidation, ego structure, and predominant defensive operations.

DSM-III AND *DSM-III-R*

DSM-III (1980, pp. 320–321) retained the *DSM-II* "antisocial" designation but shifted the diagnostic approach in some important ways. However, before commenting on this shift, I will first go over the *DSM-III* criteria for this diagnosis.

A. Current age at least 18

B. Onset before age 15 as indicated by a history of three or more of the following before that age:

(i) truancy (positive if it amounted to at least five days per year for at least two years, not including the last year of school)

(ii) expulsion or suspension from school for misbehavior

(iii) delinquency (arrested or referred to juvenile court because of behavior)

(iv) running away from home overnight at least twice while living in parental or parental surrogate home

(v) persistent lying

(vi) repeated sexual intercourse in a casual relationship

(vii) repeated drunkenness or substance abuse

(viii) thefts

(ix) vandalism

(x) school grades markedly below expectations in relation to estimated or known IQ (may have resulted in repeating a year)

(xi) chronic violations of rules at home and/or at school (other than truancy)

(xii) initiation of fights

C. At least four of the following manifestations of the disorder since age 18:

(i) inability to sustain consistent work behavior, as indicated by any of the following: (a) too frequent job changes (e.g., three or more jobs in five years not accounted for by nature of job or economic or seasonal fluctuation), (b) significant unemployment (e.g., six months or more in five years when expected to work), (c) serious absenteeism from work (e.g., average three days or more of lateness or absence per month, (d) walking off several jobs without other jobs in sight (Note: similar behavior in an academic setting during the last few years of school may substitute for this criterion in individuals who by reason of their age or circumstances have not had an opportunity to demonstrate occupational adjustment)

(ii) lack of ability to function as a responsible parent as evidenced by one or more of the following: (a) child's malnutrition, (b) child's illness resulting from lack of minimal hygiene standards, (c) failure to obtain medical care for a seriously ill child, (d) child's dependence on neighbors or nonresident relatives for food or shelter, (e) failure to arrange for a caretaker for a child under six when parent is away from home, (f) repeated squandering, on personal items, of money required for household necessities

(iii) failure to accept social norms with respect to lawful behavior, as indicated by any of the following: repeated thefts, illegal occupation (pimping, prostitution, fencing, selling drugs), multiple arrests, a felony conviction

(iv) inability to maintain enduring attachment to a sexual partner as indicated by two or more divorces and/or separations (whether legally married or not), desertion of spouse, promiscuity (ten or more sexual partners within one year)

(v) irritability and aggressiveness as indicated by repeated physical fights or assault (not required by one's job or to defend someone or oneself), including spouse or child beating

(vi) failure to honor financial obligations, as indicated by repeated defaulting on debts, failure to provide child support, failure to support other dependents on a regular basis.

(vii) failure to plan ahead, or impulsivity, as indicated by traveling from place to place without a prearranged job or clear goal for the period of travel or clear idea about when the travel would terminate, or lack of a fixed address for a month or more

(viii) disregard for the truth as indicated by repeated lying, use of aliases, "conning" others for personal profit

(ix) recklessness, as indicated by driving while intoxicated or recurrent speeding

D. A pattern of continuous antisocial behavior in which the rights of others are violated, with no intervening period of at least five years without antisocial behavior between the age 15 and the present time (except when the individual was bedridden or confined in a hospital or penal institution).

E. Antisocial behavior is not due to either Severe Mental Retardation, Schizophrenia or manic episodes.

As can be noted from these criteria, *DSM-III* altered the earlier *DSM-II* diagnostic approach in three ways. First, accommodating the epidemiological research (Glueck and Glueck 1959, Guze 1964, O'Neal et al. 1962 Robins 1966) that had demonstrated the sustained nature of antisocial behavior from childhood onward, *DSM-III* included an early age of onset requirement. Second, *DSM-III* shifted the focus from pathological personality traits to specific antisocial behaviors (Frances 1980, Hare 1983, Kernberg 1989, Millon 1981), thus leading to an excessively concrete portrayal of the disorder. Third, the *DSM-III* criteria appeared to overemphasize criminal behavior (Frances 1980, Hare 1983, Millon 1981). This caused two kinds of nosological handicaps (Kernberg 1989): it permitted the inclusion of characterologically different delinquent individuals under the rubric of antisocial personality disorder, while excluding the passive, inadequate, and parasitic types of antisocial personalities (Bursten 1989, Karpman 1941, Kernberg 1989, Wolman, 1987) altogether from the classification.

DSM-III-R (1987, pp. 344–346) offered the following diagnostic criteria:

A. Current age at least 18.

B. Evidence of Conduct Disorder with onset before age 15, as indicated by a history of three or more of the following:

(i) was often truant

(ii) ran away from home overnight at least twice while living in parental or parental surrogate home (or once without returning)

(iii) often initiated physical fights

(iv) used a weapon in more than one fight

(v) forced someone into sexual activity with him or her

(vi) was physically cruel to animals

(vii) was physically cruel to other people

(viii) deliberately destroyed others' property (other than by fire-setting)

(ix) deliberately engaged in fire-setting

(x) often lied (other than to avoid physical or sexual abuse)

(xi) has stolen without confrontation of a victim on more than one occasion (including forgery)

(xii) has stolen with confrontation of a victim (e.g., mugging, purse-snatching, extortion, armed robbery).

C. A pattern of irresponsible and antisocial behavior since age of 15, as indicated by at least four of the following:

(i) is unable to sustain consistent work behavior, as indicated by any of the following (including similar behavior in academic settings if the person is a student): (a) significant unemployment for six months or more within five years when expected to work and work was available, (b) repeated absences from work unexplained by illness in self or family, (c) abandonment of several jobs without realistic plans for others

(ii) fails to conform to social norms with respect to lawful behavior, as indicated by repeatedly performing antisocial acts that are grounds for arrest (whether arrested or not), e.g., destroying property, harassing others, stealing, pursuing an illegal occupation

(iii) is irritable and aggressive, as indicated by repeated physical fights or assaults (not required by one's job or to defend someone or oneself) including spouse- or child-beating

(iv) repeatedly fails to honor financial obligations, as indicated by defaulting on debts or failing to provide child support or support for other dependents on a regular basis

(v) fails to plan ahead, or is impulsive, as indicated by one or both of the following: (a) traveling from place to place without a prearranged job or clear goal for the period of travel or clear idea about when the travel will terminate, (b) lack of a fixed address for a month or more

(vi) has no regard for the truth, as indicated by repeated lying, use of aliases, or "conning" others for personal profit or pleasure

(vii) is reckless regarding his or her own or others' personal safety, as indicated by driving while intoxicated, or recurrent speeding

(viii) if a parent or guardian, lacks ability to function as a responsible parent, as indicated by one or more of the following: (a) malnutrition of child, (b) child's illness resulting from lack of minimal hygiene, (c) failure to obtain medical care for a seriously ill child, (d) child's dependence on neighbors or nonresident relatives for food or shelter, (e) failure to arrange for a caretaker for young child when parent is away from home, (f) repeated squandering, on personal items, of money required for household necessities

(ix) has never sustained a totally monogamous relationship for more than one year

(x) lacks remorse (feels justified in having hurt, mistreated, or stolen from another)

D. Occurrence of antisocial behavior not exclusively during the course of Schizophrenia or Manic Episodes.

Most of the changes made in *DSM-III-R* are minor or essentially semantic. For instance, the *DSM-III* criterion "running away from home overnight at least twice while living in parental or parental surrogate home" appears in *DSM-III-R* as "ran away from home overnight at least twice while living in parental or parental surrogate home (or once without returning)." Similarly, the *DSM-III* criterion "often initiated physical fights" appears in *DSM-III-R* as "initiation of fights" and the *DSM-III*'s "persistent lying" is the *DSM-III-R*'s "often lied (other than to avoid physical or sexual abuse)." Many other such examples exist but there seems little point in going over them.

The only significant addition in *DSM-III-R* is the criterion "lacks remorse (feels justified in having hurt, mistreated, or stolen from another)." Though its parenthetical "translation" may be questionable, at least the criterion itself is trait-oriented. This is an improvement over *DSM-III,* which was entirely geared toward specific behaviors and took no account of underlying psychological traits. However, as Widiger and colleagues (1988) pointed out, it may be too early to tell whether the addition of this criterion will lead to an improved diagnosis of antisocial personality disorder.

Moreover, the change might be too little to accomplish this. More needs to be done. For instance, neither *DSM-III* nor *DSM-III-R* take into account the narcissistic features (Bursten 1973a,b, 1989, Freud 1914, Kernberg 1989, Millon 1981, Stone 1989) of antisocial personality disorder. These include grandiosity, search for power and glory, self-absorption, exhibitionism, defective empathy, frequent boredom, and hypochondriacal tendencies. The outlines provided by both *DSM-III* and *DSM-III-R* also overlook the antisocial individual's cognitive peculiarities (Abraham 1925, Greenacre 1945, Rappeport 1974, Wolman 1987), such as glibness, plagiarism, superficial smattering of art, literature, and technical parlance, soft-learning defects, and a tendency to confuse intention with action. Finally, both criteria lists fail to include the fundamentally paranoid orientation of the antisocial individuals (Kernberg 1984, 1989a,b, Millon 1981, Stone 1989), who invariably believe all others to be devious, unreliable, dishonest, or honest only because of fear of social reprisals.

The following multifaceted clinical profile of antisocial personality disorder includes these three features (narcissism, paranoia, and cognitive peculiarities) omitted by *DSM-III* and *DSM-III-R*. It also takes into account the centrality of splitting and identity diffusion in such a character organization and thus brings the description of antisocial personality in phenomenological alignment with other severe personality disorders described earlier in this book.

AN ATTEMPT AT SYNTHESIS

The entire literature surveyed here was pooled and synthesized to develop a composite clinical profile of antisocial personality disorder. According to this profile (Table 8–1), the clinical features of

TABLE 8–1. Clinical Features of Antisocial Personality Disorder.

Clinical Features	*Overt Characteristics*	*Covert Characteristics*
I. *Self-Concept*	Self-assured; innocent, victimlike self-image; preoccupation with unrealistic fantasies of power, glory, and revenge; feelings of entitlement; self-sufficiency	Feelings of inferiority, confusion about self, and bleak emptiness; fluctuations between sentimental self-pity and surprising lack of concern about self; subtle body-image disturbances
II. *Interpersonal Relations*	Affability; quick in reading others for manipulation purposes; rapid intimacy with others; shallow and ill-sustained relationships; inability to genuinely participate in groups or family life; absence of nonexploitative relations; impaired capacity for respect	Pervasive mistrust of everyone; views others as dishonest; defective empathy with enduring aspects of others' characters; marked contempt toward others; lack of generational boundaries; unreliability and irresponsibility; parasitic lifestyle
III. *Social Adaptation*	Socially charming, playful, and thrill seeking; can appear earnestly interested in vocational opportunities offered; often makes big schemes; intense ambition but little effort; preoccupation with status and appearances	Checkered or barely adequate academic and employment record; chronic boredom; lacks goals and plans for future; always looking for short cuts to money and fame; seeks pleasure only in the "here and now"; uses aliases and leads double life

IV.	*Love and Sexuality*	Shrewdly manipulative seductiveness; promiscuity; fantastic infatuations that evaporate rapidly; frequent separations, divorce, and spouse abuse, if married	Inability to remain in love; incapacity to view the romantic partner as a separate individual with his/her own interests, rights, and values; inability to genuinely comprehend the incest taboo; frequent sexual perversions
V.	*Ethics, Standards, and Ideals*	Profound lack of authentic guilt and remorse; pathologic lying; disregard of social mores and law; love of gambling; impostrous and fraudulent tendencies; criminal acts	Fantastically unrealistic ideals; powerful fears of certain external figures; occasional, ill-sustained, and sentimentalized longings for direction and guidance
VI.	*Cognitive Style*	Can appear impressively polished and knowledgeable; glib and facile with language; smattering of art, literature, and technical jargon in conversation; "addiction to novelty"; quick in learning delinquent skills	Knowledge often limited to trivia ("headline intelligence"); magic beliefs; inability to learn the expected and ordinary; tends to equate intent with action; speaking used for regulating self-esteem; plagiarism

antisocial personality disorder belong to six areas of psychosocial functioning: (1) self-concept; (2) interpersonal relations; (3) social adaptation; (4) love and sexuality; (5) ethics, standards, and ideals; and (6) cognitive style. Akin to the situation in the five other severe personality disorders (Chapters 3 through 7), each of these areas has overt and covert features. It should, however, be noted that the overt and covert features are more rigidly separated in narcissistic, schizoid, hypomanic, and paranoid personalities than in borderline, antisocial, and histrionic personalities. In other words, the overt and covert features of antisocial personality disorder often fluidly and rapidly alternate in becoming surface phenomena.

Other caveats regarding the organization of symptomatology along these lines have already been mentioned in preceding chapters. These have equal application here. Nonetheless, in emphasizing the centrality of splitting and identity diffusion and in including cognitive style, pathological narcissism, and the fundamentally paranoid orientation of these patients, the diagnostic scheme provided here is richer and theoretically more sound than the checklist approach of *DSM-III* and *DSM-III-R*.

According to this profile, the overt features of antisocial personality disorder include (1) a self-righteous, victimlike self-concept that is nonetheless grandiose and filled with omnipotent fantasies of power and glory, (2) superficial charm resulting in rapid development of intimacy with others, (3) seeming earnestness regarding work and making big schemes, (4) fantastic infatuations and colorful love life, (5) profound incapacity for guilt and concern for others, and (6) impressively knowledgeable and articulate cognition. However, the covert picture is different and includes (1) inferiority, self-doubt, and chronic confusion about oneself; (2) pervasive cynicism and contempt toward others; (3) checkered career, aliases, "double life," and inability to sustain interest in job or work; (4) an inability to love and to comprehend incest taboo with tendency toward perversion; (5) occasional, ill-sustained, and sentimental longing for direction and guidance; and (6) soft-learning defects and superficiality of knowledge. This comprehensive portrait links descriptive and psychoanalytic data on antisocial personality disorder and facilitates its distinction from related conditions.

DIFFERENTIAL DIAGNOSIS

Antisocial behavior has multiple determinants, and "all that is antisocial, asocial, hedonistic, narcissistic, frustrating, or refractory to treatment is not antisocial personality" (Reid 1986, p. 3). Indeed, the differential diagnosis of antisocial personality is complex. On the one hand, the disorder needs to be distinguished from antisocial manifestations of mania, schizophrenia, dementia, and delinquent acts resulting from primary drug abuse and alcoholism, though of course the latter two conditions might coexist with antisocial personality (see Gerstley et al. 1990, for an excellent recent discussion of their complex relationships). On the other hand, antisocial personality disorder needs to be differentiated from the sociopathic behaviors associated with neurotic characters and with narcissistic, paranoid, and histrionic personality disorders. Since the psychotic disorders are recognizable without much difficulty from their clinical history and phenomenology, I will focus here on differentiation of antisocial from other personality disorders.

Neurotic Personality Disorders with Antisocial Features

Beginning with Freud's (1916) description of "criminals from a sense of guilt," many investigators (Alexander 1930, Fenichel 1945, Greenacre 1945, Kernberg 1989) have noted that antisocial behavior at times is a manifestation of an unconscious neurotic conflict. In contrast to the delinquent acts of those with a defective superego, such antisocial behavior is invariably accompanied by a thinly veiled attempt at seeking punishment. Reich's (1925) and Fenichel's (1945) description of "isolation" and "bribing" of the superego, respectively, apply largely to such patients and not to true antisocial characters. In such cases, there is evidence of profound intrapsychic conflict and hidden guilt. Their "crimes" have multilayered symbolic connections with events and fantasies of their childhood. Unlike those with antisocial personalities, these individuals have not had brutally traumatizing childhoods. They display hysterical, compulsive, phobic, or depressive character structures and have a "higher-level" (Kernberg 1970) character organization. In other words, their identity is well established and they are capable of genuinely reciprocal object relations. Their defenses center around repression, and they give evidence of a strict, indeed unduly harsh, superego. Although such cases are perhaps "relatively rare" (Kernberg 1989, p. 565), their favorable prognosis with treatment makes their distinction from antisocial personality disorder of great clinical importance.

Narcissistic Personality Disorder

Descriptive psychiatrists (Cleckley 1941, Henderson 1939, Schneider 1950) and psychoanalysts (Akhtar 1989a, Bursten 1973b, 1989, Freud 1908c, 1914, Kernberg 1989) have both noted the antisocial individual's self-centeredness, emotional coldness, grandiosity, glibness, superficial charm, sexual promiscuity, and manipulativeness. These behavioral characteristics also are associated with narcissistic personality disorder (see Chapter 3). In addition, individuals with both disorders are given to self-serving distortions of reality and pathological lying (Bursten 1973, Horowitz 1975, Kohut 1971). Neither antisocial nor narcissistic personalities are prone to regressive fragmentation (Bursten 1989). Indeed, the similarities between them are striking, and many theoreticians (Bursten 1973, 1989, Kernberg 1989) consider antisocial personality as a narcissistic personality with greater superego defects.

This brings up the issue of their differences. Essentially there are six grounds on which antisocial and narcissistic personalities differ. First, antisocial personality disorder shows more severe superego pathology resulting not only in more frequently occurring delinquent acts but also in a much greater incapacity for genuine guilt and remorse (Kernberg 1989). Second, an individual with narcissistic personality retains some capacity for reciprocal, nonexploitative relationships as well as that for idealization of others. An antisocial individual, in contrast, has practically no capacity for sustained idealization or for relationships that are nonexploitative (Bursten 1989). Third, a narcissistic individual is capable of sustained work and job-related success (Akhtar 1989a, Akhtar and Thomson 1982a), while the antisocial individual cannot retain and/or progress in sustained employment. He is always hoping to succeed by robbing, stealing, or winning lotteries. Fourth, although both narcissistic and antisocial individuals harbor contempt for others, this contempt is more "widespread and impersonal" (Bursten 1989, p. 581) in the latter. Fifth, the narcissistic individual is generally more social and more involved with others, while the antisocial person is disaffiliated and uninvolved with others. Finally, the background history of the two types of individuals is different. The antisocial individual has suffered more gross traumatic insults, such as parental death, desertion, violence, sexual abuse, and the like during his childhood than has the narcissist, who, while treated unempathically, was nonetheless held "special" in some way in his family.

Paranoid Personality Disorder

Both antisocial and paranoid individuals display grandiosity, emotional coldness, job-related difficulties, vindictiveness, and a self-serving sort of mendacity. Both may commit crimes. Both may be quite sadistic and cruel toward others. However, the paranoid individual does not possess the superficial glibness, charm, or interpersonal manipulativeness of the antisocial individual. The paranoid inclines toward destruction of his victim, the antisocial mostly toward proving his superiority by conning, thus retaining his hope for reunion (Bursten 1973a). The paranoid person also "characteristically lacks the chronicity of antisocial behavior—and the child-to-adult continuum—found in the psychopath. His acts are more consistent with projection and paranoia, without the stimulating quality usually seen in antisocial personality" (Reid 1986, p. 3). Moreover, the paranoid individual's pervasive mistrust prevents comfortable socialization (Akhtar 1990a), while the antisocial individual retains the capacity for casual banter and social relaxation. The cognitive style of the two individuals differs as well. The paranoid individual has an acutely vigilant but biased perception that is always seeking malicious intent in others (Shapiro 1965). The antisocial person also is vigilant but more interested in finding out others' innocence and vulnerability for his own exploitative reasons.

Histrionic Personality Disorder

Both histrionic and antisocial individuals display diffuse impulsivity, shallow relationships, sexual promiscuity, erratic employment records, identity conflicts, and pathological lying (Kernberg 1985, 1989). However, the histrionic individual is dependent, clinging, and highly suggestible, while the antisocial individual is uninvolved, disaffiliated, and relatively impervious to influence by others. The histrionic individual also may commit crimes but not with the chronicity, frequency, and ruthlessness of the antisocial person. It should be noted here, though, that my use of the term *histrionic personality disorder* is different from that of *DSM-III-R* and is not to be confused with the traditionally recognized hysterical personality. I will clarify this important distinction in the next chapter.

COMMENT

Four areas pertaining to the phenomenology of antisocial personality disorder need further clarification. First, the introduction in *DSM-III* of newer personality disorders (e.g., narcissistic and histrionic) that also show superego defects necessitates mapping out boundaries between them and antisocial personality proper. Even the tentatively listed *DSM-III-R* "sadistic personality disorder" may encroach on the phenomenological domain of antisocial personality. Intimidation and sadistic control of others as well as fascination with weapons, martial arts, and torture may be manifested by both antisocial and sadistic individuals. Millon (1981, pp. 182–183) points out that hostile affectivity and social vindictiveness are among the essential traits of antisocial personality. These also form the basis of the *DSM-III-R* sadistic personality disorder description. Moreover, both disorders display "malignant narcissism" (Kernberg 1984, 1989), which consists of (1) features of narcissistic personality disorder, (2) antisocial behavior, (3) ego-syntonic sadism, and (4) a fundamentally paranoid orientation toward life. Such a characterological constellation, with an admixture of narcissistic, antisocial, sadistic, and paranoid features, is frequent among murderers and, therefore, is of great forensic significance (Stone 1989). Clearly, differential diagnosis in this context is not simple and merits further investigation.

Second, the status of "dyssocial" (*DSM-II* 1968) and "asocial" (Hott 1979) characters in relation to antisocial personality proper remains unclear. The "dyssocial" category refers to individuals who, owing to a normal and/or neurotic adjustment to a criminal subgroup, come to have antisocial tendencies. Members of organized crime families in the United States, the Thugs of India, or the Berserkers of the Middle East (Reid 1981) constitute some examples of this sort. The question here is whether such individuals themselves are antisocial personalities or whether their antisocial behavior is an expectable adaptation to an abnormal situation. On the other hand, it can be argued that almost all antisocial individuals have had abnormal parents and hence are "dyssocial" to a certain extent. Some authors (Hott 1979, Reid 1981) separate the dyssocial from the antisocial, while others (Cameron 1963) regard the "dyssocial sociopathic personality" as a subgroup of antisocial personality disorder. A similar lack of clarity exists regarding the concept of "asocial" characters (Hott 1979), individuals who are totally unable to live in a social environment and maintain a solitary existence with little relationship to social reality. In this concept, there seems an admixture of narcissistic, schizoid, and antisocial elements in ways that remain understudied.

The third issue pertains to subtypes within antisocial personality disorder. Many investigators (Henderson 1939, Karpman 1941, Kernberg 1989, Schneider 1950, Wolman 1987) propose that there are at least two types of antisocial characters. One group is more overtly aggressive, actively criminal, and potentially violent, while the other group is passive, dependent, lazy, parasitic, and given to petty swindling, rather than aggressive criminality. In view of these subtypes, Millon (1981) and Kernberg (1989) criticize *DSM-III*'s overemphasis on overt criminal behavior in the diagnosis of antisocial personality disorder. They assert, and I agree with them, that such emphasis tends to delineate criminal individuals better than antisocial ones, since most antisocial individuals successfully avoid criminal involvements. They lead apparently ordinary lives marked by subtly parasitic and exploitive behaviors.

Finally, there is the issue of sex-related prevalence and the effect of gender on the overt symptomatology of antisocial personality. The disorder is three times more prevalent among men (Cloninger et al. 1975, *DSM-III-R* 1987). However, with a changing cultural climate, which provides greater freedom to women, the sex-related prevalence might change and one might see more female antisocial characters (Hott 1979, K. S. Kashyap 1989, personal communication). This assumes that greater societal restraints on women had so far prevented the occurrence or the overtness of antisocial personality among them. While this is plausible, two other hypotheses need to be considered. One is that constitutional differences between the sexes (and their effects upon psychic development) determine this differential prevalence. The second is that the disorder is less often diagnosed in women because it looks somewhat different in them (Rappeport 1974). Perhaps the passive-parasitic type of antisocial personality mentioned above is more common in women. This would be akin to the sex-related difference in the symptomatology of paranoid personality disorder discussed in Chapter 6.

9

HISTRIONIC AND SCHIZOTYPAL PERSONALITY DISORDERS

I come from where the trees
Send worms into their own fruit
I have strengthened my teeth against a hard wall
The waste of things has passed me like a chill
And the dampness of my mother is still with me.

—"The Roach," Charles Simic

I have chosen to discuss the two remaining severe personality disorders in a single chapter because these nosological newcomers (*DSM-III* 1980) have not yet accumulated a complex, rich literature of their own. Both entities are derived from older, more familiar categories, although their exact relationship with these conceptual predecessors remains unclear. For instance, is histrionic personality merely a renaming of the traditional hysterical personality, or is it a distinct entity in its own right? Is the schizotypal category a legitimate personality disorder, or is it simply a fancier name for simple and latent varieties of schizophrenia? In this chapter, I will attempt to answer these questions. I will survey the literature pertinent to these two disorders, review their *DSM-III* and *DSM-*

III-R profiles, and discuss their differential diagnoses. Finally, since this chapter concludes my discussion of the phenomenology of severe personality disorders, I will append to it a brief comment on various extraneous factors that affect the ultimate clinical picture and the level of social functioning of all eight severe personality disorders. I begin with the two disorders that remain to be addressed.

HISTRIONIC PERSONALITY DISORDER

Origins

Although the term *histrionic* existed parenthetically as a synonym for *hysterical* in the personality disorder section of *DSM-II* (1968, p. 43), it was only with the publication of *DSM-III* (1980) that "histrionic personality disorder" gained an independent status. Its widespread use in descriptive psychiatry ever since, its retention in *DSM-III-R* (1987), and its adoption by psychoanalysts (e.g., Kernberg 1985), who in the past had used various other labels for such a condition, confirm that the term is here to stay. This, of course, does not imply clarity about its usage. Indeed, there is considerable controversy (Gorton and Akhtar 1990) about whether the histrionic label is merely a synonym for the older hysterical one (Frances 1980, Spitzer et al. 1980, Widiger et al. 1988) or whether it designates a phenomenologically and psychodynamically distinct condition (Kernberg 1984, 1986). In order to elucidate this controversy and to evaluate the currently popular *DSM-III-R* portrayal of this disorder, it seems profitable to first survey the psychoanalytic literature from which the concept originated.

In a careful review of psychoanalytic literature on hysterical character, Lazare (1971) noted that while attempts at a deeper understanding of hysterical symptoms had led to the birth of psychoanalysis, Freud himself did not refer to a specific hysterical character. Behavioral traits associated with the development of conversion symptoms, such as affective instability, excitability, and suggestibility, were mentioned only in passing by him. Abraham's

(1921, 1924a,b) early papers on the relationship of character traits and libidinal stages also did not mention a hysterical personality. The first psychoanalytic description of hysterical personality was provided by Wittels (1930), who noted the relationship between hysterical symptoms and a specific type of underlying character while emphasizing that the latter could exist independently. Interestingly, although the development of hysterical symptoms had thus far been related with phallic-oedipal conflicts, Wittels saw the hysteric's developmental failure as predominantly pregenital. Wittels also pointed out the strong dependency needs of such individuals and underscored their tendencies toward depression, addiction, and suicide attempts.

In the following year, Freud (1931) published "Libidinal Types," in which he described the erotic, obsessional, and narcissistic types. Regarding the first of these, he wrote:

> Erotics are persons whose main interest—the relatively largest amount of their libido—is focused on love. Loving, but above all being loved, is for them the most important thing in life. They are governed by the dread of loss of love, and this makes them peculiarly dependent on those who may withhold their love from them. . . . When persons of erotic type fall ill they will develop hysteria. [pp. 218-220]

Thus, Freud noted the hysteric's dependent longings and, by implication, the preoedipal determinants of hysterical character. Reich (1933), on the other hand, emphasized that the hysterical character is determined by a fixation on the genital phase of infantile development, with its incestuous attachment. He associated the following traits with the hysterical character: subtle but obvious sexual behavior, coquettishness, bodily suppleness and grace, excitability, suggestibility, pathologic lying, and a perplexing withdrawal when sexual seductiveness seems close to achieving its goals. The trend to view hysterical personality in such phallic-oedipal terms continued over the next two decades. Fenichel (1945), for instance, maintained that hysterical character traits betray conflicts between intense fears of sexuality and equally intense but repressed sexual strivings. In addition, there is the conflict between the "rejection of actuality" (p. 527) and the tendency to find the infantile objects again in the external environment. Fenichel described hysterical characters as persons who are inclined to sexualize all nonsexual relations. They tend toward suggestibility, emotional outbreaks, dramatization, histrionic behavior, and even mendacity and its extreme form, pseudologia phantastica.

In 1953, Marmor challenged the notion that hysterical personality emanated predominantly from phallic-oedipal conflicts. He pointed out that certain aspects of the hysterical character, especially its resistance to change, the instability of its ego structure, and its close relationship to addictions, depression, and schizophrenia, are all best explained on the basis of deep-seated oral fixations. Marmor emphasized that deeper scrutiny of clinical material in most such cases reveals that the fixations in the oedipal phase are themselves the outgrowths of preoedipal, chiefly oral, fixations. The sexuality of the hysteric is a sham because it actually represents pregenital receptive needs, rather than genital desires. Marmor's position was upheld by Halleck (1967), who found severe maternal deprivation to be a frequent background of adult hysterical personality. Halleck too felt that the hysteric's intense desire for an ideal man disguised a search for a preoedipal mother who could satisfy her oral needs. The associated theme of certain hysterical women's desire to be held, not seduced, was further developed by Hollender (1970).

From the very beginning, then, a certain conflict existed in the views of hysterical character. Freud's (1905, 1909) views on hysterical conversion symptoms and Reich's (1933) and Fenichel's (1945) description of hysterical personality emphasized the phallic-oedipal conflicts. Freud's (1931) ideas regarding the "erotic type," coupled with Wittels's (1930), Marmor's (1953), and Halleck's (1967) assertions, painted a sicker picture of hysterical character, with greater emphasis on its preoedipal determinants. This tension was further highlighted and somewhat resolved by the following significant contributions.

Easser and Lesser (1965), while acknowledging that there is no sharp differentiating line but rather a continuum between two kinds of hysterical patients, distinguished the true hysteric from the "hysteroid." They described the individual with hysterical personality as displaying (1) labile emotionality, (2) active engagement with the human world, (3) anxiety in the face of self-created overexcitement, (4) a tendency to sexually embroider existing relationships, (5) suggestibility, (6) a dislike of the exact and the mundane, and (7) a childlike attitude of seeming naivete and inexperience. The authors noted that such persons come from intact, strongly bonded families. Their mothers have been consistent and responsible, though often regarded by the patients as drab, uninteresting, and not charming enough. Most of these patients have remained profoundly involved with their fathers, in actuality or in fantasy. Their educational and vocational concerns are steady, and they are capable of maintaining long-term friendships. While appearing seductive, these individuals are frequently sexually inhibited and frigid. The "hysteroid" patients, on the other hand, come from disturbed, often broken families where adequate maternal care was unavailable to them. Their conflicts center on their mothers, not their fathers. They have erratic academic and vocational careers and are unable to maintain friendships over time. Cross-sectionally, "the hysteroid would appear to be a caricature of the hysteric, much as the hysteric has been said to be a caricature of femininity" (pp. 398–399). Each characteristic of the hysteric appears in more exaggerated form in the hysteroid, who shows less emotional control, less ability to tolerate tension, and greater proneness to action and depression.

> The bounds of social custom and propriety are breached. The latent aggressivity of the exhibitionism, the competitiveness and the self-absorption becomes blatant, insistent and bizarre. The chic becomes the mannequin; the casual, sloppy; the bohemian, beat. . . . The hysteric has difficulty within the relationship, the hysteroid with the relationship. . . . The hysteric will often regress. The content of such regression may show oral and other pregenital trends and is used to defend against the developing sexual feelings and the erotic transference . . . conversely, the hysteroid, to defend against feared passivity and primitive orality, tends to go into action and reaction, which activity may include the use of erotic (more exactly pseudo-erotic) transference and sexual acting out. [Easser and Lesser 1965, pp. 399, 401]

A few years later, Kernberg (1967) distinguished an "infantile" personality from a hysterical personality on six grounds: (1) in the hysterical personality, hyperemotionality and impulsivity are seen only in the context of sexualized, triangular relationships; the infantile personality, in contrast, shows diffuse emotional lability and impulsivity; (2) overinvolvement and childlike clinging occur in certain selected, especially heterosexual, relationships in the hysterical personality; the infantile personality shows more desperate, inappropriate demandingness; (3) exhibitionism has a sexual implication in the hysterical personality and a narcissistic agenda in the infantile personality; (4) the sexual life of the hysteric is characterized by subtle seductiveness on the surface and inhibition underneath, while the infantile personality shows crude seductiveness and actual promiscuity; moreover, there is a general repression of sexual fantasy in the hysteric, whereas there may be conscious sexual fantasies of a polymorphous perverse nature in the infantile personality; (5) hysterical individuals show much competitiveness, especially with imagined oedipal rivals, while infantile personalities show less chronic competitiveness and overall less differentiation in their behavior toward the two sexes; and (6) masochistic tendencies are more restricted and less intense in the hysterical personality than in the infantile personality.

Zetzel (1968) elaborated further on the dynamics and phenomenology of the hysterical continuum. Zetzel divided hysterical women patients in four groups of increasing psychopathological severity. Group 1 included the "true" hysterics. Such individuals keep stable friendships, are notably successful in their academic and vocational careers, and are often the oldest, most gifted children in their families. They are frequently their fathers' favorites and have been unable to relinquish a powerful oedipal relationship. While they may be sexually seductive on the surface, they are frequently frigid and sexually inhibited in actuality. Group 2 includes persons of a somewhat wider range of character structure. They are often the youngest children in their families and have failed to achieve as stable ego-syntonic obsessional defenses as the first group. They are somewhat more passive and academically less consistent. Their friendships are more openly ambivalent. Group 3 consists of individuals with low self-esteem who feel helpless and are frequently depressed. The fourth and last group consists of so-called good hysterics. They are floridly hysterical and, when in treatment, all too readily express intense sexualized transference fantasies, regarding them as potential areas of actual gratification. They display difficulties in distinguishing between external and internal reality and therefore fail to develop a meaningful therapeutic alliance. Zetzel stated that such patients'

> major pathology is attributable to significant developmental failure in respect to basic ego functions . . . they have few areas of past or present conflict-free interest in autonomous ego functions. They seldom present a history which includes a genuine period of latency in respect of either achievement or peer relationships. Their obsessional defenses, if present, are not directed against their own ego-alien impulses . . . [but] towards ensuring their perception and control of certain aspects of external reality. [Zetzel 1968, pp. 259–260]

Zetzel pointed out that the developmental history in such individuals often reveals (1) significant separations in the first four years of life, (2) serious parental psychopathology, (3) much physical illness during childhood, and (4) absence of meaningful, sustained relations with either sex.

In 1974, Abse distinguished "hysteriform borderline personalities" from the hysterical personality proper. This group of individuals displayed "pronounced oral character traits, sometimes also undergirded by severe narcissistic ego disorder" (p. 186). Abse noted that such individuals display greater dependence needs than the usual hysterics and also have a greater vulnerability to severe regression.

Following this, Blacker and Tupin (1977) described "the more pregenitally fixated or more narcissistically vulnerable hysteric" (p. 126). Such individuals display much ego weakness and poor differentiation of internal and external reality. They show a greater regressive potential and vulnerability to psychosis and suicide.

> They have few problem-solving techniques—acting out, regression, or sickness frequently being their only resource. Negative self-concepts and poor self-esteem are common. There is poor adaptation with an unstable, unpredictable, and lonely adjustment. Relationships may be intense but quite chaotic and unpredictable with

> primitive aggressive outbursts, intense jealousy, and possessiveness. There may be grandiose beliefs in self. A variety of sexual behaviors may be attempted with little investment or satisfaction. Often there is an abuse of drugs or alcohol. The caricature of femininity or masculinity is often more bizarre. [p. 126]

Blacker and Tupin contrasted this "infantile personality organization" with the "genital or mature hysterical personality organization" (p. 136), which experienced less early deprivation, exhibited deeper object relations and fewer ego defects, and was more successful in vocational and social areas.

These important psychoanalytic contributions laid the foundation for the creation of a personality disorder superficially related to, but psychostructurally distinct from, hysterical personality proper. Another impetus to such conceptualization came from the work of Liebowitz and Klein (1981), who outlined an entity called "hysteroid dysphoria." This consisted of (1) flamboyance, seductiveness, and demandingness; (2) extreme dependence on external approval; (3) intolerance of rejection; (4) brief, atypical depressions; and (5) tendency toward substance abuse, self-mutilation, and suicidal gestures. Once again, it is clear that this entity represented a sicker state of affairs than had been associated with hysterical personality disorder.

DSM-III and *DSM-III-R*

Responding in part to these advances, as well as attempting to "avoid confusion caused by the historical relationship of the term 'hysteria' to female anatomy and conversion symptoms" (Spitzer et al. 1980, p. 161), *DSM-III* (1980, p. 315) introduced the diagnostic entity of "histrionic personality disorder" with the following diagnostic criteria:

> A. Behavior that is overly dramatic, reactive, and intensely expressed, as indicated by at least three of the following:
>
> (i) self-dramatization, e.g., exaggerated expression of emotions

(ii) incessant drawing of attention to oneself

(iii) craving for activity and excitement

(iv) overreaction to minor events

(v) irrational, angry outbursts or tantrums

B. Characteristic disturbances in interpersonal relationships as indicated by at least two of the following:

(i) perceived by others as shallow and lacking genuineness, even if superficially warm and charming.

(ii) egocentric, self-indulgent, and inconsiderate of others

(iii) vain and demanding

(iv) dependent, helpless, constantly seeking reassurance

(v) prone to manipulative suicidal threats, gestures, or attempts

Clearly, *DSM-III* took a nosologically advanced step by recognizing the sicker end of the hysterical continuum. Its description of a histrionic personality with dramatization, craving for activity, temper tantrums, affective shallowness, dependence, helplessness, and vulnerability to depression and suicidal attempts seemed to fit well with earlier descriptions of "hysteroid" (Easser and Lesser 1965), "infantile" (Blacker and Tupin 1977, Kernberg 1967), and "hysteriform borderline" (Abse 1974) personalities, and the so-called good hysterics (Zetzel 1968). Addition of crude seductiveness, identity conflicts, superego defects, and sadomasochistic tendencies would have made the description an outstanding one. The omission of these aspects, however, was not the major problem with *DSM-III*'s approach to the disorder. A bigger, more serious mistake of *DSM-III* was to view "histrionic personality disorder" as merely a renaming of the older, hysterical personality disorder. This most certainly was not the case, since the *DSM-III* histrionic personality disorder represented only the "more regressive pole of the hysterical-infantile continuum" (Kernberg 1984, p. 82). Such thinking is supported by the recent research (Lilienfeld et al. 1986) showing the association between histrionic and antisocial personality disorders.

In a critique of the *DSM-III* histrionic personality disorder criteria, Cooper (1987) noted the omission of sexual seductiveness, as well as the failure to distinguish between a healthier "hysterical" personality and a more "infantile" hysteric or "hysteroid" one. Citing Tupin's (1981) synthesis of earlier literature, he pointed out that the former type is ambitious, competitive, vain, coquettish, moral, labile, and expressive, while the latter is demanding, helpless, dependent, pouty, unpredictable, and communicatively unclear. Cooper (1987) stated that these are significantly different personalities and suggested that revised criteria consider them two separate disorders.

Instead, *DSM-III-R* (1987, p. 349) offered a slightly altered picture of histrionic personality disorder. It portrayed the disorder as a pervasive pattern of excessive emotionality and attention seeking, as indicated by at least four of the following:

(i) constantly seeks or demands reassurance, approval, or praise

(ii) is inappropriately sexually seductive in appearance or behavior

(iii) is overly concerned with physical attractiveness

(iv) expresses emotion with inappropriate exaggeration, e.g., embraces casual acquaintances with excessive ardor, uncontrollable sobbing on minor sentimental occasions, has temper tantrums

(v) is uncomfortable in situations in which he or she is not the center of attention

(vi) displays rapidly shifting and shallow expression of emotions

(vii) is self-centered, actions being directed toward obtaining immediate satisfaction; has no tolerance for the frustration of delayed gratification

(viii) has a style of speech that is excessively impressionistic and lacking in detail (e.g., when asked to describe mother, can be no more specific than "She was a beautiful person.")

This description deleted manipulative suicidal gestures and temper tantrums, which were included in *DSM-III.* It also added sexual seductiveness, which was excluded from *DSM-III.* An attempt was made to bridge the gap between the traditional hysterical and the newcomer histrionic categories. However, such criteria juggling failed to resolve the issue, since the *DSM-III-R* description appears to fit an intermediate level of psychopathology, leaving aside both the higher and the lower end of this continuum (Gorton and Akhtar 1990).

Unresolved Issues

In a recent publication, Kernberg (1986) has once again highlighted the differences between hysterical and histrionic ("infantile") personalities. He has also provided detailed descriptions of the two disorders in both male and female patients. Briefly, in his view, histrionic personality disorder corresponds to what was previously referred to as hysteroid (Easser and Lesser 1965), infantile (Kernberg 1967), and the Zetzel (1968) Types 3 and 4 hysterics. These patients show identity diffusion, generalized emotional lability, few sexual inhibitions, diffuse impulsivity, moral defects, primitive defense mechanisms centering on splitting, and marked mood swings. They basically show an underlying borderline personality organization "characterized by a lack of integration of the self-concept and concepts of significant others, reflected in an inability to differentiate relationships with other people and to evaluate others in depth, and the consequently inappropriate selection of sexual and marital partners" (Kernberg 1985, p. 1).

I concur with this portrayal of histrionic personality disorder. However, I want to add that its symptomatology, like those of other severe personality disorders (see Chapters 3 through 8), can be viewed as overt and covert in the realm of self-concept, interpersonal relations, social adaptation, love and sexuality, ethics, standards, and ideals, and cognitive style. Viewed in this manner, overtly the histrionic individuals are compliant and ingratiating, lively and friendly, readily interested in vocational opportunities, somewhat crudely seductive,[1] seemingly enthusiastic about moral and ethical issues, and cognitively quick and decisive. However, covertly they are riddled with feelings of inferiority, highly dependent yet narcissistically manipulative, corruptible, promiscuous, impulsive, vocationally erratic, and cognitively inattentive to details.

Histrionic personality disorder is distinct from hysterical personality disorder, which deserves to be included separately in future revisions of *DSM-III-R*. The distinctions (Blacker and Tupin 1977, Cooper 1987, Easser and Lesser 1965, Kernberg 1967, 1986, Lazare 1971, Tupin 1981, Zetzel 1968) have been commented on already. Borderline and antisocial personality disorders constitute other significant differential diagnoses for histrionic personality disorder. Both borderline and histrionic individuals are manipulative, dependent, action-oriented, inferiority-laden, corruptible, sexually promiscuous, substance abusing, and recklessly decisive. However, the borderline individual is chronically enraged, frequently vituperative, and more readily suicidal (Gunderson 1985a, Gunderson and Siever 1983), while the histrionic individual is, at least on the surface, easier to get along with, more suggestible, and less overtly self-destructive. Histrionic individuals share sexual promiscuity, corruptibility, shallowness of emotions, and a basically self-centered attitude with antisocial personalities (Kernberg 1989, Lilienfeld et al. 1986). However, they lack the sustained, calculated, and ruthless disregard of social mores and laws typically shown by antisocial personalities.

SCHIZOTYPAL PERSONALITY DISORDER

Origins

DSM-III (1980) introduced a new diagnostic entity, "schizotypal personality disorder," into the psychiatric nosology. The term

[1]Women with both hysterical and histrionic (infantile) characters seem vulnerable to involvement with married men. However, the two types of "other women" can be distinguished based upon identity consolidation, capacity for guilt, depth of object relations, and degree of sadomasochism (Akhtar 1985).

schizotype itself was indeed relatively new, having first been used by Rado in 1953 as a condensation of the two words *schizophrenic genotype*. However, the idea behind the delineation of such a syndrome had a long history. Basically, this idea was that certain nonpsychotic but eccentric and dysfunctional personalities were actually attenuated expressions of the same constitutional defect that underlay the full-blown forms of schizophrenia. In the following section, I will review the history of this idea, comment upon the *DSM-III* and *DSM-III-R* criteria for schizotypal personality disorder, and address the problems as well as the merits of recognizing this condition as a personality disorder.

Two traditions have originated the current conceptualization of schizotypal personality disorder (Kendler 1985). The first approach emanated from observations of behavioral peculiarities in nonpsychotic relatives of schizophrenics. The second grew out of the observation that some patients had all the core symptoms of schizophrenia but were not overtly psychotic. The first group of individuals were generally called "schizoid," and the second group "latent schizophrenics." Therefore, to grasp the origins of the current schizotypal concept, one would have to understand the history of both schizoid personality and latent schizophrenia.

Since I have already summarized the literature on schizoid personality elsewhere (see Chapter 5), my comments here will be brief. Bleuler (1908) coined the term *schizoid personality* to designate a morbidly exaggerated interest in one's inner life at the cost of turning away from external reality. Bleuler described such individuals as quiet, suspicious, incapable of sustained discussion, pursuers of vague interests, and comfortably dull while at the same time internally quite sensitive. Bleuler (1911) frequently observed such traits among the relatives of schizophrenics and stated that these peculiarities "are qualitatively identical with those of the patients themselves, so that the disease appears to be only a quantitative increase of the anomalies seen in the parents and siblings" (p. 238). Among those who made significant contributions to the description of schizoid personality following Bleuler were Hoch (1910), Kretschmer (1925), Kasanin and Rosen (1933), Terry and Rennie (1938), Kallman (1938), and Nanarello (1953). The portrait that emerged from their descriptions was one of a shy, introverted, cognitively peculiar, socially withdrawn, and affectively cold and asexual individual who was nonetheless deeply sensitive and hungry for affection from others. The characteristics of withdrawal, vivid internal life, and odd style of communication furthered the notion that the condition was related to schizophrenia.

Why was the term *schizotypal* needed? Perhaps, because in the 1940s and 1950s there developed an interest in the psychoanalytic study of the schizoid phenomena. This interest, more marked in British than in American psychoanalysis, both clarified and confused the issues involving the schizoid personality. On the one hand, it provided an astute understanding of the intrapsychic dynamics of the schizoid individual (Fairbairn 1940, Guntrip 1969, Klein 1946) and by extension opened up doors for psychoanalytic reconstruction of earliest infancy and its traumas. On the other hand, psychoanalysts caused the term *schizoid personality* to lose much of its salience with regard to its presumed relationship to schizophrenia. They included individuals who were less sick than those reported on by descriptive psychiatrists and used the term *schizoid* to describe simultaneously a normal infantile position and an adult psychopathology. Such dilution of the schizoid concept necessitated a redefinition of the personality type with kinship to schizophrenia. Attempts at such redefinition culminated in the schizotypal personality disorder concept of today.

The second impetus for this nosological innovation came from the clinical observations of individuals who displayed all the fundamental symptoms of schizophrenia but were not outwardly psychotic. In his original text on schizophrenia, Bleuler (1911) had in fact stated that

> latent schizophrenia . . . is the most frequent form, although admittedly these people hardly ever come for treatment. . . . In this form, we can see in *nuce* all symptoms and all the combinations of symptoms which are present in the manifest types of the disease. Irritable, odd, moody, withdrawn or exaggeratedly punctual people arouse, among other things, the suspicion of being schizophrenic. [p. 239]

Similar ideas were voiced by Zilboorg (1941, 1952), who later described individuals suffering from "ambulatory schizophrenia."

Such persons displayed (1) no florid symptoms of advanced schizophrenia, (2) an outward appearance of relative normality, (3) a hidden yet discernible tendency toward autistic thinking, (4) shallow interpersonal relationships, (5) hypochondriasis, (6) an incapacity to settle on one job or life pursuit, (7) an inner life suffused with hatred, and (8) a perverse and sadomasochistic sexual life. A less detailed, yet similar description of "latent schizophrenia" was subsequently provided by Federn (1947), who emphasized the feelings of depersonalization and estrangement in this condition. Individuals with latent schizophrenia also gave a history of having many overtly schizophrenic relatives. Two years later, Hoch and Polatin (1949) described what they termed "pseudoneurotic schizophrenia." Individuals with this problem had all the core symptoms of schizophrenia. In addition, they displayed multiple neurotic symptoms (panneurosis), much free-floating anxiety (pananxiety), and polymorphous perverse sexuality (pansexuality). Their cognitive peculiarities included concreteness, condensation, allusiveness, and overvalued ideas but no clearcut hallucinations or delusions. Many subsequent authors (Ekstein 1955, Noble 1951) popularized the notion of latent schizophrenia, and *DSM-I* (1952) included a "latent type" in the subtypes of schizophrenia.

These clinical descriptions received theoretical underpinnings from Rado's (1953) and Meehl's (1962) hypotheses regarding a "schizotypal" disorder and the later genetic studies of schizophrenia by Kety et al. (1968, 1975). Rado hypothesized that schizotypal individuals had essentially the same two constitutional defects that underlay schizophrenia. These were a deficiency in integrating pleasurable experiences and a distorted awareness of the bodily self. The manifest symptoms seen in schizotypal individuals emanated from these two defects. Basically, these symptoms were (1) chronic anhedonia and poor development of pleasurable emotions such as love, pride, joy, enthusiasm, and affection; (2) continual engulfment in emergency emotions such as fear and rage; (3) extreme sensitivity to rejection and loss of affection; (4) feelings of alienation from everything and everyone; (5) rudimentary sexual life; and (6) propensity for cognitive disorganization under stress. Rado felt that such individuals were chronically at risk for a breakdown into full-blown schizophrenia. In favorable circumstances, however, many such individuals lived their entire lives without such fragmentation.

Rado's ideas found a receptive exponent in Meehl (1962), who suggested that an integrative neural deficit ("schizotaxia") is actually what is inherited in both the schizotypal disorder and in schizophrenia proper. Meehl outlined four behavioral traits as being typical of schizotypal individuals: (1) cognitive slippage; (2) conviction of unlovability, expectation of rejection, and resultant social anxieties; (3) ambivalence; and (4) chronic anhedonia. Meehl felt that, depending on environmental stressors, an individual with such an inherited predisposition could develop full-blown schizophrenia or could exist as an odd and eccentric character.

The Danish adoptive studies of Kety, Wender, Rosenthal, and their colleagues (Kety et al. 1968, 1975, Rosenthal et al. 1968, 1971, Wender et al. 1974) further highlighted the syndrome of "borderline schizophrenia." These researchers developed the following characteristics to make this diagnosis: (1) strange, atypical thinking and oddities of communication; (2) brief episodes of cognitive disorganization, depersonalization, and micropsychosis, (3) chronic anhedonia, (4) shallow interpersonal relations and poor sexual life; and (5) multiple neurotic symptoms.

To recapitulate, two factors underlay the emergence of the contemporary schizotypal personality disorder concept: the dilution of the original schizoid concept with its strong association with schizophrenia, and the increasingly solid demonstration of a nonpsychotic schizophrenialike disorder that existed with great frequency among the relatives of schizophrenics. A third factor entered the scene around the late 1960s and early 1970s. This was the increasing popularity of the "borderline" concept. The term *borderline* was being used to designate marginal forms of schizophrenia (Kety et al. 1968, 1975), as well as a type of character organization (Kernberg 1967) or even a specific personality disorder (Gunderson and Singer 1975). It thus became necessary to further clarify which "borderlines" were related to the schizoid–schizotypal-latent schizophrenic categories and which were different. This galvanized the momentum of the aforementioned traditions and led to the emergence of "schizotypal personality disorder."

DSM-III and *DSM-III-R*

Spitzer and colleagues (1979), in the course of developing *DSM-III* criteria for personality disorders, were interested in the arena of personality disorders that were related to major psychoses. They also felt that the term *borderline* had come to be applied to both characterologically unstable and marginally schizophrenic individuals. They were especially interested in developing criteria that could identify the latter group and distinguish it from other personality disorders. They turned to the genetic studies of Kety et al. (1968, 1975) and from a review of their "borderline schizophrenic" cases developed eight criteria to discriminate a schizophrenia-related personality disorder. These eight criteria were (1) magical thinking, (2) ideas of reference, (3) social isolation, (4) recurrent illusions, (5) odd speech, (6) inadequate rapport, (7) suspiciousness, and (8) undue social anxiety. Spitzer et al. mixed this criteria set with another set they had developed for an "unstable" (later renamed "borderline") personality disorder. They then sent the resulting true–false questionnaire to 4,000 members of the American Psychiatric Association. From the statistical analysis of the results of this survey, Spitzer et al. (1979) concluded that two separate disorders existed in this realm: the borderline (which they previously called "unstable") and the schizotypal (a renaming of "borderline schizophrenia" of Kety et al.) personality disorders. It is largely from this study that the *DSM-III* outline for schizotypal personality disorder emerged. According to this outline (p. 373), the following are characteristics of the individual's current and long-term functioning, and may cause either significant impairment in social functioning or subjective distress.

A. At least four of the following:

(i) magical thinking, e.g., superstitiousness, clairvoyance, telepathy, "6th sense," "others can feel my feelings" (in children and adolescents, bizarre fantasies or preoccupations)

(ii) ideas of reference

(iii) social isolation, e.g., no close friends or confidants, social contacts limited to essential everyday tasks

(iv) recurrent illusions, sensing the presence of a force or person not actually present (e.g., "I felt as if my dead mother were in the room with me"), depersonalization, or derealization not associated with panic attacks

(v) odd speech (without loosening of associations or incoherence), e.g., speech that is digressive, vague, overelaborate, circumstantial, metaphorical

(vi) inadequate rapport in face-to-face interaction due to constricted or inappropriate affect, e.g., aloof, cold

(vii) suspiciousness or paranoid ideation

(viii) undue social anxiety or hypersensitivity to real or imagined criticism

Post-*DSM-III* studies of schizotypal personality disorder (Gunderson and Siever 1983, Kendler et al. 1981, Siever and Gunderson 1983) did support the notion of such a syndrome. However, these studies revealed that the *DSM-III* criteria of social isolation, inadequate rapport, suspiciousness, and undue social anxiety most accurately discriminate the schizotypal individuals from personality-disordered and neurotic controls. Cognitive-perceptual disturbances, in contrast, did not appear to be as salient as was originally thought. A somewhat similar result was obtained by McGlashan (1987) in a follow-up study of *DSM-III* schizotypal and borderline patients. He reported that the most characteristic *DSM-III* symptoms of schizotypal personality disorders are odd communication, suspiciousness, and social isolation, while the least discriminating criteria involved illusions, depersonalization, and derealization. (See Chapter 4 for further distinctions between borderline and schizotypal personality disorders.)

As a result of these and other similar findings (Gunderson 1984, Kendler 1985), *DSM-III-R* (pp. 341–342) presented a slightly revised description of schizotypal personality disorder:

A. A pervasive pattern of deficits in interpersonal relatedness and peculiarities of ideation, appearance, and behavior, beginning by early adulthood and present in a variety of contexts, as indicated by at least five of the following:

(i) ideas of reference (excluding delusions of reference)

(ii) excessive social anxiety, e.g., extreme discomfort in social situations involving unfamiliar people

(iii) odd beliefs or magical thinking, influencing behavior and inconsistent with subcultural norms, e.g., superstitiousness, belief in clairvoyance, telepathy, or "sixth sense," "others can feel my feelings" (in children and adolescents, bizarre fantasies or preoccupations)

(iv) unusual perceptual experiences, e.g., illusions, sensing the presence of a force or person not actually present (e.g., "I feel as if my dead mother were in the room with me")

(v) odd or eccentric behavior or appearance, e.g., unkempt, unusual mannerisms, talks to self

(vi) no close friends or confidants (or only one) other than first-degree relatives

(vii) odd speech (without loosening of associations or incoherence), e.g., speech that is impoverished, digressive, vague, or inappropriately abstract

(viii) inappropriate or constricted affect, e.g., silly, aloof, rarely reciprocates gestures or facial expressions, such as smiles or nods

(ix) suspiciousness or paranoid ideation

B. Occurrence not exclusively during the course of Schizophrenia or a Pervasive Developmental Disorder.

The changes from *DSM-III* to *DSM-III-R* are subtle but important. First, the number of criteria has been increased. Second, an item specifically listing "odd or eccentric behavior or appearance" has been included. Finally, even in those items retained from *DSM-III* there is a subtle shift toward underscoring odd behavior more than odd thinking. For instance, the earlier criterion of "magical thinking" now includes a reference to its "influencing behavior."

Unresolved Issues

From the foregoing survey of literature and the *DSM-III* and *DSM-III-R* criteria for schizotypal personality disorder, it seems clear that this concept refers to the intermingling of the most severe schizoid personalities and "the tail end of schizophrenia" (Kernberg 1984, p. 89). Insofar as such conceptualization illuminates the understudied overlap between psychoses and character pathology, it is a nosologically advanced step and is therefore welcome. However, in causing a parallel, artificial restriction of the definition of schizophrenia in *DSM-III* and *DSM-III-R,* the concept of schizotypal personality disorder poses conceptual difficulties. Moreover, these classifications show a logical inconsistency in including a schizophrenic-spectrum disorder in the personality disorder section while excluding affective-spectrum disorders (e.g., hypomanic, cyclothymic, and depressive characters) from personality disorders.

There are two ways to resolve this inconsistency: either the schizotypal disorder should be moved out of the personality disorder section or affective-spectrum disorders should also be included there. In other words, either both schizotypal and affective spectrum disorders should be classified with their "parent" disorders or both groups should be listed under personality disorders. My own preference is to include the two spectrum disorders in the personality disorder section. This should be clear from my advocacy

(Akhtar 1988) of the recognition of a hypomanic personality disorder. I believe that including depressive, cyclothymic, hypomanic, and schizotypal categories in the personality disorders will discourage the artificial separation of character pathology and major psychoses. It will also align us with our classic literature, which astutely recognized many personality disorders as "fundamental states" (Kraepelin 1921b) of psychotic disorders.

MIXED FORMS AND EXTRINSIC INFLUENCES ON SYMPTOMATOLOGY

Now that I have finished describing these two remaining severe personality disorders, it seems reasonable to make a few general remarks applicable to the entire group of eight disorders in order to round things out. Five issues immediately present themselves: (1) mixed forms, (2) level of social functioning, (3) sex-related differences, (4) changes in symptomatology over the life span, and (5) cultural influence on the phenomenology of these disorders. Comments on these issues are scattered here and there in the preceding chapters, but it seems worthwhile to bring them together in a succinct form here.

Mixed Forms

Although I have rather strenuously etched out separate phenomenological profiles for the eight severe personality disorders, clinical experience demonstrates that individual patients frequently present with features of more than one of these conditions at a time. Many other investigators have noted the occurrence of such admixture. Examples include the overlap of narcissistic and paranoid personality (Akhtar 1990a, Bursten 1973a), narcissistic and antisocial personality (Bursten 1989, Kernberg 1989, Wolman 1987), borderline and antisocial personality (Reid 1981), and schizoid and narcissistic personality (Akhtar 1987, Kohut and Wolf 1978). Such admixture does not invalidate the diagnostic profiles I have outlined. It only reminds us that these profiles are to be used as friendly guideposts and not as inviolable categories. Diagnosis of a specific personality disorder is not based on a complete exclusion of the characteristics of another disorder but on the predominance of those for the entity under consideration.

Level of Social Functioning

Any mention of severe character pathology is immediately associated, especially in the novice's mind, with markedly impaired social functioning. While often true, this is not necessarily the case. The fact is that individuals with severe personality disorders may function relatively well and, at times, even acquire social prominence and outstanding success. Narcissistic personalities, for instance, gravitate toward administrative positions of power and exhibitionistic vocations that gratify their need to be admired. They may become quite successful in these lines of work, and the constant adulation they receive from others may amply compensate for their inner despair (Kernberg 1975a). The same is true, though to a lesser extent, of hypomanic characters (Akhtar 1988, Akiskal 1984, 1986). Certain schizoid personalities become successful in solitary intellectual work, such as hard research and literary pursuits. Paranoid individuals may excel in politics and law, finding a socially acceptable expression of their inherent combativeness in these professions. Even the obviously impaired borderline may be capable of considerable artistic and literary contributions. Low social functioning and the existence of a severe personality disorder are therefore not correlated on a one-on-one basis. Factors other than character pathology determine social functioning. These include the presence of natural talents, socioeconomic background, intelligence, education, and the impact of significant extrafamilial later identifications in the form of teachers, neighbors, clergy, vocational mentors, and so on. This whole area of the relationship between the levels of character organization and social functioning, however, is ill-understood and merits further investigation.

Sex-Related Differences

Some sex-related differences seem to exist in the incidence and prevalence of these severe personality disorders. For instance, narcissistic, antisocial, and paranoid personality disorders are more common in men (Akhtar 1989a, Akhtar and Thomson 1982a, Reich 1987, Robins et al. 1984, Wolman 1987), while histrionic and borderline personality disorders occur more often in women (Akhtar et al. 1986, Reich 1987). It remains unclear, though, what such differences really represent. A multitude of factors including diagnostic biases, referral artifacts, and pathoplastic effects of gender must be ruled out before it can be declared that there are actual sex-related differences in incidence of certain personality disorders. Only then a search for deeper meaning of such findings can begin. Moreover, men and women may manifest each of these syndromes differently. In my discussion of paranoid personality (see Chapter 6), for instance, I pointed out that the subdued, brooding, and cynical picture of the disorder is more common in women, while the arrogant, litigious, and actively combative picture occurs more often in men. There might be similar sex-related differences of symptomatology in the other severe personality disorders. This too needs further investigation.

Changes in Symptomatology Over the Life Span

The diagnostic profiles proposed here, as well as those in *DSM-III-R,* refer to adult patients. However, adulthood is not static. The onset of middle age, especially, introduces newer developmental tasks (Erikson 1959, Kernberg 1980b), and this challenge may prove too difficult for individuals with already compromised ego functions. Newer symptoms may emerge and relatively established behavioral patterns may recede in the background. For instance, narcissistic patients who were promiscuous in their youth may now begin to settle down, while those who had remained inhibited so far may, for the first time, begin a life of amorous adventures (Kernberg 1980). An occasional mid-life crossover between the overt pictures of narcissistic and schizoid personalities has also been noted (Akhtar 1987). Paranoid individuals may fare better than expected (Bergman 1971, 1978), borderline individuals may become anergic and less restless (Snyder et al. 1983), and antisocial individuals may give up overt criminality (Wolman 1987) during later phases of life. All this suggests a greater phenotypal flexibility in severe personality disorders than has been suspected. Phenomenological refinements are needed, however, not only to cover the second half of life but also to map out the childhood behavioral warnings of these disorders; this work is especially crucial for the purposes of prevention and early intervention. There is some literature on early schizoid (Wolff and Chick 1980), antisocial (Robins et al. 1966), borderline (Rinsley 1980), and narcissistic (Bleiberg 1984, Kernberg 1989) phenomena, but it is far from enough.

Cultural Factors

By and large, personality disorders described here are universal in their prevalence. However, a particular culture might facilitate a particular type of phenotypal outcome of severe character pathology. In other words, it is conceivable that approximately similar inner pathology may end up manifesting as borderline in one culture and schizoid in another. It is also possible that the surface manifestations of the same personality disorder vary according to culturally provided vehicles of self-expression. For instance, I have noted (see Chapter 3) that a grandiose asceticism may be a more frequent accompaniment of narcissistic personality in the Orient and a materialistically acquisitive picture more common in the West. Further transcultural studies of personality disorders may bring other such differences to attention. Even within a culture, subcultural differences may exist. The lesser frequency with which the diagnosis of borderline personality is used among blacks in this country (Akhtar et al. 1986) is an unanswered case in point.

In conclusion, the eight severe personality disorders outlined here are not watertight compartments. Admixtures among them occur frequently, and their level of functioning depends on many factors other than the nature of psychopathology itself. Age, sex, and cultural differences seem to affect the ultimate clinical picture of these syndromes. Armed with detailed phenomenological profiles of these disorders and alerted by certain caveats, we are now ready to address ways to their amelioration.

Part III

PSYCHOTHERAPY

10

INITIAL EVALUATION AND EARLY TREATMENT DECISIONS

The wild thyme unseen, or the winter lightning
Or the waterfall, or music heard so deeply
That it is not heard at all, but you are the music
While the music lasts. These are only hints and guesses.
Hints followed by guesses: and the rest
Is prayer, observance, discipline, thought and action.

—"The Dry Salvages," T. S. Eliot

In the preceding chapters, I have reviewed and synthesized the vast literature highlighting the historical evolution, psychostructural foundations, and clinical phenomenology of severe personality disorders. My emphasis has been on other researchers' contributions and how they confirm, consolidate, and enhance each other. My own role in these essays largely has been one of an interpreter of these works. However, the final synthesis in the form of the various clinical profiles (consisting of overt and covert manifestations in six psychosocial areas) is, of course, mine.

While this most certainly has been influenced by my clinical experience, my own voice has been muted so far. From this chapter onward, the tone of my writing will shift a bit. While I will still refer to the pertinent literature, especially to Kernberg's (1984) technique of "structural interview," which has profoundly influenced me, my voice will be more personal. This is partly due to the fact that this and the following chapter deal with treatment issues, and treating patients involves personal responsibility and authenticity. Writing about such matters cannot be impersonal.

With this as the backdrop, let me briefly outline the issues I intend to address in this chapter. I will begin with a thorough discussion of the technique of initial evaluation, taking into account the six tasks that constitute this process from its beginning to its end. These are (1) responding to the first telephone call from the patient and setting up an appointment; (2) observing the patient's appearance and overall behavior, including his manner of arrival for the appointment; (3) collecting the core information; (4) establishing and protecting the therapeutic framework, (5) assessing psychological-mindedness, including the use of trial interpretations; (6) sharing the diagnostic conclusions and making treatment recommendations. The entire process takes two to three sessions of 45 to 50 minutes each, and I have found it useful to conduct these sessions on consecutive days.

Following a discussion of these six tasks, I will attempt to answer questions that frequently arise toward the end of the initial evaluation. These questions include the following: (1) Should the patient be treated at all? (2) Should the patient be treated as an outpatient or as an inpatient? (3) Should the patient be put on medications, and If so, which ones and for how long? (4) Is the patient suitable for psychoanalysis? (5) If not, what alternative psychotherapeutic strategies might be indicated and/or useful? This last question leads me to a consideration of psychoanalytic psychotherapy, which is the topic of my next chapter.

THE TECHNIQUE OF INITIAL EVALUATION

Responding to the First Phone Call

The first contact between a patient and his or her therapist almost invariably occurs via telephone. While I do not wish to overemphasize its importance, I do believe that during this contact many things can be learned, impressions formed, trends discerned, and, at times, even some help given. Yet there is little in the psychiatric or psychoanalytic literature on this dialogue. The six things I say here are largely from my own clinical experience and should therefore be taken as collegial counsel rather than as self-evident pedagogy.

First and foremost, it seems advisable to return a phone call from a potential patient only when one can spare a reasonable amount, say 15 minutes or so, of peaceful and uninterrupted time. While lengthy phone contact at this point is generally inadvisable, having the cushion of a few extra minutes comes in handy if unexpected complications begin to arise.

Second, attention should be paid to both the form and content of what the patient is saying. One might note that the patient is cryptic and reticent to give information, or conversely, is talkative and has difficulty ending the conversation. Surely no definite conclusions can be drawn from these observations, nor can the patient be immediately confronted with these. Still, these bits and pieces of information should be tucked into the back of one's mind to be used either as comparative background or as topics of specific investigation during the evaluation proper.

Case 1: While setting up an appointment via telephone, a patient asked me twice whether my office building had a name, such as the Pan Am Building, the Chrysler Building, and so on. I was intrigued by his insistence, since I had already given him the street number of my building. I also noted that both the buildings he mentioned were in New York and not in Philadelphia, where I practice. I politely repeated that my building did not have a name, keeping my sense of curiosity for later. Indeed, during my first evaluative session with him I noted that despite having an older brother, it was he who was named after his father. Upon my inquiring about it, he agreed that this was not customary but said that he had never thought about the reasons for this unusual situation. Further questioning revealed that his older brother was mildly mentally retarded. At this point, I ventured a hypothesis. Could it be that his older brother had at first been named after their father, only to be given a different name after the discovery of his retardation? The patient was moved by this suggestion and, though he did not remember hearing any such thing while growing up, began talking about his sadness about his brother and his guilt over his own

> success, which, I must say, he had impressively attempted to undermine on many occasions. As this came out, I became aware that he had unconsciously given me a clue to his problem by insisting that my building (me) have a bigger, better name than merely a number. Now I brought up our telephone conversation, thus attempting to demonstrate the workings of the unconscious to him.

What this dramatic example demonstrates is that by paying close attention to the patient's phone call, one can pick up important clues regarding his or her problem. These can be used to clarify and document the hypotheses that one begins to develop during the evaluative sessions.

Third, it is advisable to involve the patient in choosing the time for the first appointment. Asking such questions as "How urgent do you think the situation is?" or "When was it that you were planning to see me?" permits the patient to negotiate a realistically needed and feasible appointment. More importantly, allowing the patient to exercise some control subtly emphasizes the mutuality of the therapeutic undertaking and may restore, at least to a certain extent, the patient's sense of self-respect at a time of difficulty and self-doubt.

My fourth point involves the converse issue, that is, how to deal with conditions that some patients put forth on the telephone. Here, what is needed is neither undue flexibility nor dogmatic rigidity but a firm adherence to the therapeutic stance of neutrality, curiosity, and respect for the complexity of mental processes.

> *Case 2:* A young woman, while calling to make an appointment for consultation, said that she would come only if I agreed to three conditions: she would never tell me her name, she would always pay in cash, and no records of any sort could be kept on her by me. I responded by saying: "I cannot accept these conditions, but I cannot reject them either. In other words, I am not saying 'yes,' nor am I saying 'no' to what you are asking of me. I am certain that you are asking for something profoundly important, but since I do not truly understand what it is, I cannot jump into quick actions. Now, if you can tolerate my insistence on understanding before action, I will be glad to discuss when we might get together."

The important thing is neither to lose one's therapeutic stance under the sway of being helpful nor close the door to patients who, for reasons often beyond their control, are compelled to be demanding.

Fifth, it is considerate to inform the patient right away of any constraints from one's own side. For instance, if one does not have time to take a new patient, it is wise to let the patient know that on the phone rather than during or after the initial consultation. This allows the patient either to seek consultation with someone else or to be narcissistically prepared for being referred elsewhere after the consultation. Similarly, when someone calls for an appointment when one is about to leave town for a while, it seems reasonable either not to begin a consultation before the break or to let the patient know of the upcoming interruption in one's schedule. Such forthrightness will prevent feelings of betrayal and may preclude more serious complications in truly regressed, chaotic, and needy patients.

Finally, one should give clear and specific directions about the location of one's office to patients and not assume that they know their way around. At times, patients' lateness for their first appointment is reflective more of the vague directions given them than of their inner resistances, fantasies, and enactments. Of course, at other times, the story is different. This brings me to my next point.

Observing the Patient's Appearance, Behavior, and Manner of Arrival

Like an experienced internist who observes his patient's skin color, gait, speech, scars, congenital anomalies, and so on, before a formal physical examination, we can begin making observations before the formal interview. I have already mentioned the informative potential of the first phone contact in this regard. A second area pertains to the appearance and overall behavior of the patient, including his manner of arrival for the initial evaluation. There are many things to be noted here: Is the patient appropriately dressed? How is his personal hygiene? Are there any outstanding mannerisms, scars, or tattoos? Does he look angry, sad, happy, nervous? Also, does he come on time? Does he arrive late or, conversely, too early? Or does the patient come at a completely different time than was agreed upon? Why?

Case 3: After having waited for a young woman who had sought a consultation with me for about 20 minutes, I received a frantic phone call from her. She was looking for my office in a building five blocks away. Where did I say my office was? When I repeated my address, she realized her "mistake" and wanted to know if she could still come over for her appointment. Thinking that not much time would be left by the time she arrived, I offered her an appointment on a subsequent day. She apologized for her "mistake" and accepted my offer.

On the day before her second appointment, I came out of my office after the last patient of the day had left to find her sitting in my waiting room. She was enraged and said that she felt very humiliated by my having "abused" her in this fashion! Puzzled, I asked what it was that she felt I had done to her. She responded by saying that I had kept her waiting for an entire hour while seeing another patient. It took her a few minutes to realize that she had come a day earlier than her scheduled appointment!

Now, there were these two enactments even before we "began" a consultation. First, she went to the wrong building and was frantically looking for me. Second, she came at the wrong time and felt "abused" by me. I kept these in mind and decided to see what in our "third" encounter (i.e., our first formal interview) might shed light on the communications contained in these enactments. (Besides, of course, I noted the propensity toward acting out, resistance, sadomasochism, and use of paranoid defenses.)

In her subsequent appointment, for which she arrived punctually, she told me that her main difficulty was constant anger at men, sexual disinterest, and depressive mood swings with occasional suicidal thoughts. She revealed that her father, to whom she was very attached, had abruptly left the family when she was 5 years old. She never saw him afterwards and was always "searching" for him. When she was 8 years old, her mother remarried. Her stepfather sexually abused her until she was 13 years old. At this time, the patient herself arranged to start living with an aunt. As this material came out, I brought to her attention that her frantically searching for me the first time and feeling "abused" by me the second time were perhaps her ways of putting me in the place of her real father and stepfather, respectively. Until the time I was in either position, I added, she could not relate to me. Perhaps she needed a third chance, a new experience. The patient began to cry and, after composing herself, revealed more details of a successful but anguished life.

The point I am trying to make here is that enactments as gross as those mentioned above cannot be ignored. They must be thought about and brought into the initial evaluation for discussion. Vigilance combined with tact is the key here.

There are other things to observe about the patient's arrival. For instance, the arrival of an adult patient (who is not psychotic or organically impaired, or is not a fresh immigrant) in the company of a relative or friend should raise question in the consultant's mind. Is there ego impairment here? Paranoia? Separation anxiety? Some phobia? Enactment of some unconscious fantasy? Such behavior could reflect any of these or might imply something completely different. The point is to observe it, consider it data. Similarly, the observation that the patient arrives carrying too many things should be silently registered. It may lead to something or it may not, but it cannot simply be ignored. Finally, our own very first feelings about the patient should be jotted down in the back of our minds for further private exploration. This may yield significant information about either or both parties in the transactional dyad of a consultation.

Collecting the Core Information

In agreement with Kernberg's (1984) recommendations for a "structural interview," I combine a thorough exploration of the presenting symptomatology with an investigation of the level of the underlying character organization. I too make simple clarifications and interpretations as the interview proceeds and observe the patient's response to these in order to assess his intelligence, flexibility, capacity for therapeutic alliance, psychological-mindedness, and level of character organization. Somewhat differently from Kernberg, though to a certain extent as a matter of style, I conceive of collecting the information, necessary for arriving at a descriptive diagnosis and a dynamic formulation, as occurring in three steps.

The first step consists of a relatively straightforward exploration of the patient's presenting symptoms. Kernberg (1984) recommends that such inquiry might begin with a statement like: "I am interested to hear what brought you here, what is the nature of your difficulties or problems, what you expect from treatment, and where you are now in this regard" (p. 31). While such an opening may be well utilized by relatively sophisticated, "experienced," and intelligent patients, it may appear too comprehensive, even intimidating, to others who are anxious and unclear about their purpose for psychiatric consultation. It may be preferable to begin with a more modest question, for example, "What seems to be the problem that has led you to coming here?" This would lead the patient to describe his or her predominant difficulties. The interviewer, after listening patiently for 5 to 10 minutes, should summarize for the patient the main symptoms and, in doing so, organize the relevant clusters of complaints. For instance, the interviewer might say: "From what you have told me so far, it seems that you are experiencing three main difficulties: first, depression, including crying spells, hopelessness, and occasional suicidal thoughts; second, an increasing alienation with your family involving disagreements about your boyfriend and your place of residence; and third, some confusion about whether you wish to continue your education or drop out from school altogether." Such an intervention helps the patient organize his or her thinking, demonstrates to the patient that the therapist has already begun his work, and, by providing identifiable categories to the often diffuse distress, gives the patient an intellectual handle on it. It might limit the patient's freedom somewhat, but this can be rectified by asking open-ended questions pertaining to what one might have missed somewhat later in the interview.

Once the patient's main symptoms are identified, more detailed investigation of each should follow. Continuing with the abovementioned example of the woman patient with depression, family disputes, and indecision about career goals, the interviewer might now ask her to elaborate about each of the three areas separately and in somewhat greater detail. The account now provided by the patient might be fleshed out further by the interviewer's asking more direct questions, preventing the patient from becoming too tangential, and exploring the presence or absence of secondary and related symptoms. In the case of depression, for instance, these might include excessive drinking, suicidal ideation, incapacity for caring for children, and manic episodes. As the details of each symptom cluster is becoming clear, the interviewer might begin thinking about the possible connections between the various clusters. However, it is preferable to keep such rudimentary hypotheses to oneself at this time and proceed to the next step.

The second step involves the assessment of character organization. It should be noted here that the presence of a psychotic condition or organic brain syndrome forces the interview in the direction of a traditional psychiatric history taking (Kernberg 1984) and by and large eliminates this second step, whose main purpose is to distinguish between a neurotic and borderline level of personality organization. The main distinguishing features between these two groups pertain to the degree of identity consolidation and the nature of defensive operations (Kernberg 1970, 1975a, 1980b). In the neurotic character organization, there is a well-established identity and the defenses center on repression, while in the borderline organization there is identity diffusion (see Chapter 2 for its detailed phenomenology) and a predominance of splitting and related defenses over repression (Akhtar and Byrne 1983, Kernberg 1967, 1975a, 1976, Volkan 1976). The assessment of these two features is, therefore, of crucial importance in arriving at a meaningful characterological diagnosis. How is this to be done? What are the clinical markers of identity diffusion and splitting? How can they be elicited?

The features of identity diffusion include markedly contradictory character traits, temporal discontinuity in the self-experience, feelings of emptiness, gender dysphoria, subtle body-image disturbances, and inordinate ethnic and moral relativism (Akhtar 1984). Not all of these features can be elicited and explored to an equal degree through formal questioning. Some (e.g., feelings of emptiness) are more evident in the patient's complaints, while others (e.g., temporal discontinuity in the self-experience) become clear only through obtaining a longitudinal account of the patient's life. Still other features (e.g., subtle disturbances of gender identity) are discernible, at least in the beginning, mainly through the overall manner of the patient's relating to the interviewer. Yet it is almost always helpful to ask the patient to describe himself or herself. One might say something like this: "Well, now that you have told me about your difficulties and we have talked about them for a while, can you please describe yourself as a person?" In the description offered, one should look for consistency versus contradiction; clarity versus confusion; solidity versus emptiness; well-developed and comfortably experienced masculinity or femininity versus gender confusion and dysphoria; and a sense of ethnicity, inner morality, and belonging to a group versus the lack of any historical or communal anchor. However, if the patient is unable to provide a coherent self-description, this should not be automatically construed as showing identity diffusion. This could be due to anxiety, lack of psychological-mindedness, cultural factors, poor verbal skills, or low intelligence. These factors should be ruled out before making a conclusion regarding the presence or absence of identity diffusion. Moreover, a less than forthcoming patient is often helped in this regard by a piecemeal inquiry. For instance, the interviewer might ask about the patient's religious beliefs, practices, and their continuity with what was handed down to him during childhood; feelings of ethnicity and of belonging to a certain regional or communal group; continuity with friends and associates from earlier periods of life; clarity and stability of vocational goals; various sublimations and hobbies; legal record; drug use and drinking, and so on. He may then surmise about the patient's identity based on the information gathered. A patient might not be able to describe himself well, yet may turn out to possess a consolidated identity. Conversely, one might come across in a patient

> peripheral areas of self-experience that are contradictory to a well-integrated, central area of subjective experience, peripheral areas that the patient experiences as ego-alien or ego-dystonic, not fitting into his otherwise integrated picture of himself. These isolated areas may be an important source of intrapsychic conflict or interpersonal difficulties but should not be equated with identity diffusion. [Kernberg 1984, p. 37]

Next is the issue of splitting. Here too the interviewer would benefit from keeping in mind the various clinical manifestations (Akhtar and Byrne 1983) associated with extensive use of this defense: inability to tolerate much ambivalence, intensification of affects, impairment of the decision-making process, ego-syntonic impulsivity, and marked oscillations of self-esteem. Unlike the compromise-formation tendency typical of those with higher order defenses, the individual using splitting as the predominant defense tends to have an all-or-nothing approach to life. He sees good and bad as mutually exclusive, is either overly controlled or loses all control, attacks the entire problem or avoids it altogether, and has a tendency toward "now or never; murderous rage or total denial of anger; either my way or your way; either this way or not at all" (Schulz 1980, p. 184).

In the interview situation, the patient's verbal productions, as well as his overall attitudes (toward others and the interviewer), give hints toward the existence, or more accurately the predominance, of splitting. Confronting the patient with contradictions in the information provided by him and seeing his response also helps discern the tendency toward splitting. It may help distinguish borderline from potentially psychotic levels of organization (Kernberg 1984). Demonstrating such contradictions to the patient leads in the former instance to anxiety and awkwardness coupled with recognition of contradictions and a temporarily improved observing ego. In the latter, however, such confrontation leads to a greater tenacity of compartmentalizations and the production of increasingly odd "logic" to defend their validity. Once some assessment of identity diffusion and splitting has been made, the interviewer can begin to put together his earlier notions about the dynamics of the patient's symptomatology and his beginning ideas about the level of the patient's character organization. Such telescoping of the two sets of inferences would lead to a deeper appreciation of the nature and meaning of the patient's difficulties.

The third step involves obtaining a family history (including the prevalence of major psychiatric disorders, suicide, and addictions) and a brief chronological account of the patient's life. This provides a gross, somewhat defensively altered, but nonetheless useful first version of what things were like in the formative years of the patient's life. While exceptions exist, hereditary predisposition to major mental illness and the existence of severe, unmitigated, major, and sustained trauma in early childhood are usually associated with severe personality disorders. Individuals with higher levels of character organization usually do not give histories of such traumatic events in early childhood. Taking the family history helps in another way. The existence of certain features in the patient's descriptions of family members suggests splitting, primitive object relations, and hence a lower level of character organization. These features include (1) an emphasis on one's own feelings and views about the person one is describing rather than on that person's independent attributes (e.g., "I do not like my husband," or "I love my wife" versus "My husband is a 33-year-old attorney who . . ." or "My wife is from the Midwest and . . ."); (2) an extreme and affectively charged verdict rather than a balanced account that permits mixed feelings (e.g., "She is wonderful," or "He is a son of a bitch" versus "My father is a hard-working, decent man but somewhat awkward and . . ." or "My wife is a generally unpleasant, irritable, and miserable person, but she is a talented pianist and a remarkable cook . . ."); and (3) an inability to see motivations in others independent of their feelings about oneself (e.g., "My wife does not keep up her appearance because she knows it hurts me and of course she does not love me" versus "She does so because she comes from a poor family"). The main thing here is not that the patient's "explanations" are actually correct, only that they show an ability to consider that others may have reasons of their own.

The last piece of information to be gathered is a brief chronological account of the patient's life. This can reveal recurrent patterns that may give further support to the dynamics being suspected. When such patterns begin to emerge, the interviewer should make remarks that highlight their existence and invite the patient to say what he thinks about them. With this, the interviewer has finished collecting information about (1) the presenting symptoms, (2) the character organization, and (3) the patient's family background and life up to the current time. Putting these three together helps him consolidate his dynamic formulation, and he may now share this hypothesis with the patient. However, before discussing this last step of the evaluation, I will digress a bit and discuss two other important tasks that are part and parcel of a comprehensive initial evaluation. The first is safeguarding the therapeutic framework; the second is assessing psychological-mindedness. These tasks actually go on concurrently with collecting the core information. Discussing them separately is merely for didactic ease.

Safeguarding the Therapeutic Framewor

Another important task during the initial interview, besides collecting information in the manner outlined above, is to establish, maintain, and protect the therapeutic framework. A patient's naivete and/or psychopathology often exert a pull on the interviewer's work ego in this regard. No hard-and-fast rules exist for dealing with complex situations that may unexpectedly arise during an initial evaluation. However, a useful guideline is that a temporary giving up of one's neutral stance is almost always preferable over risking harm to the patient or oneself, carrying on an interview under bizarre circumstances, and colluding with someone's pathological agenda. Let me give a few examples of such situations and their technical handling.

A minor, though frequent and tricky, situation is when a patient asks for permission to smoke. In such a situation the therapist might respond with something like "No, you may not smoke a cigarette. If you wish, I will gladly explain the reasons for my stance." If the patient takes one up on this offer, one might say that "for the kind of work we have undertaken today, some degree of tension is necessary. Anxiety is the fuel of our work and your smoking, by diminishing it, will render our work pale." Depending on the degree of the patient's psychological-mindedness and the affective tone prevailing in the interview, one might invite the patient to be curious about the timing of this request. On the other hand, if such a request is made by a patient who is truly panicked, becoming psychotic in front of one's eyes, one might permit him or her to smoke.

A more serious situation is when a patient refuses to give identifying information about himself or herself, while insisting on talking about his or her problems and receiving help. Two examples, with notably different outcomes, follow.

Case 4: Within the first few minutes of his consultation with me, a middle-aged man revealed that what he had told me was not his true name. I asked him his reasons for having hidden his name from me as well as for acknowledging this lie to me. He explained, quite convincingly, that he could not tell me his name because he was involved in a certain covert operation of the government and could not risk revealing his name to someone he did not know well and could not yet trust fully. At the same time, he felt bad about telling me a lie while seeking help from me. As we talked further, it became clear that despite his narcissistic and antisocial tendencies, he was desperately attempting to relate honestly to me. I told him that I agreed that there was no reason for him to trust me automatically. However, I went on to ask if he could conceptualize telling me his true name if, with the passage of time, he could trust me more. "Of course," he replied. With this, we proceeded to explore issues that were troubling him and had led to his setting up an appointment with me. As a footnote, I might add that the patient did subsequently reveal his real name and turned out to be quite treatable in psychotherapy.

Case 5: As I began the evaluation by asking for some basic identifying information, a middle-aged man refused to give me his address. I asked him his reasons for such secrecy. He said that he worked as a live-in chauffeur cum butler for an extremely wealthy older couple who prohibited him from revealing their address to anyone. The most he could tell me, he said, was that he lived in such-and-such part of the city. In the next breath, he began talking about the problems for which he was seeking help from me. I interrupted him and asked if he noted that there was a contradiction in his not trusting me with his address and his readiness to reveal his innermost anxieties to me. He dodged my question, again offering the reality excuse for withholding his address. Not convinced, yet willing to be flexible, I asked for his phone number so that I would at least have some way of reaching him should the need arise. The patient refused to tell me this too, offering the same reason. Upon my insistence, he finally did tell me his phone number. Now, as it happens, I immediately realized that the phone number he had given me was for an entirely different part of the city. I put down my yellow pad, looked at him, and confronted him with his giving me false information. He apologized profusely and said that from now on he would tell me everything truly. As if to prove his earnestness, he revealed that even the name that he had given me was actually not his true name. He now told me a different name and offered to tell me his address and phone number as well. However, in view of what had transpired so far, I had no way of knowing that what he was about to tell me was the truth. I decided to take a firm stance and check out things for myself. I asked him to show me his driver's license so that I could make sure that he was not telling me another lie. He blushed and refused to show me his driver's license; it was obvious that even this second name was not real. As his refusal persisted, I felt that there was no point in our continuing this dialogue and I would have to call this session off. And I did.

Although the outcome was different in these two cases, the technical stance was essentially the same. Maintaining curiosity, showing flexibility, insisting on honesty, confronting pathological defenses, appealing to the healthy sector of the patient's personality, and setting firm limits characterized the technique with both cases. The second patient was lost because of his greater severity of superego defect and lack of a healthy ego to form a therapeutic alliance. To continue the interview in the face of such outstanding lies would have been of little use, since all subsequent information would be suspect. Terminating the interview seemed the best measure.

Similarly, if a patient reveals a definite suicidal plan during the evaluative interview, active measures, often at the cost of aborting the interview proper, need to be taken to prevent such occurrence.

Case 6: A tall, attractive college student in her twenties revealed within a few moments of beginning her first interview with me that she was going to blow her head off that evening. She had already bought a gun and bullets. There was no point in our conducting this interview, she said. I told her that I agreed with her. There was no point in talking further; what needed to be done was for her to be hospitalized, the gun to be immediately removed from her possession, and her situation to be evaluated thoroughly, including the indication of her being put on antidepressant medications. I asked her for her room keys and the phone number of a trusted friend or relative so that I could arrange for the gun to be removed; meanwhile, I myself would begin arranging for her hospitalization. When she protested my firm and active stance, I explained to her that clearly she had run out of ability to protect her life and had sought me out to be the temporary custodian of this function for her. Therefore, I had to act on her behalf. After some further back and forth, she permitted me to proceed with my treatment plan.

All these vignettes attempt to convey one major point: the fundamentally therapeutic nature of our work must be safeguarded despite the patient's attempts to challenge and distort it. Minor transgressions, such as smoking, major attacks on the setting, such as marked lateness or deliberate lying, and life-threatening situations should all be met with a basically similar attitude of curiosity, flexibility, firmness, and refusal to collude, an effort to protect the patient and ourselves, and an attempt to pave the way for further therapeutic intervention.

Assessing Psychological-Mindedness

Since greater psychological-mindedness is usually associated with the favorable outcome of psychoanalysis, psychoanalytic psychotherapy, and even insight-oriented group therapy (Abramowitz and Abramowitz 1974, Coltart 1988, Ryan and Cicchetti 1985), its assessment constitutes an important task during the initial evaluation. But what is psychological-mindedness? A quick survey of the literature reveals that different people mean different things by it or at least emphasize different aspects. Reiser (1971), for instance, delineated three components of psychological-mindedness. These were (1) sensitivity to symbolic meanings and to situational resemblances between life events in historical context, (2) empathy for people, particularly for their affective experiences, and (3) interest and curiosity about human behavior and the motives that underlie it. Reiser emphasized that psychological-mindedness, in contrast to curiosity, is inwardly directed. It is more passive, reflective, and receptive than curiosity, which is driving and compelling. Following Reiser, Lower, Escoll, and Huxster (1972) described psychological-mindedness as including "a capacity for insight, introspection, intuition, verbality, remembering dreams and fantasies, awareness of transference, of internal conflict; sensitivity to own feelings and curiosity about drives" (p. 615). Appelbaum (1973) noted that such words and phrases as *reflectiveness, insightfulness, capacity for introspection, psychological grasp* (Loewenstein, quoted in Joseph 1967), *self-awareness,* and *capacity for self-observation* were often used interchangeably with *psychological-mindedness.* In an attempt to clarify the usage and practical application of this term, Appelbaum proposed the following definition: "A person's ability to see relationships among thoughts, feelings, and actions, with the goal of learning the meanings and causes of his experience and behavior" (p. 36). He noted that psychologically minded individuals show interest in the way minds work, capacity for concern, and ability to allow emotions their rightful place. He distinguished such psychological interest for purposes of understanding oneself and others from the intellectualized, exhibitionistic, merely playful, or self-condemnatory uses of introspection. Subsequent to Appelbaum's contribution, Werman (1979) noted that psychological-mindedness is evident not only in one's capacity for self-observation but also in one's view of the external world. Exploration of this latter aspect, however, is often neglected in the assessment of a patient's psychological-mindedness. Werman observed that the inability to accept chance occurrences and intolerance of ambiguity in the external world are often the outward manifestations of poor psychological-mindedness. The ability to believe in chance and to tolerate ambiguity interestingly are consequences of the development of secondary-process thinking and may be regarded as specialized aspects of reality testing.

While the papers by Reiser (1971), Lower et al. (1972), Appelbaum (1973), and Werman (1979) contain many "clinical pearls," it is Coltart (1988) who, to the best of my knowledge, has provided the most detailed guidelines about the assessment of psychological-mindedness in the diagnostic interview. Though acknowledging that the whole is often greater than the sum of its parts, she outlines nine points "in an approximate order of discovery, rather than importance, under two headings" (p. 819): the history, and developments in the interview arising from the history. Under the first heading, Coltart suggests that the diagnostician should look for

> 1. The capacity to give a history which deepens, acquires more coherence, and becomes textually more substantial as it goes on. . . . 2. The capacity to give such a history without much prompting, and a history which gives the listener an increasing awareness that the patient feels currently related in himself, to his own story; properly—if unhappily—the product of the connective aetiology of his life's circumstances . . . [and] 3. The capacity to bring up memories with appropriate affects. [p. 819]

Under the second heading, Coltart includes the following:

> 4. Some awareness in the patient that he has an unconscious mental life. . . . 5. Some capacity to step back, if only momentarily, from self-experience, and to observe it reflectively—either spontaneously, or with the help of a simple interpretation from the assessor, who should make opportunity for this sort of intervention. . . . 6. A capacity, or more strongly a wish, to accept and handle increased responsibility for the self. . . . 7. Imagination. . . . 8. Some capacity for achievement, and some realistic self-esteem. . . . 9. Overall impression . . . something deeply recognizable, but ultimately not fully definable, about the assessor's experience of a thorough, intense, working consultation with a psychologically minded person. [pp. 819–820]

I am in agreement with Coltart. However, I think that she becomes a bit overinclusive in listing capacity for achievement under psychological-mindedness. On the other hand, she does not include some other ways to assess the patient's psychological-mindedness. For instance, a patient who reveals having kept an ongoing journal displays a capacity for reflectiveness, a wish for psychic dialogue, and a respect for mental life. The same applies to a patient who spontaneously offers a dream during the initial evaluation. This is especially significant if the patient is not in the mental health field and thus is not biased in that direction. Yet another evidence of psychological-mindedness is the patient's spontaneous offering of a genetic explanation of either his or her own or someone else's behavior.

To summarize, it seems that psychological-mindedness is best assessed by observing the following things: (1) *a capacity for reflective self-observation* as evidenced by the patient's giving a coherent and affectively resonant history as well as by his or her ability to be aware (or become aware during the assessment interview) of internal conflicts; (2) *an interest in one's mental life* as evidenced by a history of having kept journals, and by spontaneously mentioning dreams and fantasies in the initial interview; (3) *a belief in psychic causality* as evidenced by the patient's offering a genetic explanation of his or her own or another's behavior and by his or her capacity to entertain mental basis for certain accidents, onset of a physical illness, and so on; (4) paradoxically, *an ability to accept ambiguity and chance occurrences in the external reality* without feeling compelled to explain everything; and (5) *a readiness to see symbolic meanings* and enter into a metaphorical dialogue as evidenced by a positive, even welcoming, response to a trial interpretation.

This last point cannot be overemphasized. I have already given two examples demonstrating the use of such interpretations (Cases 1 and 3 above). Here I will include one more example.

> *Case 7:* As he entered my office for his first evaluative session, a well-dressed businessman in his mid-fifties quipped half-jokingly about the unclear reasons of his having brought an umbrella on a bright, sunny day. I responded by saying that perhaps we will discover these too during our conversation. He dropped the subject, however, and went on to describe the problems that had led him to call me. These included vague feelings of depression, gastrointestinal symptoms for which no clear explanation had been found, and sleeplessness. After having talked about these for a while, he told me that these actually were the least of his problems. His real problem was profoundly shame-laden and a secret from everyone, including his wife, to whom he appeared otherwise devoted. With some encouragement, he went on to reveal a complex sexual perversion. Although it was difficult for him to talk about it, he felt relieved having unburdened himself. At a point when he was expressing his deep shame in revealing his perversion, I said: "I wonder if you brought an umbrella to protect yourself from the shower of criticism you feared will fall upon you as you reveal this matter." He laughed in a most congenial way and added that, in his commenting on the sunny day, he was also showing his certainty that such a "shower" would not occur, that is, I would not criticize him. (The point is not that my comment was "correct" but that it alluded metaphorically to his defenses and tapped, successfully, on his capacity to see symbolic meanings. Of course, if he had looked at me askance, had failed to see the playful allusion, it would have shown a poorer psychological-mindedness.)

Two caveats are in order here: First, the presence of only one factor should not lead to the estimation of psychological-mindedness; all five evidences outlined above should be considered. Two, an attempt should be made to distinguish an actual deficiency in psychological-mindedness from its compromise out of the anxiety of the interview situation. Supportive, empathic remarks may diminish the anxiety and improve psychological-mindedness in the latter but not in the former instance.

Sharing Diagnostic Conclusions and Recommending Treatment

The initial evaluation enters its terminal phase once the core information has been gathered, a working hypothesis about the nature of the patient's suffering has been developed, and the patient's psychological-mindedness has been assessed. At this point, the interviewer should inform the patient that his diagnostic evaluation is over and share his conclusions with the patient in simple, jargon-free language. He might include in his comments hints of how he arrived at his conclusions. Quoting something the patient had said, recounting a particular emotional outburst, reminding the patient of a slip of tongue, and so on, enhance the patient's sense of participation and mutuality even at this phase. This, in turn, facilitates the patient's receptivity to the information being given.

Two other things should be kept in mind: One, it might be useful, besides being true, to preface one's comments with the caveat that conclusions arrived at in one to three sessions are necessarily a bit tentative. The interviewer might also indicate at this time the need for further investigations of a social (i.e., family interview), psychometric, or laboratory kind, if he thinks that these might help to clarify the situation. Two, while using ordinary language is preferable, there is no reason to be wishy-washy or apologetic if a patient asks for a specific psychiatric diagnosis. Exploring the patient's reasons for asking this might reveal further, significant information. However, such exploration should not be used as delay tactics, and a patient who wants to know his diagnosis should be told. Much is made of a patient's misunderstanding diagnostic terminology or being narcissistically injured by it. What is overlooked is that the interviewer's cryptic attitude, fudging, and uncomfortable avoidance too can have alienating and adverse effects on the patient.

Following the discussion of the nature of the patient's problems, the focus should shift to issues of its treatment. The interviewer should now inform the patient of what he thinks is the ideal treatment for the patient's malady, explaining, especially if asked, the reasons for this recommendation. The patient should also be informed, especially if things are unclear, of alternate approaches to treating the condition involved. Questions raised by the patient should be answered factually, and the interviewer should not derail or mystify the patient by "interpreting" the reasons behind such questions. For instance, the patient may frequently ask about the difference between psychoanalysis and psychotherapy. Subtle controversies in the field notwithstanding, it is possible to answer this question in a simple, straightforward way. One might explain the difference not only in terms of frequency of visits and the use of couch but, to a certain extent, in terms of the nature of the patient's expected role and the therapist's stance vis-à-vis the patient's report of his thoughts, feelings, fantasies, and dreams.

Once the treatment strategy has been discussed, the interviewer should explore with the patient the feasibility of carrying out such treatment. A quick survey of the patient's daily schedule, financial resources, geographical stability, ease of arriving at the therapist's office, and so on, should be undertaken at this point. Equipped with this information, the interviewer can fine-tune his recommendations. At this point, based on the nature of the treatment modality selected and/or the various factors in the patient's external reality, either a referral elsewhere might become necessary or one may elect to treat the patient oneself. In the latter instance, it is my own practice to give the patient some further time, say one to two weeks, to mull over what has transpired in the consultation, what has been recommended, and what treatment plan has been agreed upon. After this interval, I meet with the patient to discuss further business arrangements (schedule of appointments, fees, methods of emergency communication, etc.), as well as to explain what is expected of him or her in order for our work to be optimally helpful.

FREQUENT QUESTIONS AT THE END OF EVALUATION

There are certain questions that frequently arise as one nears the end of the diagnostic part of the initial consultation. If the interview has been conducted carefully, these questions should be easily answerable by the interviewer. Formulating the answers in one's mind is essential before proceeding to the last step (sharing diagnostic conclusions and recommending treatment) of the initial consultation. These questions include the following:

Should the Patient Be Treated at All?

Certain realistic conditions must be met before one agrees to treat a patient in intensive psychotherapy or psychoanalysis. Some certainty of sustained financial resources, for instance, is necessary. Another requirement is the patient's willingness and ability to regularly attend the required number of sessions per week. The patient's residing within a reasonable distance of the therapist's office is therefore helpful. In the absence of these basic requirements of money, attendance, and ease of travel, it is preferable not to accept the patient for treatment. A patient who lives a long distance from the therapist's office may at times make earnest promises to maintain regular attendance for the sessions. In general, this should not be acceptable. Such resolve, well-meaning though it might be in the beginning, is soon eroded by bad weather, traffic difficulties, and, more importantly, the emergence of negative transference and resistance during treatment. Rather than accepting such a patient for treatment, the therapist should encourage him or her to seek help at a geographically more reasonable locale. Even in those rare situations in which such help is truly not available nearby, the patient should be offered psychotherapeutic help on an emergency basis only instead of being accepted in an ongoing regular treatment conducted far away in a less than optimal fashion. On the other hand, one must be willing to reconsider the treatment strategy should there be a change in the patient's residential status.

Yet another situation that should preclude the patient's being accepted for intensive treatment is when there is a move in the near future. It may be worthwhile to explore with the patient the conflict underlying this pattern of seeking help while planning to leave town. This may identify for the patient hitherto unrecognized anxieties regarding intimacy and distance (Akhtar 1990b, 1992, Bouvet 1958, Escoll 1992, Mahler 1970, Melges and Swartz 1989). While this information might become a useful nidus for future treatment, the temptation to start a brief but "deep" treatment while the patient is leaving in a few weeks or months must be resisted.

Besides such difficulties in external reality, there are internal factors that should alert the therapist about accepting the patient for intensive psychotherapeutic intervention. Pronounced antisocial tendencies are almost always a contraindication to in-depth treatment (Kernberg 1984). A markedly deficient capacity for verbal communication, regardless of its etiology, also precludes such intervention. Low intelligence levels do the same. Prominent secondary gains from the illness, excessive drinking, drug abuse, refusal to attend sessions as recommended, and relentless sadomasochistic acting out constitute relative contraindications. However, with a firm initial contract (Kernberg et al. 1990, Selzer et al. 1987) and the concurrent development of adjunctive treatment measures (e.g., medications, Alcoholics Anonymous, or hospitalization) it may be possible to engage some of these patients in a meaningful, long-term treatment.

A less frequent situation in which the recommendation of no treatment is valid applies to a patient who is truly not sick enough, was misguidedly referred to a psychiatrist, or is well on the way to a spontaneous recovery from a transient disturbance in psychic homeostasis. More often, it turns out that the recommendation is actually no further treatment, since the process of initial evaluation has itself been therapeutic enough.

Should the Patient Be Treated as an Outpatient or as an Inpatient?

Another important early decision pertains to treating the patient as an outpatient or as an inpatient. A pivotal consideration here is that of associated psychosis. Individuals with severe personality disorders often seek help during transient psychotic regressions. These may be drug-related or stress-induced. The symptomatology of such psychoses may be schizophreniform, affective, or like an organic brain syndrome. The treatment of such psychotic symptomatology takes precedence over that of the underlying personality disorder (Kernberg 1984) and raises the question of hospitalization. The presence of psychosis in the setting of limited social supports (to monitor treatment and to prevent major mishaps during this period of impaired reality testing) generally indicates the need for hospitalization. If the psychotic symptoms are mild, ample social networks exist, and the patient is willing to comply with the recommended psychotropic regime, then hospitalization may be avoided.

An assessment of suicidal risk is also necessary in considering hospitalization. If the patient is suicidal, then the decision is clearly in favor of hospitalization (voluntary or involuntary). If the patient is not suicidal, then the treatment can be conducted on an outpatient basis. However, a clinical challenge is posed by situations in which the therapist feels unclear about the extent of suicidal risk. Here, it is helpful to remember that there are five *D*s (*drinking, drug* abuse, severe *depression,* presence of physical *disease* or deformity, and a *disorganized* social life leading to anomie and isolation) that almost always speak for a problematic outcome. When a dubiously suicidal patient displays even two or three of these symptoms, it is preferable to err on the side of caution and choose hospitalization. At the same time, the extent to which the patient has been honest during the evaluation should be considered. That the patient is dishonest is often revealed by (1) a history of withholding information from previous therapists, (2) a history or record of legal offenses, (3) evidence of breaking moral commitments (e.g., an honor code violation on campus or an extramarital affair), (4) gross discrepancies in the historical account provided by the patient and others, (5) the patient's not acknowledging anything about himself that will put him in a somewhat socially negative light. If any of these indicators of dishonesty exist, then the patient's information about his suicidal intent cannot be relied on (Kernberg 1984). Under such circumstances, it is preferable to hospitalize him for further evaluation. If the patient refuses voluntary admission, the therapist must initiate involuntary commitment. If this is not granted due to the way in which the pertinent laws are interpreted in a given community, at least the therapist would have tried in good faith to implement what seemed the best treatment option. Such caution and integrity would not only protect the therapist legally, they would minimize his anxiety in assessing alternative ways of managing the situation.

Finally, as Kernberg (1984) emphasizes, distinction should be made between the objectives for short-term and long-term hospitalization for individuals with severe personality disorders. Short-term hospitalization is indicated for averting suicide risk, controlling psychotic symptoms, doing a comprehensive diagnostic workup, mobilizing family supports, and planning future outpatient treatment (Kernberg 1984). Long-term hospitalization, in contrast, is aimed at

> the modification of personality features of these patients that militate against their capacity to engage in and maintain outpatient psychotherapy. The key personality features to be modified in long-term hospital treatment include the patient's attitudes toward his illness and the treatment, that is, lack of introspection or insight, poor motivation for treatment, and significant secondary gain of illness. The prognostically most negative features for outpatient psychotherapy, namely, severe antisocial tendencies and deterioration or absence of residual, good, internalized object relations, may be additional indications for long-term hospital treatment. [Kernberg 1984, p. 173]

Once the patient has been accepted for treatment and the locale of this treatment has been decided upon, the clinical ground is ripe for yet another important question.

Should The Patient Be Put On Medication?

The basic problems of individuals with severe personality disorders are not affected by medications. These problems are integral to their character and are not merely responses to external events or inner, biological triggers. At the same time, certain features do force one to consider psychopharmacologic interventions. First is the matter of genetic links that some of these disorders (e.g., paranoid, schizotypal, schizoid, hypomanic) definitely and others (e.g., borderline) most likely have with major psychiatric disorders, such as schizophrenia and bipolar affective disorder. This makes it tempting to view them as potentially drug-responsive. Second, most such patients seek help during a major crisis and with intense dysphoria; the sheer intensity of their behavior disturbance often warrants the quick alteration offered by various psychotropic medications. Finally, a comprehensive diagnostic workup might yield results that indicate the need for pharmacologic intervention. Such indicators may include a family history of positive response to psychotropic medication, an abnormal EEG, a positive dexamethasone test, a suggestive Rorschach profile, and the presence of "soft" neurological signs. These three factors—the genetic background, the severity of disturbance, and the results of diagnostic workup in the hospital—may not only suggest a need for medication but affect the choice of psychotropic agents used (Stone 1983). For instance, if there is a family history of schizophrenia, character symptomatology is schizotypal, and Rorschach is suggestive of covert thought disorder, then low-dose antipsychotic medication might be useful. If there is a family history of affective disorders, symptomatology includes affective lability, a dexamethasone test is positive, and there is cyclic quality to the "borderline" phenomenology, then antidepressants or lithium might be used. If there are subtle EEG abnormalities, "soft" neurological signs, and symptoms of episodic dyscontrol, then anticonvulsant medications might be useful (Andrulonis et al. 1981).

One thing is quite clear: while putting patients with severe personality disorders on medication may reflect the therapist's inexperience, anxiety, and countertransference, this is not always the case. Carefully thought-out, brief, and target symptom–oriented drug intervention might indeed be useful in the management of patients on the severe end of this spectrum. A brief list of psychotropic medications and their target symptoms in the setting of personality disorders includes the following: (1) low-dose antipsychotic agents for transitory psychotic episodes, paranoia, intense depersonalization, uncontrollable impulsivity, and marked cognitive disorganization (Goldberg et al. 1986, Hymowitz et al. 1986); (2) lithium for affective lability, hypomanic excitement, "hysteroid dysphoria" (Liebowitz and Klein 1981), marked impulsivity, and refractory depression (Stone 1983); (3) tricyclic antidepressants for depression, panic attacks, and compulsive symptoms (Stone 1983); and (4) monoamine oxidase inhibitors (MAOIs) for agoraphobia (Kocsis and Mann 1986), atypical depression, and panic attacks. Other medications, including benzodiazapines, newer antidepressants, beta blockers, carbamazepine, and anticonvulsants, have been used with personality disorder patients (Eichelman 1988, Kocsis and Mann 1986, Liebowitz et al. 1986) with mixed results. Ideally, a careful literature review and consultation with a pharmacologically up-to-date colleague should precede one's use of medications.

This brings up the issue of caveats about drug treatment of personality disorders. From the growing literature in this area, Gorton and I (Gorton and Akhtar 1990) culled several such reservations. I take the liberty to quote from our work at some length:

> First, drug treatment should not be presented to patients as a panacea—it is better to profess a cautious uncertainty about possible benefit, even if this attitude mitigates placebo effect. Second, careful consideration should be given to risks versus benefits before instituting medication for patients with ongoing substance abuse, suicidal ideation, or inability to comply with required diet, blood levels, dosing schedule, or follow-up visits. Third, a consistent focus on unrealistic expectations is crucial to maximize both compliance and evaluation of efficacy. Fourth, concurrent treatments should remain firmly in place because drug therapy alone is rarely globally effective. Fifth, drugs should be introduced into treatment as a single variable: they should be used for preplanned periods with a clear beginning and end-point related to agreed-on target symptoms. Sixth, serial substitution of alternative drugs is preferable to concurrent use of alternative drugs. Seventh, drugs and dosages that may cause tardive dyskinesia, paradoxical dyscontrol, or lowering of seizure threshold should, if possible, be reserved as final treatment options. Eighth, informed consent for drug trials should be obtained continually over the course of treatment. Ninth, worsening symptoms should alert the clinician to the possible presence of some other disorder, a negative therapeutic reaction, a drug interaction with illicit agents, paradoxical aggravation of target symptoms, or the presence of an undiagnosed medical illness. [p. 47]

On the one hand are these caveats about the drug treatment of personality disorders; on the other hand are the considerations pertaining to the next question.

Is the Patient Suitable for Psychoanalysis?

From a careful and systematic review of sixteen clinical and eight quantitative-predictive studies of analyzability, Bachrach and Leaff (1978) concluded that individuals most suitable for psychoanalysis are those

> whose functioning is generally adequate; they have good ego strength, effective reality testing and subliminatory channels, and are able to cope flexibly, communicate verbally, think in secondary-process terms, and regress in the service of the ego with sufficient intellect to negotiate the tasks of psychoanalysis; their symptoms are not predominantly severe, and their diagnoses fall within a "neurotic" spectrum. Such persons are able to form a transference neurosis and therapeutic alliance, are relatively free of narcissistic pathology, have good object relations with friends, parents, and spouses, and have been able to tolerate early separations and deprivations without impairment of object constancy; they are therefore able to experience genuine triangular conflict. They are motivated for self-understanding, change, and to relieve personal suffering. They are persons with good tolerance for anxiety, depression, frustration, and suffering and are able to experience surges of feeling without loss of impulse control or disruption of secondary-process mooring of thought. Their character attitudes and traits are well-suited to the psychoanalytic, i.e., psychological mindedness. Superego is integrated and tolerant. They are mainly in their late twenties or early thirties and have not experienced past psychotherapeutic failure or difficulties. Of all these qualities, those relating to ego strength and object relations are most important. [pp. 885–886]

This portrayal of an analyzable individual is in accord with Freud (1905), who stated that one should possess "a reasonable degree of education and a fairly reliable character" (p. 263) in order to be suitable for psychoanalysis. Bachrach and Leaff's conclusions are also largely upheld by the studies (Erle 1979, Erle and Goldberg 1984, Rothstein 1982, Zimmerman 1982) that have appeared since the publication of their work. There seems a fair amount of consensus that factors that reasonably indicate analyzability include greater ego strength, deeper object relations, psychological-mindedness, achievement of object constancy, realistic expectations, and the capacity for developing both transference and therapeutic alliance. Clearly, all this implies that psychoanalysis is, by and large, the treatment of choice for patient's with neurotic or "higher level" (Kernberg 1970) personality organization and is not indicated for those with borderline personality organization. Indeed, Bachrach and Leaff (1978) concluded that "persons not likely to benefit come to analysis seeking magical fulfillments consistent with their infantile attitudes, character traits, and impoverished, need-satisfying relations with people; their ego functioning is likely within a 'borderline' (Kernberg 1975a) or 'psychotic' range" (p. 885).

This is still considered to be valid. Yet two recent developments make the picture somewhat more optimistic. First, there is an increasing awareness that analyzability may depend not only on intrinsic factors in the patient but also on the match between the patient and the analyst, and even on the person of the analyst himself (Bachrach 1983). This makes it conceivable that a patient deemed unanalyzable by one analyst may indeed turn out to be analyzable by another. Second, the increasing assimilation into psychoanalytic theory of the inferential data of child observation research and of conceptual models other than traditional structural theory (e.g., object relations theory, self psychology, and the Kleinian approach) has led to a more refined psychoanalytic technique (Abrams 1978, Blum 1981, Kernberg 1975, 1976, 1984, Killingmo 1989, Kohut 1971, Kramer and Akhtar 1988, Searles 1986, Stone 1954, Strenger 1989, Volkan 1976) that seems applicable, in flexible and modified forms, to more severe psychopathology. Indeed, Kernberg (1984) declares that he has "recently become more optimistic" (p. 165) about the application of psychoanalysis to severe character pathology. He feels that narcissistic personalities not functioning on an overt borderline level and infantile personalities with hysterical features, even when functioning on a borderline level, may be quite analyzable. The presence of natural talents, industriousness, honesty, a track record of perseverance, and a genuine desire to change oneself may enhance analyzability in the setting of severe character pathology. However, even with this optimistic note, the fact remains that psychoanalysis proper may be indicated for only a small proportion of individuals with severe personality disorders.

What Other Psychotherapeutic Strategies Might Be Indicated?

Most patients are potential candidates for psychoanalytic psychotherapy. However, for this they must meet certain basic criteria (Kernberg 1984, Kernberg et al. 1990), including (1) at least normal intelligence, (2) psychological-mindedness, (3) honesty, (4) absence of significant substance abuse, (5) willingness and ability to attend two to three sessions per week for a length of time, and (6) reasonably stable external circumstances so that minimal structuring of the treatment hours is necessary. In addition, the therapist should have access to support personnel who can make environmental interventions on his behalf and thus safeguard his neutrality. In the absence of these criteria, psychoanalytic psychotherapy is contraindicated.

Under such circumstances supportive psychotherapy should be considered. Supportive psychotherapy judiciously combined with adjunctive measures (e.g., group therapy, medication, brief hospitalization) might actually be a better approach to patients with severe social isolation (where there is a risk of the patients' developing unresolvable transference relationships that threaten to become "too real") and to patients with grossly disorganized external lives (where frequent environmental interventions are inevitable).

One last point: since supportive psychotherapy is "an ideal modality for crisis intervention" (Kernberg 1984, p. 169) and since some patients, owing to geographical restrictions, poor motivation, gross ego impairment, insufficient psychological-mindedness, and specific characterological constellations (e.g., severely schizoid, schizotypal, inadequate), cannot be engaged in ongoing treatment of any sort, it might be worthwhile to offer them only supportive intervention, though on a lifelong basis. In other words, instead of permitting certain patients to become, what is sometimes derogatorily called "lifers," one may actively select this strategy for some grossly ego-impaired and yet marginally socially adapted, geographically remote, reclusive, and unmotivated patients. These patients should be seen "on demand" (Winnicott 1971) for a few sessions during crisis situations only, every few months, or perhaps even every few years. The reassuring though "silent" availability of the therapist during intervals from these brief interventions is itself their ongoing treatment.

11

PSYCHOANALYTIC PSYCHOTHERAPY

To find the origin
trace back the manifestations.
When you recognize the children
and find the mother,
you will be free of sorrow.

—Tao-te-ching, Lao-tzu

The level of psychosocial integration even within the realm of severe personality disorders is quite variable, and this affects the choice of treatment modality for these conditions. At the healthiest pole of this spectrum are those narcissistic, histrionic, and schizoid patients who possess great psychological-mindedness, talents, honesty, and perseverance, and who do not display signs of generalized ego weakness (i.e., poor impulse control, lack of anxiety tolerance, and lack of sublimatory channels). Despite their rather severe psychopathology, such individuals are reasonable candidates for psychoanalysis. At the opposite pole are those schizotypal and borderline patients who show much ego weakness, profound affective turmoil, chronic self-destructiveness, disorganized social lives, cognitive disorganization, and tendency toward psychotic break downs. They need to be treated with supportive psychotherapy judiciously combined with psychotropic medication and other adjunctive measures, including brief hospitalization, day programs, and group therapy. Also located at this end of the spectrum are the markedly negativistic paranoid personalities who resist treatment efforts of any sort, the severe antisocial characters who seem untreatable by psychotherapeutic means, and the highly reclusive, geographically remote, sensitive schizoid individuals who are better treated on an emergency basis only for their entire lives. Most individuals with severe personality disorders, however, belong somewhere between these extremes. For them, especially if they possess honesty and psychological-mindedness, the treatment of choice is psychoanalytic psychotherapy.

The literature on this subject has grown enormously over the past two or three decades. Individual articles on the topic are too numerous to count. Even the list of books on it is quite long. However, it should be noted that the definition of psychoanalytic psychotherapy in these books is not uniform; even such designation is not consensually agreed upon. Authors have varying theoretical bents and often seem to be talking about considerably dissimilar patients. While it is not my intent to review this literature comprehensively, I must emphasize its diverse nature while considering its clinical applications. Among the theoretical views represented here, for instance, are those based on classical structural theory (Abend et al. 1983), object relations theory (Kernberg 1975a, Kernberg et al. 1990, Volkan 1976, 1987), Kleinian metapsychology (Grotstein 1981, Rosenfeld 1987), views of the "independent" British psychoanalysts (Balint 1968, Guntrip 1969, Khan 1974, 1983) and their exponents in this country (Adler 1985, Modell 1984), therapeutic approaches evolving from the impact of the interpersonal tradition on mainstream psychoanalysis (Searles 1986) and from certain specific developmental paradigms (Masterson 1976, Rinsley 1982), self psychology (Kohut 1971, 1977), and other mixed theoretical viewpoints (Boyer and Giovacchini 1967, 1980, Chatham 1985, Gunderson 1985). The patients whose treatments are reported on by these authors are equally diverse. They include higher functioning narcissistic personalities (Kernberg 1976, Kohut 1971, 1977);

lonely, anguished, and sensitive borderlines (Adler 1985); angry, impulsive, self-destructive, *DSM-III-R*-type borderlines (Gunderson 1985, Kernberg et al. 1990); "psychosis-prone individuals" (Volkan 1987); outrageously infantile and perverse characters (Khan 1983); withdrawn schizoid personalities (Balint 1968, Guntrip 1969, Khan 1974); and other types of troubled individuals for whom the use of "borderline" diagnosis has been questioned (Abend et al. 1983).

The differences in these books, however, are not restricted to their theoretical allegiances and their patient samples. The degree to which the psychotherapeutic procedure described in them remains akin to psychoanalysis proper versus the extent to which it departs from the latter also varies considerably. Moreover, some of these books offer ample clinical material (Adler 1985, Kernberg et al. 1990, Volkan 1976, 1987) while others (Grotstein 1981, Kohut 1971, 1977) provide very little. Some (Adler 1985, Kernberg 1975a) give only brief vignettes, while others (e.g., Volkan 1987) describe one particular treatment in great detail. Finally, some of these monographs are largely theoretical discourses on the subject (Grotstein 1981, Kohut 1971, 1977), while others (e.g., Khan 1983) are poignant but idiosyncratically personal accounts of cases. Still others are written, either in part (Volkan 1987) or in full (Kernberg et al. 1990), as treatment manuals outlining various interventions in a step-by-step fashion. However, these do not disregard theory and repeatedly emphasize that the complexities and nuances of psychotherapy are difficult to describe or legislate as guidelines. Freud's (1913) warning in regard to psychoanalysis proper is equally valid here:

> The extraordinary diversity of the psychical constellations concerned, the plasticity of all mental processes and the wealth of determining factors oppose any mechanization of the technique; and they bring it about that a course of action that is a rule justified may at times prove ineffective, whilst one that is usually mistaken may once in a while lead to the desired end. [p. 123]

Therefore, in discussing the psychoanalytic psychotherapy of individuals with severe personality disorders, I will avoid laying down rules. Instead, I will discuss theoretical issues that might yield certain guidelines for such an undertaking as well as for psychoanalysis of such individuals, when that seems possible. I will not describe the entire course of the psychotherapeutic process in a step-wise fashion. I recognize that it is tempting to divide the process into a beginning phase, a phase of predominantly preoedipal transferences, a transitional period where preoedipal and oedipal transferences alternate, a phase of oedipal transferences, a pretermination phase, and a termination phase proper. The fact is that there is no such thing as a purely preoedipal transference or a purely oedipal transference. Both elements coexist in each transference manifestation; at a given time one or the other may be addressed beneficially. Besides, there is another reason for avoiding a tight sequential conceptualization such as the one outlined above. The psychotherapeutic process, especially in its middle part, appears too complex for such neat categorization. I will therefore discuss only the beginning and the ending as clearcut phases.

I must also point out that I regard psychoanalytic psychotherapy as a river separating the two banks of psychoanalysis and supportive psychotherapy. It is a little bit like both, being sometimes closer to psychoanalysis, at other times to supportive psychotherapy. Like psychoanalysis, it involves a deep and intimate dialogue focusing on the transference relationship, which it seeks to resolve largely through interpretation in a neutral setting. Unlike psychoanalysis, however, it may involve departures from technical neutrality and occasionally a predominance of confrontations and clarifications over interpretations. Moreover, psychoanalytic psychotherapy pays considerably more attention to the patient's current difficulties, often leaving the genetic interpretations either incomplete or to much later in the course of the treatment. The therapist's interventions generally deal with bigger chunks of transference material rather than the finer associative links between various thoughts and feelings as is more characteristic of the psychoanalytic method proper (Gray 1983). Like supportive psychotherapy, psychoanalytic psychotherapy permits mild idealizing transferences to be left untouched, allows certain "legitimate and well-controlled gratifications" (Stone 1954, p. 57), and, at times, includes interventions basically directed toward improving reality testing, even reassurance. Unlike supportive psychotherapy, however, it does not deflect or dilute the transference but deals with it interpretively. It should be noted that such distinctions depend on the kinds of patients with whom one is working. For instance, the amount of limit setting, confrontation, and overall activity on the part of the therapist is greater with impulsive and self-destructive borderlines (Kernberg et al. 1990) than with "thin-skinned" (Rosenfeld 1987) narcissistic patients, especially if they happen to be highly psychologically minded. In the latter instance, the treatment becomes more akin to psychoanalysis. In general, it is the dialectical tension between psychoanalytic and supportive principles that guides the interventions in psychoanalytic psychotherapy. These vary from patient to patient and from time to time with the same patient, depending on the possible level of continuing dialogue.

Since I have pointed out the diversity of clinical samples in the pertinent literature, I must delineate the subgroup with which I have the most clinical experience and to the treatment of whom my views might apply. My experience is mostly with individuals of mild to medium severity within severe personality disorders. These are not neurotic characters with well-internalized structural conflicts and the capacity to develop and resolve a transference neurosis with the help of a neutral analyst's interpretations alone. Nor are they chaotic, marginally functional, frequently suicidal, severe borderlines needing repeated hospitalizations, psychotropic medication, or partial programs. My patients have been individuals who, while psychologically minded and seemingly well functioning, are in chronic anguish, often angry, sometimes suicidal, searching for love but frightened of intimacy, ruthlessly self-lacerating yet inordinately confident, unrealistically pessimistic and fantastically optimistic at the same time, hurting, sulking, and mistrustful. Their conflicts involve unresolved issues pertaining to both separation-individuation and the Oedipus complex. They act out, are subject to "emotional flooding" (Volkan 1976), often enact the unconscious scenarios of their conflicts during the sessions, walk out of them, sometimes call me names, once in a while make late-night phone calls, and (less frequently) need hospitalization. Their diagnoses include milder borderline personalities, histrionic ("infantile") personalities, and narcissistic personalities functioning on an overt borderline level.

Although I will focus on the treatment of such patients, I will comment from time to time on certain issues involving sicker patients. I will assume the reader's familiarity with basic concepts of psychoanalytic theory and technique and will hope that the intellectual collage of the following sections provides useful guidelines for the novice and food for thought for the experienced. These sections are (1) synthesizing two contrasting approaches; (2) the skills, attitude, and personality of the therapist; (3) beginning the treatment; (4) the emergence of transference and its handling; (5) needs versus wishes; (6) the issue of suicide; (7) the concept of "holding environment" (Winnicott 1965) and its technical consequences; (8) the beginning of the end; and (9) termination.

SYNTHESIZING TWO CONTRASTING APPROACHES

In a paper remarkable for its lucidity, Strenger (1989) noted that a tension between a "classic" and a "romantic" vision of human nature exists within the psychoanalytic thought since its beginnings. He traced this tension within psychoanalysis from the early Freud-Ferenczi struggles (see also Haynal 1988) to the current Kernberg-Kohut controversy (see also Akhtar 1989b) while acknowledging that the roots of the debate went as far back as the rationalist streak of the Enlightenment and the romantic reaction against it. The classic view, found most clearly in Kant's thought, held striving toward autonomy and the reign of reason to be the essence of being human. The romantic view, developed by Rousseau and Goethe, valued authenticity and spontaneity over logic and reason. The powerful impact of these two visions on psychoanalytic theory was summarized by Strenger in the following two paragraphs:

> The classic view sees man as governed by the pleasure principle and the development towards maturity is that towards the predominance

> of the reality principle. Neurosis is the result of the covert influence of the pleasure principle. The analyst's attitude towards the patient is a combination of respect and suspicion and the analyst takes the side of the reality principle. The ethic is stoic: maturity and mental health depend on the extent to which a person can acknowledge reality as it is and be rational and wise.
>
> The romantic view sees man as striving towards becoming a cohesive self. Development aims at a self which consists of a continuous flow from ambitions to ideals, from a sense of vitality towards goals which are experienced as intrinsically valuable. Mental suffering is the result of the failure of the environment to fulfill the self-object function and the patient's symptoms are the desperate attempt to fill the vacuum in his depleted self. The analyst's attitude towards the patient is one of trust in his humanity and the analyst takes the side of joy and vitality. The ethic is romantic: maturity and mental health consist in the ability to sustain enthusiasm and a sense of meaning. [p. 601]

This is not mere theoretical brainstorming. It has profound effects on the technique of psychoanalysis and psychoanalytic psychotherapy, especially in the following areas: (1) *listening attitude:* the classic attitude prompts skepticism and a listening geared to decipher "the ways in which the patient's wishes and fantasies colour his perception of reality, past and present" (Strenger 1989, p. 603); the romantic attitude mobilizes credulousness and a listening attitude geared to discern "the healthy striving for wholeness and psychic survival" (Strenger 1989, p. 603) in his communications; (2) *nature of interventions:* the classic attitude yields interventions that address resistance, facilitate uncovering, and pertain to the intrapsychic "here and now," while the romantic attitude yields interventions aimed at enhancing plausibility of the patient's experience by empathic affirmation and reconstruction.

Certain other aspects of technique, not spelled out by Strenger, also reveal the differences in these two approaches. Among these are (1) *the therapist's personality:* one approach regards it significant only in so far as it is a constituent of the technique (Kernberg 1984), while the other approach regards the warmth, tact, and authenticity of the therapist to be of central importance (Guntrip 1969); (2) *the model of psychopathology:* one approach views psychopathology, even its severe forms, largely in terms of internal conflict (Abend et al. 1983, Kernberg 1975a), while the other (Kohut 1977, Winnicott 1960, 1965) in terms of deficit; (3) *deep regression during the treatment:* one view deems it undesirable since it threatens therapeutic alliance and contaminates reason (Kernberg 1975, 1984), while the other (Balint 1968, Guntrip 1969, Searles 1986, Volkan 1987, Winnicott 1960) regards it essential for a new beginning to become possible; (4) *acting out:* while both views acknowledge it to be inevitable, one view deems it an undesirable spilling over into the life of material that should be brought to awareness in treatment (Abend et al. 1983, Kernberg 1975, 1984, Volkan 1987), while the other approach views it as a "manifestation of hope" (Winnicott 1963, p. 208) that the environment (now embodied by the therapist) will reverse the damage it has done; (5) *the recognition of the therapist's role as a new object* is lesser in the first than in the second approach; and (6) *the goal of the treatment* (hence the indications for termination) are also subtly different, with the first approach valuing rationality and realism and the second approach authenticity and vitality in this regard.

These two approaches are strikingly distinct. In regard to borderline personality, for instance, their differences are exemplified in the treatment paradigms outlined by Kernberg (1975a, 1984) and Adler (1985), respectively. Kernberg emphasizes conflict; Adler focuses on deficit. Kernberg advocates confrontation; Adler painstakingly warns against its misuses. Kernberg views regression with suspicion; Adler regards it as offering a possibility of psychic "rebirth" (p. 157). Approximately the same dichotomy is evident in the treatment of narcissistic personality disorder as outlined by Kernberg (1975) and Kohut (1977). I have summarized the differences in their approaches elsewhere (Akhtar 1989b):

> Kohut emphasizes empathy as therapeutic tool; Kernberg regards it as a technical necessity for interpretation. Kohut makes a reductionistic, linear reconstruction of childhood traumata from patients' conscious recall; Kernberg posits that narcissistic transferences at first activate past defenses against deeper relationships with parents and only then the real past relationships. Kohut appears to decode dreams from manifest content and does not provide adequate associative material to substantiate his conclusions; Kernberg pro-

> poses no deviation from traditional technique in the handling of dreams. When rage appears in treatment, Kohut views it as reactive to emphatic failures of the analyst that reactivate similarly traumatizing experiences from past; Kernberg views pregenital aggression as the basic, inciting agent against which the grandiose self is built as a defense. His suggested technique insists upon a thorough interpretation of negative transference developments in their defensive as well as recapitulation aspects. [p. 356]

In the same essay, I pointed out that the treatment approaches of Kohut and Kernberg hint at important differences in the underlying views of human nature.

> For Kohut, man is born whole, full of potential, even happy and eager to joyfully actualize the blueprint of his destiny. If he is unhappy, it is because of environmental failure. All his conflicts are the end result of unfortunate, tragic disorganization caused by lack of parental empathy. For Kernberg, conflict is embedded in normal development. Lifelong struggle with intrapsychic and reality conflicts is unavoidable. There is no escape from aggression, both from within and from outside. Life, comprising the constant reactivations of the infantile conflicts as well as renewed challenges posed by reality, is, however, still interesting and possesses the potential for that greatest of human experiences, love. However, even love can never be totally free of early transferences. [pp. 356–357]

The Kernberg–Adler and Kernberg–Kohut comparisons amply illustrate the profound influence of the classic and the romantic visions of psychotherapeutic technique. The resulting differences are summarized (admittedly, with some oversimplification) in Table 11–1. It will be noted that the table refers to the approach resulting from the classic vision as Approach 1 and to that emanating from the romantic vision as Approach 2. This is to avoid the mistranslation of classic as the older approach and to minimize sentimentalization of the label romantic.

The distinctions between the two approaches notwithstanding, it should be acknowledged that the proponents of each approach do take the features of the other approach into account. In the early writings of Kohut (1971), for instance, a parallel and equal

TABLE 11–1. Two Contrasting Therapeutic Approaches.

Variables	*Approach 1*	*Approach 2*
Fundamental view of human nature	Classic: man is intrinsically limited but can be disciplined by tradition to something fairly decent	Romantic: man is intrinsically good and capable, only restricted and injured by circumstances
Philosophical progenitors	Kant	Rousseau
Psychoanalytic progenitors	Freud	Ferenczi
Later exponents	Anna Freud, Melanie Klein,[1] American Ego psychologists, (e.g., Hartmann, Kris, Loewenstein)	The British "middle" group (e.g., Balint, Winnicott, Guntrip)
*Treatment of NPD**	Kernberg	Kohut/Modell[2a]
*Treatment of BPD***	Kernberg/Volkan[2b]	Adler
Model of psychopathology	Conflict	Deficit
Oedipus complex	Recognized	Minimized

Therapist's role	Transference object; dispassionate guide	New object; compassionate healer
Listening attitude	Skeptical	Credulous
Deep regression	Undesirable	Necessary for a "new beginning"
Acting out	Undesirable; to be controlled	A sign of patient's hope that someone will listen
Countertransference risks	Judgmental and rejecting attitude	Overidentification; rescue attempts
Therapist's personality	Significant only insofar as it makes it possible to practice technique	Crucial ingredient
Curative factor	Insight	Empathy
Treatment goal	Autonomy and self-control by heightened realism and dominance of reason	Increased meaning, freedom, and joy in life by enhanced authenticity

*narcissistic personality disorder ** borderline personality disorder

[1]Despite their enormous differences, Anna Freud and Melanie Klein both exemplify the classic vision in emphasizing innate givens, drives, and fantasies over environmental influences.

[2a and b]Modell and Volkan represent two hybrid approaches. Modell's stance is largely "romantic" but acknowledges the role of the Oedipus complex, a proposition of the classic vision. Volkan's approach is largely "classical" but includes the restorative value of deep regression, a proposition of the romantic vision.

importance is given to self-esteem and oedipal issues in the treatment of narcissistic personalities. Kohut emphasized that

> following relationships may exist between the phallic-oedipal structures in which the child's wounded narcissism plays only a secondary role, and the narcissistic structures (phallic and prephallic) which are the leading pathogenic determinants of a narcissistic transference. (1) Either (a) the narcissistic or (b) the object-transference pathology is clearly predominant; (2) a dominant narcissistic fixation coexists with an important object-transference pathology; (3) a manifestly narcissistic disorder hides a nuclear oedipal conflict; and (4) a narcissistic personality disorder is covered by manifestly oedipal structures. [pp. 154–155]

In this passage, Kohut seems to accommodate both classic and romantic perspectives outlined above. Similarly, while recommending a full exploration, interpretation, and working through of negative transference in the treatment of narcissistic individuals, Kernberg (1976) emphasizes that the positive, growth-seeking, and libidinal aspects of the patient's experience must not be overlooked, since

> focusing on such remnants as exist of a capacity for love and object investment, and for realistic appreciation of the analyst's efforts, prevents an almost exclusive focus on the latent negative transference, which can be misinterpreted by the patient as the psychoanalyst's conviction that the patient is "all bad." [p. 263]

An admixture of classic and romantic visions is evident in these brief passages from Kohut and Kernberg. It is even more clear in the writings of Modell and Volkan. Modell (1976), while betraying a romantic bent, recognizes the importance of oedipal transferences, a proposition of the classical type. Volkan (1987), though aligned with Kernberg's classic style, emphasizes the redemptive power of a deep regression, a proposition of the romantic type. Other hybrid approaches also exist (Killingmo 1989, Strenger 1989), and most clinicians perhaps intuitively attempt to strike their own variety of a balance between these two positions.

My own sense is that the two approaches can be reconciled on three levels of increasing complexity. The simplest, though not necessarily incorrect, stance would be to view them as being applicable to different kinds of patients. Approach 1 would appear more applicable to truly analyzable neurotics and, within the severe character pathology realm, to "thick-skinned" (Rosenfeld 1987) narcissistic and borderline patients. Approach 2 would seem suited for fragile borderline, retiring schizoid, and "thin-skinned" (Rosenfeld 1987) narcissistic patients. At a more complex level, both approaches would seem suitable for one and the same patient, only at different times during the treatment. Approach 1, with its emphasis on the search for hidden meaning, would work better when the patient is more organized and allied with the therapist. Approach 2, with its accent on empathy, would be the preferred mode of engaging the patient during states of extraordinary turmoil, self-absorption, and regression. Along similar lines, though in an even more sophisticated manner, it can be said that every patient's every association and every behavior can, and should, be understood from both approaches. The choice of which perspective to address the material from and what facet to bring to the patient's attention then depends on the therapist's intuitive evaluation of the patient's capacity to hear and assimilate the information. Issues of optimal distance (Bouvet 1958, Mahler 1975) and tact (Poland 1975) are clearly of paramount importance here. One thing, however, is certain and that is that the

> choice between the classic and the romantic attitude is not to be made once and for all. It must depend at every moment on an assessment of where the patient is in this respect . . . this tension is not to be resolved, as it reflects the tension between the human ability and need for full experience and the capacity for self-reflection which is essential to maturity and wisdom. [Strenger 1989, pp. 607, 609]

In a different but overlapping context, Wallerstein (1983) voices reservations about an exclusive focusing upon the oedipal or preoedipal determinants of psychopathology. Wallerstein emphasizes that

> in the flow and flux of analytic clinical material we are always in the world of "both/and." We deal constantly, and in turn, both with the

> oedipal where there is a coherent self, and the preoedipal, where there may not yet be; with defensive regressions and with developmental arrests; with defensive transferences and defensive resistances and with recreations of earlier traumatic and traumatized states. [p. 31]

Another reminder of this sort, this time about the conflict–deficit controversy (and deciphering and interpreting transferences related to these), comes from Killingmo (1989), who states:

> As the structural level will fluctuate within one and the same patient from one point of time to another or from one area of the personality to another, the analyst has to be in a state of constant receptivity to oscillate between the two strategic positions. [p. 77]

Therefore, it seems that whether it be the polarity between classic and romantic (Strenger 1989), oedipal and preoedipal (Wallerstein 1987), conflict and deficit (Killingmo 1989), or insight (Kernberg 1975a) and empathy (Kohut 1977), the ideal to be strived for is the acceptance of complexity, of paradox, of multiple determination, and by implication, of a fluid though informed and thoughtful technique.

THE SKILLS, ATTITUDE, AND PERSONALITY OF THE THERAPIST

Intensive treatment of individuals with severe personality disorders requires a lot from both parties involved in it. The patient needs to be psychologically minded and motivated for changing not only his life but his own self. He should be prepared to sacrifice time and money and honestly reveal his own self. The therapist too needs to possess the personality characteristics of honesty, authenticity, and warmth. Indeed, the therapist's skills should include

> a capacity to integrate creatively his personality traits and countertransference reactions into the technique . . . the most crucial factor

in the outcome of the treatment of patients with low level of psychic functioning, that is, ego weakness. [Kernberg 1975a, p. 147]

Kernberg's stance in this regard is neither new nor idiosyncratic. Freud (1910), in stating that "no psychoanalyst goes further than his own complexes and resistances permit" (p. 145), clearly implied connections between the technique, the depth, and the results of analysis on the one hand, and the analyst's personality on the other. Many subsequent investigators (Guntrip 1969, Klauber 1968, Little 1957) also commented on this issue. However, it must be emphasized that the therapist cannot help the patient simply by his warmth, understanding, and kindness. The significance of these qualities resides in their complex connections with the therapist's technical skills. Many factors are involved here.

First is the matter of knowledge and experience. Conducting psychoanalytic psychotherapy with severely ill patients requires much clinical experience as well as familiarity with the basic psychoanalytic theory, developmental concepts, theory of technique, and literature on intensive psychotherapy of such individuals. Of course, a mastery of this literature is not essential, but a more than elementary knowledge and continued study of it is definitely required.

Second, it should be remembered that work with severely ill patients is difficult and frequently disheartening. Improvement is slow to occur. The patient often has little reason for hope and, for long periods of time the function of maintaining optimism rests solely with the therapist. The therapist, therefore, must have "great patience for absence of change" (Kernberg 1984, p. 252), as well as a firmly held conviction that "loss, severe illness, and failure can be tolerated and worked through" (p. 249). Seasoned clinicians draw such conviction from their knowledge and prior experience. The novice, however, must survive on "borrowed faith," that is, a conviction drawn from the beneficial experience of his own analysis, the useful counsel of his clinical supervisors, and his respect, even idealization, of prominent workers in the field. All three sources function as antidotes to pessimism until authentic trust in one's work develops. Needless to say that a "forward projection" (Chasseguet-

Smirgel 1984) of infantile narcissism and idealization of the father are essential for drawing faith from such sources.

Third, the therapist must have overcome his narcissistic tendencies. While this is helpful for intensive work with all kinds of patients, its importance is even greater for treating patients with borderline personality organization. Kernberg (1975a) emphasizes that the tendency toward massive regression in these patients and

> their intense, predominantly negative transference reactions, and the particular transference, countertransference complications which develop in their treatment process put a maximum of stress on the psychotherapist. The lowered capacity for sustaining object relationships under frustrating conditions, so typical for narcissistic personalities, is a major liability for therapists with important unresolved narcissistic tendencies who attempt to treat borderline patients. [p. 149]

Overcoming his own narcissism helps the therapist seek supervision either on a continuing basis or at least during times of doubt and difficulty while treating a patient. It prevents the therapist from having unrealistically high expectations from his treatment of the patient. More importantly, resolving narcissistic issues deepens the therapist's acceptance of himself as he truly is, which "may permit him to express in his behavior the conviction that the patient will also be able to accept truths about himself and his life" (Kernberg 1984, p. 250).

Fourth, the therapist must be capable of a genuine and specific emotional response to the patient (Little 1957, Winnicott 1947). There is no place in psychotherapy for phony, as-if emotions, even those with a rosy hue of helpful sentimentality. The therapist's inner range of emotions needs to be wide. He must be capable of experiencing curiosity, anger, sympathy, sadness, erotic interest and arousal, jealousy, pity, disgust, horror, love, friendliness, and so on, though, of course, the degree to which these affects become manifest in his interventions is highly limited. The therapist's inner emotional freedom will not only lend authenticity to his work but will also enhance his capacity to use his countertransference reactions productively (Kramer and Akhtar 1988).

Fifth, the therapist must have achieved "object constancy" (Mahler 1972). This capacity is repeatedly tested in psychotherapeutic work with severely ill patients. Ticho (1972a), in elaborating on this point, goes even further and states:

> The therapist of a borderline case should have a capacity for a true object relationship. The treatment of borderline cases requires a great deal of security in the analyst; and there is no question that on a continuum from the treatment of neurotics to borderline cases to psychotics, there is an increasing requirement that the therapist be in control of his hostility. The analyst's attitude toward the unavoidable acting out of the patient makes a great deal of difference. If the analyst is unconcerned, the acting out gets worse; if he is overconcerned, he also encourages acting out. There is also need for a clear sense of the analyst's moral values, and any lack of conviction in the analyst about his moral values can lead to difficulties in the treatment, while a moralistic attitude is detrimental. [pp. 148–149]

Comfort with aggression, both from within and without, is of utmost importance. Individuals with severe personality disorders are often chronically self-destructive and may generate much countertransference hatred (Maltsberger and Buie 1974, Winnicott 1947). Such emotions in the therapist, if unrecognized, may spill over into his technique (e.g., through a reaction formation manifesting as oversolicitousness), his self-estimation (e.g., turning against the self, resulting in depression), or his outside behavior (e.g., displacement resulting in irritability toward others). The therapist's capacity to face his occasional feelings of hostility, even malice, paradoxically diminishes the chance of his unwittingly putting them into action.

Finally, the therapist, while always keeping an eye on the clinical data, should possess a certain intellectual flexibility when it comes to their interpretation. He must firmly believe in the "principle of multiple function" (Waelder 1930). Distinct from theoretical wishy-washiness, such latitude would allow him to accommodate various perspectives on the patient's psychopathology, for example, oedipal versus preoedipal (Greenspan 1977), defensive versus instinctual, romantic versus classical (Strenger 1989), conflict-related versus deficit-based (Killingmo 1989). These oscillations would prevent the therapist from being lured into believing "personal myths" (Kris 1956) of the patient, as well from succumbing to either–or, simplistic, unifactorial explanations of the patient's psychopathology offered by his own mind.

BEGINNING THE TREATMENT

Once the initial evaluation is over and the recommendation of psychoanalytic psychotherapy has been accepted, a relatively businesslike session should be held to explain certain aspects of the procedure to the patient. First and foremost among these are the frequency and duration of the sessions and their precise scheduling in the week. Although estimates of an optimal frequency (Kernberg et al. 1990, Volkan 1987) vary, my own preference is for conducting three 50-minute sessions each week. Also, I prefer to see the patient in a face-to-face position, although I recognize that many treatments conducted on the couch are actually psychoanalytic psychotherapies rather than psychoanalysis proper, since either the patient is unable to follow the "fundamental rule" (Freud 1913) or the analyst has had to depart frequently from technical neutrality. Other matters that need to be discussed at this time include the therapist's yearly vacation schedule, the policy regarding payments for missed appointments, and the billing procedure. A method of emergency communication between the two parties should also be established (Glover 1955). One must inform the patient of the location of the water fountain and restrooms. In addition, the patient should be given some instruction regarding what is expected of him during the sessions. The directions for this purpose outlined by Kernberg et al. (1990) are exemplary, and I quote them at length:

> What I expect you to do is to talk as freely as you can about the problems and difficulties that are affecting you at the time of our session; or, if there are no particular problems or difficulties affecting you at the time, to talk as freely as you can about everything that is on your mind. That may include thoughts and memories and perceptions, dreams and feelings, and questions. The more openly

> and freely you talk about yourself, the more you try to communicate fully what is on your mind to the limits of your own awareness, the better. When one talks freely about what comes to mind, the important issues tend to emerge naturally. Thus, regardless of whether what comes to mind seems important or trivial, it will help in the long run if you go ahead and talk about it. [p. 27]

The only additional thing that I have found useful is an advance warning about the expected development of transference and the need to discuss it openly. A comment such as the following often serves as an orienting device, a reality anchor, and a gentle push toward candor, especially for patients with somewhat less than optimal psychological-mindedness.

> As our work proceeds, you might begin to develop some feelings, curiosities, and fantasies about me. This is natural and expected in any sustained dialogue between two people. What is different here is that you are expected to talk about all such feelings and fantasies, since these too might give us clues to the nature of the difficulties that have brought you here. Talking about them, therefore, will also be a facet of your treatment.

Finally, the therapist might briefly explain his own role to the patient by saying that his task will be to help the patient gain an understanding of himself, that he will be listening to what the patient is saying, and that he will indeed make comments when he has something significant to contribute. The therapist should also tell the patient that, at times, he will treat the latter's questions like any other of his thoughts. Consequently, he may not answer them factually, his silence in this regard being an invitation to the patient to explore what in his mind gave rise to the question in the first place.

Such guidelines are generally enough for most patients. However, for severe borderline patients who present with marked impulsivity, antisocial tendencies, and grossly disorganized lives, an even more structured, "initial contract" (Kernberg et al. 1990, Selzer et al. 1987) might be required. This involves the therapist's setting up realistic conditions for starting and continuing the treatment. The therapist should explain to the patient (1) how the treatment ied by his psychopathology, and (2) how his to the therapist to take control of the situation. If the difficulty persists after such clarifica- should introduce conditions to starting treat- ent. Such a firm stance

> not only challenges the patient's sense of specialness and desire to avoid responsibility but also addresses the health-seeking aspect of the patient, which wishes to join with the therapist. By the same token, the therapist is allotted rights as well as responsibilities. In this way the therapist provides the patient with a figure for identification who, over time, can aid him or her in forming a more realistic sense of entitlement. [Kernberg et al. 1990, p. 39]

THE EMERGENCE OF TRANSFERENCE AND ITS HANDLING

In order to anticipate, decipher, and interpret the transference developments of the patients with severe personality disorders, it is necessary to have a clear understanding of the deeper nature of their psychopathology. While the earlier chapters have discussed this separately for each of the eight severe personality disorders, it may be worthwhile to make some comments now about their common characteristics. Elsewhere I have stated:

> Descriptively, such individuals exhibit chronic restlessness, unstable emotions, vacillating relationships, unrealistic goals, excessive self-absorption, defective empathy, egocentric perception of reality, impaired capacity for mourning, inability to love, sexual difficulties, and moral defects of varying degrees. Dynamically, splitting or active dissociation of mutually contradictory self- and object representations is a major defensive operation in these conditions. This is accompanied by the subsidiary mechanisms of denial, primitive idealization, and projective identification. Psychostructurally, at this level of character organization there is a restriction of the conflict-free ego, poor superego internalization and integration, blurring of the ego–superego delimitation, and, most importantly, the lack of an

> integrated self-concept, resulting in the syndrome of identity diffusion. [Akhtar 1991c, p. 261]

Individuals with severe personality disorders also share a common developmental background, although with some differences of the nuance, timing, and intensity of traumata and their intrapsychic elaboration. By and large, their conditions are associated with an aborted separation-individuation process with fixation in the rapprochement subphase (Mahler and Kaplan 1977, Settlage 1977), resulting in persistence of splitting mechanisms, lack of object constancy, problems of optimal distance, nonrenunciation of infantile omnipotence, and much unneutralized aggression. The continued internal clinging to the all-good mother representation of the symbiotic phase (Mahler et al. 1975) prompts a chronic search for such an object in external reality. It also gives rise to the fantasy that "someday" (Akhtar 1991c) everything will become all right; that is, there will be no disappointment in others and no aggression from within. On an overt level, patients differ in the manner in which they strive to reach this "someday":

> Those with a narcissistic personality (Akhtar 1989b) actively seek to bring this "someday" to life by devoting themselves to hard work and social success. Those with an antisocial bent seek similar magic through swindling, gambling, and other get-rich-quick schemes. Paranoid individuals (Akhtar 1990a) focus on the obstacles in their path to "someday." Borderline individuals frantically look for this "someday" through intense infatuations, perverse sexuality, and the use of mind-altering drugs. Schizoid individuals (Akhtar 1987), in contrast, adopt a passive stance in which they are constantly waiting for a magical happening, a windfall, a chance encounter with a charismatic guru, or a sexual explosion of idiosyncratic transcendental connotations. All individuals with severe personality disorder—be it narcissistic, antisocial, paranoid, borderline, or schizoid—seem to be seeking a restitution of an inner homeostasis that was disturbed years ago. All are in chronic pursuit. [Akhtar 1991c, p. 269]

Parallel to this unrealistic search is a difficulty in assimilating self- and object representations tinged with aggression. These lay their own claims on fantasy and behavior, resulting in profoundly angry ("monster," "serial killer," etc.) self-images and intense revenge fantasies. The contradictory nature of seeking "someday" and revenge simultaneously and of the ongoing conflict between their respective affects and self-representations leads to an inner world that is unstable and chaotic. Identity is uncertain. There is an intolerance of ambivalence and a tendency to react to realistic setbacks with intensely negative mood swings (Mahler 1970, Mahler and Kaplan 1977).

Since the preoedipal phase invariably affects and sometimes even determines the shape of the Oedipus complex (Kramer and Akhtar 1988, Loewald 1979, Mahler 1975, Parens 1980, Ritvo 1974), it is not surprising that the developments described above have markedly deleterious effects upon later psychic configurations of these patients. A profound lack of libidinal ministrations by the mother, perhaps going as far back as the symbiotic phase, often results in a tragic "lack of activation of early eroticism" (Kernberg, quoted in Akhtar 1991a, p. 751). Such neglect, if continued over the later part of infancy and childhood, may preclude a substantial enough oedipal experience from occurring. This seems to be the case in profoundly sadomasochistic schizoid and paranoid characters who show an obliteration of gender markers and a life-style altogether devoid of tenderness, romance, and sexuality. Such structural "thinness" of the oedipal experience is also evident in profoundly infantile and as-if characters with a background of unstable, shifting, and multiple caretakers during the first few years of life. On the other hand, evidence of a precocious and extraordinarily intense Oedipus complex is often discernible in narcissistic and borderline individuals. In both these characterological formations, there is a condensation of oedipal and preoedipal conflicts under the overriding influence of pregenital, especially oral, aggression (Kernberg 1975a). The orally tinged craving for the "all-good" mother intensifies the oedipal longing, while the projection of oral rage establishes exaggerated castration fears in the mind. Among the various phenomenological outcomes (Kernberg 1967) is sexual promiscuity, to obtain oral supplies through oedipal aims, and homosexuality, to renunciate oedipal competition altogether and through this perversely deny the differences between sexes. More often, one sees poorly object-related, desperate heterosexuality covering up a tenuous and fluctuating sexual orientation in borderline and narcissistic patients. Among male narcissistic patients, however, one sometimes comes across a peculiarly split oedipal configuration, with an attitude of oedipal triumph (often facilitated by an overindulgent mother and a weak father) on the one hand, and terrifying castrating anxiety on the other. The resulting clinical picture comprises, on the one hand, irreverence, undue bravado, sexual promiscuity, an inability to respect the institution of marriage, and an atemporal life-style with little regard for generational differences, and, on the other hand, secret and intense fear of authority, bouts of sexual impotence, doubts regarding physical integrity and prowess, feeling like a little boy, a lifelong hunger for an admirable father, and unconscious seeking of punishment over one's transgressions. Highly relevant in the context of such a split oedipal picture (see Chapter 3) are the contributions of Rothstein (1979) and Chasseguet-Smirgel (1984). Also important is Jacobson's (1954) early reminder that much unconscious guilt and self-destructive tendency exist among those who treat themselves as "exceptions" (Freud 1916).

This quick overview of the psychopathological makeup of severe personality disorders should serve as an aid in discerning the transference developments that await the therapist once the treatment gets underway. A therapist familiar with this material would not be surprised that in treating such individuals, the fundamental transference themes include (1) a search for an all-good object, often felt as a pressing and unquestionable need; and (2) a revenge motif, involving an all-bad object representation and permitting guilt-free attacks on the therapeutic setting. The former transference propensity manifests as sustained idealization in certain narcissistic and schizoid patients, defensive and superficial collusion in as-if and infantile patients, and worshipping awe coupled with hungry pleading for love and guidance in borderline patients. The latter transference propensity manifests as cold and haughty devaluation of the therapist in narcissistic and paranoid patients, outbursts of contempt and impulsive destructive actions in borderline patients, and a pouting withdrawal into futility in schizoid patients. Regardless of their phenotypic manifestations, the basically contradictory nature of these transferences sooner or later leads to both idealization and devaluation of the therapist. In the more ego-impaired patients, the two attitudes are consciously, though alternately, experienced with comparable conviction (Kernberg 1975a). In better integrated patients, such fluctuations are mild, and/or one side is experienced in relation to the therapist and the other in relation to some real figure outside the treatment, and/or one attitude is emphatically professed and felt while the behavior gives evidence to the contrary. Alongside this, regression mobilized by the intimacy of the treatment situation also begins to bring out the covert self-representations (see Chapter 3 through 9) into the open. The narcissist begins to be aware of his shame-laden self, the schizoid of his needy and curious self, the paranoid of his gullibility and masochism, and the borderline of his sadistic and smug haughtiness. This awareness is defended by denial and projective identification; the latter mechanism induces the therapist rather than the patient to experience these self-views (Akhtar 1991b, Goldstein 1991, Hamilton 1986, Kernberg 1975a, Klein 1946, Ramchandani 1989). Only with the sustained interpretation of these mechanisms does the patient begin to own his dissociated self-representations, a movement resulting in a salutary deepening of his identity.

Another difficulty arises from the fact that while the patient constantly asks for love, his hate and lust for revenge make it difficult for him to acknowledge the therapist's ongoing concern for him. To feel loved is to give up the sadomasochistic gratification in hating and feeling unloved. Also, to feel loved stirs up further dependent longings and the associated fear of betrayal. The acknowledgment that one is receiving care challenges the patient's cynical world view and in a sense becomes a progressive step leading him away from his pathology. It may stir up fears of premature abandonment by the therapist (Akhtar 1992, Grunert 1979). All this needs to be interpreted in due course of time: (1) that the patient seems to need unconditional and unlimited love; (2) that the limits of the therapist's availability cause him severe pain; (3) that his belief that such love is possible is itself a defense against recognizing that even if he did not get unconditional love when it was perhaps essential (and one cannot be certain about it), the past cannot be changed and such love cannot be provided now; (4) that his rage comes in the way of his recognizing the sustained concern, devotion, and care he is indeed getting from the therapist; (5) that his ongoing wish for revenge negates his own responsibility (admittedly little in the beginning of his psychopathology) and puts the blame for what is now happening to him on others; (6) that his idealization of the therapist also serves as a shield against his hate and that his rage protects him from his envy. Clearly, such an interpretive line is not to be imparted didactically and can, indeed must, vary its sequence with each individual patient, depending on his specific metaphors and on what he is able to hear and assimilate and when.

Even more complexity results from the inevitable intermingling of oedipal themes in the two transferences mentioned above. The longing for an "all-good" symbiotic mother is frequently condensed with desires for oedipal gratification; the persistence of infantile omnipotence seriously interferes with the establishment of an incest barrier. The refusal to comprehend that some things are prohibited is the inevitable legacy of the inability to accept that some things are impossible. In transference, this oedipal and preoedipal condensation complicates things immensely. The patient asking for a tangible token of love from the therapist, for instance, insists that he "needs" it, is entitled to it like a baby to a mother. At the same time, the patient shows evidence that the desired gratification is also related in his mind with an oedipal transgression. Consequently, the entitlement felt by the patient is tacitly colored by its opposite and leads to his feeling confused. This echoes in the powerful ambivalence often felt by the therapist under such circumstances. The issue, however, is not restricted to oedipal or preoedipal determinants being intermingled. Also existing in intermingled and alternating form are transferences related to conflict and deficit. While the former are to be handled in the traditional interpretive manner, the latter require a somewhat different sort of response. The first thing, though, is to distinguish them. In a highly astute clinical paper, Killingmo (1989) outlined the following cues of a deficit-based transference:

> First of all, there is a quality of monotonous *persistence* in the patient's way of demanding. . . . It is like playing a simple melody on an instrument with few strings. . . . Secondly, there is a special quality

> of *directness* both in style and in choice of the words. It is the "frankness" of the person who has nothing to hide and therefore in an obstinate way can press his point without risking the burden of evidence being turned back on himself. . . . Thirdly, the emotional flavor is one of *oscillation* between desperate hope and resignation, leaving no room for a moderate position in between. . . . it is a matter of vital importance. . . . [pp. 72–73]

In addition, in the deficit-based sector of personality and the transferences emanating from it, the patient feels no responsibility, not even on the unconscious level, and therefore assumes the self-righteous stance of a victim. Killingmo noted that usually the patient oscillates between conflict- and deficit-type transferences and ideally the therapeutic interventions should also move in tandem: the usual interpretative interventions for conflict transferences and "affirmative interventions" (p. 74) for the deficit transferences. The latter are comprised of (1) *an objectifying element,* which conveys the sense to the patient that the therapist can feel what it is to be in the former's shoes (e.g., "Your tense silence, distraught appearance, and avoidance of me all tell me that you are profoundly upset and find the situation unbearably painful"); (2) *a justifying element,* which introduces a cause-and-effect relation (e.g., "No wonder you feel so upset at my announcing my vacation since you do feel desperately lost without me and on top of that feel so helplessly excluded from my decisions in this regard"); and (3) *an accepting element,* which imparts an historical context to the current distress by including the mention of similar experiences from the patient's childhood (e.g., "I know that my leaving hurts you deeply since it reminds you of the time when you were 4 or 5 years old and your parents would go away for weeks at a time, leaving you pining for them"). It should be emphasized that such interventions do not require any special indulgence in the patient and can be made while maintaining a neutral position. They strengthen therapeutic alliance, prevent treatment relationship from becoming "too real," and enhance the recognition of the emotional turmoil as a transference reaction, which thus becomes amenable to more traditional interpretative intervention. Such "oscillation in strategy" (Killingmo 1989, p. 75) between affirmative and interpretive interventions seems to me to be based on a subtle though potentially problematic theoretical distinction between the patient's needs and wishes, although with a full realization that in the clinical situation "needs" might largely be indistinguishable from "wishes," hence unsatisfiable in a direct, action-oriented manner.

NEEDS VERSUS WISHES

One factor that may crucially affect the therapist's handling of the patient's demands is whether the therapist views them as representing wishes or needs. Each perspective has its technical consequences. Classical psychoanalysis and the psychotherapies derived from it regard the patient's demands (e.g., for personal information from the therapist, extra sessions, longer sessions, or contact during a long break) as disguised derivatives of conflicted, unconscious wishes (Brenner 1976, Fenichel 1945, Freud 1912, 1913, 1915, Menninger 1958). Such benevolent skepticism, coupled with a steadfast focus on the patient's intrapsychic life, prompts the traditional interpretive stance toward these requests. The therapist points out their resistance value, indicates their evocative functions, or invites the patient to join him in a mutual attempt at discovering their actual meanings. His stance is one of skepticism, abstinence, curiosity, and interpretation. In the realm of severe personality disorders, Kernberg's (1975a, 1984, Kernberg et al. 1990) approach is an excellent example of this stance.

A minority opinion within psychoanalysis, however, holds that just as there are physical needs (e.g., air, food, sleep) and wishes (e.g., ice cream, a firm mattress), there are psychological needs (e.g., being understood and affirmed, causality, vitality) and wishes (e.g., to be humiliated, to be "number one"). This viewpoint does not readily reduce the patient's demands to conflicted wishes needing interpretation; instead, it allows for the possibility of their being based on genuine needs. Such a distinction impels the therapist to take a more benevolent stance toward those of the patient's requests that he deems related to his needs. The therapist might even choose to gratify them. Examples of such gratification include increasing the length of sessions for patients who need a long time to warm up (Kurtz 1989, Little 1990) and dropping a note or making a phone call to patients who need some contact during a long summer break. The attitude is one of trust, empathy, and affirmation, occasionally even gratification, of the patient's needs. This viewpoint began with Ferenczi (1919, 1926a,b, 1929, 1930) and is evident in the works of Suttie (1935), Winnicott (1960, 1963), Balint (1968), Guntrip (1969), and Casement (1990), and in the later writings of Kohut (1977, 1982).

The fact is that while needs and wishes are perhaps distinguishable during early childhood, in adults such a distinction is extremely hard to make. For instance, a narcissistic patient's idealization contains both his need for admirable parents and a defensive wish to ward off aggression toward them. In the course of development, needs and wishes become condensed and alter each other in the process. Consequently, a person driven by entitlement tends to experience wishes as pressing needs, and one with an ascetic bent often denounces needs as mere wishes. Also, unmet needs during development result not in psychic gaps or holes but in powerful affects, fantasies, and compensatory structures (Curtis 1983). A "therapist of supply" (Killingmo 1989, p. 76) cannot fill such lacunae by kindness toward the patient. The patient's rage over unmet needs (and guilt over this rage) are also activated in the transference and fiercely combat such benevolent attempts at solace. What, then, is to be done?

Here is a situation that frequently raises this question. The therapist is about to leave for vacation. The patient insists on being told where the therapist is going. He says that he needs to know, is beside himself. The therapist's inviting him to explore the meanings of this demand holds no appeal. "What does it *mean* to be thirsty?" the patient retorts cynically. Now, should the therapist tell the patient his destination? If one views the patient as being in the midst of a symbioticlike oneness with the therapist, where self- and object boundaries have merged and the separation is indeed tearing the patient apart, causing him much "psychic pain" (Freud 1926a, p. 123), then one would be inclined to see a need element in this request. However, if one sees this request as an angry refusal to permit a love object its autonomy, or a disguised attempt at sadistic penetration into the romantic and sexual privacy of the parental couple, then one would see more wish elements in it. The former stance might tilt the balance toward considering gratification (providing ego support), the latter toward deprivation (restraining an id upsurge). The situation, however, is more complex. In accordance with the "principle of multiple-determination" (Waelder 1930), a request or demand of this sort generally has both need and wish elements. Therefore, in gratifying or not gratifying one, something is also being done to the other. Consequently, whatever one does ends up with advantages and disadvantages. For instance, in letting the patient know where one is going, one may enhance the patient's sense of safety and diminish his pain. At the same time, however, it may disappoint him since it has not satisfied his contradictory need for the therapist to be able to withstand his assaults. In addition, having thus caused the therapist to depart from neutrality may stir up much guilt in the patient because it has satisfied a prohibited wish involving a primal-scene fantasy. Of course, the therapist's doing the opposite would have its own pros and cons, most likely in reverse order.

The guideline in such situations emanates from the therapist's understanding the following: (1) ego support and id gratification are different, even if not easily separable, (2) transference is affected by gratification as well as deprivation, (3) gratification of one "need" might thwart a competing "need" *and* gratify a problematic wish at the same time, (4) the intervention chosen should match the patient's ego strength and serve the "technical" (Bibring 1954) function of preserving the treatment alliance, and (5) the effects of one's intervention should be looked for and subsequently handled in an interpretive manner.

THE ISSUE OF SUICIDE

The theme of suicide crops up in many different ways during the intensive treatment of individuals with severe character pathology. First and foremost is the acute situation of a patient's beginning to talk seriously of suicide. This poses a technical challenge for the therapist, who is faced with the difficult task of assessing the actual risk to the patient's life. The therapist must gauge the intensity of the patient's suicidal ideation, the existence and clarity of plans, the availability of means, the depth of depression, the extent of social isolation, the amount of alcohol and drug intake, and the degree to which the patient's communications are trustworthy. If there are definite plans, available means, insufficient social support, heavy drinking and drug abuse, severe depression, including the ominous feeling of having no alternative, and if there is doubt regarding the patient's reliability, then the therapist must act decisively. The course open to the therapist under such circumstances includes putting the patient on antidepressant medication, informing relatives, assuring the removal of the means for intended suicide, and hospitalizing the patient, which may have to be against the patient's wishes. Whether such radical departure from neutrality threatens the future possibility of the patient's continuing in psychoanalytic psychotherapy with the same therapist is something that can await assessment at a later time. At the moment of a serious suicidal risk, however, protecting the patient is the prime consideration.

A second manner in which the theme of suicide enters the treatment is by self-destructive threats becoming incorporated in the patient's way of life. Kernberg et al. (1990) emphatically suggest that faced with such a situation,

> the therapist should tell the family that the patient is chronically apt to commit suicide, indicating to them that the patient suffers from a psychological illness with a definite risk of mortality. The therapist should express to those concerned the willingness to engage in a therapeutic effort to help the patient overcome the illness, but should neither give firm assurance of success nor guarantee protection from suicide over the long period of treatment. This realistic circumscription of the treatment may be the most effective way to protect the therapeutic relationship from the destructive involvements of family members and from the patient's efforts to control the therapy by inducing in the therapist a countertransference characterized by guilt feelings and paranoid fears regarding third parties. [pp. 156–157]

The two situations mentioned here necessitate action-oriented interventions and departures from neutrality on the therapist's part. However, the fact is that patients often talk about suicide and express wishes to die and/or to be killed in less than urgent and acutely life-threatening ways. Such situations do not require the therapist to act in the manners outlined above. Instead, these situations challenge his understanding and interpreting capacities. It is important to keep in mind the three paradigmatic affect constellations that exist in this regard: those pertaining to hopelessness, impotent rage, and guilt. Respectively, these represent the wish to die, the inverted wish to kill, and the wish to be killed, that is, the three fundamental motifs of suicide (Menninger 1938). The first of these, namely, hopelessness leading to a wish to die, has been most meaningfully addressed by the independent group of British analysts. This group sees the individual with a "false self" (Winnicott 1960) or a "basic fault" (Balint 1968) in his psychostructural organizations as being involved in a lifelong quest. This quest is for a relationship that will provide optimal conditions for a safe regression, containment of aggression, shedding of lifelong pretenses, and regrowth of the core personality. The therapeutic relationship should, and usually does, offer such a possibility and therefore enhances the patient's hope. Empathic failures of the therapist and ruptures of the continuity of the therapeutic hours dash the patient's hope and precipitate a painful sense of futility. Life appears worthless, and the theme of suicide enters the scene. The following passage from Winnicott (1960) eloquently summarizes this dynamic constellation:

> The False Self has as its main concern a search for conditions which will make it possible for the True Self to come into its own. If conditions cannot be found, then there must be reorganized a new defence against exploitation of the True Self, and if there be doubt, then the clinical result is suicide. Suicide in this context is the destruction of the total self in avoidance of annihilation of the True Self. When suicide is the only defence left against betrayal of the True Self, then it becomes the lot of the False Self to organize the suicide. This, of course, involves its own destruction but at the same time eliminates the need for its continued existence, since its function is the protection of the True Self from insult. [pp. 143]

The second paradigmatic constellation involves impotent rage and the inverted wish to kill oneself, "coupled with a fantasy that one's death will make the significant object either recognize one's worth or be crushed by guilt feelings" (Kernberg et al. 1990, p. 154).

The transferences related to the wish for revenge seem the prime motivator of such behavior. Suicidal threats and gestures become ways to coercively "dominate, manipulate, or control the environment" (Kernberg et al. 1990, p. 155). Finally, there is the dynamic constellation based on feelings of guilt and the resultant wish to be killed (punished). This guilt, though involving oedipal issues as well, is largely based on the patient's arrival, after months or years of psychotherapeutic work, at a "depressive position" (Klein 1934). The patient may become increasingly aware of his aggression toward the therapist and begin to develop a genuine human concern for the latter.

> At this point, an extremely difficult emotional situation comes about for the patient: he must acknowledge the realistically good aspects of the analyst (mother) which he has previously denied and devaluated and bring upon himself a shattering feeling of guilt because of his previous aggression toward the analyst. The patient may feel despair because he has mistreated the analyst and all the significant persons in his life, and he may feel that he has actually destroyed those whom he could have loved and who might have loved him. Now he may have intense suicidal thoughts and intentions. [Kernberg 1975a, p. 258]

This brief overview of the triad of hopelessness, rage, and guilt that underlies suicidal feelings is intended to sharpen the awareness of the varying motives of such thoughts and actions. It is worth considering whether the three dynamic constellations could be responded to by matching psychotherapeutic strategies. For instance, the hopelessness dynamic may be met with "affirmative interventions" (Killingmo 1989), the impotent rage dynamic with limit setting and interpretive interventions, and the guilt dynamic with a mixture of facilitation of mourning and interpretive interventions. However, this line of thinking tends to oversimplify things, since in clinical practice the three constellations neither exhaust the list of motivations underlying suicidal intent nor occur in pure forms. The greater advantage of knowing them is that such knowledge might enhance the therapist's ability to

> empathize with the patient's suicide temptations, with his longing for peace, with his excitement of self-directed aggression, with his pleasure in taking revenge against significant others, with his wish to escape from guilt and with the exhilarating sense of power involved in suicidal urges. Only that kind of empathy on the part of the therapist may permit the patient to explore these issues openly in treatment. [Kernberg, 1984, p. 263]

Clearly, such exploration can be conducted only in an environment that accepts and contains the patient's aggression, that empathizes with his agony, that respects his autonomy, and that is safe, trustworthy, and reliable.

THE CONCEPT OF *HOLDING ENVIRONMENT* AND ITS TECHNICAL CONSEQUENCES

The term *holding environment* was coined by Winnicott (1960) in connection with the ordinary function of a mother holding her infant. Holding in this context meant "not only the actual physical holding of the infant, but also the total environmental provision prior to the concept of *living with*" (p. 43, author's emphasis). Winnicott (1960) noted that the holding environment's main function is "the reduction . . . of impingements to which the infant must react with resultant annihilation of personal being" (p. 47).

The holding environment meets physiological needs and is reliable. Its reliability, however, is not in its mechanical predictability but in its remaining empathically attuned to the child's needs, which vary from moment to moment. It does not abandon, nor does it impinge; it facilitates growth. Moreover, it extends beyond the infantile period to the broader caretaking functions of the parents in relation to the older child. Winnicott came to believe that the psychotherapeutic situation should be like such a holding environment and should provide safety, security, and containment of affects and offer an opportunity for one's growth potential to be reactivated. His notions in this regard have been further developed by Guntrip (1969), Khan (1974, 1983), and more recently Casement (1991) in England, and Modell (1976, 1984) and Adler (1985) in the United States. A review of this literature reveals that the concept of the holding environment has a significant impact on the psychoanalytic and psychotherapeutic technique. This impact is discernible in at least four areas.

First and foremost, the awareness of the importance of the holding environment would affect the therapist's attitude toward the physical environment in which his and the patient's mutual work is to be carried out. Thus, in setting up his office, the therapist would avoid both ostentatiousness and undue asceticism. He would make his office a comfortably appointed place that authentically represents him without being unduly revealing and that has little impingements of noise. He would avoid frequently altering the decor of the office. He would safeguard the physical integrity of this environment and not permit the patient to destroy it. A striking example of such protection of the physical environment without rupturing the emotional bond between the patient and the therapist comes from Winnicott (1947). Winnicott once physically removed a child patient who was destroying things in his office, telling him that he could ring the door bell and be let in if and when he felt calm enough to talk and play, and not be destructive.

The physical limits of the holding environment can be extended metaphorically. A common situation that requires such an intervention is when a patient abruptly and angrily walks out of a session, slamming the office door behind him. Faced with such a situation, the therapist should neither stay put in his chair nor run after the patient. The former allows the patient's attack on the setting (Limentani 1989) to rupture the therapeutic connection, and exposes the patient to the humiliation of having to knock on the door should he wish to return. The latter is an impingement on the patient's autonomy, permissible only if there is a serious suicidal risk and not otherwise. Better than either of these options is walking up to the door, opening it, and returning to one's chair. This way the office has been "extended" to include the hallway or wherever the patient has gone.

Second, the notion of the holding environment is evident in the necessity for the therapist to provide a psychological atmosphere of trust, emotional security, and acceptance, attributes akin to the early maternal care of the child. Modell (1976) eloquently spells out these elements in the analyst's technique:

> [The] analyst is constant and reliable; he responds to the patients' affects; he accepts the patient, and his judgment is less critical and more benign; he is there primarily for the patient and not for his own; he does not retaliate; and he does at times have a better grasp of the patient's inner reality than does the patient himself and therefore may clarify what is bewildering and confusing. [p. 291]

Modell's remarks, though made in connection with psychoanalysis proper, are equally applicable to the psychoanalytic psychotherapy of severe personality disorders.

Third, the concept of the holding environment guides the content of interpretations in some instances. Winnicott (1963) notes that the therapist's holding function "often takes the form of conveying in words at the appropriate moment something that shows that the analyst knows and understands the deepest anxiety that is being experienced, or that is waiting to be experienced" (p. 240).

In clinical practice, this translates into an empathically attuned commentary on the patient's anxieties not only about his inner drives but also, and at times especially, about his use of the therapist and his office as a much-needed environmental provision.

To a patient who was profoundly upset about an upcoming separation, I once said: "It seems to me that sometimes I am like an ocean to you, in which you swim freely like a fish, at other times, I am like a jar and you the water nicely contained in it. In either case, my leaving feels profoundly threatening to you, since it is like an ocean drying up for a fish or a jar breaking for the water in it." The patient sobbed but indicated feeling understood.

A significant thing to note about this interpretation is that it referred to the transference relationship as one to an environment rather than to a specific person and in doing so relied heavily on the concept of the holding environment. Another example involves a narcissistic patient struggling with the issue of optimal distance (Akhtar 1992, Bouvet 1958, Escoll 1992, Mahler 1968), especially as it threatened her with fears of fusion on the one hand and of stark aloneness on the other.

Once, when such a patient described her chronic hesitation in relating deeply to me as perpetually standing on a diving board without jumping in the pool, I said: "Perhaps in this picture I am the pool. I think what frightens you is that the pool is so deep that you may drown or so shallow that you may crash against its bottom and hurt yourself. If somehow you could be reassured that the pool is neither too shallow nor too deep, then you might jump in and swim around."

Of course, having discerned a different anxiety might have led me to include her concern, for instance, over her own swimming skills, the presence or absence of a swimming instructor in the pool, or the elegance of her diving. However, my sense was that she was not relating to me in transference as a specific individual but more as a somewhat uncertain containing environment—hence, the choice of my phrases.

Finally, it should be remembered that the holding and caretaking functions of the therapist might themselves become the foci of patient's fantasies and that these will require interpretive resolution of their own, especially toward the end of the treatment (Modell 1976).

THE BEGINNING OF THE END

The end of the therapeutic process begins to be in sight with the occurrence of certain structural achievements. At the minimum, such changes include (1) a newly developed or enhanced capacity for experiencing and tolerating ambivalence; (2) a greater ability to empathize with others and the resultant deepening of object relations; (3) the emergence of a more realistic view of oneself; (4) a working through and renunciation of the "someday" and revenge fantasies, at least in their more intense and literal forms; (5) a strengthening of ego as evidenced by better impulse control, greater anxiety tolerance, and enhanced sublimatory tendencies; (6) a diminution of reliance on magical acts or fantasies and alcohol or drugs to control anxiety; (7) a greater capacity for peaceful aloneness; and (8) the gradual replacement of intense, predominantly preoedipal transferences by relatively subtle, oedipal transferences. These developments, however, only herald the beginning of the end, not the end itself. The increasing evidence of these capacities, both within the patient–therapist dyad and in the patient's outside life, is tantamount to the first flickering of the proverbial light at the end of the tunnel.

This process has emotional and cognitive reverberations in both the patient and the therapist. From the patient's perspective, there is (1) a greater trust in the therapist; (2) a true fondness for him—still based on idealization but now including an awareness of the therapist's occasional failures and his more sustained quirks and limitations; (3) a marked diminution or removal of presenting symptoms; (4) a deeper capacity for, and interest in, the process of understanding his own self, resulting from an identification with the analyzing functions of the therapist; this is akin to what Giovacchini (1972) called the formation of an "analytic introject"; (5) a diminution in the felt need of the therapist, a development often accompanied by some anxiety and regressive movements to cling to the therapist; (6) a deeper, more complex view of the patient's parents and a changed relationship with them; and (7) a pleasurable increase in the range of both work- and leisure-related activities.

These structural changes in the patient affect the overall ambience of the treatment hours. Cold silence, pouting withdrawal, hungry pleading, desperate clinging, and sulking bitterness gradually give way to nervous giggling, shy withholding, counterphobic cockiness, sensual teasing, and jealous competitiveness. There is more verbalization and less enactment, more collaboration and less negativism. Parallel to these developments in the patient are those in the therapist. He too begins to feel somewhat relaxed, finding himself freer from the countertransference pull toward taking or avoiding this or that stance. The therapist's experience is analogous to that of a mother during the later phases of separation-individuation:

> These feelings are twofold in nature. The parent feels a lessening of the demand for attention and libidinal gratification from the child who has successfully negotiated rapprochement; the analyst of the termination-ready patient feels a decrease in the transference de-

> mands. The analyst is less likely to be drawn into transference–countertransference enactments and feels less pressure to behave in ways foreign to himself. In addition to this direct response, the parent, by identification, senses the child's readiness to do more on his own; he can, for example, envision the child's spending the afternoon with a friend with the excitement that he himself feels about such activities rather than anxiety. Similarly, the analyst can picture the autonomous activities the patient describes with pleasure rather than with the feeling that this is a defensive retreat from the relationship. [Pulver 1991, pp. 402–403]

Yet another development is a dawning awareness on the part of both parties that time is passing. The patient begins to mention various life goals (Ticho 1972a) more frequently, and the therapist too, often for the first time, becomes aware of time's passage. This development in part reflects the structural changes noted above. It is also related to the fact that oedipal transferences, which now begin to occupy center stage with greater clarity and persistence (Kernberg 1984, Kernberg et al. 1990, Modell 1976, Volkan 1976, 1987), themselves inherently involve the matter of time. After all, the Oedipus complex at its roots involves generational (temporal) differences. Its successful negotiation results in a strengthened capacity to wait.

The emergence of oedipal transferences is of crucial importance to the overall course of treatment. Two outcomes are possible. First, patients who were very ego-impaired and whose treatments were characterized by profound sadomasochistic enactments, seen in the therapist's frequent departure from neutrality, might end the treatment at this point. Their treatment appears to them as having reached a point of diminishing returns. They feel the exhilaration in their burgeoning ego capacities to be sufficient reward to consider termination. Paradoxically, psychic growth here takes the patients away from introspection. The need to exercise some of the newly acquired capacities in the external world becomes predominant. Another reason for such patients' wanting termination at this point is their inability to sustain the more refined, subtle transferences of the oedipal phase in connection with the therapist with whom they have charted the bloody seas of preoedipal transferences. Many patients return for work on oedipal issues, though at times with a different therapist.

A second outcome is witnessed in less ego-impaired patients. Here, after the mending of splitting of self- and object representations and with the achievement of object constancy, oedipal transferences can be handled in the customary interpretive fashion (Modell 1976, Volkan 1987). However, even these cases may present special difficulties. The oedipal transferences may continue to have a "narcissistic tinge" (Volkan 1987), which may need only a gentle recognition or a proper interpretive handling if it is marked. More importantly, there may be a continued tendency toward regressive reification of preoedipal structures. The deprived, hungry baby and the ruthless avenger self-images tend to be activated repeatedly, but now their transference aim is one of a regressive defense against the more subtle, oedipal issues with less familiar incestuous anxieties. A related development is the tendency toward a negative therapeutic reaction (Freud 1923a) based on the fear that mastery of preoedipal issues might lead to a premature abandonment by the therapist (Akhtar 1991c, 1992, Grunert 1979). As a result, there might follow a transitional phase during which there is much back and forth activity between preoedipal and oedipal transferences. This is especially true, in my experience, for women who felt traumatically "dropped" by their mothers around age 2 or so and whose mothers also appeared to be unduly powerful oedipal rivals. Increasing psychosocial autonomy during treatment frightens them with premature loss of the therapist. Pleasure in newly acquired skills also becomes quickly associated with oedipal, hence guilt ridden, ambitions. Together such dynamic forces lead to frequent, often tenacious regressions into a victimized babylike posture. Empathic comments conveying the therapist's awareness of these anxieties diminish the patients' aloneness with such fears. This, in turn, renders them amenable to interpretive resolution. Killingmo's (1989) recommendation of "oscillations in technique" (p. 77) between affirmation and interpretation is highly pertinent in this context. As the oedipal component of these issues is analyzed, termination becomes a real possibility.

TERMINATION

A proper handling of termination is extremely important in the analytic treatment of individuals with severe character pathology. It should be done gradually and carefully, with the process of termination being divided into two subphases (Novick 1982, Rangell 1966, Ticho 1972a, Volkan 1987). The first subphase would extend from the day on which the therapist and the patient agree that the treatment may indeed be ended to the day an actual ending date is decided upon. The second subphase would extend from the setting of this date to the end of the last session. The duration of the first subphase is harder to determine since it depends on the unfolding of new feelings and their interpretive resolution. The duration of the second subphase is more a matter of choice; four to six months seems a reasonable amount of time to work through the deeper mourning process mobilized by the setting of the actual termination date.

Many difficult and complex issues need to be tackled during the first subphase. The end of treatment for the patient means separating from a highly valued object, the therapist. It stirs up feelings of anxiety, rage, and mourning, the characteristic "termination triad" (Pulver 1991, p. 401). The patient may feel that the therapist is permitting the final separation because he, the patient, is not valued. His self-esteem is hurt and he feels angry. This anger often remobilizes the earlier preoedipal and oedipal transferences of aggressive type. Anxiety is experienced in regard to the patient's ability to sustain autonomous psychic welfare. This leads the patient to seek reassurances that he can return for "emotional refueling" (Mahler et al. 1975). The patient may also voice convictions that once the treatment is over, he can never return to the therapist for help. Such fears may be based on superego reactions to dependent wishes, but they may also contain a kernel of historical truth of having experienced less than "optimal emotional availability" (Mahler et al. 1975) during the rapprochement subphase of separation-individuation. At this time, the patient needs to be reminded of such relevant reconstructions made during earlier periods of the treatment. As anger and anxiety recede, the patient's curiosity and desire for setting the actual date for termination returns. A mutually convenient date, perhaps four to six months in the future, may now be agreed upon.

With the advent of the second subphase, increasing sadness begins to set in. A mourning process is now clearly evident, and this manifests in various ways. On the encouraging side are feelings of sadness and gratitude; "review dreams" (Glover 1955) that contain evidence of the structural changes made; the patient's utilization of his own observing ego in understanding his symptom revival and his wish for continued attachment to the therapist; a capacity for the patient to experience happiness in the prospects of being on his own; and a beginning awareness by the patient of his own positive contributions to the process and outcome of the treatment. On the problematic, though inevitable, side are the resurgence of symptoms as a way of holding onto the therapist (Miller 1965); the continued use of "magical links" (Volkan 1987, p. 104) with the therapist; and the persistent, even renewed, idealization of the therapist. With attention to these issues and their reasonable amelioration, the actual end of the treatment is at hand. Mourning over termination, of course, may continue. However, the patient's ego is now strong enough to deal with this on its own.

Part IV

CODA

12

SUMMARY, CONCLUSION, AND RECOMMENDATIONS

A list of some observations. In a corner, it's warm.
A glance leaves an imprint on anything it's dwelt on.
Water is glass's most public form.
Man is more frightening than his skeleton.

—"A Part of Speech," Joseph Brodsky

In this book I have attempted to present a comprehensive view of the pathology, phenomenology, evaluation, and treatment of severe personality disorders. I have tried to synthesize the descriptive and psychoanalytic viewpoints and to demonstrate the continuing validity of the classic literature within both these traditions. I have cast my net wide and have covered a vast area. Now is the time to summarize, reflect, propose some ideas for the future, and conclude. Perhaps a good way to begin this process of ending is to go over the major points made here.

RECAPITULATING THE IMPORTANT POINTS

1. The term *identity* has an ambiguous place in psychoanalytic theory. This is because the concept is two-sided, having both intrapsychic and interpersonal ramifications. The tension between the views of identity as self-objectivation and as a relationship of each soul to its mere existence exists in most writings on the subject.

2. Identity originates within the earliest mother–infant interactions; gains structure from primitive introjections; refines itself through differentiation from early objects; is strengthened by more selective later identifications; acquires filiation, generational boundaries, and temporality in the passage through the Oedipus complex; and arrives at its more or less final shape through further synthesis of contradictory identifications, greater individuation, and renunciation of negative oedipal strivings during adolescence.

3. A well-established identity consists of sustained self-sameness, display of roughly similar traits to varied others, realistic body image, temporal continuity in the self-experience, authenticity, a sense of inner solidity and the associated capacity for mature aloneness, clarity regarding one's gender, inner solidarity with a familial and ethnic group's ideals, and a well-internalized conscience.

4. Individuals with identity diffusion display markedly contradictory character traits, subtle body-image disturbances, feelings of emptiness, lack of authenticity, temporal discontinuity in the self-experience, gender dysphoria, and inordinate ethnic and moral relativism.

5. This syndrome is present in all severe personality disorders, although the degree to which it is readily manifest varies greatly. Also, the various manifestations of identity diffusion do not occur to an equal degree in all types of severe personality disorders.

6. The syndrome of identity diffusion needs to be distinguished from psychotic disturbances of identity, multiple personality, and adolescent identity crisis. Psychotic identity disturbances are usually bizarre and occur in the setting of gross personality disorganization with regressive loss of self- and non-self-discrimination. Identity diffusion and multiple personality do have some overlaps, but the former lacks fugues, trancelike states, physiognomic alternations, and automatic writing often associated with the latter. Also, individuals with identity diffusion do not display the elaboration, naming, personification, and dramatization of their dissociated attributes typical of those with multiple personality disorder.

7. There are eight types of severe personality disorders: narcissistic, borderline, schizoid, paranoid, hypomanic, antisocial, histrionic, and schizotypal.

8. Each severe personality disorder involves overt and covert characteristics in six areas of psychosocial functioning: self-concept; interpersonal relations; social adaptation; ethics, standards, and ideals; love and sexuality; and cognitive style. Overt and covert designations in this context do not imply conscious or unconscious existence, although such topographical distribution might exist. In general, the overt and covert designations denote contradictory phenomenological aspects that are more or less discernible. This manner of organizing the symptomatology of severe personality disorder emphasizes the centrality of splitting and identity diffusion in these conditions. It also presents a modern, dimensional system of personality diagnosis while retaining the traditional, categorical system of nosology.

9. The overt and covert clinical features are more rigidly separated in narcissistic, schizoid, hypomanic, and paranoid personalities than in borderline, antisocial, and histrionic personalities. In the latter three personality disorders, these sets of features often fluidly alternate in becoming surface phenomena.

10. The individual with a narcissistic personality disorder is overtly grandiose, scornful of others, successful, enthusiastic about ideologies, seductive, and often strikingly articulate. However, covertly he is doubt-ridden, envious, bored, incapable of genuine sublimations, unable to love, corruptible, forgetful, and impaired in the capacity for genuine learning.

11. A borderline individual overtly views himself as a victim, is self-righteously indignant and chronically enraged, is intensely involved in idealizing and hating others, is superficially adapted to reality though highly impulsive, is transiently zealous about moral and ethical issues, is very romantic and sexually promiscuous, and is recklessly decisive and smugly knowledgeable. However, covertly he feels inherently defective, is frequently suicidal, is incapable of truly depending on others, is impaired in his capacity for aloneness, is unable to experience genuine guilt, is incapable of sustained love, and is vulnerable to magical thinking and psychoticlike episodes.

12. The schizoid individual is overtly detached, self-sufficient, absentminded, uninteresting, asexual, and idiosyncratically moral. Covertly, the person is exquisitely sensitive, emotionally needy, acutely vigilant, creative, often perverse, and vulnerable to corruption.

13. The individual with a paranoid personality disorder is overtly arrogant, mistrustful, suspicious of others, driven, at times successful in solitary professions, moralistic, and sharply vigilant toward the external environment. However, covertly he is frightened, timid, gullible, chronically experiencing interpersonal difficulties, corruptible, vulnerable to erotomania and sadomasochistic perversions, and cognitively unable to grasp the totality of actual events in their proper context.

14. The individual with a hypomanic personality is overtly cheerful, highly social, given to idealization of others, work-addicted, flirtatious, and articulate. Covertly, the person is guilty over his aggression toward others, incapable of aloneness, defective in empathy, unable to love, corruptible, and lacking a systematic approach in his cognitive style.

15. The individual with antisocial personality disorder is overtly grandiose, charming, affable, earnest, seductive, strikingly unburdened by social mores, and impressively knowledgeable and articulate. However, covertly he is inferiority-laden and confused about himself, scornful of others, incapable of love and loyalty, profoundly lacking in the capacity for remorse and guilt, unable to sustain any vocational interest, and possessing only exhibitionistic tidbits of knowledge. Active or passive criminal tendencies often accompany the condition, but since criminality is not a psychological concept these should not form the basis for the diagnosis.

16. Histrionic personality disorder is distinct from the hysterical personality disorder. The individual with hysterical personality disorder, though affectualized and unwittingly seductive, possesses an intact identity, a capacity for stable, discriminating, and empathic interpersonal relationships, and a predominance of defense mechanisms centering on repression. The individual with histrionic personality disorder, in contrast, shows an underlying borderline personality organization with identity diffusion, predominance of splitting over repression, inability to integrate the contradictory aspects of self and others, marked superego defects, and restriction of autonomous ego functions. This corresponds to what was earlier termed infantile, hysteroid, hysteroid dysphoric, and sick hysteric personalities.

17. Overtly the histrionic individual is compliant and ingratiating, lively and friendly, readily interested in vocational opportunities, crudely seductive, enthusiastic about moral and ethical issues, and cognitively quick and decisive. However, covertly he is ridden with feelings of inferiority, highly dependent yet narcissistically manipulative, corruptible, promiscuous, impulsive, vocationally erratic, and cognitively inattentive to details.

18. Schizotypal personality disorder seems to refer to the intermingling of the most severe schizoid personalities with the earlier categories of simple and latent schizophrenia. Insofar as such conceptualization illuminates the understudied overlap between psychoses and character pathology, it is a nosologically advanced step and is therefore welcome. However, the introduction of this category does lead to two difficulties. First, in what appears to be an historically regressive step, it causes an artificial restriction of the definition of schizophrenia. Second, it is logically inconsistent for the current psychiatric nosology to include a schizophrenic-spectrum disorder in personality disorders while excluding affective-spectrum disorders (e.g., hypomanic, cyclothymic, and depressive characters) from personality disorders. Either both spectrum disorders should be classified with their parent disorders or both should be listed under personality disorders. My preference is for the latter alternative, as would be clear from my advocacy of the hypomanic personality disorder entity.

19. While I have outlined separate phenomenological profiles for the eight severe personality disorders, in clinical reality patients almost always present with features of more than one of these conditions at a time. Such admixture does not invalidate these diagnostic profiles; it only reminds us that these are to be used as friendly guideposts and not inviolable categories.

20. Severe character pathology is automatically associated, especially in the novice's mind, with markedly impaired social functioning. While often true, this is not necessarily the case. The fact is that individuals with severe personality disorders may function relatively well and, at times, even acquire social prominence and outstanding success.

21. Factors other than the specific nature of psychopathology can affect the ultimate clinical picture and the level of social functioning associated with severe personality disorders. These include age, sex, presence of natural talents, socioeconomic background, intelligence, education, and the impact of cultural institutions and significant extrafamilial identifications.

22. A thorough initial evaluation is needed to decide whether a patient should be accepted for treatment and, if he or she is accepted, what treatment modality would be most useful in each particular case. Such an evaluation usually requires two or three sessions of 45 to 50 minutes each, conducted preferably on consecutive days.

23. The technique of initial evaluation is complex. It includes six tasks: (1) responding to the first telephone call from the prospective patient and setting up an appointment; (2) observing the patient's appearance and overall behavior, including his manner of arrival for the first interview; (3) collecting the core information; (4) establishing and protecting the therapeutic framework; (5) assessing psychological-mindedness; and (6) sharing the diagnostic impressions and recommending treatment.

24. The core interview is a three-step process: (1) a thorough exploration of the presenting symptomatology; (2) an investigation of the extent of identity consolidation and splitting mechanisms, leading to some idea of the underlying level of character organization; and (3) the telescoping of these two sets of data with a comprehensive family history and a chronological account of the patient's life.

25. The assessment of psychological-mindedness is a very important task during the initial evaluation. This is best done by observing the patient's capacity for reflective self-observation, interest in his or her own mental life, belief in psychic causality, ability to accept chance occurrences in external reality, and readiness to see symbolic meanings and enter into metaphorical dialogue. Greater psychological-mindedness indicates treatability and better prognosis with psychoanalysis or psychoanalytic psychotherapy.

26. Toward the end of the initial evaluation, the interviewer is faced with certain questions. These include the following: Should the patient be treated at all? Should the patient be treated as an outpatient or as an inpatient? Should the patient be put on medication? If so, which ones and for how long? Is the patient suitable for psychoanalysis? If not, what alternative psychotherapeutic strategies might be indicated and/or useful? The answers to these questions, evident to the interviewer if the evaluation has been conducted properly, are discussed at length in Chapter 10.

27. Despite their rather severe psychopathology, those narcissistic, histrionic, and schizoid patients who possess great psychological-mindedness, talent, honesty, and perseverance, and who do not display signs of generalized ego weakness, are candidates for psychoanalysis.

28. The schizotypal and borderline patients who show much ego weakness, affective turmoil, chronic self-destructiveness, social disruption, cognitive disorganization, and "micropsychotic" episodes need to be treated with supportive psychotherapy judiciously combined with psychotropic medication and other adjunctive measures.

29. Most individuals with severe personality disorders are not appropriate candidates for either psychoanalysis or psychopharmacological intervention. If they possess honesty, psychological-mindedness, and strong motivation, however, and do not have substance abuse as a major aspect of their problem, they can be treated with psychoanalytic psychotherapy.

30. The literature on psychoanalytic psychotherapy of severe personality disorders has grown enormously over the past two or three decades. It consists of numerous papers, book chapters, and books written from opposing theoretical perspectives and often referring to considerably dissimilar groups of patients. The diverse nature of this literature must be kept in mind in considering its clinical applications.

31. Psychoanalytic psychotherapy is like a river separating the two banks of psychoanalysis proper and psychotherapy. Like psychoanalysis, it involves a deep, intimate, and prolonged dialogue focusing on the transference relationship which it seeks to resolve largely through interpretation in a neutral setting. Unlike psychoanalysis, it pays more attention to the patient's current difficulties, deals with bigger chunks of transference material, and often leaves the genetic interpretations incomplete. Like supportive psychotherapy, it leaves certain defenses and transferences unquestioned and, at times, includes interventions aimed at improving reality testing, even reassurance. Unlike supportive psychotherapy, it does not deflect or dilute the transference but deals with it interpretively. The dialectic between psychoanalytic and supportive principles guides the interventions characteristic of psychoanalytic psychotherapy.

32. Two approaches to this kind of work seem to exist. These appear guided by a classic versus romantic vision of the fundamental nature of man. The approaches differ in the listening attitude, the focus of interventions, the recognition of the importance of the therapist's personality, the model of psychopathology, the viewpoint regarding deep regression and acting out during the treatment, and the treatment goals themselves.

33. It is proposed that these two approaches can be reconciled on three levels of increasing complexity. The simplest stance is to view them as being applicable to different kinds of patients. At a more complex level of conceptualization, both approaches appear suitable for one and the same patient, only at different times during the treatment. At a still higher level, it can be said that every patient's every association and every behavior can and should be understood from both approaches. Factors determining the choice of one such perspective over the other are discussed in Chapter 11.

34. Intensive work with an individual having severe character pathology is always characterized by struggles with polarities. The patient is seeking not only unconditional love but also revenge for the imagined and real traumas of childhood. He idealizes yet devalues the therapist. He presents with both deficit and conflict, though neither in a pure and exclusive form. His needs are indistinguishable from his wishes, and his preoedipal and oedipal issues are condensed. From the therapist's perspective there are constant choices to be made between attending to either oedipal or preoedipal issues, between responding with empathy or insight, between offering an interpretive response to a conflict-based transference or an affirmative response to a deficit-based transference, and between an overall classic or romantic attitude. The ideal to be strived for, of course, is the acceptance of complexity, of paradox, of multiple determination, and of an oscillating though informed technique.

35. When the patient expresses acute self-destructive thoughts, the therapist is faced with the difficult task of assessing the risk of actual suicide. He must estimate the depth of depression, the intensity of suicidal ideation, the existence and clarity of plans, the availability of means, the extent of alcohol and drug use, the strength of social support, and the degree of the patient's trustworthiness. Based on the assessment of these factors, if the suicide risk appears considerable, the patient may have to be put on psychotropic medication and/or hospitalized, at times even against his will.

36. When the suicidal threats occur repeatedly and as a part of a manipulative characterological style, the therapist must meet with the family and inform them of the potentiality of an actual suicide. The therapist can assure them of his efforts but not of his ability to definitely prevent such an occurrence.

37. In less urgent circumstances, listening empathically to the patient's talk of suicide often reveals three affect and fantasy constellations. These include the wish to die emanating from hopelessness, the wish to kill oneself manifesting impotent rage, and the wish to be killed (punished) resulting from feelings of guilt. These coexist, generally but there may be occasions when one or the other is clearly the predominant constellation. Under such circumstances, different strategic interventions might be indicated (see Chapter 11). More importantly, the awareness of these dynamic constellations enhances the therapist's capacity to empathize with the multiple facets of the patient's torment and agony.

38. The psychotherapeutic setting functions as a "holding environment" (Winnicott 1960) insofar as it provides safety, security, and containment of affects and offers an opportunity for the patient's growth potential to be activated.

39. The impact of this concept on technique is discernible in four different areas: (1) the therapist's attitude toward the physical setting in which his and the patient's work is done; (2) the provision of a psychological atmosphere of trust, emotional security, nonretaliation, comprehension, and acceptance; (3) the therapist's ability to convey in words at the appropriate moment something that shows that he knows that the patient may be relating to him not as a person, but as a dimly perceived though necessary environmental provision; and (4) the therapist's awareness that his holding function might itself become the focus of the patient's fantasies, which may require interpretation, especially toward the later part of treatment.

40. Termination appears on the horizon, with consolidation of the following structural changes: an enhanced capacity for empathy; a realistic view of oneself; an establishment of optimal distance; a strengthening of ego; a capacity for peaceful aloneness; and a gradual replacement of intense, predominantly preoedipal transferences by relatively subtle oedipal transferences. The patient feels more trusting of the therapist, symptom-free, more capable of introspection, less needy of the therapist, and capable of a wider range of work- and leisure-related activities. The therapist too feels a decrease in the transference demands and can picture the patient's autonomy with pleasure rather than view it solely as a defensive flight from their relationship.

41. Two outcomes are possible: (1) Patients who were much ego-impaired to begin with and whose treatments were characterized by profound sadomasochistic enactments often end the treatment at this point. Their burgeoning ego capacities appear to them to be a sufficient reward. Many such patients return for further work on unresolved oedipal transferences, though often to a different therapist. (2) Other patients do not interrupt the treatment at this point. Their oedipal transferences can be handled in the customary interpretive fashion, with the treatment becoming increasingly akin to psychoanalysis. As the oedipal issues are analyzed, a proper termination becomes a real possibility.

42. The termination phase should be divided into two subphases, with the first extending from the agreement to stop treatment until the setting of the actual date of termination; the second, from this point until the end of termination itself. The duration of the first phase is quite variable. It depends on the resolution of separation anxiety, rage, mourning, and occasional symptom revival and negative therapeutic reactions. The second subphase should last at least four to six months. During this time a deeper working through of the mourning process should be facilitated, with the realization that such mourning may continue after the treatment has actually ended.

A NEW CLASSIFICATION OF PERSONALITY DISORDERS

In the foregoing section, I have reiterated the major points of the book and thus synthesized the past and present knowledge in this area into a composite whole. Now I will outline a complex but clinically meaningful and theoretically sound, classification of personality disorders that I hope will contribute to future investigation and understanding of these conditions. While anchored in Kernberg's (1970) hierarchical scheme of character organizations (and borrowing its designation of the three main groups), this classification includes much more. It draws on the contributions of the large number of psychiatrists and psychoanalysts mentioned throughout this book. It aims at a conceptual elaboration of Kernberg's work and also at its phenomenological adaptation by "translating" psychoanalytic metapsychology into an easier clinical language.

According to this scheme, personality disorders can be viewed as belonging to higher, intermediate, and lower levels. These broad categories are seen as developmentally, structurally, dynamically, and prognostically distinct. Moreover, they contain the various diagnostic entities customarily included in descriptive classifications. The higher, intermediate, and lower levels of personality disorders are compared in the following dimensions (see Table 12-1).

Heredity and Early Childhood

Genetic proximity with psychotic disorders and history of early, unmitigated, major traumatic events is not characteristic of higher level personality disorders and is typically found in the backdrop of lower level personality disorders. The intermediate group may give evidence of one or the other, but generally not both.

Preoedipal Factors

Certain psychological capacities originate largely during preoedipal development, though these also receive contributions from later phases of development. These capacities include self- and non-self-discrimination, basic trust and reasonable optimism, concern and empathy, self- and object constancy, optimal distance, renunciation of infantile omnipotence, capacity for ambivalence, capacity for mourning, and core gender identity. This cluster of psychological capacities is intact in higher level personality disorders. At the intermediate level the self- and non-self-discrimination is intact, but all other capacities contained in this cluster are only weakly established, being easily lost under stress. At the lower level, even the self- non-self-discrimination may be lost under throes of powerful emotions and/or psychoactive substance use.

Oedipal Factors

Passage through the Oedipus complex results in the establishment of incest barrier, capacity to respect generational boundaries, entry into a temporal order of life, and capacity for experiencing genuine inner guilt. These capacities are established but affectively charged and inwardly questioned in the higher level personality disorders. At the intermediate and lower levels, respectively, these capacities are questionably established and not established at all. In some intermediate and lower level personalities, one comes across a clinical picture of contradictory nature regarding these capacities. On the one hand, the individual gives evidence of an irreverent bravado and promiscuity typical of oedipal triumph. On the other hand, he shows intense castration anxiety, hunger for an admirable father, and unconscious search for punishment.

Factors Derived from Latency and Adolescence

These include capacity for play and work, further inner disengagement from parents, softening of childhood morality, beginning clarity of vocational goals, appropriate sexual object choice, and capacity for mature love. At the lower level, these capacities are often grossly impaired. At the higher level, the capacity for work, clarity of vocational goals, and capacity for mature love are generally intact. However, playing is often restricted, and disengagement from early parental imagoes is less than optimally complete. Consequently, morality continues to be concretely tied to childhood parental dictates, and the sexual object choice is often unconsciously an incestuous one. At the intermediate level, the clinical picture is usually mixed with their attention of vocational and work-related ideals and impairment of the capacity for mature love.

Psychostructural Characteristics

At the higher level, there is a well-consolidated identity. At the lower level, there is identity diffusion. At the intermediate level, the disturbances of identity are subtle and covert; in certain gifted

TABLE 12-1. A Contemporary Psychoanalytic Classification of Personality Disorders.

Variables	*Higher level*	*Intermediate level*	*Lower level*
Heredity and Early Childhood			
Genetic proximity to major mental disorders	–	–	+
Early, unmitigated, major traumatic events	–	+	++
Preoedipal Factors			
Self-/non-self-discrimination	+	+	+
Basic trust and reasonable optimism	+	?	–
Concern and empathy	+	?	–
Self- and object constancy	+	?	–
Optimal Distance	+	?	–
Renunciation of infantile omnipotence	+	?	–
Capacity for ambivalence	+	?	–
Capacity for mourning	+	?	–
Gender identity	+	+	?

Oedipal Factors			
Recognition and acceptance of generational boundaries	?	–	–
Incest barrier	+	?	–
Entry into temporal order; familial and ethnic affiliation	+	?	–
Capacity for experiencing guilt	+	?	–
Factors Derived from Latency and Adolescence			
Capacity for play	+	+	–
Capacity for sublimation and work	+	?	–
Further internal separation from parents; softening of childhood morality	?	?	–
Consolidation of ideals; beginning clarity of vocational goals	+	?	–
Appropriate sexual object choice	?	?	–
Capacity for mature love	+	–	–

(continued)

TABLE 12-1. *(Continued)*

Variables	*Higher level*	*Intermediate level*	*Lower level*
Psychostructural Characteristics			
Identity diffusion	Not present	Hidden	Present
Ego defenses	Repression Rationalization Projection Isolation Reaction-formation	Splitting Reaction-formation Some repression Some use of manic defense	Splitting Denial Projective identification Primitive idealization Omnipotent-control Manic defenses
Nature of conflicts	Structural Fully internalized	Intrasystematic Partially internalized Object-relations conflicts	Object-relations conflicts
Response to stress	Symptom formation	Acting out	Psychoticlike regression
Creativity	"Daily"/Scientific	Scientific/Artistic	Artistic/Autistic

Diagnostic Categories/ Treatment/Prognosis			
Corresponding diagnostic	Obsessive Hysterical Phobic (avoidant) Masochistic (Type I)	Narcissistic Masochistic (Type II)	Borderline Infantile (histrionic) Paranoid Hypomanic Antisocial As-if Schizoid Schizotypal
Treatment of choice	Psychoanalysis	Psychoanalysis Psychoanalytic/ Psychotherapy	Psychoanalytic Psychotherapy/ Supportive Psychotherapy/ Medication Other adjunctive measures
Prognosis	Excellent	Good	Guarded

\+ = Capacity fully achieved
\- = Capacity not achieved
? = Capacity weak and often lost

individuals they form the basis of extraordinary versatility. Defenses center on repression at the higher level, a mixture of reaction formation and splitting at the intermediate level, and a predominance of splitting, denial, and projective identification at the lower level. It is not that there is no tendency whatsoever toward splitting at the higher level and repression at the lower level, it is the matter of predominance and pervasiveness of one or the other form of defensive operation. The higher level gives evidence of fully internalized, structural conflicts. The intermediate level gives evidence of partially internalized conflicts of both intrasystemic and object-relations types. The lower level shows a predominance of object-relation conflicts. The characteristic response of the three groups to stress is also different. Stress leads to symptom formation, acting out, and psychoticlike regression in the personality disorders of higher, intermediate, and lower levels, respectively. Finally, there is often a difference in the nature of creativity displayed by individuals at these three levels: creativity of daily life and of scientific type at the higher level, creativity of scientific and of artistic type at the intermediate level, and creativity of artistic type tending to merge into creativity of idiosyncratic forms and autistic origins at the lower level.

As already stated, these three groups contain within them the customary descriptive diagnostic categories of personality disorders. The higher level contains within it obsessive, hysterical, phobic (avoidant), and Type I–masochistic personality disorders. The term *avoidant* as used here is somewhat different than that used in *DSM-III-R* (for details, see Chapter 5). Type I–masochistic personality refers to a neurotic character organization with an intact gender identity and capacity for love and work, but with a difficulty in achieving and enjoying success and a tendency toward self-depreciation. The intermediate level contains within it narcissistic and Type II–masochistic personality. The latter refers to a more pervasive anhedonia and asceticism, coupled with near obliteration of gender identity and a life geared toward suffering and dedication to lost causes. The lower level contains within it borderline, infantile (histrionic), paranoid, hypomanic, antisocial, as-if, schizoid, and schizotypal personality disorders.

Regarding treatment and prognosis, the treatment of choice at the higher level is psychoanalysis, at the intermediate level psychoanalysis and/or psychoanalytic psychotherapy, and at the lower level psychoanalytic psychotherapy or supportive psychotherapy either alone or in combination with medication and other adjunctive measures. Prognosis is excellent at the higher level, quite good at the intermediate level, and somewhat guarded at the lower level.

This brings us to the final point of this book.

THE PARABLE OF TWO FLOWER VASES

This incident happened about 10 years ago. I was teaching a course on severe character pathology to a group of psychiatric residents and clinical psychology interns and usually ended each session by taking questions from the group. One afternoon, after I had spoken enthusiastically about psychoanalytic treatment of such conditions, a young man posed this question: "After the successful completion of a most intensive psychoanalytic treatment conducted by a most skillful psychoanalyst under the best of circumstances, would an individual with severe character pathology become indistinguishable from a person who has always been psychologically well adjusted and healthy?"

I thought for a moment. Then, prompted by an inner voice, I spontaneously came up with the following answer: "Well, let us suppose that there are two flower vases made of fine china. Both are intricately carved and of comparable value, elegance, and beauty. Then a wind blows and one of them falls from its stand, and is broken into pieces. An expert from a distant land is called. Painstakingly, step by step, the expert glues the pieces back together. Soon the broken vase is intact again, can hold water without leaking, is unblemished to all who see it. Yet this vase is now different from the other one. The lines along which it had broken, a subtle reminder of yesterday, will always remain discernible to an experienced eye. However, it will have a certain wisdom since it knows something that the vase that has never been broken does not: it knows what it is to break and what it is to come together. Does this answer your question?"

REFERENCES

Abend, S. M., Porder, M. S., and Willick, M. S. (1983). *Borderline Patients: Psychoanalytic Perspectives*. New York: International Universities Press.

Abraham, K. (1911a). On the determining power of names. In *Clinical Papers and Essays on Psychoanalysis*, pp. 31-32. New York: Brunner/Mazel.

_____ (1911b). Notes on the psychoanalytic investigation of manic-depressive insanity and allied conditions. In *Selected Papers on Psychoanalysis*, pp. 137-156. London: Hogarth Press, 1927.

_____ (1921). Contributions to the theory of the anal character. In *Selected Papers of Karl Abraham, M. D.*, pp. 370-392. London: Hogarth Press, 1927.

_____ (1924a). A short study of the development of the libido, viewed in the light of mental disorders. In *Selected Papers on Psychoanalysis*, pp. 418-502. London: Hogarth Press.

_____ (1924b). The influence of oral erotism on character formation. In *Selected Papers of Karl Abraham, M. D.*, pp. 393-406. London: Hogarth Press, 1927.

_____ (1925). The history of an imposter in the light of psychoanalytic knowledge. In *Clinical Papers and Essays on Psychoanalysis*, pp. 291-305. New York: Brunner/Mazel.

_____ (1926). Character formation on the genital level of libido development. *International Journal of Psycho-Analysis* 7:214-222.

Abramowitz, S. I., and Abramowitz, C. V. (1974). Psychological-mindedness and benefits from insight-oriented group therapy. *Archives of General Psychiatry* 30:610-615.

Abrams, S. (1978). The teaching and learning of psychoanalytic developmental psychology. *Journal of the American Psychoanalytic Association* 26:387–406.

Abse, D. W. (1974). Hysterical conversion and dissociative syndromes and the hysterical character. In *American Handbook of Psychiatry,* vol. 3, ed. S. Arieti and E. B. Brodie, 2nd ed., pp. 155–194. New York: Basic Books.

——— (1983). Multiple personality. In *New Psychiatric Syndromes: DSM-III and Beyond,* ed. S. Akhtar, pp. 339–361. New York: Jason Aronson.

Adler, G. (1980). Transference, real relationship and alliance. *International Journal of Psycho-Analysis* 61:547–558.

——— (1981). The borderline-narcissistic personality disorders continuum. *American Journal of Psychiatry* 138:46–50.

——— (1985). *Borderline Psychopathology and Its Treatment.* New York: Jason Aronson.

Agoston, T. (1946). The fear of post-orgastic emptiness. *Psychoanalytic Review* 33:197–214.

Aichhorn, A. (1925). *Wayward Youth* (English ed., 1935). New York: Viking.

Akhtar, S. (1984). The syndrome of identity diffusion. *American Journal of Psychiatry* 141:1381–1385.

——— (1985). The other woman: phenomenological, psychodynamic and therapeutic considerations. In *Contemporary Marriage,* ed. D. Goldberg, pp. 215–240. Homeswood, IL: Dow-Jones Irwin.

——— (1986). Differentiating schizoid and avoidant personality disorders (letter to editor). *American Journal of Psychiatry* 143:1061–1062.

——— (1987). Schizoid personality disorder: A synthesis of developmental, dynamic and descriptive features. *American Journal of Psychotherapy* 41:499–518.

——— (1988a). Hypomanic personality disorder. *Integrative Psychiatry* 6:37–52.

——— (1988b). Some reflections on the theory of psychopathology and personality development in Kohut's self psychology. In *New Concepts in Psychoanalytic Psychotherapy,* ed. J. M. Ross and W. A. Myers, pp. 227–252. Washington, DC: American Psychiatric Press.

——— (1989a). Narcissistic personality disorder. *Psychiatric Clinics of North America* 12:505–529.

——— (1989b). Kohut and Kernberg: a critical comparison. In *Self Psychology: Comparisons and Contrasts,* ed. D. W. Detrick and S. P. Detrick, pp. 329–362. Hillsdale, NJ: Analytic Press.

——— (1990a). Paranoid personality disorder: a synthesis of developmental, dynamic, and descriptive features. *American Journal of Psychotherapy* 44:5–25.

——— (1990b). Concept of interpersonal distance in borderline personality disorder (letter to editor). *American Journal of Psychiatry* 147:2.

——— (1991a). Panel report: sadomasochism in the perversions. *Journal of the American Psychoanalytic Association* 39:741–755.

——— (1991b). Comments on projective identification (letter to editor). *American Journal of Psychiatry* 148:1407–1408.

——— (1991c). Three fantasies related to unresolved separation-individuation: a less recognized aspect of severe character pathology. In *Beyond the Symbiotic Orbit: Advances in Separation-Individuation Theory—Essays in Honor of Selma Kramer, M.D.,* ed. S. Akhtar and H. Parens, pp. 261-284. Hillsdale, NJ: Analytic Press.

_____ (1992). Tethers, orbits, and invisible fences: clinical, developmental, sociocultural, and technical aspects of optimal distance. In *When the Body Speaks: Psychological Meanings in Kinetic Clues,* ed. S. Kramer and S. Akhtar, pp. 21-57. Northvale, NJ: Jason Aronson.

Akhtar, S., and Byrne, J. P. (1983). The concept of splitting and its clinical relevance. *American Journal of Psychiatry* 140:1013-1016.

Akhtar, S., Byrne, J. P., and Doghramji, K. (1986). The demographic profile of borderline personality disorder. *Journal of Clinical Psychiatry* 47:196-198.

Akhtar, S., and Thomson, A. J. (1982a). Overview: narcissistic personality disorder. *American Journal of Psychiatry* 139:12-20.

_____ (1982b). Akhtar and Thomson reply (letter to editor). *American Journal of Psychiatry* 139:1078.

Akiskal, H. D. (1984). Characterologic manifestations of affective disorders: toward a new conceptualization. *Integrative Psychiatry* 2:83-88.

_____ (1986). The clinical significance of the "soft" bipolar spectrum. *Psychiatric Annals* 16:667-671.

_____ (1987). The milder spectrum of bipolar disorders: diagnostic, characterologic and pharmacologic aspects. *Psychiatric Annals* 17:32-37.

_____ (1988). Commentary. *Integrative Psychiatry* 6:46-47.

Akiskal, H. D., Djenderedjian, A. H., Rosenthal, A. H., et al. (1977). Cyclothymic disorder—validating criteria for inclusion in the bipolar affective group. *American Journal of Psychiatry* 134:1227-1233.

Akiskal, H. D., Hirshfeld, R. M. A., and Yerevanian, B. I. (1983). The relationship of personality to affective disorders. *Archives of General Psychiatry* 40:801-810.

Alexander, F. (1930). The neurotic character. *International Journal of Psycho-Analysis* 11:292-311.

Allodi, F. (1982). Acute paranoid reaction (bouffee delirante) in Canada. *Canadian Journal of Psychiatry* 27:366-373.

Andrulonis, P. A., Glueck, B. C., Stroebel, C. F., et al. (1981). Organic brain dysfunction and the borderline syndrome. In *Borderline Disorders,* ed. M. H. Stone, pp. 47-66. Philadelphia: W. B. Saunders.

Angel, A. (1934). Einige bemerkungen über den optismismus. *International Journal of Psycho-Analysis* 20:191-199.

Anthony, E. J. (1981). The paranoid adolescent as viewed through psychoanalysis. *Journal of the American Psychoanalytic Association* 29:745-787.

Appelbaum, S. A. (1973). Psychological-mindedness: word, concept and essence. *International Journal of Psycho-Analysis* 54:35-46.

Asperger, H. (1944). Die autistichen psychopathen im kindesalter. *Archieve fur Psychiatrie und Nerven Krankheiten* 177:76-137.

Bach, S. (1977). On narcissistic state of consciousness. *International Journal of Psycho-Analysis* 58:209-233.

_____ (1985). *Narcissistic states and the therapeutic process.* New York: Jason Aronson.

Bachrach, H. (1983). Concepts of analyzability. *Psychoanalytic Quarterly* 52:180-204.

Bachrach, H., and Leaff, L. (1978). "Analyzability": a systematic review of the clinical and quantitative literature. *Journal of the American Psychoanalytic Association* 26:881-920.

Bak, R. (1946). Masochism in paranoia. *Psychoanalytic Quarterly* 15:285-301.

Balint, M. (1968). *The Basic Fault: Therapeutic Aspects of Regression.* London: Tavistock.

Barasch, A., Frances, A., Hurt, S., et al. (1985). Stability and distinctness of borderline personality disorder. *American Journal of Psychiatry* 142:1484-1486.

Baron, M., Asnis, L., and Gruen, R. (1981). The schedule for schizotypal personalities (SSP): a diagnostic interview for schizotypal features. *Psychiatry Research* 4:213-228.

Benner, D. G., and Joscelyne, B. (1984). Multiple personality as a borderline disorder. *Journal of Nervous and Mental Disease* 172:98-104.

Bergman, K. (1971). The neuroses of old age. In *Recent Developments in Psychogeriatrics,* ed. D. W. Kay and A. Walk, pp. 39-50. *British Journal of Psychiatry* spec. pub. 6.

_____ (1978). Neurosis and personality disorder in old age. In *Studies in Geriatric Psychiatry,* ed. A. D. Issacs and F. Post, pp. 41-76. New York: Wiley.

Bergman, R. E. (1968). *The Sociopath.* New York: Exposition Press.

Bibring, E. (1954). Psychoanalysis and the dynamic psychotherapies. *Journal of the American Psychoanalytic Association* 2:745-770.

Blacker, K. H., and Tupin, J. P. (1977). Hysteria and hysterical structures: developmental and social theories. In *Hysterical Personality,* ed. M. J. Horowitz, pp. 95-142. New York: Jason Aronson.

Blashfield, R., and McElroy, R. (1987). The classification of personality disorders. *Comprehensive Psychiatry* 28:536-546.

Bleiberg, E. (1984). Narcissistic disorders in children. *Bulletin of the Menninger Clinic* 48:501-517.

Bleuler, E. (1908). *Textbook of Psychiatry.* Trans. A. A. Brill. New York: Macmillan.

_____ (1911). *Dementia Praecox, or the Group of Schizophrenias.* Trans. J. Zinkin. New York: International Universities Press.

Bleuler, M. (1954). The concept of schizophrenia (letter to editor). *American Journal of Psychiatry* 11:382-383.

Blos, P. (1957). Preoedipal factors in the etiology of female delinquency. *Psychoanalytic Study of the Child* 12:229-249. New York: International Universities Press.

_____ (1962). *On Adolescence.* New York: Free Press.

_____ (1965). The initial state of male adolescence. *Psychoanalytic Study of the Child* 20:145-164. New York: International Universities Press.

_____ (1967). The second individuation process of adolescence. *Psychoanalytic Study of the Child* 22:162-186. New York: International Universities Press.

_____ (1972). The function of the ego ideal in adolescence. *Psychoanalytic Study of the Child* 27:92-97. New Haven, CT: Yale University Press.

_____ (1974). The genealogy of the ego ideal. *Psychoanalytic Study of the Child* 29:43-88. New Haven, CT: Yale University Press.

_____ (1984). Father and son. *Journal of the American Psychoanalytic Association* 32:301-324.

Blum, H. (1980). Paranoia and beating fantasy: psychoanalytic theory of paranoia. *Journal of the American Psychoanalytic Association* 28:331-361.

_____ (1981). Object inconstancy and paranoid conspiracy. *Journal of the American Psychoanalytic Association* 29:789-813.

Bouvet, M. (1958). Technical variations and the concept of distance. *International Journal of Psycho-Analysis* 39:211-221.

Bowlby, J. (1940). The influence of early environment in the development of neurosis and neurotic character. *International Journal of Psycho-Analysis* 21:154-178.

_____ (1969). *Attachment and Loss.* Vol. 1. *Attachment.* New York: Basic Books.

_____ (1973). *Attachment and Loss.* Vol. 2. *Separation: Anxiety and Anger.* New York: Basic Books.

Boyer, L. B., and Giovacchini, P. L. (1967). *Psychoanalytic Treatment of Characterological and Schizophrenic Disorders.* New York: Jason Aronson.

_____ (1980). *Psychoanalytic Treatment of Schizophrenic, Borderline, and Characterological Disorders.* New York: Jason Aronson.

Brenner, C. (1976). *Psychoanalytic Technique and Psychic Conflict.* New York: International Universities Press.

Buck, O. D. (1983). Multiple personality as a borderline state. *Journal of Nervous and Mental Disease* 117:62-65.

Burland, A. J. (1986). The vicissitudes of maternal deprivation. In *Self and Object Constancy,* ed. R. Lax, S. Bach, and A. J. Burland, pp. 324-348. New York: Guilford.

Burnham, D. L., Gladstone, A. E., and Gibson, R. W. (1969). *Schizophrenia and the Need-Fear Dilemma.* New York: International Universities Press.

Bursten, B. (1973a). Some narcissistic personality types. *International Journal of Psycho-Analysis* 54:287-290.

_____ (1973b). *The Manipulator: A Psychoanalytic View.* New Haven, CT: Yale University Press.

_____ (1989). The relationship between narcissistic and antisocial personalities. *The Psychiatric Clinics of North America* 12:571-584.

Cadoret, R. (1978). Psychopathology in adopted-away offspring of biologic parents with antisocial behavior. *Archives of General Psychiatry* 35:176-184.

Cameron, N. (1963). *Personality Development and Psychopathology.* Boston: Houghton Mifflin.

Capote, T. (1965). *In Cold Blood.* New York: Random House.

Carpenter, W. T., Gunderson, J. G., and Strauss, J. S. (1977). Considerations of the borderline syndrome: a longitudinal comparative study of borderline and schizophrenic patients. In *Borderline Personality Disorders: The Concept, the Syndrome, the Patient,* ed. P. Hartocollis, pp. 231-253. New York: International Universities Press.

Casement, P. J. (1991). *Learning from the Patient.* New York: Guilford.

Chasseguet-Smirgel, J. (1983). Perversion and the universal law. *International*

Review of Psycho-Analysis 10:293–302.
_____ (1984). *Creativity and Perversion.* New York: Norton.
_____ (1985). *The Ego Ideal: A Psychoanalytic Essay on the Malady of the Ideal.* New York: Norton.
Chatham, P. (1985). *Treatment of Borderline Personality.* Northvale, NJ: Jason Aronson.
Christ, J., and Solomon, P. (1974). Character disorders. In *Handbook of Psychiatry,* ed. P. Solomon and V. D. Patch, 3rd ed., pp. 232–242. Los Altos, CA: Lange Medical Publications.
Clarkin, J. P., Widiger, T. A., Frances, A., et al. (1983). Prototypic typology and the borderline personality disorder. *Journal of Abnormal Psychology* 92:263–275.
Cleckley, H. (1941). *The Mask of Sanity.* St. Louis: Mosby.
Cloninger, C. R., Reich, T., and Guze, S. B. (1975). The multifactorial model of disease transmission. II. Sex differences in the familial transmission of sociopathy (antisocial personality). *British Journal of Psychiatry* 127:11–22.
Cohen, M. B., Baker, G., Cohen, R. A., et al. (1954). An intensive study of twelve cases of manic depressive psychosis. *Psychiatry* 17:103–137.
Coltart, N. E. (1988). The assessment of psychological-mindedness in the diagnostic interview. *British Journal of Psychiatry* 153:819–820.
Conlon, G. B. (1984). The paranoid psychopath (letter to editor). *New Zealand Medical Journal* 97:90–91.
Cooper, A. M. (1987). Histrionic, narcissistic, and compulsive personality disorders. In *Diagnosis and Clarification in Psychiatry: A Critical Appraisal of DSM-III,* ed. G. Tischler, pp. 290–299. New York: Columbia University Press.
_____ (1988). The narcissistic-masochistic character. In *Masochism: Current Psychoanalytic Perspectives,* ed. R. A. Glick and D. I. Meyers, pp. 117–138, Hillsdale, NJ: Analytic Press.
Craft, M. (1965). *Ten Studies into Psychopathic Personality.* Bristol, England: John Wright & Sons.
_____ (1966). *Psychopathic Disorders and Their Assessment.* New York: Pergamon Press.
_____ (1969). The natural history of psychopathic disorder. *British Journal of Psychiatry* 115:39–44.
Curtis, H. C. (1983). Book review: "The Search for the Self: Selected Writings of Heinz Kohut," ed. P. H. Ornstein. *Journal of the American Psychoanalytic Association* 31:272–285.
Deutsch, H. (1933). The psychology of manic-depressive states with particular reference to chronic hypomania. In *Neuroses and Character Types,* pp. 203–217. New York: International Universities Press, 1965.
_____ (1942). Some forms of emotional disturbance and their relationship to schizophrenia. *Psychoanalytic Quarterly* 11:301–321.
_____ (1955). The imposter—a contribution to the ego psychology of a type of psychopath. *Psychoanalytic Quarterly* 24:383–505.
Diagnostic and Statistical Manual of Mental Disorders (1952). Washington, DC: American Psychiatric Association.

_____ (1980). 3rd ed. Washington, DC: American Psychiatric Association.

_____ (1987). 3rd ed. revised. Washington, DC: American Psychiatric Association.

Dorpat, T. L. (1976). Structural conflict and object relations conflict. *Journal of the American Psychoanalytic Association* 24:855–874.

Dunn, W. H. (1941). The psychopath in the armed forces: review of the literature and comments. *Psychiatry* 4:251–259.

Durkheim, E. (1951). *Suicide.* New York: Free Press.

Easser, B. R., and Lesser, S. R. (1965). Hysterical personality: a re-evaluation. *Psychoanalytic Quarterly* 34:390–405.

Eichelman, B. (1988). Toward a rational pharmacotherapy for aggressive and violent behavior. *Hospital and Community Psychiatry* 39:31–39.

Eisnitz, A. (1980). The organization of the self representation and its influence on pathology. *Psychoanalytic Quarterly* 49:361–392.

Eissler, K. R., ed. (1949a). *Searchlights on Delinquency: Essays in Honor of August Aichhorn.* New York: International Universities Press.

_____ (1949b). Some problems of delinquency. In *Searchlights on Delinquency: Essays in Honor of August Aichhorn.* New York: International Universities Press.

_____ (1950). Ego psychological implications of the psychoanalytic treatment of delinquents. *Psychoanalytic Study of the Child* 6:97–121. New York: International Universities Press.

_____ (1953). The effects of the structure of the ego on psychoanalytic technique. *Journal of the American Psychoanalytic Association* 1:104–143.

_____ (1958). Problems of identity, abstracted in panel: problems of identity (reported by D. L. Rubinfine). *Journal of the American Psychoanalytic Association* 6:131–142.

Ekstein, R. (1955). Vicissitudes of the "internal image" in the recovery of a borderline schizophrenic adolescent. *Bulletin of the Menninger Clinic* 19:86–92.

Erikson, E. H. (1950a). Growth and crises of the healthy personality. In *Identity and the Life Cycle,* pp. 50–100. New York: International Universities Press, 1959.

_____ (1950b). *Childhood and Society.* New York: Norton.

_____ (1956). The problem of ego identity. In *Identity and the Life Cycle,* pp. 104–164. New York: International Universities Press, 1959.

_____ (1958). *Young Man Luther: A Study in Psychoanalysis and History.* New York: Norton.

_____ (1959). *Identity and the Life Cycle.* New York: International Universities Press.

_____ (1962). *Identity: Youth and Crisis.* New York: Norton.

Erle, J. (1979). An approach to the study of analyzability and analyses: the course of forty consecutive cases selected for supervised analysis. *Psychoanalytic Quarterly* 48:198–228.

Erle, J., and Goldberg, D. A. (1984). Observations on the assessment of analyzability by experienced analysts. *Journal of the American Psychoanalytic Association* 32:715–737.

Escoll, P. J. (1992). Vicissitudes of optimal distance through the life cycle. Discussion of Salman Akhtar's chapter "Tethers, Orbits, and Invisible Fences:

Clinical, Developmental, Sociocultural, and Technical Aspects of Optimal Distance." In *When the Body Speaks: Psychological Meanings in Kinetic Clues,* ed. S. Kramer and S. Akhtar, pp. 59–87. Northvale, NJ: Jason Aronson.

Essen-Moller, E. (1946). Concept of schizoidia. *Monatsschrift fur Psychiatrie und Neurologie* 112:258–271.

Eysenck, H. J. (1964). *Crime and Personality.* Boston: Houghton Mifflin.

Fairbairn, W. R. D. (1940). Schizoid factors in the personality. In *An Object Relations Theory of the Personality,* pp. 3–27. New York: Basic Books.

_____ (1952). *Psychoanalytic Studies of the Personality.* London: Tavistock.

Fast, I. (1974). Multiple identities in borderline personality organization. *British Journal of Medical Psychology* 47:291–300.

Faust, D., and Miner, R. A. (1986). The empiricist and his new clothes: *DSM-III* in perspective. *American Journal of Psychiatry* 143:962–967.

Federn, P. (1947). Principles of psychotherapy in latent schizophrenia. *American Journal of Psychotherapy* 1:129–139.

_____ (1952). *Ego Psychology and the Psychoses.* New York: Basic Books.

Fenichel, O. (1937). Early stages of ego development. In *The Collected Papers of Otto Fenichel,* vol. 2, pp. 25–48. New York: Norton.

_____ (1939). Trophy and triumph. In *The Collected Papers of Otto Fenichel,* vol. 2, pp. 141–162. New York: Norton.

_____ (1945). *The Psychoanalytic Theory of Neurosis.* New York: Norton.

Ferenczi, S. (1919). On the technique of psychoanalysis. In *Further Contributions to the Theory and Technique of Psychoanalysis,* pp. 177–189. London: Maresfield Library, 1950.

_____ (1923). The dream of the "clever baby." In *Further Contributions to the Theory and Technique of Psychoanalysis,* pp. 349–350. London: Hogarth Press, 1950.

_____ (1926a). Psychoanalysis of sexual habits. In *Further Contributions to the Theory and Technique of Psychoanalysis,* pp. 259–297. London: Hogarth Press, 1950.

_____ (1926b). Contraindications to the "active" psychoanalytical technique. In *Further Contributions to the Theory and Technique of Psychoanalysis,* pp. 217–230. London: Maresfield Library, 1950.

_____ (1929). The unwelcomed child and his death instinct. In *Final Contributions to the Problems and Methods of Psychoanalysis,* pp. 102–107. London: Maresfield Library, 1980.

_____ (1930). The principle of relaxation and neocatharsis. In *Final Contributions to the Problems and Methods of Psychoanalysis,* pp. 108–125. London: Maresfield Library, 1980.

Fisher, V. E. (1944). Psychic shock treatment for early schizophrenia. *American Journal of Orthopsychiatry* 14:358–367.

Fraiberg, S. (1969). Libidinal object constancy and mental representation. *Psychoanalytic Study of the Child* 24:9–47. New York: International Universities Press.

Frances, A. J. (1980). The *DSM-III* personality disorders section: a commentary. *American Journal of Psychiatry* 137:1050–1054.

_____ (1982). Categorical and dimensional systems of personality diagnosis: a comparison. *Comprehensive Psychiatry* 23:516–527.

Frances, A. J., and Widiger, T. (1986). The classification of personality disorders: an overview of problems and solutions. In *Psychiatry Update: American Psychiatric Association Annual Review,* vol. 5, ed. A. J. Frances and E. Hales, pp. 240-257. Washington, DC: American Psychiatric Press.

Frances, L., Widiger, T., Manning, D., and Fyer, M. (1988). Commentary. *Integrative Psychiatry* 6:47-48.

Frankenstein, C. (1959). *Psychopathy.* New York: Grune & Stratton.

Freeman, T. (1964). Some aspects of pathological narcissism. *Journal of the American Psychoanalytic Association* 12:540-561.

Freud, A. (1949). Certain types and stages of social maladjustment. In *Searchlights on Delinquency: Essays in Honor of August Aichhorn,* ed. K. R. Eissler, pp. 193-204. New York: International Universities Press.

Freud, S. (1887-1902). *The Origins of Psychoanalysis.* New York: Basic Books, 1954.

_____ (1905). Three essays on the theory of sexuality. *Standard Edition* 7:135-243.

_____ (1908a). Character and anal erotism. *Standard Edition* 9:167-176.

_____ (1908b). Hysterical fantasies and their relation to bisexuality. *Standard Edition* 9:155-166.

_____ (1908c). "Civilized" sexual morality and modern nervous illness. *Standard Edition* 9:177-204.

_____ (1909). Some general remarks on hysterical attacks. *Standard Edition* 9:227-234.

_____ (1910). The future prospects of psycho-analytic therapy. *Standard Edition* 10:141-151.

_____ (1911). Psychoanalytic notes on an autobiographical account of a case of paranoia. *Standard Edition* 12:1-82.

_____ (1912). The dynamics of transference. *Standard Edition* 12:97-108.

_____ (1913). On beginning the treatment (further recommendations on the technique of psycho-analysis I). *Standard Edition* 12:123-144.

_____ (1914). On narcissism: an introduction. *Standard Edition* 14:67-103.

_____ (1915). Repression. *Standard Edition* 14:141-158.

_____ (1916). Some character-types met with in psychoanalytic work. *Standard Edition* 14:310-333.

_____ (1917). Mourning and melancholia. *Standard Edition* 14:237-260.

_____ (1919). A child is being beaten: A contribution to the study of the origins of sexual perversions. *Standard Edition* 17:175-204.

_____ (1921). Group psychology and the analysis of the ego. *Standard Edition* 18:67-144.

_____ (1922). Some neurotic mechanisms in jealousy, paranoia and homosexuality. *Standard Edition* 18:221-232.

_____ (1923a). The ego and the id. *Standard Edition* 19:12-68.

_____ (1923b). Femininity. *Standard Edition* 22:122-135.

_____ (1924). The dissolution of the Oedipus complex. *Standard Edition* 19:173-179.

_____ (1925a). Preface to Aichhorn's *Wayward Youth. Standard Edition* 19:271-275.

_____ (1925b). Some psychical consequences of the anatomical distinction between the sexes. *Standard Edition* 19:243–258.

_____ (1926a). Inhibitions, symptoms and anxiety. *Standard Edition* 20:77–174.

_____ (1926b). Address to the society of B'nai B'rith. *Standard Edition* 20:271–274.

_____ (1931). Libidinal types. *Standard Edition* 21:215–220.

Friedlander, K. (1945). Formation of the antisocial character. *Psychoanalytic Study of the Child* 1:189–203. New York: International Universities Press.

Fromm, E. (1955). *The Sane Society*. New York: Rinehart.

Galenson, E., and Roiphe, H. (1971). The impact of early sexual discovery on mood, defensive organization, and symbolization. *Psychoanalytic Study of the Child* 26:195–216. New Haven, CT: Yale University Press.

Gediman, H. K. (1985). Imposter, inauthenticity and feeling fraudulent. *Journal of the American Psychoanalytic Association* 33:911–936.

Gerstley, L. J., Alterman, A. I., McLellan, A. T., and Woody, G. (1990). Antisocial personality disorder in patients with substance abuse disorders: a problematic diagnosis? *American Journal of Psychiatry* 147:173–178.

Giovacchini, P. L. (1972). Interpretation and definition of the analytic setting. In *Tactics and Technique in Psychoanalytic Therapy*, pp. 291–304. New York: Science House.

_____ (1979). *Treatment of Primitive Mental Status*. New York: Jason Aronson.

Glover, E. (1950). *On the Early Development of Mind*. New York: International Universities Press.

_____ (1955). *Technique of Psychoanalysis*. New York: International Universities Press.

Glueck, B. (1918). A study of 608 admissions to Sing-Sing prison. *Mental Hygiene* 2:85–151.

Glueck, S., and Glueck, E. (1956). *Physique and Delinquency*. New York: Harper Books.

_____ (1959). *Predicting Delinquency and Crime*. Cambridge, MA: Harvard University Press.

Goldberg, A. (1983). On the nature of the "misfit." In *The Future of Psychoanalysis*, pp. 293–308. New York: International Universities Press.

Goldberg, S., Schultz, C., Schulz, P., et al. (1986). Borderline and schizotypal personality disorders treated with low-dose thiothixene vs. placebo. *Archives of General Psychiatry* 43:680–686.

Goldstein, W. N. (1991). Clarification of projective identification. *American Journal of Psychiatry* 148:153–161.

Gorton, G., and Akhtar, S. (1990). The literature on personality disorders, 1985–88: trends, issues, and controversies. *Hospital and Community Psychiatry* 41:39–51.

Gottesman, I. T., Shields, J., and Heston, L. L. (1976). Characteristics of the traits of schizophrenics as fallible indicators of schizoidia. *Acta Grenitical Medical et Cremellogie* 25:225–236.

Gouster, M. (1878). Moral insanity. *Journal of Nervous and Mental Disease* 5:181–182.

Gray, K. C., and Hutchinson, H. C. (1964). The psychopathic personality: a survey of Canadian psychiatrists' opinions. *Canadian Psychiatric Association Journal* 9:452–461.

Gray, P. (1983). Psychoanalytic technique and ego's capacity to view intrapsychic activity. *Journal of the American Psychoanalytic Association* 21:474-489.

Green, A. (1986). Moral narcissism. In *On Private Madness,* pp. 115-141. New Haven, CT: International Universities Press.

Green, R. (1975). Sexual identity research strategies. *Archives of Sexual Behavior* 4:337-352.

Greenacre, P. (1945). Conscience in the psychopath. *American Journal of Orthopsychiatry* 15:495-509.

_____ (1958a). Problems of identity, abstracted in Panel: Problems of identity (reported by D. L. Rubinfine). *Journal of the American Psychoanalytic Association* 6:131-142.

_____ (1958b). The impostor. *Psychoanalytic Quarterly* 17:359-381.

_____ (1958c). Early physical determinants in the development of the sense of identity. *Journal of the American Psychoanalytic Association* 6:612-627.

Greenspan, S. I. (1977). The oedipal-preoedipal dilemma: a reformulation in the light of object relations theory. *International Review of Psycho-Analysis* 4:381-391.

Grinker, R. (1979). Diagnosis of borderlines: a discussion. *Schizophrenia Bulletin* 5:47-52.

Grinker, R., and Werble, B. (1977). *The Borderline Patient.* New York: Jason Aronson.

Grinker, R., Werble, B., and Drye, R. C. (1968). *The Borderline Syndrome: A Behavioral Study of Ego Functions.* New York: Basic Books.

Grotstein, J. S. (1981). *Splitting and Projective Identification.* New York: Jason Aronson.

Grotstein, J. S., Solomon, M. F., and Long, J. A., eds. (1987). *The Borderline Patient: Emerging Concepts in Diagnosis, Psychodynamics, and Treatment.* Vols. I & II. Hillsdale, NJ: Analytic Press.

Grunberger, B. (1975). *Narcissism: Psychoanalytic Essays.* New York: International Universities Press.

Grunert, U. (1979). The negative therapeutic reaction as a reactivation of a disturbed process of the separation in the transference. *Bulletin of the European Psychoanalytic Federation* 16:5-19.

Gunderson, J. G. (1982). Empirical studies of the borderline diagnosis. *Psychiatry* 5:415-437.

_____ (1984). Engagement of schizophrenic patients in psychotherapy. In *Attachment and the Evolution of a Self,* ed. Y. Akabana, Y. Sacksteder, and D. Schwartz, pp. 139-153. New York: International Universities Press.

_____ (1985a). *Borderline Personality Disorder.* Washington, DC: American Psychiatric Press.

_____ (1985b). Biological markers in schizotypal personality disorder. *Schizophrenia Bulletin* 11:564-574.

_____ (1989). Afterword. In *Review of Psychiatry,* vol. 8, ed. A. Tasman, R. Hales, and A. J. Frances, pp. 123-125, Washington, DC: American Psychiatric Press.

Gunderson, J. G., and Kolb, J. E. (1978). Discriminating features of borderline patients. *American Journal of Psychiatry* 135:792-796.

Gunderson, J. G., Kolb, J. E., and Austin, V. (1981). The diagnostic interview for borderline patients. *American Journal of Psychiatry* 138:896–903.

Gunderson, J. G., and Siever, L. J. (1983). The search for a schizotype: crossing the border again. *Archives of General Psychiatry* 40:15–22.

Gunderson, J. G., and Singer, M. (1975). Defining borderline patients: an overview. *American Journal of Psychiatry* 133:1–10.

Guntrip, H. (1969). *Schizoid Phenomena, Object Relations and the Self.* New York: International Universities Press.

_____ (1971). *Psychoanalytic Theory, Therapy and the Self.* New York: Basic Books.

Guttman, S. A., Jones, R. L., and Parrish, S. M. (1980). *The Concordance to the Standard Edition of the Complete Psychological Works of Sigmund Freud.* Vol. I. Boston, MA: G. K. Hall.

Guze, S. B. (1964). Conversion symptoms in criminals. *American Journal of Psychiatry* 121:580–583.

_____ (1971). Diagnostic consistency in antisocial personality. *American Journal of Psychiatry* 128:360–361.

Halleck, S. L. (1967). Hysterical personality traits. *Archives of General Psychiatry* 16:750–757.

Hamilton, M., ed. (1974). *Fish's Clinical Psychopathology.* Bristol, England: John Wright & Sons.

_____ (1978). *Fish's Outline of Psychiatry,* 3rd ed. Bristol, England: John Wright & Sons.

Hamilton, N. G. (1984). *Fish's Schizophrenia,* 3rd ed. Boston: Wright PGS.

_____ (1986). Positive projective identification. *International Journal of Psycho-Analysis* 67:489–496.

Hankoff, L. D. (1982). Response to overview on narcissism (letter to editor). *American Journal of Psychiatry* 139:1078.

Hare, R. D. (1970). *Psychopathy: Theory and Research.* New York: Wiley.

_____ (1983). Diagnosis of antisocial personality disorder in two prison populations. *American Journal of Psychiatry* 140:887–890.

Hare, R. D., and Shalling, D. (1978). *Psychopathic Behavior: Approaches to Research.* New York: Wiley.

Hartmann, H. (1948). Comments on the psychoanalytic theory of instinctual drives. In *Essays on Ego Psychology,* pp. 69–89. New York: International Universities Press.

_____ (1949). Notes on the theory of aggression. In *Papers on Psychoanalytic Psychology,* pp. 56–85. New York: International Universities Press.

_____ (1950). Comments on the psychoanalytic theory of the ego. In *Essays on Ego Psychology,* pp. 113–141. New York: International Universities Press.

_____ (1952). The mutual influences on the development of ego and id. In *Essays on Ego Psychology,* pp. 151–181. New York: International Universities Press.

_____ (1955). Notes on the theory of sublimation. In *Essays on Ego Psychology,* pp. 215–240. New York: International Universities Press.

Hartmann, H., Kris, E., and Loewenstein, R. (1946). Comments on the formation of psychic structure. In *Papers on Psychoanalytic Psychology,* pp. 27–55. New York: International Universities Press.

Hartmann, H., and Loewenstein, R. M. (1962). Notes on the superego. In *Papers on Psychoanalytic Psychology,* ed. H. Hartmann, E. Kris, and R. Loewenstein, pp. 144–181. New York: International Universities Press.

Hartocollis, P., ed. (1977). *Borderline Personality Disorders: The Concept, the Syndrome, the Patient.* New York: International Universities Press.

Haynal, A. E. (1988). *The Technique at Issue: Controversies in Psychoanalysis from Freud and Ferenczi to Michael Balint.* London: Karnac Books.

Heimann, P. (1952). Preliminary notes on some defence mechanisms in paranoid states. *International Journal of Psycho-Analysis* 33:206–213.

Henderson, D. K. (1939). *Psychopathic States.* New York: Norton.

Heston, L. L. (1966). Psychiatric disorders in foster home-reared children of schizophrenic mothers. *British Journal of Psychiatry* 112:819–825.

_____ (1970). The genetics of schizophrenia and schizoid disease. *Science* 167:249–256.

Hoch, P. (1909). A study of the mental makeup in the functional psychosis. *Journal of Nervous and Mental Disorders* 36:230–236.

_____ (1910). Constitutional factors in dementia praecox group. *Review of Neurology Psychiatry* 8:463–474.

Hoch, P., and Polatin, P. (1949). Pseudoneurotic forms of schizophrenia. *Psychoanalytic Quarterly* 23:248–276.

Hoffer, W. (1949). Deceiving the deceiver. In *Searchlights on Delinquency: Essays in Honor of August Aichhorn,* ed. K. R. Eissler, pp. 150–155. New York: International Universities Press.

Hollender, M. H. (1970). The need or wish to be held. *Archives of General Psychiatry* 22:445–453.

Horowitz, M. J. (1975). *The Psychoanalytic Theory of Neurosis.* New York: Norton.

Hott, L. R. (1979). The antisocial character. *American Journal of Psychoanalysis* 39:235–244.

Hutchings, B., and Mednick, S. (1974). Registered criminality in the adoptive and biological parents of registered male adoptees. In *Genetics, Environment and Psychopathology,* ed. S. A. Mednick, F. Schulsinger, J. Higgins, and B. Bell, pp. 215–230. Amsterdam: North Holland Publishing Co.

Hymowitz, P., Frances, A., and Jacobsberg, L. (1986). Neuroleptic treatment of schizotypal personality disorders. *Comprehensive Psychiatry* 27:267–271.

The International Classification of Diseases (1980). Vol. 1, 2nd ed. Washington, DC: U.S. Department of Health and Human Services.

Jack, R. A., Nicassio, P. M., and West, W. S. (1984). Acute paranoid disorder in a Southeast Asian refugee. *Journal of Nervous and Mental Diseases* 172:495–597.

Jacobson, E. (1953a). The affects and their pleasure—unpleasure qualities in relation to the psychic discharge processes. In *Affects, Drives, Behavior,* ed. R. Loewenstein, pp. 38–66. New York: International Universities Press.

_____ (1953b). Contribution to the metapsychology of cyclothymic depression. In *Affective Disorders: Psychoanalytic Contribution to Their Study,* ed. P. Greenacre, pp. 49–83. New York: International Universities Press.

_____ (1954a). The self and the object world. *Psychoanalytic Study of the Child* 9:75–127. New York: International Universities Press.

_____ (1954b). Contribution to the metapsychology of psychotic identification. *Journal of the American Psychoanalytic Association* 2:239–262.

_____ (1954c). The "exceptions": an elaboration of Freud's character studies. *Psychoanalytic Study of the Child* 14:135–154. New York: International Universities Press.

_____ (1957). Denial and repression. *Journal of the American Psychoanalytic Association* 5:61–92.

_____ (1959). Depersonalization. *Journal of the American Psychoanalytic Association* 7:581–610.

_____ (1964). *The Self and the Object World.* New York: International Universities Press.

_____ (1971). *Depression.* New York: International Universities Press.

Jacobson, L. B., Hymowitz, P., Barasch, A., and Frances, A. J. (1986). Symptoms of schizotypal personality disorder. *American Journal of Psychiatry* 143:1222–1227.

Jaspers, K. (1949). *General Psychopathology.* Trans. M. W. Hamilton. London: Manchester University Press.

Johnson, A. M. (1949). Sanctions for superego lacunae of adolescents. In *Searchlights on Delinquency: Essays in Honor of August Aichhorn,* ed. K. R. Eissler, pp. 225–245. New York: International Universities Press.

Johnson, A. M., and Szurek, S. A. (1952). The genesis of antisocial acting out in children and adults. *Psychoanalytic Quarterly* 21:323–343.

Johnson, F. A. (1977). Psychotherapy of the alienated individuals. In *The Narcissistic Condition,* ed. M. C. Nelson, pp. 127–161. New York: Human Sciences Press.

Jones, E. (1913). The God complex. In *Essays in Applied Psycho-Analysis,* vol. 2, pp. 244–265. New York: International Universities Press, 1973.

_____ (1918). Anal erotic character traits. In *Papers on Psychoanalysis,* pp. 413–437. London: Bailliere, Tindall & Cox, 1950.

Joseph, E., ed. (1967). *Indications for Psychoanalysis* (Kris Study Group Monograph 2). New York: International Universities Press.

Jung, C. (1923). *Psychological Types.* New York: Harcourt Brace.

Kallman, F. J. (1938). *The Genetics of Schizophrenia.* New York: Augustin.

Karpman, B. (1941). On the need for separating psychopathy into two distinct clinical types: symptomatic and idiopathic. *Journal of Clinical Psychopathology* 3:112–137.

_____ (1947). *Case Studies in the Psychopathology of Crime.* Vol. 1–4. Washington, DC: Medical Science Press.

_____ (1948). Myth of psychopathic personality. *American Journal of Psychiatry* 104:523–534.

Kasanin, K., and Rosen, Z. A. (1933). Clinical variables in schizoid personalities. *Archives of Neurology Psychiatry* 30:538–566.

_____ (1985). Diagnostic approaches to schizotypal personality disorder: a historical perspective. *Schizophrenia Bulletin* 11(4):538–553.

Kendler, K., Gruenberg, A. M., and Strauss, J. S. (1981). An independent analysis of the Copenhagen sample of the Danish adoption study of schizophrenia: II. The relationship between schizotypal personality disorder and schizophrenia. *Archives of General Psychiatry* 38:982–987.

Kendler, K., and Grunberger, A. (1975). The splitting defense mechanism of the borderline adolescent: developmental and clinical aspects. In *Borderline States in Psychiatry,* ed. J. E. Mack, pp. 93–101. New York: Grune & Stratton.

_____ (1982). Genetic relationship between paranoid personality disorder and the "schizophrenic spectrum" disorders. *American Journal of Psychiatry* 139:1185–1186.

Kendler, K., Masterson, C. S., Ungaro, R., and Davis, K. L. (1984). A family history study of schizophrenia-related personality disorders. *American Journal of Psychiatry* 141:424–427.

Kendler, K., and Rinsley, D. B. (1975). The borderline syndrome: the role of the mother in the genesis and psychic structure of the borderline personality. *International Journal of Psycho-Analysis* 56:163–177.

Kernberg, O. F. (1967). Borderline personality organization. *Journal of the American Psychoanalytic Association* 15:641–685.

_____ (1970). A psychoanalytic classification of character pathology. *Journal of the American Psychoanalytic Association* 18:800–822.

_____ (1971). Prognostic considerations regarding borderline personality organization. *Journal of the American Psychoanalytic Association* 19:595–635.

_____ (1975a). *Borderline Conditions and Pathological Narcissism.* New York: Jason Aronson.

_____ (1975b). Melanie Klein. In *Comprehensive Textbook of Psychiatry,* vol. 1, ed. A. M. Freedman, H. I. Kaplan, and B. J. Sadock, pp. 641–650. Baltimore: Williams & Wilkins.

_____ (1976). *Object Relations Theory and Clinical Psychoanalysis.* New York: Jason Aronson.

_____ (1977). The structural diagnosis of borderline personality organization. In *Borderline Personality Disorders: The Concept, the Syndrome, the Patient,* ed. P. Hartocollis, pp. 87–121. New York: International Universities Press.

_____ (1978). The diagnosis of borderline conditions in adolescence. *Adolescent Psychiatry* 6:298–319.

_____ (1980a). Factors in the treatment of narcissistic personality disorder. *Journal of the American Psychoanalytic Association* 18:51–85.

_____ (1980b). *Internal World and External Reality.* New York: Jason Aronson.

_____ (1984). *Severe Personality Disorders.* New Haven, CT: Yale University Press.

_____ (1985). Hysterical and histrionic personality disorders. In *Psychiatry,* vol. 1, ed. R. Michels and J. O. Cavenar, pp. 1–12. Philadelphia: Lippincott.

_____ (1989). The narcissistic personality disorder and the differential diagnosis of antisocial behavior. *The Psychiatric Clinics of North America* 12:553–570.

Kernberg, O. F., Burstein, E., Coyne, L., et al. (1972). Psychotherapy and psychoanalysis: final report of the Menninger Foundation's psychotherapy research project. *Bulletin of the Menninger Clinic* 36:1–275.

Kernberg, O. F., Goldstein, G., Carr, A. C., et al. (1981). Diagnosing borderline personality: a pilot study using multiple diagnostic methods. *Journal of Nervous and Mental Disease* 169:225–231.

Kernberg, O. F., Selzer, M. A., Koenigsberg, et al. (1990). *Psychodynamic Psychotherapy of Borderline Patients.* New York: Basic Books.

Kernberg, P. (1989). Narcissistic personality disorder in childhood. *The Psychiatric Clinics of North America* 12:671–294.

Kety, S. S., Rosenthal, D., Wender, P. H., and Schulsinger, F. (1968). The types and prevalence of mental illness in the biological and adoptive families of adopted schizophrenics. In *The Transmission of Schizophrenia,* ed. D. Rosenthal and S. S. Kety, pp. 345-362. Oxford, England: Pergamon Press.

_____ (1975). Mental illness in biological and adoptive families of adopted individuals who have become schizophrenic: a preliminary report based on psychiatric interviews. In *Genetic Research in Psychiatry,* ed. R. R. Fieve, D. Rosenthal, and H. Brill, pp. 147–165. Baltimore: Johns Hopkins University Press.

Khan, M. M. R. (1963). The concept of cumulative trauma. *Psychoanalytic Study of the Child* 18:286–306. New York: International Universities Press.

_____ (1969). On symbiotic omnipotence. In *The Privacy of the Self,* pp. 82–92. New York: International Universities Press, 1974.

_____ (1974a). *The Privacy of the Self.* New York: International Universities Press.

_____ (1980). *Alienation in Perversion.* New York: International Universities Press.

_____ (1983). *Hidden Selves.* New York: International Universities Press.

Killingmo, B. (1989). Conflict and deficit: implications for technique. *International Journal of Psycho-Analysis* 70:65–79.

Kinston, W. (1980). A theoretical and technical approach to narcissistic disturbance. *International Journal of Psycho-Analysis* 61:383–394.

_____ (1982). An intrapsychic developmental scheme for narcissistic disturbance. *International Review of Psycho-Analysis* 9:253–261.

Klass, D. B., and Offenkrantz, W. (1976). Sartre's contribution to the understanding of narcissism. *International Journal of Psychoanalytic Psychotherapy* 5:547–565.

Klauber, J. (1968). The psychoanalyst as a person. In *Difficulties in the Analytic Encounter,* pp. 123–139. New York: Jason Aronson.

Klein, D. (1975). Psychopharmacology and the borderline patient. In *Borderline States in Psychiatry,* ed. J. Mack, pp. 75–92. New York: Grune & Stratton.

_____ (1977). Psychopharmacological treatment and delineation of borderline disorders. In *Borderline Personality Disorders: The Concept, the Syndrome, the Patient,* ed. P. Hartocollis, pp. 365–384. New York: International Universities Press.

Klein, M. (1935). A contribution to the psychogenesis of manic-depressive states. In *Love, Guilt and Reparation and Other Works, 1921–1945,* pp. 262–289. New York: The Free Press.

_____ (1940). Mourning and its relation to manic-depressive states. In *Love, Guilt and Reparation and Other Works, 1921–1945,* pp. 344–369. New York: Free Press.

_____ (1946). Notes on some schizoid mechanisms. In *Envy and Gratitude and Other Works, 1946–1963,* pp. 1-24. New York: Free Press, 1975.

_____ (1948). *Contributions to Psychoanalysis, 1921–1945.* London: Hogarth Press.

_____ (1955). On identification. In *Envy and Gratitude and Other Works, 1946–1963,*

pp. 141-175. New York: Free Press, 1975.
_____ (1960). *The Psychoanalysis of Children.* New York: Grove Press.
Knight, R. (1953). Borderline states. *Bulletin of the Menninger Clinic* 17:1-12.
_____ (1954). Borderline states. In *Psychoanalytic Psychiatry and Psychology,* ed. R. P. Knight, and C. R. Friedman, pp. 110-122. New York: International Universities Press.
Koch, J. L. A. (1891). *Die Psychopathischen Minderwertigkeiten.* Ravensburg, Germany: Maier.
Kocsis, J., and Mann, J. (1986). Drug treatment of personality disorders and neuroses. In *Psychiatry: The Personality Disorders and Neuroses,* ed. A. Cooper, A. Frances, and M. Sacks, pp. 33-57. New York: Basic Books.
Kohut, H. (1971). *The Analysis of the Self.* New York: International Universities Press.
_____ (1972). Thoughts on narcissism and narcissistic rage. *Psychoanalytic Study of the Child* 27:360-400. New Haven, CT: International Universities Press.
_____ (1977). *Restoration of the Self.* New York: International Universities Press.
_____ (1982). Introspection, empathy and the semi-circle of mental health. *International Journal of Psycho-Analysis* 63:395-407.
_____ (1984). *How Does Analysis Cure?* Chicago: University of Chicago Press.
Kohut, H., and Wolf, E. (1978). The disorders of the self and their treatment: an outline. *International Journal of Psycho-Analysis* 59:413-425.
Kolb, J., and Gunderson, J. (1980). Defining borderline patients with a semistructured interview. *Archives of General Psychiatry* 37:37-41.
Kolb, J., and Wolff, E. (1978). The disorders of the self and their treatment: an outline. *International Journal of Psycho-Analysis* 59:413-426.
Kolb, L. C. (1973). *Modern Clinical Psychiatry,* 8th ed. Philadelphia: Saunders.
Kovel, J. (1981). *The Age of Desire.* New York: Pantheon.
Kraepelin, E. (1905). *Einfuehrung in die Psychiatrische Klinik,* 2nd ed. Leipzig, Germany: Barth.
_____ (1909-1913). *Psychiatry,* 8th ed. Leipzig, Germany: Thieme.
_____ (1921a). *Manic Depressive Illness and Paranoia.* Edinburgh, Scotland: E. S. Livingstone.
_____ (1921b). *Clinical Psychiatry,* 4th ed. Leipzig, Germany: Thieme.
Kramer, P. (1955). On discovering one's identity. *Psychoanalytic Study of the Child* 10:47-74. New York: International Universities Press.
Kramer, S. (1974). Panel report: vicissitudes of infantile omnipotence. *Journal of the American Psychoanalytic Association* 22:588-602.
Kramer, S., and Akhtar, S. (1988). The developmental context of internalized preoedipal object relations. Clinical applications of Mahler's theory of symbiosis and separation-individuation. *Psychoanalytic Quarterly* 42:547-575.
Kretschmer, E. (1925). *Physique and Character.* Trans. W. J. H. Sprott. New York: Harcourt Brace.
_____ (1927). *Der sensitive Bezihungswahn,* vol. 2. Berlin: Springer.
Kris, E. (1956). The personal myth. A problem in psychoanalytic technique. *Journal of the American Psychoanalytic Association* 4:653-681.

Kroll, J. (1988). *The Challenge of the Borderline Patient: Competency in Diagnosis and Treatment.* New York: Norton.

Kurtz, S. (1989). *The Art of Unknowing.* Northvale, NJ: Jason Aronson.

Laing, R. D. (1965). *The Divided Self.* London: Tavistock.

Lampl-de Groot, J. (1949). Neurotics, delinquents and ideal formation. In *Searchlights on Delinquency,* ed. K. R. Eissler, pp. 225–245. New York: International Universities Press.

Lasch, C. (1978). *The Culture of Narcissism: American Life in an Age of Diminishing Expectations.* New York: Norton.

Laughlin, H. P. (1956). *The Neuroses in Clinical Practice.* Philadelphia: Saunders.

Lazare, A. (1971). The hysterical character in psychoanalytic theory. *Archives of General Psychiatry* 25:131–137.

Leaff, L. A. (1978). The antisocial personality: psychodynamic implications. In *The Psychopath: A Comprehensive Study of Antisocial Disorders and Behaviors,* ed. W. H. Reid, pp. 79–117. New York: Brunner/Mazel.

Leichtman, M. (1989). Evolving concepts of borderline personality disorders. *Bulletin of the Menninger Clinic* 53:229–249.

Leonhard, K. (1959). *Die Aufteilung der Endogenen Psychosen,* 2nd ed. Berlin: Akademie.

Levy, K. (1949). The eternal dilettante. In *Searchlight on Delinquency,* ed. K. R. Eissler, pp. 65–76. New York: International Universities Press.

Levy, S. T. (1984). Psychoanalytic perspectives on emptiness. *Journal of the American Psychoanalytic Association* 32:387–404.

Lewin, B. D. (1937). A type of neurotic hypomanic reaction. *Archives Neurology Psychiatry* 37:868–873.

_____ (1941). Comments on hypomanic and related states. *Psychoanalytic Review* 28:238–246.

_____ (1950). *The Psychoanalysis of Elation.* New York: Norton.

Lichtenstein, H. (1961). Identity and sexuality: a study of their interrelationship in man. *Journal of the American Psychoanalytic Association* 9:179–260.

_____ (1963). The dilemma of human identity: notes on self-transformation, self-objectivation and metamorphosis. *Journal of the American Psychoanalytic Association* 11:173–223.

Liebowitz, M. R. (1979). Is borderline a distinct entity? *Schizophrenia Bulletin* 5:23–37.

Liebowitz, M. R., and Klein, D. F. (1981). Interrelationship of hysteroid dysphoria and borderline personality disorder. *Psychiatric Clinics of North America* 4:67–87.

Liebowitz, M. R., Stone, M., and Turkat, I. (1986). Treatment of personality disorders. In *Psychiatry Update: American Psychiatric Association Annual Review,* vol. 5, ed. A. Frances and R. Hales, pp. 356-393. Washington, DC: American Psychiatric Press.

Lifton, R. J. (1971). Protean man. *Archives of General Psychiatry* 24:298–304.

Lilienfeld, S. O., Van Volkenburg, C., Larntz, K., and Akiskal, H. S. (1986). The relationship of histrionic personality disorder to antisocial personality and

somatization disorders. *American Journal of Psychiatry* 143:718–722.
Limentani, A. (1989). *Between Freud and Klein: The Psychoanalytic Quest for Knowledge and Truth.* London: Free Association Books.
Little, M. (1957). "R"—the analyst's total response to his patient's needs. *International Journal of Psycho-Analysis* 38:240–254.
_____ (1990). *Psychotic Anxieties and Containment.* Northvale, NJ: Jason Aronson.
Livesley, W. J., West, M., and Tanney, A. (1986). Historical comment on *DSM-III* schizoid and avoidant personality disorders. *American Journal of Psychiatry* 142:1344–1346.
Loewald, H. W. (1951). Ego and reality. *International Journal of Psycho-Analysis* 32:10–18.
_____ (1974). Current status of the concept of infantile neurosis. *Psychoanalytic Study of the Child* 29:183–188. New Haven, CT: International Universities Press.
_____ (1979). The waning of the Oedipal complex. *Journal of the American Psychoanalytic Association* 27:751–775.
Lombroso, C. (1876). *Crime, Its Causes and Remedies.* Trans. H. P. Horton. Boston: Little, Brown, 1911.
Lowenthal, M. F. (1968). The relationship between social factors and mental health in the aged. In *Aging in Modern Society,* ed. A. Simon and L. J. Epstein, pp. 187–197. Washington, DC: American Psychiatric Association.
Lower, R., Escoll, P., and Huxster, H. (1972). Bases for judgments of analyzability. *Journal of the American Psychoanalytic Association* 20:610–621.
Lynd, H. M. (1958). *On Shame and the Search for Identity.* New York: Harcourt Brace.
Mack, J. E. (1975). Borderline states: an historical perspective. In *Borderline States in Psychiatry,* ed. J. E. Mack, pp. 1–27. New York: Grune & Stratton.
Mackinnon, R. A., and Michaels, R. (1971). *The Psychiatric Interview in Clinical Practice.* Philadelphia: Saunders.
Magnan, V. (1893). *Leçons Cliniques sur les Maladies Mentales,* 2nd ed. Paris: Bataille.
Mahler, M. S. (1958a). Autism and symbiosis: two extreme disturbances of identity. *International Journal of Psycho-Analysis* 39:77–83.
_____ (1958b). On two crucial phases of integration of the sense of identity: separation-individuation and bisexual identity. *Journal of the American Psychoanalytic Association* 6:136–139.
_____ (1966a). *Discussion of "Problems of overidealization of the analyst and analysis."* Abstracted in *Psychoanalytic Quarterly* 37:637.
_____ (1966b). Notes on the development of basic moods: the depressive affect. In *Psychoanalysis—A General Psychology,* ed. R. Loewenstein, L. M. Newman, M. Schur, and A. J. Solnit, pp. 152–168. New York: International Universities Press.
_____ (1967). On human symbiosis and the vicissitudes of individuation. In *The Selected Papers of Margaret S. Mahler,* vol. 2, pp. 77–98. New York: Jason Aronson.
_____ (1968). *On Human Symbiosis and the Vicissitudes of Individuation.* Vol. 1. Infantile Psychosis. New York: International Universities Press.
_____ (1971). A study of the separation-individuation process and its possible application to borderline phenomena in the psychoanalytic situation. *Psychoana-*

lytic Study of the Child 26:402–424. New Haven, CT: International Universities Press.

_____ (1972). Rapprochement subphase of the separation-individuation process. *Psychoanalytic Quarterly* 41:487–506.

_____ (1975). On the current status of the infantile neurosis. In *The Selected Papers of Margaret S. Mahler,* vol. 2, pp. 189–194. New York: Jason Aronson.

Mahler, M. S., and Kaplan, L. (1977). Developmental aspects in the assessment of narcissistic and so-called borderline personalities. In *Borderline Personality Disorders: The Concept, the Syndrome, the Patient,* ed. P. Hartocollis, pp. 71–86. New York: International Universities Press.

Mahler, M. S., Pine, F., and Bergman, A. (1975). *The Psychological Birth of the Human Infant.* New York: Basic Books.

Maltsberger, J. T., and Buie, D. H. (1974). Countertransference hate in the treatment of suicidal patients. *Archives of General Psychiatry* 30:625–633.

Marmor, J. (1953). Orality in the hysterical personality. *Journal of the American Psychoanalytic Association* 1:656–671.

Marx, K. (1867). *Das Kapital.* Hamburg, Germany: Verlog Von Otto Meissner.

Masterson, J. F. (1967). *The Psychiatric Dilemma of Adolescence.* Boston: Little, Brown.

_____ (1972). *Treatment of the Borderline Adolescent: A Developmental Approach.* New York: Wiley Interscience.

_____ (1976). *Psychotherapy of the Borderline Adult: A Developmental Approach.* New York: Brunner/Mazel.

Masterson, J. F., and Rinsley, D. (1975). The borderline syndrome: the role of the mother in the genesis and psychic structure of the borderline personality. *International Journal of Psycho-Analysis* 56:163–177.

Maudsley, H. (1896). *Responsibility in Mental Disease.* London: King and Company.

Mawson, D., Grounds, A., and Tantam, D. (1985). Violence and Asperger's syndrome: a case study. *British Journal of Psychiatry* 147:566–568.

McCord, W., and McCord, J. (1956). *Psychopathy and Delinquency.* New York: Grune & Stratton.

_____ (1964). *The Psychopath: An Essay on the Criminal Mind.* Princeton, NJ: Van Nostrand.

McGlashan, T. H. (1983). The borderline syndrome: I. Testing three diagnostic systems: II. Is it a variant of schizophrenia or affective disorder? *Archives of General Psychiatry* 40:1311–1323.

_____ (1986). Schizotypal personality disorder. The Chestnut Lodge follow-up study: VI. Long-term follow-up perspectives. *Archives of General Psychiatry* 43:329–334.

_____ (1987). Testing *DSM-III* symptom criteria for schizotypal and borderline personality disorders. *Archives of General Psychiatry* 44:143–148.

Meehl, P. E. (1962). Schizotaxia, schizotypy, schizophrenia. *American Psychologist* 17:827–838.

Meissner, W. W. (1978a). Notes on some conceptual aspects of borderline personality organization. *International Review of Psycho-Analysis* 5:297–311.

_____ (1978b). *The Paranoid Process*. New York: Jason Aronson.
_____ (1978c). Theoretical assumptions of concepts of the borderline personality. *Journal of the American Psychoanalytic Association* 26:559–598.
_____ (1982). Notes on the potential differentiation of borderline conditions. *International Journal of Psychoanalytic Psychotherapy* 9:3–49.
_____ (1984). *The Borderline Spectrum: Differential Diagnosis and Developmental Issues*. New York: Jason Aronson.
Melges, F. T., and Swartz, M. S. (1989). Oscillations of attachment in borderline personality disorder. *American Journal of Psychiatry* 146:1115–1120.
Mellsop, G., and Varghesi, F. (1982). The reliability of Axis II of *DSM-III*. *American Journal of Psychiatry* 139:1360–1361.
Menninger, K. A. (1938). *Man Against Himself*. New York: Harcourt.
_____ (1958). *Theory of Psychoanalytic Technique*. New York: Basic Books.
Meyer, J. K. (1980). Body image, selfness, and gender sense. *Psychiatric Clinics of North America* 3:21–36.
_____ (1982). The theory of gender identity disorders. *Journal of the American Psychoanalytic Association* 30:381–418.
Miller, A. (1981). *Prisoners of Childhood*. New York: Basic Books.
Miller, I. (1965). On the return of symptoms in the terminal phase of psychoanalysis. *International Journal of Psycho-Analysis* 45:487–501.
Millon, T. (1969). *Modern Psychopathology: A Biosocial Approach to Maladaptive Learning and Functioning*. Philadelphia: Saunders.
_____ (1981). *Disorders of Personality: DSM-III, Axis-II*. New York: Wiley.
Millon, T., and Millon, R. (1974). *Abnormal Behavior and Personality*. Philadelphia: Saunders.
Modell, A. (1963). Primitive object relationships and the predisposition to schizophrenia. *International Journal of Psycho-Analysis* 44:282–292.
_____ (1976). The holding environment and the therapeutic action of psychoanalysis. *Journal of the American Psychoanalytic Association* 24:285–307.
_____ (1984). *Psychoanalysis in a New Context*. New York: International Universities Press.
Moore, B. E., and Fine, B. D., eds. (1967). *A Glossary of Psychoanalytic Terms and Concepts*. New York: American Psychoanalytic Association.
Morey, L. C. (1985). An empirical comparison of interpersonal and *DSM-III* approaches to classification of personality disorders. *Psychiatry* 48:358–364.
_____ (1988). Personality disorders in *DSM-III* and *DSM-III-R:* convergence, coverage and internal consistency. *American Journal of Psychiatry* 154:573–577.
Morris, D., Soroker, E., and Burrus, G. (1954). Follow-up studies of shy, withdrawn children: I. Evaluation of later adjustment. *American Journal of Orthopsychiatry* 24:743–750.
Munro, A. (1987). Paranoid (delusional) disorders: *DSM-III-R* and beyond. *Comprehensive Psychiatry* 28:35–39.
Nakdimen, K. A. (1986). Borderline personality disorder and *DSM-III* (letter to editor). *American Journal of Psychiatry* 144:254.
Nanarello, J. J. (1953). Schizoid. *Journal of Nervous and Mental Diseases* 118:237–249.

Ndtei, D. M. (1986). Paranoid disorder—environmental, cultural or constitutional phenomenon? *Acta Psychiatrica Scandinavia* 74:50–54.

Nemiah, J. C. (1961). *Foundations of Psychopathology.* New York: Oxford University Press.

Niederland, W. G. (1956). Clinical observations on the "little man" phenomenon. *Psychoanalytic Study of the Child* 11:381–395. New York: International Universities Press.

Noble, D. (1951). A study of dreams in schizophrenia and allied states. *American Journal of Psychiatry* 107:612–616.

Novick, J. (1982). Termination. *Psychoanalytic Inquiry* 2:329–365.

O'Connell, M., Cooper, S., Perry, J. C., and Hoke, L. (1989). The relationship between thought disorder and psychotic symptoms in borderline personality disorder. *Journal of Nervous and Mental Disease* 177:273–278.

Offer, D. (1969). *The Psychological World of the Teenager: A Study of Normal Adolescent Boys.* New York: Basic Books.

_____ (1971). Rebellion and antisocial behavior. *American Journal of Psychoanalysis* 31:13–19.

Olden, C. (1941). About the fascinating effect of the narcissistic personality. *American Imago* 2:347–355.

_____ (1946). Headline intelligence. *Psychoanalytic Study of the Child* 2:263–269. New York: International Universities Press.

O'Neal, P., Robins, L. M., King, L. J., and Schaefer, J. (1962). Parental deviance and the genesis of sociopathic personality. *American Journal of Psychiatry* 118:1114–1124.

Ovessey, L. (1955). Pseudohomosexuality, the paranoid mechanism and paranoia. *Psychiatry* 18:163–173.

Pao, P. N. (1969). Pathological jealousy. *Psychoanalytic Quarterly* 38:616.

_____ (1971). Elation, hypomania and mania. *Journal of the American Psychoanalytic Association* 19:787–798.

Parens, H. (1980). An exploration of the relations of instinctual drives and the symbiosis/separation-individuation process. *Journal of the American Psychoanalytic Association* 28:89–114.

Partridge, G. E. (1930). Current conceptions of psychopathic personalities. *American Journal of Psychiatry* 10:53–99.

Perry, J. C., and Klerman, G. L. (1978). The borderline patient. *Archives of General Psychiatry* 35:141–150.

_____ (1980). Clinical features of the borderline personality disorder. *American Journal of Psychiatry* 137:165–173.

Person, E. S. (1986). Manipulativeness in entrepreneurs and psychopaths. In *Unmasking the Psychopath: Antisocial Personality and Related Syndromes,* ed. W. H. Reid, D. Dorr, J. I. Walker, and J. W. Bonner III, pp. 256–273. New York: Norton.

Pfeiffer, E. (1974). Borderline states. *Diseases of the Nervous System* 35:212–219.

Pfohl, B., Coryell, W., Zimmerman, M., and Strangel, D. (1986). *DSM-III* personality disorders: diagnostic overlap and internal consistency of individual

DSM-III criteria. *Comprehensive Psychiatry* 27:21–34.

Piaget, J. (1937). *The Construction of Reality in the Child.* New York: Basic Books. 1954.

Pinel, P. (1801). *Abhandlung uber Geisteverirrunger oder Manie.* Wien, Austria: Carl Schaumburg.

Plakum, E. M., Burkhardt, P. E., and Muller, J. P. (1985). Fourteen-year follow-up of borderline and schizotypal personality disorders. *Comprehensive Psychiatry* 26:448–455.

Poland, W. (1975). Tact as a psychoanalytic function. *International Journal of Psycho-Analysis* 56:155–162.

Polatin, P. (1975). Paranoid states. In *Comprehensive Textbook of Psychiatry,* vol. 1, ed. A. M. Kaplan, H. I. Kaplan, and B. J. Sadock, pp. 992–1002. Baltimore: Williams & Wilkins.

Pope, H. G., Jonas, J. M., Hudson, J. I., et al. (1983). The validity of *DSM-III* borderline personality disorder: a phenomenologic, family history, treatment response and long-term follow-up study. *Archives of General Psychiatry* 40:23–30.

——— (1985). An empirical study of psychosis in borderline personality disorder. *American Journal of Psychiatry* 142:1285–1290.

Prichard, J. C. (1835). *Treatise on Insanity.* London: Sherwood Gilbert and Piper.

——— (1837). *A Treatise on Insanity and Other Disorders Affecting the Mind.* Philadelphia: Carey, Hart.

Pulver, S. E. (1970). Narcissism: the term and the concept. *Journal of the American Psychoanalytic Association* 18:319–342.

——— (1978). Survey of psychoanalytic practice 1976: some trends and implications. *Journal of the American Psychoanalytic Association* 26:615–631.

——— (1991). Termination and separation-individuation. In *Beyond the Symbiotic Orbit: Advances in Separation-Individuation Theory—Essays in Honor of Selma Kramer, M. D.,* ed. S. Akhtar and H. Parens, pp. 389–404. Hillsdale, NJ: Analytic Press.

Rado, S. (1927). Das problem der Melancholie. *Internationale Zeitschrift für Psychoanalyse* 13:439–455.

——— (1953). Dynamics and classification of disordered behavior. *American Journal of Psychiatry* 110:406–416.

Ramchandani, D. (1989). The concept of projective identification and its clinical relevance. *American Journal of Psychotherapy* 43:238–247.

Rangell, L. (1955). The borderline case. *Journal of the American Psychoanalytic Association* 3:285–298.

——— (1966). An overview of the ending of an analysis. In *Psychoanalysis in the Americas,* ed. R. E. Litmin, pp. 141–173. New York: International Universities Press.

——— (1980). *The Mind of Watergate.* New York: Norton.

Rapaport, D., Gill, M., and Schafer, R. (1945–1946). *Diagnostic Psychological Testing: The Theory, Statistical Evaluation, and Diagnostic Evaluation of a Battery of Tests,* vol. 1, pp. 16–28; vol. 2, pp. 24–31, 329–366. Chicago: Year Book Publishers.

Rappeport, J. R. (1974). Antisocial behavior. In *The American Handbook of*

Psychiatry, vol. 3, ed. S. Arieti and E. B. Brody, 2nd ed., pp. 255–269. New York: Basic Books.

Ray, I. (1838). *A Treatise on the Medical Jurisprudence of Insanity.* Cambridge, MA: Harvard University Press, 1962.

Regier, B., Myers, J., Kramer, M., et al. (1984). The NIMH epidemiologic catchment area program: historical context, major objectives, and study population characteristics. *Archives of General Psychiatry* 41:934–941.

Reich, A. (1954). Early identification as archaic elements in the superego. *Journal of the American Psychoanalytic Association* 2:218–238.

_____ (1960). Pathologic forms of self-esteem regulation. *Psychoanalytic Study of the Child* 15:215–232. New York: International Universities Press.

Reich, J., and Noyes, R. (1986). Differentiating schizoid and avoidant personality disorders (letter to editor). *American Journal of Psychiatry* 143:1002.

_____ (1987). Sex distribution of *DSM-III* personality disorders in psychiatric outpatients. *American Journal of Psychiatry* 144:485–488.

Reich, W. (1925). *Der Triebhafte Charakter.* Leipzig: Internationaler Psychoanalytischer Verlag.

_____ (1933). *Character Analysis.* Trans. V. R. Carfagno, 3rd ed. New York: Farrar, Straus and Giroux.

Reid, W. H. (1978). The sadness of the psychopath. *American Journal of Psychotherapy* 32:496–509.

_____ (1981). Antisocial personality and related syndromes. In *Personality Disorders: Diagnosis and Management,* ed. J. R. Lion, 2nd. ed., pp. 133–162. Baltimore: Williams & Wilkins.

_____ (1985). Antisocial personality. In *Psychiatry,* vol. 1, ed. R. Michels and J. O. Cavenar, pp. 1–11. Philadelphia: Lippincott.

Reiser, M. F. (1971). Psychological issues in training for research in psychiatry. *Journal of Psychiatric Review* 8:531–537.

Rettersol, N. (1985). Paranoid disorders. In *Psychiatry,* vol. 2, ed. R. Michels and J. O. Cavenar, pp. 1–19. Philadelphia: Lippincott.

Rey, J. (1979). Schizoid phenomena in the borderline. In *Advances in Psychotherapy of the Borderline Patient,* ed. J. LeBoit and A. Capponi, pp. 449–484. New York: Jason Aronson.

Rinsley, D. B. (1977). An object relations view of borderline personality. In *Borderline Personality Disorders: The Concept, the Syndrome, the Patient,* ed. P. Hartocollis, pp. 47–70. New York: International Universities Press.

_____ (1978). Borderline psychopathology: a review of etiology dynamics and treatment. *International Review of Psycho-Analysis* 5:45–54.

_____ (1980). The developmental etiology of borderline and narcissistic disorders. *Bulletin of the Menninger Clinic* 44:127–134.

_____ (1981). Dynamic and developmental issues in borderline and related "spectrum" disorders. *Psychiatric Clinics of North America* 4:117–132.

_____ (1982). *Borderline and Other Self Disorders: A Developmental and Object Relations Perspective.* New York: Jason Aronson.

Ritvo, S. (1974). The current status of the infantile neurosis. *Psychoanalytic Study of the Child* 29:159–191. New Haven, CT: International Universities Press.

Robbins, L. L. (1956). Panel report: the borderline case. *Journal of the American Psychoanalytic Association* 4:550–563.

Robbins, M. D. (1982). Narcissistic personality as a symbiotic character disorder. *International Journal of Psycho-Analysis* 63:457–473.

——— (1983). Toward a new mind model for the primitive personalities. *International Journal of Psycho-Analysis* 64:127–148.

Robins, L. R. (1966). *Deviant Children Grown Up*. Baltimore: Williams & Wilkins.

Robins, L. R., Helzer, J., Weissman, M., et al. (1984). Lifetime prevalence of specific psychiatric disorders in three sites. *Archives of General Psychiatry* 41:949–958.

Rosenberger, P. H., and Miller, G. A. (1989). Comparing borderline definitions: DSM-III borderline and schizotypal personality disorders. *Journal of Abnormal Psychology* 98:161–169.

Rosenfeld, H. (1964). On the psychopathology of narcissism: a clinical approach. *International Journal of Psycho-Analysis* 45:332–337.

——— (1971). Theory of life and death instincts: aggressive aspects of narcissism. *International Journal of Psycho-Analysis* 52:169–183.

——— (1987). The influence of projective identification in the analyst's task. In *Impasse and Interpretation*, pp. 157–261. London: Tavistock.

Rosenthal, D. (1975). The genetics of schizophrenia. In *Generic Research in Psychiatry*, ed. R. R. Fieve, D. Rosenthal, and H. Brill, pp. 199–208. Baltimore: Johns Hopkins University Press.

Rosenthal, D., Wender, P. H., Kety, S. S., et al. (1968). Schizophrenics' offspring reared in adoptive homes. In *The Transmission of Schizophrenia*, ed. D. Rosenthal and S. S. Kety, pp. 377–391. Oxford: Pergamon Press.

——— (1971). The adopted-away offspring of schizophrenics. *American Journal of Psychiatry* 128:307–311.

Ross, N. (1967). The "as-if" personality. *Journal of the American Psychoanalytic Association* 15:59–82.

Rothstein, A. (1979). Oedipal conflicts in narcissistic personality disorders. *International Journal of Psycho-Analysis* 60:189–199.

——— (1982). Analyzability. *International Journal of Psycho-Analysis* 63:177–188.

Ryan, R., and Cicchetti, D. V. (1985). Predicting quality of Alliance in the initial psychotherapy interview. *Journal of Nervous and Mental Disease* 173:717–725.

Rycroft, C. (1960). The analysis of a paranoid personality. *International Journal of Psycho-Analysis* 41:59–69.

Salzman, L. (1974). Other character personality syndromes: schizoid, inadequate, passive-aggressive, paranoid, dependent. In *American Handbook of Psychiatry*, vol. 3, ed. S. Arieti and E. B. Brody, 2nd ed., pp. 224–234. New York: Basic Books.

Schmideberg, M. (1947). The treatment of psychopathic and borderline patients. *American Journal of Psychotherapy* 1:45–71.

——— (1949). The analytic treatment of major criminals: therapeutic results and technical problems. In *Searchlights on Delinquency*, ed. K. R. Eissler, pp. 174–192. New York: International Universities Press.

Schneider, K. (1950). *Psychopathic Personalities.* Trans. M. W. Hamilton. Springfield, IL: Charles C Thomas, 1958.

Schulsinger, F. (1977). Psychopathy: heredity and environment. In *Biosocial Basis of Criminal Behavior,* ed. S. A. Mednick, and K. O. Christiansen, pp. 109–141. New York: Gardener Press.

Schulz, C. (1980). All-or-none phenomena in the psychotherapy of severe disorders. In *The Psychotherapy of Schizophrenia,* ed. J. Strauss, M. Bowers, T. Downey, et al. pp. 181–189. New York: Plenum.

Schwartz, L. (1974). Narcissistic personality disorders—a clinical discussion. *Journal of the American Psychoanalytic Association* 22:292–306.

Searles, H. F. (1960). *The Non-human Environment in Normal Development and in Schizophrenia.* New York: International Universities Press.

_____ (1969). A case of borderline thought disorder. *International Journal of Psycho-Analysis* 50:655–664.

_____ (1978). Psychoanalytic therapy with the borderline adult: some principles concerning technique. In *New Perspectives on Psychotherapy of the Borderline Adult,* ed. J. F. Masterson, pp. 41–65. New York: Brunner/Mazel.

_____ (1979). *Countertransference and Related Subjects: Selected Papers.* New York: International Universities Press.

_____ (1986). *My Work with Borderline Patients.* Northvale, NJ: Jason Aronson.

Selzer, M. A., Koenigsberg, H. W., and Kernberg, O. F. (1987). The initial contract in the treatment of borderline patients. *American Journal of Psychiatry* 144:927–930.

Settlage, C. F. (1977). Narcissistic and borderline personality disorders. *Journal of the American Psychoanalytic Association* 25:805.

Shapiro, D. (1965). *Neurotic Styles.* New York: Basic Books.

Shapiro, E., Zinner, J., Shapiro, R., et al. (1975). The influence of family experience on borderline personality development. *International Review of Psycho-Analysis* 2:399–411.

Sheehy, M., Goldsmith, I., and Charles, E. (1980). A comparative study of borderline patients in a psychiatric outpatient clinic. *American Journal of Psychiatry* 137:1374–1379.

Sheldon, W. H. (1970). *Varieties of Delinquent Youth.* Vol. 1. Darien, CT: Hafner.

Shepherd, M. (1961). Morbid jealousy: some clinical and social aspects of psychiatric symptoms. *British Journal of Psychiatry* 107:687–714.

Siever, L. J., and Gunderson, J. G. (1983). The search for a schizotypal personality: historical origins and current status. *Comprehensive Psychiatry* 24:199–212.

Siever, L. J., and Kendler, K. S. (1987). An evaluation of the *DSM-III* categories of paranoid, schizoid and schizotypal personality disorders. In *Diagnosis and Classification in Psychiatry,* ed. G. Tischler, pp. 300–320. London: Cambridge University Press.

Siever, L. J., and Klar, H. (1986). A review of DSM-III criteria for the personality disorders. In *Psychiatry Update—American Psychiatric Association Annual Review,* vol. 5, ed. A. J. Frances and E. R. Hales, pp. 279–314. Washington, DC: American Psychiatric Press.

Simons, R. D., Rubinstein, M., and Franks, R. D. (1985). Depression and depressive disorders. In *Understanding Human Behavior in Health and Illness,* ed. R. C. Simons, 3rd ed., pp. 297–712. Baltimore: Williams & Wilkins.

Singer, M. (1975). The borderline delinquent: the interlocking of intrapsychic and interactional determinants. *International Review of Psycho-Analysis* 2:429–440.

_____ (1977a). The experience of emptiness in narcissistic and borderline states: deficiency and ego defect versus dynamic-defensive models. *International Review of Psycho-Analysis* 4:459–470.

_____ (1977b). The experience of emptiness in narcissistic and borderline states: the struggle for a sense of self and the potential for suicide. *International Review of Psycho-Analysis* 4:471–479.

_____ (1979). Some metapsychological and clinical distinctions between borderline and neurotic conditions with special consideration to the self experience. *International Journal of Psycho-Analysis* 60:489–499.

_____ (1981). Anal sadism, rapprochement and self representation: analysis of preverbal complaint of emptiness. *Bulletin of the Philadelphia Association for Psychoanalysis* 8:173–192.

Singer, M. T. (1977). The borderline diagnosis and psychological tests: review and research. In *Borderline Personality Disorders,* ed. P. Hartocollis, pp. 193–212. New York: International Universities Press.

Slater, E., and Roth, M. (1969). *Clinical Psychiatry,* 3rd ed. Baltimore: Williams & Wilkins.

_____ (1977). *Clinical Psychiatry.* London: Bailliere, Tindal.

Snyder, S., Pitts, W. M., and Gustin, Q. (1983). Absence of borderline personality disorder in later years (letter to editor). *American Journal of Psychiatry* 140:1527–1529.

Socarides, C. (1966). On vengeance: the desire to "get even." *Journal of the American Psychoanalytic Association* 14:356.

_____ (1970). A psychoanalytic study of the desire for sexual transformation (transsexualism): the plaster of paris men. *International Journal of Psycho-Analysis* 51:341–349.

Soloff, P. H., George, A., Nathan, S., et al. (1989). Amitriptyline versus haloperidol in borderlines: final outcomes and predictors of response. *Journal of Clinical Psychopharmacology* 9:238–246.

Spiegel, L. A. (1959). The self, the sense of the self and perception. *Psychoanalytic Study of the Child* 14:81–112. New York: International Universities Press.

Spitz, R. (1957). *No and Yes: On the Genesis of Human Communication.* New York: International Universities Press.

Spitzer, R. L., and Endicott, J. (1979). Justification for separating schizotypal and borderline personality disorders. *Schizophrenia Bulletin* 5:95–102.

Spitzer, R. L., Endicott, J., and Gibbon, M. (1979). Crossing the border into borderline personality and borderline schizophrenia: the development of criteria. *Archives of General Psychiatry* 36:17–24.

Spitzer, R. L., Forman, J. B. W., and Nee, J. (1979). DSM-III field trials. I: initial interrater diagnostic reliability. *American Journal of Psychiatry* 136:815–817.

Spitzer, R. L., Williams, J. B. W., and Skodol, A. E. (1980). *DSM-III:* the major achievements and an overview. *American Journal of Psychiatry* 137:151–164.

Spruiell, V. (1975). Three strands of narcissism. *Psychoanalytic Quarterly* 44:577–595.

Stanton, A. H. (1978). Personality disorders. In *The Harvard Guide to Modern Psychiatry,* ed. A. M. Nicholi, pp. 283–295. Cambridge, MA: Belknap Press.

Starcevic, V. (1989). Contrasting patterns in the relationship between hypochondriasis and narcissism. *British Journal of Medical Psychology* 62:311–323.

Stern, A. (1938). Psychoanalytic investigation and therapy in borderline group of neuroses. *Psychoanalytic Quarterly* 7:467–489.

Stoller, R. (1968). *Sex and Gender.* New York: Science House.

_____ (1972). The "bedrock" of masculinity and femininity: bisexuality. *Archives of General Psychiatry* 26:207–212.

Stone, L. (1954). The widening scope of indications for psychoanalysis. *Journal of the American Psychoanalytic Association* 2:564–594.

Stone, M. H. (1980). *The Borderline Syndrome.* New York: McGraw-Hill.

_____ (1983). Borderline personality disorder. In *New Psychiatric Syndromes:* DSM-III *and Beyond,* ed. S. Akhtar, pp. 19–48. New York: Jason Aronson.

_____ (1989). Murder. *Psychiatric Clinics of North America* 12:643–652.

Strenger, C. (1989). The classic and romantic visions in psychoanalysis. *International Journal of Psycho-Analysis* 70:595–610.

Suttie, I. (1935). *The Origins of Love and Hate.* London: Keegan Paul, Trench, Trubner.

Svrakic, D. M. (1985). Emotional features of narcissistic personality disorder. *American Journal of Psychiatry* 142:720–724.

_____ (1986). Dr. Svrakic replies (letter to editor). *American Journal of Psychiatry* 143:269.

Szurek, S. A. (1942). Notes on the genesis of psychopathic personality trends. *Psychiatry* 5:1–6.

_____ (1949). Some impressions from clinical experience with delinquents. In *Searchlights on Delinquency,* ed. K. R. Eissler, pp. 115–127. New York: International Universities Press.

Tartakoff, H. (1966). The normal personality in our culture and the Nobel Prize complex. In *Psychoanalysis: A General Psychology,* ed. R. M. Loewenstein, L. M. Newman, and M. Schur, pp. 222–252. New York: International Universities Press.

Tausk, V. (1919). Uber die entstehung des beeinflussungsapparates in der schizophrenie. *International Journal of Psycho-Analysis* 5:1–33.

Terry, G. C., and Rennie, T. (1938). Analysis of paraergasia. *American Journal of Orthopsychiatry* 9:817–818.

Thompson, G. N. (1953). *The Psychopathic Delinquent and Criminal.* Springfield, IL: Charles C Thomas.

Ticho, E. (1972a). The effects of the psychoanalyst's personality on the treatment. *Psychoanalytic Forum* 4:221–247.

_____ (1972b). Termination of psychoanalysis: treatment goals, life goals. *Psychoanalytic Quarterly* 41:315–333.

Tienari, P. (1963). Psychiatric illness in identical twins. *Acta Psychiatria Scandinavica* 171:39.

Tobak, M. (1989). Lying and the paranoid personality (letter to editor). *American Journal of Psychiatry* 146:125.

Torgersen, S. (1984). Genetic and nosological aspects of schizotypal and borderline personality disorders: a twin study. *Archives of General Psychiatry* 1:546–554.

_____ (1985). Relationship of schizotypal personality disorder to schizophrenia: genetics. *Schizophrenia Bulletin* 11:554–563.

Tupin, J. P. (1981). Histrionic personality. In *Personality Disorders: Diagnosis and Management,* ed. J. R. Lion, 2nd ed., pp. 85–96. Baltimore: Williams & Wilkins.

Tyson, P. (1982). A developmental line of gender identity, gender role, and choice of love object. *Journal of the American Psychoanalytic Association* 30:61–86.

Tyson, R., and Tyson, P. (1984). Narcissism and superego development. *Journal of the American Psychoanalytic Association* 32:75–91.

van der Waals, H. G. (1965). Problems of narcissism. *Bulletin of the Menninger Clinic* 29:293–311.

Volkan, V. D. (1976). *Primitive Internalized Object Relations.* New York: International Universities Press.

_____ (1980a). Narcissistic personality organization and "reparative" leadership. *International Journal of Group Psychotherapy* 30:131–152.

_____ (1980b). Transsexualism: as examined from the point of view of internalized object relations. In *On Sexuality: Psychoanalytic Observations,* ed. T. Karasu and C. Socarides, pp. 189–121. New York: International Universities Press.

_____ (1981). *Linking Objects and Linking Phenomena.* New York: International Universities Press.

_____ (1982). Narcissistic personality disorder. In *Critical Problems in Psychiatry,* ed. J. O. Cavenar and H. K. H. Brodie, pp. 332–350. Philadelphia: Lippincott.

_____ (1986). The narcissism of minor differences in the psychological gap between opposing nations. *Psychoanalytic Inquiry* 6:175–191.

_____ (1987). *Six Steps in the Treatment of Borderline Personality Organization.* Northvale, NJ: Jason Aronson.

Waelder, R. (1925). The psychoses, their mechanisms and accessibility to influence. *International Journal of Psycho-Analysis* 6:259–281.

_____ (1930). The principle of multiple function: observations on overdetermination. *Psychoanalytic Quarterly* 5:45–62.

Wallerstein, R. S. (1983). Self psychology and "classical" psychoanalytic psychology: the nature of their relationship. In *The Future of Psychoanalysis,* ed. A. Goldberg, pp. 19–63. New York: International Universities Press.

Walsh, F. (1977). The family of the borderline patient. In *The Borderline Patient,* ed. R. Grinker and B. Werble, pp. 149–177. New York: Jason Aronson.

Walters, O. (1955). Metapsychological critique of Freud's Schreber analysis. *Psychoanalytic Review* 42:321–342.

Wender, P. H., Rosenthal, D., Kety, S. S., et al. (1974). Crossfostering: A research strategy for clarifying the role of genetic and experiential factors in the etiology of schizophrenia. *Archives of General Psychiatry* 30:121–128.

Werman, D. S. (1979). Chance, ambiguity, and psychological mindedness. *Psychoanalytic Quarterly* 48:107–115.

Wheelis, A. (1958). *The Quest for Identity.* New York: Norton.

_____ (1966). *The Illusionless Man.* New York: Colophon Books/Harper & Row.

Widiger, T. A., and Frances, A. (1985). Axis II personality disorders: diagnostic and treatment issues. *Hospital and Community Psychiatry* 36:619–627.

_____ (1987). Interviews and inventories for the measurement of personality disorders. *Clinical Psychological Review* 7:49–75.

_____ (1989). "Epidemiology, Diagnosis, and Comorbidity of Borderline Personality Disorder." In *Review of Psychiatry,* vol. 8., ed. A. Tasman, R. Hales, and A. J. Frances, pp. 8–24. Washington, DC: American Psychiatric Press.

Widiger, T. A., Frances, A., Spitzer, R. L., and Williams, J. B. W. (1988). The *DSM-III-R* personality disorders: an overview. *American Journal of Psychiatry* 145:786–795.

Widiger, T. A., Frances, A., Warner, L., and Bluhm, C. (1986). Diagnostic criteria for the borderline and schizotypal personality disorders. *Journal of Abnormal Psychology* 95:43–51.

Wing, L. (1981). Asperger's syndrome: a clinical account. *Psychological Medicine* 11:115–129.

Winnicott, D. W. (1935). The manic defense. In *Collected Papers: Through Paediatrics to Psychoanalysis,* pp. 129–144. London: Tavistock, 1958.

_____ (1947). Hate in the countertransference. In *Collected Papers: Through Paediatrics to Psychoanalysis,* pp. 194–203. London: Tavistock, 1958.

_____ (1949). Mind and its relation to the psychesoma. In *Collected Papers: Through Paediatrics to Psychoanalysis,* pp. 243–255. London: Hogarth Press, 1958.

_____ (1952). Psychosis and child care. In *Collected Papers: Through Paediatrics to Psychoanalysis,* pp. 219–228. London: Tavistock, 1958.

_____ (1953). Transitional objects and transitional phenomena: a study of the first not-me possession. *International Journal of Psycho-Analysis* 34:89–97.

_____ (1956). The antisocial tendency. In *Collected Papers: Through Paediatrics to Psychoanalysis,* pp. 306–315. London: Tavistock, 1958.

_____ (1960). Ego distortion in terms of true and false. In *The Maturational Process and the Facilitating Environment,* pp. 140–152. New York: International Universities Press, 1965.

_____ (1963). The development of the capacity for concern. In *The Maturational Processes and the Facilitating Environment,* pp. 73–82. New York: International Universities Press.

_____ (1965). *The Maturational Process and the Facilitating Environment.* New York: International Universities Press.

_____ (1971). *Playing and Reality.* London: Penguin Books.

Winokur, G. (1977). Delusional disorder. *Comprehensive Psychiatry* 18:511–521.

_____ (1985). Familial psychopathology in delusional disorder. *Comprehensive Psychiatry* 26:241–248.

Winokur, G., Clayton, P. J., and Reich, T. (1969). *Manic Depressive Illness.* St. Louis: C. V. Mosby.

Winokur, G., and Crowe, R. R. (1975). Personality disorders. In *Comprehensive*

Textbook of Psychiatry, vol. 2, ed. A. M. Freedman, H. I. Kaplan, and B. J. Sadock, pp. 1279-1297. Baltimore: Williams & Wilkins.

Wittels, F. (1930). The hysterical character. *Medical Review of Reviews,* 36:186-190.

Wolberg, A. R. (1973). *The Borderline Patient.* New York: Intercontinental Medical Books.

Wolff, S. (1973). *Children Under Stress.* 2nd ed. Harmondsworth, England: Penguin.

Wolff, S., and Barlow, A. (1970). Schizoid personality in childhood: a comparative study of schizoid, autistic and normal children. *Journal of Child Psychology and Psychiatry* 20:29-46.

Wolff, S., and Chick, J. (1980). Schizoid personality in childhood. *Psychological Medicine* 10:85-101.

Wolman, B. B. (1987). *The Sociopathic Personality.* New York: Brunner/Mazel.

Wurmser, L. (1981). Phobic care in the addictions and the paranoid process. *International Journal of Psychoanalytic Psychotherapy* 8:311-335.

Yochelson, S., and Samenow, S. (1976). *The Criminal Personality. 1: A Profile for Change.* New York: Jason Aronson.

——— (1977). *The Criminal Personality. 2: The Change Process.* New York: Jason Aronson.

Zanarini, M. C., Frankenburg, F. R., Chauncey, D. L., and Gunderson, J. G. (1987). The diagnostic interview for personality disorders: interrater and test-related reliability. *Comprehensive Psychiatry* 28: 467-480.

Zetzel, E. (1968). The so-called good hysteric. *International Journal of Psycho-Analysis* 49:256-260.

Ziehen, T. (1905). Theory of psychopathic contribution. *Charité Ann* 29:279.

Zilboorg, G. (1941). Ambulatory schizophrenia. *Psychiatry* 4:149-155.

——— (1952). The problem of ambulatory schizophrenias. *American Journal of Psychiatry* 113:519-525.

Zimmerman, D. (1982). Analyzability in relation to early psychopathology. *International Journal of Psycho-Analysis* 63:189-200.

CREDITS

The author gratefully acknowledges permission to reprint the following:

Lines from the poems "The Face Behind Face" and "Love of Solitude," by Yevgeny Yevtushenko, in *The Face Behind the Face*, translated by Arthur Boyars and Simon Franklin. Copyright © 1979 by Marion Boyars Publishers Ltd. Used by permission of Marion Boyars Publishers Ltd.

Lines from the poem "Mea Culpa," by Patricia Goedicke. Copyright © 1984 by Patricia Goedicke. Originally in *The New Yorker*. Used by permission.

Lines from the poem "Open House," by Theodore Roethke, in *The Collected Poems of Theodore Roethke*. Copyright © 1941 by Theodore Roethke. Used by permission of Doubleday, a division of Bantam Doubleday Dell Publishing Group, Inc.

Lines from the poem "Conditions," by Pablo Neruda, in *Late and Posthumous Poems*. Copyright © 1988 by Foundación Pablo Neruda. Used by permission of Grove Press, Inc.

Lines from the poem "Soliloquy of the Solipsist," by Sylvia Plath, in *The Collected Poems of Sylvia Plath*, edited by Ted Hughes. Copyright © 1956 by Ted Hughes. Used by permission of HarperCollins Publishers.

Lines from the poem "The Dry Salvages," by T. S. Eliot, in *Four Quartets*, Copyright © 1943 by T. S. Eliot and renewed 1971 by Esme Valerie Eliot. Reprinted by permission of Harcourt Brace Jovanovich, Inc.

Lines from the poem "Tao-te-ching," by Lao-tzu, in *Tao Te Ching.* Copyright © 1988 by Stephen Mitchell. Used by permission of Harper & Collins Publishers.

Lines from "A Part of Speech," by Joseph Brodsky. Translation copyright © 1973, 1974, 1976, 1977, 1978, 1979, 1980 by Farrar, Straus & Giroux, Inc. Used by permission of Farrar, Straus & Giroux, Inc.

Material from the *Diagnostic and Statistical Manual of Mental Disorders,* Second Edition (1968), Third Edition (1980), and Third Edition Revised (1987). Copyright © 1968, 1980, 1987 by the American Psychiatric Association. Used by permission of the American Psychiatric Association.

"The Syndrome of Identity Diffusion," by Salman Akhtar, in the *American Journal of Psychiatry,* vol. 141, pp. 1381–1385. Copyright © 1984 by the American Psychiatric Association. Used by permission of the American Psychiatric Association.

"Schizoid Personality Disorder: A Synthesis of Developmental Dynamics and Descriptive Features," by Salman Akhtar, in the *American Journal of Psychiatry,* vol. 41, pp. 499–518. Copyright © 1987 by the American Psychiatric Association. Used by permission of the American Psychiatric Association.

"Paranoid Personality Disorder: A Synthesis of Developmental Dynamics and Descriptive Features," by Salman Akhtar, in the *American Journal of Psychiatry,* vol. 44, pp. 5–25. Copyright © 1990 by the American Psychiatric Association. Used by permission of the American Psychiatric Association.

"Hypomanic Personality Disorder" by Salman Akhtar, in *Integrative Psychiatry,* vol. 6, p. 3746. Copyright © 1988 by *American Journal of Hypertension,* Inc. Used by permission of Elsevier Publishing Company, Inc.

"Narcissistic Personality Disorder: Descriptive Features and Differential Diagnosis," by Salman Akhtar, in *Psychiatric Clinics of North America,* vol. 12, pp. 505–529. Copyright © 1989 by W. B. Saunders. Used by permission.

INDEX

ABOUT THE AUTHOR

Salman Akhtar, M.D., is Professor of Psychiatry at Jefferson Medical College, Lecturer on Psychiatry at Harvard Medical School, and Training and Supervising Analyst at the Philadelphia Psychoanalytic Institute. He is the Book Review Editor of the *Journal of Applied Psychoanalytic Studies,* an associate editor of the *Journal of Psychotherapy Practice and Research,* member of the editorial board of the *Journal of the American Psychoanalytic Association,* past member of the editorial board of the *International Journal of Psycho-Analysis,* and an editorial reader for *Psychoanalytic Quarterly.* He is the author of *Quest for Answers: A Primer for Understanding and Treating Severe Personality Disorders* (1995), *Inner Torment* (1999), and *Immigration and Identity: Turmoil, Treatment, and Transformation* (1999). His more than 140 scientific publications also include fifteen edited or co-edited books. Dr. Akhtar is the recipient of the Journal of the American Psychoanalytic Association's Award (1995) and the Margaret Mahler Literature Prize (1996), and was named the 1998 Clinician of the Year by IPTAR, New York. He has also published five volumes of poetry.